Eugène de La Gournerie

Christian Rome

A historical view of its memories and monuments, 41-1867

Eugène de La Gournerie

Christian Rome
A historical view of its memories and monuments, 41-1867

ISBN/EAN: 9783742897442

Manufactured in Europe, USA, Canada, Australia, Japa

Cover: Foto ©ninafisch / pixelio.de

Manufactured and distributed by brebook publishing software (www.brebook.com)

Eugène de La Gournerie

Christian Rome

CHRISTIAN ROME.

A HISTORICAL VIEW

OF ITS

MEMORIES AND MONUMENTS

41—1867

BY

EUGÈNE DE LA GOURNERIE.

TRANSLATED AND ABRIDGED

BY

THE HON. LADY MACDONALD.

WITH A PREFACE BY H. E. CARDINAL VAUGHAN.

Imperium sine fine dedi.
Virgil.

VOLUME I.

LONDON:
P. ROLANDI.
20, BERNERS STREET, W.
1898.

Printed in Germany.

Nihil obstat:

    H. S. BOWDEN
    CENSOR DEPUTATUS.

Imprimatur:

    HERBERTUS CARDINALIS VAUGHAN
    ARCHIEPISCOPUS WESTMONAST.

Die 19 Jan. 1898.

PREFACE
BY HIS EMINENCE THE CARDINAL ARCHBISHOP.

THE translation of Eugène de la Gournerie's well known work on Christian Rome will be read with pleasure. The original has been through many editions and was for several generations the most popular guide book to Rome. Its characteristic is that it gives a very readable historical sketch of all the chief events in the lives of the Popes as they were connected with Rome. It is a history of the Papacy written in the monuments of the Eternal City. There may be certain details that need revision in the light of modern research, especially where the popular traditions, alive at the time when the book was written, have undergone correction. But the spirit of the work is admirable and the narrative of the innumerable scenes and thrilling events, of which these volumes are made up, is pleasant and even exciting.

HERBERT CARDINAL VAUGHAN.

Archbishop's House. March 22, 1898.

TRANSLATOR'S PREFACE.

THE following pages present an abridged English version of Eugène de la Gournerie's work in three volumes, "Rome Chrétienne." Though the original publication appeared some forty years since, it contains so much matter of theological, historical, and artistic interest in a popular form, that its translation seemed to supply a want for English readers. In its pages we learn how the Catholic Church first took its formal, fixed, visible organization. In Rome grew, age after age, its ritual and its feasts, a history in themselves. There written in stone, we can watch its birth in the Catacombs, its growth in the time-honoured Basilicas, with their pagan columns and Christian vaults, its full development in the architectural triumph of S. Peter's, while side by side with black Madonnas attributed to S. Luke and the Apostolic age, we find the masterpieces of Michael Angelo, of Raphael, and the leading artists of the Renaissance. Its "Ospizii" alone, record the varied labours of Christian charity towards the sick and afflicted, the poor, the friendless, the ignorant, foundlings and slaves. In Rome are the head houses of the Religious Orders, the great theological schools, and the learned congregations who decide the vexed questions in faith, morals, and discipline of the world-wide Church. Within the seven hills has been fought the battle between the Church and the world. It has been at once the cradle of sanctity, and the hot bed of vice. It has been in its 2000 years "signum contradictionis" a butt of offence to the pride and sensuality of fallen man, for it is the seat of the Vicar of Christ. Hardly a century has passed without some invasion or usurpation of the Eternal City. Goths and Vandals, Arians, Lombards, Emperors of Tusculum, the great Roman families, the Orsini, Cenci, Colonna, above all, the Roman people themselves, have in turn tried to make the City their own, and have seemed to succeed. Nine times has Rome been in the hands of usurpers, it has been seven times sacked and ruined, once it was laid waste. Again in the sixth century it was given up to desolation, no creature walked within its walls. How then has it survived these perpetual assaults? Of its Pontiffs, thirty were martyred, thirty banished, four imprisoned, four unable to set foot in Rome, seven reigned at Avignon, nine were driven out of the City. However great or holy its guardians may have been, they were not humanly speaking successful, nor did they secure a permanent triumph; nay the work before us shows that in the tenth, eleventh and sixteenth centuries especially, unworthy Pontiffs sat in Peter's chair. And the marvel is, that while the private lives of her rulers were a scandal, the truth of the living Church should have been maintained in its integrity.

According to the ancient ritual, after a new Pope had been enthroned and reverenced in the apse of S. John Lateran, he was led to the vestibule and placed on a seat level with the ground, while a voice cried, "Raising up the needy from the earth, and lifting up the poor from the dunghill, that he may place him with Princes, even the Princes of the people." Thus the Popes were taught that their strength lay in God alone, and the book before us teaches this truth, a truth worthy of study in our present age.

The translator is fully conscious that notwithstanding the best endeavours the present version is by no means free from defects. They would have been, however, far more numerous but for the help and encouragement of many friends.

Amongst those to whom grateful thanks are due, must specially be mentioned His Eminence Cardinal VAUGHAN for the condescension and kindness of his valuable commendatory Preface; Rev. H. S. BOWDEN, the theological Censor; Hon. GEORGE ELLIOT for much valuable advice; Mr. VICTOR COLLINS for his excellent Index, and for all the trouble he has taken throughout.

ADELAIDE L. MACDONALD.

25 March, 1898.

CONTENTS OF VOLUME I.

Introduction, XXIII—XXIV.
Catalogue of the Roman Pontiffs, 1—20.

CHAPTER I.

First Century. — First view of Rome: S. Peter's dome, Tiber, monuments. 21—25. — Preaching of S. Peter and S. Paul in Rome. 25—28. — Simon the Magician. 29. — Domine, quò vadis; the burning of Rome; Nero's persecution. 31. — Mamertine prison. 32. — Martyrdom of S. Peter and S. Paul. 33—36. — Meetings of the first Christians. 37. — Devotion of the women. 38. — The destruction of Jerusalem; Titus's triumph. 40. — The Arch of Titus; Coliseum. 43. — The persecution by Domitian; martyrdom of S. John the Evangelist. 44.

CHAPTER II.

Second Century. — The reigns of Imperial philosophers. 46. — Martyrdom of S. Ignatius. 47. — of S. Symphorosa. 50. — of S. Felicitas. 51. — of S. Eustachius. 52. — The Thundering Legion. 53. — Heresies. 54. — S. Justin and his school at Rome. 55. — Family of Pudens: S. Praxedes, S. Pudentiana; their legend, their churches. 56—61. — The Catacombs. 61—65. — Paintings in the Catacombs. 66—68.

CHAPTER III.

Third Century. — Doctors of the Church. 69—70. — Sanctity of the Roman Pontiffs. 71. — Foundation of the first churches: S. Maria-trans-Tiberim. 72. — S. Calixtus; S. Cæcilia. 73. — S. Pancras. 77. — S. Prisca; S. Suzanna. 78. — Penitential laws. 80. — Christians in Cæsar's house. 81. — Persecutions: S. Tarcisius. 83. — S. Chrysanthus and S. Daria. 84. — SS. Rufina and Secunda; S. Zoe; S. Eugenius. 85. — S. Martina. 86. — S. Laurence. 87. — S. Hippolytus. 89. — S. Sebastian. 90. — S. Aglais and S. Boniface. 91. — S. Agnes. 92. — S. Emerentiana. 94.

CHAPTER IV.

Fourth Century. — Sufferings and death of S. Marcellus. 95. — Constantine's triumph. 96. — Changes in the laws of the Empire. 97. — Roman Basilicas: The Lateran. 98—102. — S. Peter's. 103—108. — S. Paolo-fuori-le-mura. 109—111. — S. Lorenzo-fuori-le-mura. 111—113. — S. Croce-in-Gerusalemme. 114. — Relics of the Passion. 115. — Constantine's gifts to the Roman Basilicas. 116. — Church of S. Agnes. 117. — S. Sylvester's Oratory. 118. — S. Athanasius at Rome. 121. — S. Ambrose. 122. — S. Augustine. 123. — S. Augustine's last interview with S. Monica. 124. — S. Jerome; S. Paula; S. Eustochia. 126. — S. Paulinus. 129. — Abduction and exile of Pope Liberius. 132. — Families of saints. 134. — Persecution by Julian: SS. John and Paul. 135. — New churches: S. Eusebius, S. Maria Maggiore. 137.

CHAPTER V.

Fifth Century. — Ostentation of the last Romans. 139. — Combats of gladiators: Martyrdom of S. Telemachus. 140. — First hospitals. 142. — Family of

S. Melania. 142–144. — Alaric sacks Rome; S. Marcella; The sacred vases of S. Peter. 146–147. — Lamentations of S. Jerome. 148. — Spell cast by Rome's name. 150. — Mission of new apostles: Celestius before Pope Zozimus. 151. — Liturgy. 152. — S. Leo the Great. 152–153. — Attila; Genseric. 153–155. — New churches: S. Maria-in-Aquiro, S. Vitalis. 156. — Legend of S. Alexis. 157. — Contrast between heathen and Christian memories. 158. — Mosaics at S. Maria Maggiore. 159–161. — Pontifical Library. 163. — S. Pietro-in-Vincoli. 163–164. — S. Bibiana. 165. — Quatro Santi Coronati. 165–166. — Rules for the election of Pontiffs. 167–168.

CHAPTER VI.

Sixth Century. — Theodoric: his character. 170. — Boethius: his labours and death. 171. — Symmachus: virtues of his family, his death. 173. — S. Benedict: his residence at Rome, withdraws to Subiaco and Monte-Cassino. 176. — The "Sacro Speco." 179. — Totila; Vitiges; Belisarius; Narses; Taking and retaking of Rome. 180–183. — Lombard invasion; Grief of S. Gregory. 183–184. — Progressive abolition of slavery. 185. — Banishment of Pope Sylverius. 187.— Repentance of Belisarius. 188. — Aratore's poem. 189. — Inundation and plague at Rome: Great Litany. 189–190. — Character and pontificate of S. Gregory the Great. 191. — S. Gregorio-Magno. 194. — New churches: S. Martino. 195. Fountain of S. Peter's. 196. — SS. Cosmo-e-Damiano. 196. — Ruin of Monte-Cassino. 197. — Churches of S. Cæsario, S. Adriano, S. Georgio-in-Velabro, S. Nicolo-in-Carcere. 199. — S. Salvatore-in-lacu. 200. — Patriarchal Churches and Basilicas; Deaconries. 201. — Liturgical constitutions. 202. — Stations. 203. — Institution of Gregorian Chant. 204.

CHAPTER VII.

Seventh Century. — Consecration of the Pantheon under the title of S. Maria-ad-Martyres. 208. — S. Teodoro. 209. — The column of Phocas. 210. — Rise of Mahomet. 211. — Foreigners in Rome: Cædwalla of Wessex. 213. — Monothelism: action of Pope S. Martin. 216. — His removal from Rome, sufferings, and death. 217. — Constans II at Rome. 218. — Persecution of Pope Sergius. 221. — S. Maria-in-via-Lata. 221. — S. Angelo-inter-nubes; SS. Vincenzio-ed-Anastasio; SS. Vito-e-Modesto. 222.

CHAPTER VIII.

Eighth Century. — Partition of Italy. 224. — Decay of the Eastern Empire. 224—228. — Domains of S. Peter: origin of the temporal power of the Popes. 228. — Outrages by Iconoclasts. 230. — S. Boniface at Rome. 231. — Noble character of Gregory II. 232. — The "Acheiropoietos" image of Our Lord. 234. — Virgin of S. Maria-in-Cosmedin. 235. — Statue of S. Peter. 236. — Rome menaced by Liudprand. 236. — The Popes' appeal to the Franks. 237. — S. Zachary: his constructions at the Lateran. 239. — Hospital of King Ina; Pilgrims from Great Britain. 241. — Astolf invests Rome; Violation of the cemeteries. 242. — Stephen II appeals to Pepin le Bref. 243. — Pepin's donation to the Church. 244. — Daunou and Gibbon on Papal temporal power. 244—245. — S. Denis; S. Sylvestro-in-Capite. 245. — S. Petronilla; S. Maria-Nuova. 246. — Adrian I: his character, his virtues, his foundations. 248—252. — Charlemagne's entry into Rome. 249. — Quarrel between French and Roman choristers. 250. — Attack on Leo III. 253. — Leo III at Paderborn. 254. — Second journey of Charlemagne to Rome. 255. — His solemn coronation as Emperor. 256. — S. Angelo-in-pescaria. 258. —

Princes retiring into monasteries. 258—259. — Principal constitutions of the Councils. 259—260.

CHAPTER IX.

Ninth Century. — Charlemagne in Rome; extent of his power. 261. — His testament. 263. — Works of Leo III; his Triclinium. 263. — Acknowledged dominion of the Popes over Rome. 264. — S. Paschal I. 264—265. — Invention of S. Cæcilia's relics, and restoration of her Basilica. 266. — Restoration of the church of S. Praxedes: its riches. 267. — Mosaics. 268—269. — Eugenius II: public schools in every parish. 270. — Invasion by the Saracens. 270. — Leo IV; Leonine City. 272—273. — Benedict III; Fable of Pope Joan. 274. — Anastasius the antipope. 275. — Nicholas I; Lothair and Waldrada. 277. — The Emperor Louis II at Rome. 278. — Hilduin's insolent entry to S. Peter's. 279. — Lothair excommunicated. 279. — His sacrilegious communion and death. 280. — Political power of the Popes. 280. — Humility and disinterestedness of a great number of Pontiffs. 281. — The temple of Fortuna Virilis. 282. — Stephen V; Pillage of the Lateran. 284. — Pope Formosus: his trial after death. 286. — Decoration of churches. 287. — The Septizonium. 289. — The "tempi bassi." 290. — Saints in the ninth century. 290.

CHAPTER X.

Tenth Century. — Depravity of morals. 292. — Domination of Theodora and Marozia. 293. — Sergius III. 294. — John X. 295. — Revolt of Alberic. 297. — S. Maria-Aventina. 298. — S. Odo of Cluny at Rome: his life and virtues. 298—300. — Otho the Great crowned Emperor. 302. — Irregularities of John XII. 302. — Conventicle deposes the Pope; John drives out the intruded Leo VIII. 303. — S. Mayeul, S. Dunstan, and S. Udalric at Rome. 306. —

S. Adalbert of Prague. 307. — Tomb of Otho the Red at S. Peter's. 308. — Crescentius master of S. Angelo; he opposes the antipope Philagathus to Gregory V; Philagathus is captured and mutilated. 309. — Death of Crescentius; S. Romuald; Penances given to princes in the middle ages. 311. — Sylvester II: his life and labours. 312. — First idea of the Crusades. 314. — S. Bartolomeo-in-Isola. 315. — History of S. Nilus of Rossano. 316. — Foundation of Grotta-Ferrata. 317. — Ruins of the temple of Jupiter Capitolinus. 319. — Aracœli. 320. — Vision of Augustus; Feast of Christmas at Aracœli; Sermon by children. 321. — Alarm of nations at the end of the tenth century. 322.

CHAPTER XI.

Eleventh Century. — Political state of Europe: royalty clergy, nobility. 324—326. — Penances. 327. — Intestine wars: Truce of God, refuges. 328. — General corruption; simony. 329. — Tomb of Sylvester II at the Lateran. 330. — Coronation of S. Henry and S. Cunegund. 330. — Chanting the Creed. 333. — Benedict VIII and the Saracens. 334. — Anarchy at Rome: S. Peter's is infested by brigands. 336. — S. Peter Damian denounces the luxurious lives of the clergy. 337. — Election of Leo IX. 338. — His efforts to reform the clergy. 340. — Hildebrand: his childhood and his character. 344. — Stephen IX. 346. — Nicholas II; Rules for election of Popes. 347. — The Roman Cardinals. 348. — Bérenger's condemnation. 349. — Alexander II. 350. — Rome besieged by Cadalous. 351. — Election of Gregory VII. 352. — Character and life of Henry IV of Germany. 353. — Reforms by Gregory VII. 355. — Violences exercised against him. 357. — Henry attempts to depose him. 358. — Gregory deposes and excommunicates him. 359. — Canossa. 360. — The Countess Matilda. 362. — Siege and taking of Rome. 363. — Robert Wiscard. 364. — Death of S. Gregory VII; his character. 366. — Misfortunes of Henry IV. 368. — King Robert at Rome. 369. — S. Odilon; S. Hugo. 369. — Halinard; Cardinal Humbert. 370. — The Kings Canute and Macbeth; S. Elfege. 371. — Æthelnoth and S. Anselm; the Empress Agnes. 372. — Peter the Hermit at the Coliseum. 373. — First Crusade; S. Peter's at the mercy of schismatics. 373—374. — Paschal II; S. Maria-del-Popolo. 374. — Renaissance of art; Churches of Monte Cassino, Cluny, etc. 375—376. — Guido of Arezzo. 376. — Many saints on the throne; All Soul's day. 377.

CHAPTER XII.

Twelfth Century. — Question of investitures. 378. — Paschal II: his capture, captivity, and return to Rome. 382-383. — Death of Countess Mathilda; her donation to the Church. 385—386. — Violent scenes under the Pontificate of Gelasius II. 387. — Flight of Gelasius. 388. — Entry of Calixtus II into Rome. 389. — Peter of Leon. 392. — Innocent II and Lothair encamped on Mt. Aventine. 392. — S. Norbert; S. Bernard. 393. — Monastery of SS. Vincenzio-ed-Anastasio; Scala Cœli. 394. — Republican unrest in Rome. 395. — Arnold of Brescia. 397. — Eugenius III: entrance into Rome, his character and antecedents. 398—400. — Death of Arnold of Brescia. 402. — Coronation of Frederick Barbarossa: struggle between the Romans and the Germans. 403. — Adrian IV. 403. — John of Salisbury at Rome. 404. — Election of Alexander III; schism and violence of Octavian. 405. — Alexander III and Frederick Barbarossa. 406. — Lombard League. 407. — Siege of Rome. 408. — Alexander III at Venice and Ferrara. 409. — Reconciliation of Pope and Emperor. 411. — Outrages under Lucius III. 413. — Destruction of Tusculum. 414. — Fall of

Jerusalem; Albigeois. 414—415. — Coronation of Henry VI. 415. — Lepers; S. Lazaro-fuori-di-Porta-Angelica. 417. — Grand order of the Trinity; S. John of Matha. 419. — Military orders. 420. — Catholicism at the head of social progress. 421. — Fine arts; cathedrals. 422. — Canonizations. 423. — Ceremonials at the enthronement of Pontiffs. 424—426.

CHAPTER XIII.

Thirteenth Century. — Increasing power of the aristocracy. 427. — Great Roman families: Frangipani, Cenci, Annibaldi, Colonna, Orsini, Savelli, Cajetani, Conti. 428—430. — Innocent III: his election, character, and administration. 431—433. — Coronations of Peter II of Aragon and of Otho of Bavaria. 434—435. — Justice of Innocent III; his charity and austerity. 435—437. — Foundation of the hospital of S. Spirito. 438. — Solemn procession. 439. — Fourth Lateran Council. 440. — Canons against the Patarines, Catharists, and Albigenses. 441. — Disciplinary canons. 443. — S. Dominic; S. Francis of Assisi. 443—448. — Character of the reign of Innocent III. 449. — Honorius III. 450. — Coronation of Pierre de Courtenay, Emperor of Constantinople. 451. — Coronation of Frederick II: his revolt against the Church and excommunication by Gregory IX. 452—453. —. Troubles at Rome. 455. — Innocent IV, deceived by Frederick, takes refuge at Genoa and then at Lyons. 456—457. — Deposition of Frederick. 457. — Siege of Parma; Death of Frederick. 458—459. — Death and obsequies of S. Clare. 459. — S. Rose of Viterbo. 460. — Flagellants. 461. — Brother John of Vicenza, S. Anthony, S. Bonaventure, S. Thomas Aquinas. 462—465. — Institution of the Feast of the Blessed Sacrament. 465. — Clement IV: his lofty character. 467. — Charles of Anjou at

Rome. 469. — Conradin at Rome: pillage of some
churches. 470. — Confraternity of the Gonfalone. 471.
— Martin IV a Roman senator. 473. — S. Maria-
in-Via; Palace of S. Sabina; Election of Nicholas IV;
Mosaics in S. Maria Maggiore and the Lateran. 475.
— Life of Pietro di Morone (Pope Celestine V). 477.
Weakness of his administration. 478. — Boniface VIII:
his character. 479—480. — War with the Colonna.
482—483. — S. Raymond Nonnatus, SS. Hyacinth
and Ceslar, S. Raymond of Penafort. 484. —
S. Louis of Toulouse at Rome. 485. — Great
Jubilee of 1300. 486.

CHAPTER XIV.

Fourteenth Century. — Development of civilization. 489.
— Fine arts: character of Christian architecture. 490.
— Dante; Petrarch. 490—491. — Dispute between
Boniface VIII and Philippe le Bel: the Bull *Unam
Sanctam*. 491. — The Pope arrested at Anagni. 492.
— His deliverance and death. 493. — His character.
494. — His works at Rome. 496. — Clement V
remains in France; desolation of Italy and Rome. 496.
— Conflagration of S. John Lateran. 497. —
Coronation of the Emperor Henry of Luxembourg;
Organized tyranny in the Italian cities. 499. —
Expedition of Louis of Bavaria; Petrarch's grief. 500.
— Louis of Bavaria at Rome. 501. — Louis pretends
to depose the Pope: protestation of Giacomo Colonna.
503. — Intrusion of Pietro di Corbario. 504. —
He leaves Rome: excesses following his departure.
505. — Colà di Rienzi: his character. 507. —
Rienzi proclaimed tribune. 509. — Coronation of
Rienzi; Petrarch's poem. 512. — Flight of Rienzi;
Jubilee of 1350. 513. — Return of Rienzi. 515. —
His death; Cardinal Albornoz. 516. — Urban V
in Italy. 517. — He enters Rome. 518. — State
and population of Rome at this period; Bull fight
in the Coliseum. 519. — Invention of the heads of

SS. Peter and Paul; Blessing of the Golden Rose. 520. — Charles IV and John Palaiologos at Rome. 521. — Departure of Urban V. 522. — S. Brigit and S. Catherine of Sweden. 523—525. — S. Catherine of Siena. 525—527. — Gregory XI at Rome. 529. — His death. 530. — Election of Urban VI; his character. 531—532. — Great schism. 533—536. — Froissart quoted. 534—536. — Political constitution of Rome under Boniface IX. 537. — Rebellions. 538. — The White Penitents. 539. — The Angelus; S. Maria-di-Grotta-Pinta. 540. — Consecration of the ancient temple of Vesta. 541. — Servites, Olivetains, Jesuats; Extension of the devotion to the Blessed Virgin. 542. — Foundation of La Sapienza. 543. — Petrarch's triumph. 544. — Progress of science; Celebrated miniature painters. 545. — Giotto's paintings at Rome. 546. — Works of Cavallini. 547. — S. Maria-dell'-Anima; National churches at Rome; Rome the living image of Christianity. 549.

Index of names. 550—571.

INTRODUCTION.

THE idea which prompted this work was to give a historical review of those Christian memories which bind us to Rome, that "maîtresse des gloires augustes" as Lacordaire so aptly calls her. Those memories are various; some refer to her monuments, others to her saints and to the great deeds of the Papacy. According to Pliny the naturalist, Rome bore two names, one of these was never to be uttered, it being considered a crime to do so during secret pagan rites (cujus nomen alterium dicere). This mysterious name was Valentia, which means strength in Latin, as does 'Ρώμη in Greek. Macrobius tells us that it was the name of the god beneath whose protection Rome was placed. Pagan Rome crushed the nations beneath the full weight of her corruption and tyranny, but after a while a day dawned when a new city arose, another Rome.

"Veuve du peuple-roi, mais reine encore du monde!" Such is the grand spectacle presented by Christian Rome from her earliest days. This new age dates from Nero's era; justly called by Bossuet, this "renewed creation," it purified feeling and thought, touched souls with holy passion, and raised mankind to the high level of the Gospel.

It must not be supposed that because industry and the fine arts collapsed for a long period, that all intellectual activity came to a standstill, it was at work, but rather on the moral than on the material portion of humanity, slavery was being abolished, and laws and institutions established which have made Europe what she is.

I have written this book in the strong, simple faith of a Christian, therefore my readers must not be surprised at my recording miracles and at my professing greater admiration for holy than valorous deeds; all within and around us is miraculous, if by the word miracle we understand that which cannot be proved by reason alone. We cannot explain how we become conscious of sound, sight, or will-power, neither can we fathom life or death. We therefore may not venture to limit Omnipotence! No period has, however, existed more prolific than ours in producing presumptuous thinkers, who by the aid of philosophical systems, or by some mathematical equation will pretend that they can solve mysteries which have been accepted by faith for centuries. To many persons God is a myth, to others a useless hypothesis, so they smile in disdainful pity upon that ignorant herd of believers in heaven, mysteries and miracles, while in point of fact they themselves are far more credulous than those whom they ridicule, because their faith is to believe nothing at all.

———✳———

CATALOGUE OF THE ROMAN PONTIFFS.

A great number of Popes have been honoured with the title of saint; but the Catalogues do not agree as to all those who have obtained it. So I have in this matter followed the books which I consider of most authority. In this, as indeed in all things, I defer completely and absolutely to the sovereign decisions of the Church, mother and mistress.

The Catalogues also vary occasionally as to the precise duration of the pontificates of the first centuries. The dates I give are generally those adopted by the authors of "l'Art de vérifier les dates," 3rd edition, Paris, in-folio, 1783.

Ao. Domini

41   S. PETER, born at Bethsaida in Galilee, established his seat towards A. D. 41. He suffered martyrdom under NERO and was buried on the Via Triumphalis, at the foot of the Vatican Hill.

67   S. LINUS, a Tuscan, buried near S. Peter at the Vatican.

A.o. Domini

78	S. CLETUS, a Roman of the region Vicus Patricii, (1) buried at the Vatican. Several authors consider him to be the same as S. ANACLETUS.
80	S. CLEMENT, a Roman of the region of Mount Cœlius, buried at the Vatican.
91	S. ANACLETUS, a Greek of Athens, buried at the Vatican.
100	S. EVARISTUS, a Greek of Antioch, buried at the Vatican.
109	S. ALEXANDER, a Roman of the region Caput Tauri, (2) suffered martyrdom and was buried on the Via Nomentana, on the estate of a lady named SEVERINA, seven miles from Rome. This Catacomb has lately been discovered.
119	S. XYSTUS, or SIXTUS, a Roman of the region Via Lata, (3) buried at the Vatican.
127	S. TELESPHORUS, a Greek of Anachorita, buried at the Vatican.
139	S. HYGINUS, a Greek of Athens, buried at the Vatican.
142	S. PIUS, an Italian of Aquileia, buried at the Vatican.
157	S. ANICETUS, a Syrian of Amisa, buried at the Vatican.

(1) The Vicus Patricii comprised the site and surroundings of the present church of S. Pudentiana.

(2) The region Caput Tauri comprised the present Porta S. Lorenzo and its neighbourhood.

(3) The Via Lata ran from the Forum of Antoninus to the Macellum corvorum, that is to say it served as a means of communication between the columns of Trajan and Antoninus.

Ao. Domini	
168	S. Soter, of the town of Fondi in Campania, buried at the Vatican.
177	S. Eleutherius, a Greek of Nicopolis, buried at the Vatican.
193	S. Victor, an African, buried at the Vatican.
202	S. Zephyrinus, a Roman, buried on the Via Appia, in a crypt belonging to him, near the Catacomb of Calixtus.
219	S. Calixtus, a Roman of the Ravennati Quarter, (1) buried in the Cemetery of Calepodius on the Via Aurelia.
223	S. Urban, a Roman, buried in the Cemetery of Prætextatus on the Via Appia.
230	S. Pontanus, a Roman, buried in the Cemetery of Calixtus on the Via Appia.
235	S. Antherus, a Greek, buried in the Cemetery of Calixtus.
236	S. Fabian, a Roman, buried in the Cemetery of Calixtus.
251	S. Cornelius, a Roman, buried in a crypt which belonged to him on the Via Appia, near the Cemetery of Calixtus.
251	Novatian, the first anti-pope.
252	S. Lucius, a Roman, buried in the Cemetery of Calixtus.
253	S. Stephen, a Roman, buried in the Cemetery of Calixtus.
257	S. Sixtus II, a Greek, buried in the Cemetery of Calixtus.

(1) The Ravennati Quarter comprised the site and neighbourhood of the present church of S. Maria in Trastevere.

A.o. Domini	
259	S. Dionysius, a Greek, buried in the Cemetery of Calixtus.
269	S. Felix, a Roman, buried in a crypt belonging to him on the Via Aurelia.
275	S. Eutychian, a Tuscan, buried in the Cemetery of Calixtus.
283	S. Caius, a Dalmatian, buried in the Cemetery of Calixtus.
296	S. Marcellinus, a Roman, buried in the Cemetery of Priscilla on the Via Salaria, three miles from Rome.
308	S. Marcellus, a Roman, buried in the Cemetery of Priscilla.
310	S. Eusebius, a Greek, buried in the Cemetery of Calixtus.
311	S. Melchiades, an African, buried in the Cemetery of Calixtus.
314	S. Sylvester, a Roman, buried in the Cemetery of Priscilla. (1)
336	S. Mark, a Roman, buried in the Cemetery of Balbinus on the Via Ardentina. (2)
337	S. Julius, a Roman, buried in the Cemetery of Calepodius on the Via Aurelia. (3)

(1) His body has since been transferred to the church of SS. Martino-e-Sylvestro on the declivity of the Esquiline Hill.

(2) His body has since been transferred to the church of S. Marco which he founded, if an ancient tradition is to be believed.

(3) His relics, as also those of S. Calixtus and S. Cornelius, have been transferred to the church of S. Maria in Trastevere.

A.D.	
352	S. LIBERIUS, a Roman, buried in the Cemetery of Priscilla. (1)
355	S. FELIX II, during the exile of Liberius. By some he is considered as the Vicar of Liberius, by others as an anti-pope. He relinquished his functions on the return of the Pope and died a martyr. His tomb is in the church of SS. Cosimo-e-Damiano.
366	S. DAMASUS, a Spaniard, buried with his mother and sister in the church of S. Lorenzo in Damaso which he had restored.
366	URSINUS, an anti-pope.
384	S. SERICIUS, a Roman, buried in the Cemetery of Priscilla.
398	S. ANASTASIUS, a Roman, buried in the Cemetery ad ursum Pileatum, near the present church of S. Bibiana.
402	S. INNOCENT, of Albano, buried in the Cemetery ad ursum Pileatum.
417	S. ZOZIMUS, a Greek, buried in the Catacomb of S. Lorenzo on the Via Tiburtina.
418.	S. BONIFACE, a Roman, buried in the Catacomb of S. Felicitas on the Via Salaria.
418	EULALIUS, an anti-pope.
422	S. CELESTINE, of Campania, buried in the Cemetery of Priscilla.
432	S. SIXTUS III, a Roman, buried in the Catacomb of S. Lorenzo.
440	S. LEO, a Tuscan, buried in the Basilica of S. Peter.

(1) We have given LIBERIUS the title of saint on the evidence of several ancient martyrologies.

Ao. Domini

461	S. Hilary, of Sardinia, buried in the Catacomb of S. Lorenzo.
467	S. Simplicius, of Tibur, buried in S. Peter's.
483	S. Felix III, (1) a Roman, buried in the Basilica of S. Paul.
492	S. Gelasius, an African, buried in S. Peter's.
496	S. Anastasius II, a Roman, buried in S. Peter's.
498	S. Symmachus, a Sardinian, buried in S. Peter's.
498	Laurence, an anti-pope.
514	Hormisdas, of Frosinone in Campania, buried in S. Peter's.
523	S. John, a Tuscan, died at Ravenna and buried in S. Peter's.
526	S. Felix IV, of Samnium, buried in S. Peter's.
530	Boniface II, a Roman, son of a Goth, buried in S. Peter's. (2)
533	John II, a Roman of Mt. Cœlius, buried in S. Peter's. (3)
535	S. Agapetus, a Roman, died at Constantinople, buried in S. Peter's.
536	S. Sylverius, of Campania, son of Pope Hormisdas, died and was buried in the island of Palmaria.
537	Vigilius, an anti-pope.
538	Vigilius, a Roman, recognised as Pope after the death of Sylverius. He died at Syracuse,

(1) The custom prevails to call this Pope Felix III though the legality of Felix II is much in doubt.

(2) Boniface Sigisvult or Sigisbund of the title of S. Cæcilia.

(3) John II is called John-Mercury in an ancient catalogue of the Vatican gallery.

A.D. Domini	
	and his body was brought to Rome to the Cemetery of Priscilla. (1)
555	PELAGIUS I, a Roman, buried in S. Peter's.
560	JOHN III, a Roman, buried in S. Peter's.
574	BENEDICT I, a Roman, buried in S. Peter's.
578	PELAGIUS II, a Roman, buried in S. Peter's.
590	S. GREGORY the Great, of Norcia, in Umbria, buried at the end of the gallery of the Basilica of S. Peter, and transferred by GREGORY IV to a chapel of the same Basilica.
604	SABINIAN, a Tuscan, of the town of Blera, buried in S. Peter's.
607	BONIFACE III, a Roman, buried in S. Peter's.
608	S. BONIFACE IV, of Valeria in the country of the Marsi, buried in S. Peter's.
615	S. DEODATUS, a Roman, buried in S. Peter's.
618	BONIFACE V, a Neapolitan, buried in S. Peter's.
625	HONORIUS, of Capua, buried in S. Peter's.
640	SEVERINUS, a Roman, buried in S. Peter's.
640	JOHN IV, a Dalmatian, buried in S. Peter's.
642	THEODORUS, a Greek, born at Jerusalem, buried in S. Peter's.
649	S. MARTIN I, of Todi in Tuscany, died in exile in the Chersonesus. His body was subsequently brought to Rome and deposited in the church of SS. Martino-e-Silvestro.
655	S. EUGENIUS, a Roman, buried in S. Peter's.
657	S. VITALIANUS, of Segni, buried in S. Peter's.
672	DEODATUS II, a Roman, buried in S. Peter's.

(1) Afterwards transferred to S. Peter's, or, according to some authorities, S. Marcellus's.

Ao. Domini	
676	Donus I, a Roman, buried in S. Peter's.
679	S. Agatho, a Greek, buried in S. Peter's.
682	S. Leo II, a Sicilian, buried in Peter's.
684	S. Benedict II, a Roman, buried in S. Peter's.
685	John V, a Syrian of the Province of Antioch, buried in S. Peter's.
685	Peter and Theodorus, anti-popes.
686	Conon, a Sicilian, a native of Thrace, buried in S. Peter's.
687	S. Sergius, of Palermo, a native of Antioch, buried in S. Peter's.
687	Theodorus and Paschal, anti-popes.
701	John VI, a Greek, buried in S. Peter's.
705	John VII, a Greek, buried in S. Peter's.
708	Sisinnius, a Syrian, buried in S. Peter's.
708	Constantinus, a Syrian, buried in S. Peter's.
715	S. Gregory II, a Roman, buried in S. Peter's.
731	S. Gregory III, a Syrian, buried in S. Peter's.
741	S. Zachary, a Greek, buried in S. Peter's.
752	Stephen II, died before consecration. (1)
752	Stephen II or III, a Roman, buried in S. Peter's.
757	S. Paul I, a Roman, buried first at S. Paul's, then translated to S. Peter's.
757	Theophylactus, Constantine, and Philip, anti-popes.
768	Stephen III or IV, a Sicilian, buried in S. Peter's.
772	Adrian I, a Roman, buried in S. Peter's.
795	S. Leo III, a Roman, buried in S. Peter's.

(1) This Pontiff, not having been consecrated, cannot be counted. Some chronologists nevertheless have given him rank, and this has thrown doubt upon the number belonging to his successors of the same name.

CATALOGUE OF THE ROMAN PONTIFFS.

A.c. Domini

816	STEPHEN IV or V, a Roman, buried in S. Peter's.
817	S. PASCHAL I, a Roman, buried in S. Peter's.
824	EUGENIUS II, a Roman, buried in S. Peter's.
824	SISINNIUS, an anti-pope.
827	VALENTINUS, a Roman of the Via Lata Quarter, buried in S. Peter's.
827	GREGORY IV, a Roman, buried in S. Peter's.
844	SERGIUS II, a Roman, buried in S. Peter's.
847	S. LEO IV, a Roman, buried in S. Peter's.
855	BENEDICT III, a Roman, buried in S. Peter's.
858	S. NICHOLAS I, the Great, a Roman, buried before the gates of S. Peter's Basilica.
867	ADRIAN II, a Roman, buried in S. Peter's.
872	JOHN VIII, a Roman, buried before the Judgment Gate of S. Peter's Basilica.
882	MARINUS or MARTIN II, a Tuscan, buried in S. Peter's.
884	ADRIAN III, a Roman, buried in S. Peter's.
885	STEPHEN V or VI, a Roman, buried in S. Peter's.
885	ANASTASIUS, an anti-pope.
891	FORMOSUS, a Roman, Bishop of Porto, buried in S. Peter's. (1)
891	SERGIUS, an anti-pope.
896	BONIFACE VI, a Roman, buried in S. Peter's.
896	STEPHEN VI or VII, a Roman, buried in S. Peter's.
897	ROMANUS, a Tuscan, buried in S. Peter's.
898	THEODORUS II, a Roman, buried in S. Peter's.
898	JOHN IX, of Tibur, buried in S. Peter's before the Guidonean Gate, (ante portam Guidoneam).

(1) This is the first Pope who was a Bishop before ascending the Apostolic See.

Ao. Domini

900	BENEDICT IV, a Roman, buried in S. Peter's.
903	LEO V, of Ardea. (1)
903	CHRISTOPHERUS, a Roman, an anti-pope.
904	SERGIUS III, a Roman, buried in the Basilica of S. John Lateran.
911	ANASTASIUS III, a Roman, buried in S. Peter's.
913	LANDO, of Sabina, buried in S. Peter's.
914	JOHN X, of Ravenna.
928	LEO VI, a Roman, buried in S. Peter's.
929	STEPHEN VII or VIII, a Roman.
931	JOHN XI, a Roman.
936	LEO VII, a Roman, buried in S. Peter's.
939	STEPHEN VIII or IX, a Roman, buried in S. Peter's.
942	MARINUS or MARTIN III, a Roman.
946	AGAPETUS II, a Roman.
956	JOHN XII (Octavian) (2), a Roman.
963	LEO VIII, elected by the influence of OTHO I during the pontificat of JOHN XII, an anti-pope.
964	BENEDICT V, a Roman, died at Hamburgh, and was buried in the Cathedral.
965	JOHN XIII, a Roman.
972	BENEDICT VI, a Roman.
974	BONIFACE (Franco), an anti-pope.
974	DONUS II, a Roman.

(1) The unfortunate disturbances at this period have caused all traces of the burial of several Popes to disappear, notably of LEO V, who died in prison, of JOHN X and of JOHN XII, who were assassinated or perished miserably, and of some others.

(2) He was the first Pope who changed his name on ascending the Apostolic See.

A.D.	
974	BENEDICT VII, a Roman, buried in the Basilica of S. Croce in Gerusalemme.
983	JOHN XIV, (Peter, (1) Bishop of Pavia), buried in S. Peter's.
985	JOHN XV, died before consecration. (2)
985	JOHN XVI, a Roman.
996	GREGORY V (Bruno), a German, buried in S. Peter's near S. GREGORY the Great.
999	JOHN (Philagathus), an anti-pope.
999	SYLVESTER II (Gerbert), of Auvergne, (3) buried in S. John Lateran.
1003	JOHN XVII (Sicco), a Roman, buried in the church of S. Saba.
1003	JOHN XVIII (Fasan), a Roman, died in the Abbey of S. Paul.
1009	SERGIUS IV (Peter, Bishop of Albano), a Roman, buried in S. John Lateran.
1012	BENEDICT VIII (John of Tusculum, Bishop of Porto), a Roman, buried in S. Peter's.
1012	LEO or GREGORY, anti-pope.
1024	JOHN XIX, (John of Tusculum), a Roman.
1033	BENEDICT IX, (Theophylactus of Tusculum), died at Grotta-Ferrata.
1044	GREGORY VI, (John Gratian), a Roman, died and was buried at the Abbey of Cluny.

(1) The second Pope who changed his name; he did so out of respect to the Apostle S. PETER whose name he bore.

(2) Although this Pope should not be counted, his successor is known as JOHN XVI.

(3) He was the first French Pontiff who ascended the Apostolic See.

Ao. Domini

1046 CLEMENT II, (Suidger, Bishop of Bamberg), a Saxon.

1048 DAMASUS II, (Poppo, Bishop of Brixen), a Bavarian, died at Præneste, and was buried in the Basilica of S. Lorenzo fuori le mura.

1049 S. LEO IX, (1) (Bruno, Bishop of Toul), a German, buried in S. Peter's, near the altar of S. Gregory in front of the door of the Basilica.

1055 VICTOR II, (Gebhard, Bishop of Eichstadt), a German, died in Tuscany.

1057 STEPHEN IX or X, (Frederick, Abbot of Monte Cassino), of Lorraine, died at Florence, buried in the Cathedral.

1058 NICHOLAS II, (Gerard of Burgundy, Bishop of Florence), buried at Florence in the church of S. Reparata.

1058 BENEDICT X, an anti-pope.

1061 ALEXANDER II, (Anselmo, Bishop of Lucca), a Milanese, buried in S. Peter's.

1061 CADALOUS, called HONORIUS II, an anti-pope.

1073 S. GREGORY VII, (Hildebrand), born at Soano in Tuscany, buried at Salerno in the Cathedral of S. Matthew.

1080 GUIBERT, called CLEMENT III, an anti-pope.

1086 Blessed VICTOR III, (Didier, Abbot of Monte Cassino), born at Benevento, died and was buried at Monte Cassino.

1088 URBAN II, (Otho, Bishop of Ostia), of Châlons-

---

(1) Custom has given to this holy Pope the number IX; LEO VIII, whose name appears in several catalogues, is not however considered otherwise than as an anti-pope.

A.o. Domini	
	sur-Marne, died at S. Nicolò in carcere, buried in S. Peter's.
1099	PASCHAL II, (Reinier) a Tuscan, buried in S. John Lateran.
	ALBERT and THEODORIC, anti-popes after Guibert.
1118	GELASIUS II, (John of Gaeta), died and was buried in the Abbey of Cluny.
1118	MAURICE BURDIN, called GREGORY VIII, an anti-pope.
1119	CALIXTUS II, (Guy, Bishop of Vienne), a Burgundian, buried in S. John Lateran.
1124	HONORIUS II, (Lambert, Bishop of Ostia), a Bolognese, buried in S. John Lateran.
1124	CALIXTUS, an anti-pope.
1130	INNOCENT II, (Gregory, Cardinal of S. Angelo), a Roman, buried in S. John Lateran, then translated to S. Maria trans Tiberim.
1130	PIETRO DI LEONE, called ANACLETUS II, an anti-pope. After him, VICTOR IV, an anti-pope.
1143	CELESTINE II, (Guido di Castello), a Tuscan, buried in S. John Lateran.
1144	LUCIUS II, (Gerardo), a Bolognese, buried in S. John Lateran.
1145	Blessed EUGENIUS III, (Bernardo), a Pisan, died at Tibur, buried in S. Peter's.
1153	ANASTASIUS IV, (Conrad, Bishop of Sabina), a Roman, buried in S. John Lateran.
1154	ADRIAN IV, (Nicholas Breakspeare), an Englishman, Bishop of Albano, (1) died at Anagni, buried in S. Peter's.

(1) He is the only Englishman who ever occupied the Apostolic See.

A.o. Domini

1159 ALEXANDER III, (Rolando Bandinelli), of Siena, died at Città di Castello, buried in S. John Lateran.

OCTAVIAN, GUIDO di Crema and JOHN of Sturm, successively anti-popes under the names of VICTOR IV, PASCHAL III and CALIXTUS III.

1181 LUCIUS III, (Ubaldo Allucingolo, Bishop of Ostia), of Lucca, died and buried at Verona.

1185. URBAN III, (Uberto Crivelli), Archbishop of Milan, born at Milan, died and buried at Ferrara.

1187 GREGORY VIII, (Alberto), born at Benevento, died at Pisa.

1187 CLEMENT III, (Paolo, Bishop of Palestrina), a Roman.

1191 CELESTINE III, (Hyacinto Bobo), a Roman, buried in S. John Lateran.

1198 INNOCENT III, (Lotario Conti), of Anagno, died, at Perugia, buried in the Cathedral.

1216 HONORIUS III, (Cencio Savelli), a Roman, buried in S. Maria Maggiore.

1227 GREGORY IX, (Ugolino Conti), of Anagno, Bishop of Ostia, buried in S. Peter's.

1241 CELESTINE IV, (Geoffrey, Bishop of Sabina), a Milanese, buried in S. Peter's.

1243 INNOCENT IV, (Sinibaldo Fieschi), a Genoese, died at Naples and buried in the Cathedral.

1254 ALEXANDER IV, (Rinaldo Conti), of Anagno, Bishop of Ostia, died at Viterbo and buried in the Cathedral.

1261 URBAN IV, (Jacopo Pantaleone), of Troyes in Champagne, died at Perugia, buried in the Cathedral of S. Lorenzo.

CATALOGUE OF THE ROMAN PONTIFFS.

Ao. Domini

- 1265   CLEMENT IV, (Guido Fulcodi or Foulques), born at Saint-Gilles-sur-Rhone in Languedoc, buried in the Dominican church of Viterbo.
- 1271   Blessed GREGORY X, (Thibaud), born at Piacenza, buried in S. Donato at Arezzo.
- 1276   INNOCENT V, (Pierre de Champagny), born at Moutier in Savoy, buried in S. John Lateran.
- 1276   ADRIAN V, (Fieschi), of Genoa, buried in the Franciscan church of Viterbo.
- 1276   JOHN XXI, (1) (Pietro Juliano), a Portuguese buried in the church of S. Lorenzo at Viterbo.
- 1277   NICHOLAS III, (Giovanni Gaetano Orsini), a Roman, buried in S. Peter's.
- 1281   MARTIN IV, (Simon de Brion), born in the Castle of Montpincé in Brie, buried in the Cathedral of Perugia.
- 1285   HONORIUS IV, (Giacopo Savelli), a Roman, buried in S. Peter's.
- 1288   NICHOLAS IV, (Girolamo d'Ascoli), born at Ascoli, buried in S. Maria Maggiore.
- 1294   S. CELESTINE V, (Pietro di Morone), born in Apulia, buried at Ferentino, afterwards translated to the church of the Celestines of Aquila.
- 1294   BONIFACE VIII, (2) (Benedict Cajetani), born at Anagni, buried in S. Peter's.

(1) This Pope is wrongly called JOHN XXI, for the last Pope of this name was JOHN XIX, in 1024. In order to make the number XXI, we must reckon the anti-pope PHILAGATHUS who took the name of JOHN in 999.

(2) Custom gives this Pope the name of BONIFACE VIII, although BONIFACE VII was an anti-pope.

A.o. Domini

1303   S. BENEDICT XI, (1) (Boccasini), born at Treviso, buried in the Dominican church of Perugia.

1305   CLEMENT V, (Bertrand de Goth), Archbishop of Bordeaux, born at Villandreau in Guyenne, buried at Useste in the diocese of Bazas.

1316   JOHN XXII, (Jacques d'Euse), born at Cahors, buried in the Cathedral of Avignon.

1328   PIETRO DI CORBARIO, an anti-pope.

1334   BENEDICT XII, (Jacques de Nouveau surnamed Fournier), born at Saverdun, in the county of Foix, buried in the Cathedral of Avignon.

1342   CLEMENT VI, (Pierre Roger), of Limoges, buried in the monastery of La Chaise Dieu in Auvergne.

1352   INNOCENT VI, (Etienne Aubert), born at Beyssac, in the diocese of Limoges, buried in the Chartreuse of Avignon.

1362   URBAN V, (Guillaume de Grimoard), born at Grisac in Gévaudan, buried in S. Victor's of Marseilles.

1370   GREGORY XI, (Pierre Roger), born in the Castle of Montmort in Limousin, buried at Rome in the church of S. Maria Novella.

1378   URBAN VI, (Barthélemy Prignano), born at Naples, buried in S. Peter's at Rome.

1378   CLEMENT VII, elected at Fondi, removed to Avignon and began the great Western Schism. Neither he nor his successors are reckoned in the Catalogue of the Popes.

---

(1) Custom gives this Pope the name of BENEDICT XI, although BENEDICT X was an anti-pope.

CATALOGUE OF THE ROMAN PONTIFFS.

Ao. Domini

1389   BONIFACE IX, (Tomacelli), a Neapolitan, buried in S. Peter's.

1394   BENEDICT XIII, (Pierre de Lune), elected at Avignon after the death of CLEMENT VII.

1404   INNOCENT VII, (Cosimo Megliorati), born at Sulmone, in the Abruzzi, buried in S. Peter's.

1406   GREGORY XII, (Angelo Corrario), a Venetian, buried at Recanati.

1409   ALEXANDER V, (Peter of Crete), born in the island of Crete, buried in the Franciscan church of Bologna.

1410   JOHN XXIII, (Baldassare Cossa), a Neapolitan, buried in the Baptistery of Florence.

1417   MARTIN V, (Ottone Colonna), a Roman, buried in S. John Lateran.

1424   CLEMENT VIII, elected in Avignon by the schismatical Cardinals after Pierre de Lune's death.

1431   EUGENIUS IV, (Gabriele Condolmero), a Venetian buried in the monastery of the Canons Regular of S. Salvadore.

1439   FELIX V, (Amadeus of Savoy), elected by the schismatical Council of Basle.

1447   NICHOLAS V, (Thomas of Sarzana), born at Sarzana, buried in S. Peter's.

1445   CALIXTUS III, (Alfonso Borgia), born at Xativa (San-Felipe) in Spain, buried in S. Peter's. (1)

1458   PIUS II, (Æneas Sylvius Piccolomini), born at Corsigni, now Pienza, in the territory of Siena, died at Ancona, buried in S. Andrea della Valle.

(1) Transferred to S. Maria of Montserrat.

Vol. I.

Ao. Domini

1464   PAUL II, (Pietro Barbo), a Venetian, buried in S. Peter's.

1471   SIXTUS IV, (Francesco d'Albezuola della Rovere), born at Savona, buried in S. Peter's.

1484   INNOCENT VIII, (Giovanni Battista Cibo), a Genoese, buried in S. Peter's.

1492   ALEXANDER VI, (Roderigo Lenzuoli Borgia), born at Valencia in Spain, buried in S. Peter's.

1503   PIUS III, (Francesco Todeschini Piccolomini), a Siennese, buried in S. Peter's.

1503   JULIUS II, (Giuliano della Rovere), born at Savona, buried in S. Pietro in Vincoli.

1513   LEO X, (Giovanni de' Medici), a Florentine, buried at S. Maria della Minerva.

1522   ADRIAN VI, (Adrian Florent van Trusen), born at Utrecht, buried at S. Maria dell'Anima.

1523   CLEMENT VII, (Giulio de' Medici), a Florentine, buried at S. Maria della Minerva.

1534   PAUL III, (Alessandro Farnese), born at Carino, in Tuscany, buried in S. Peter's.

1550   JULIUS III, (Giovanni Maria Giocchi del Monte), a Roman, buried in S. Peter's.

1555   MARCELLUS II, (Marcello Cervius), born at Montepulciano, buried in S. Peter's.

1555   PAUL IV, (Giovanni Pietro Caraffa), a Neapolitan, buried in S. Peter's.

1559   PIUS IV, (Giovanni-Angelo Medici), a Milanese, buried in S. Peter's.

1566   S. PIUS V, (Michele Ghislieri), born at Bosco, in the diocese of Tortona, buried in S. Peter's and afterwards translated to S. Maria Maggiore.

CATALOGUE OF THE ROMAN PONTIFFS.

Ao. Domini.

1572   GREGORY XIII, (Ugo Buoncompagno), a Bolognese, buried in S. Peter's.

1585   SIXTUS V, (Felice Peretti), born near Montalto in the March of Ancona, buried in S. Maria Maggiore.

1590   URBAN VII, (Giovanni Battista Castagna), a Roman, buried in S. Peter's.

1590   GREGORY XIV, (Nicolò Sfondrato), of Cremona, buried in S. Peter's.

1591   INNOCENT IX, (Giovanni-Antonio Facchinetti), a Bolognese, buried in S. Peter's.

1592   CLEMENT VIII, (Ippolito Aldobrandini), born at Fano, buried in S. Maria Maggiore.

1605   LEO XI, (Alessandro-Ottaviano de' Medici), a Florentine, buried in S. Peter's.

1605   PAUL V, (Camillo Borghese), of Siena, buried in S. Maria Maggiore.

1621   GREGORY XV, (Alessandro Ludovisi), a Bolognese, buried in S. Ignacio.

1623   URBAN VIII, (Maffeo Barbarini), a Florentine, buried in S. Peter's.

1644   INNOCENT X, (Giovanni-Battista Pamfili), a Roman, buried in S. Agnese nella Piazza Navona.

1655   ALEXANDER VII, (Fabio Chigi), of Siena, buried in S. Peter's.

1667   CLEMENT IX, (Giulio Rospigliosi), of Pistoja, in Tuscany, buried in S. Maria Maggiore.

1670   CLEMENT X, (Giovanni-Battista-Emilio Altieri), a Roman, buried in S. Peter's.

1676   INNOCENT XI, (Benedetto Odescalchi), (1) born at Como, in the Milanese, buried in S. Peter's.

(1) Sometimes styled The Venerable.

A.o. Domini.		
1689	ALEXANDER VIII, (Pietro Ottoboni), a Venetian, buried in S. Peter's.
1691	INNOCENT XII, (Antonio Pignatelli), a Neapolitan, buried in S. Peter's.
1700	CLEMENT XI, (Giovanni Francesco Albani), born at Pesaro, buried in S. Peter's.
1721	INNOCENT XIII, (Michele Angelo Conti), a Roman, buried in S. Peter's.
1724	BENEDICT XIII, (Vicenzio-Maria Orsini), a Roman buried in S. Maria della Minerva.
1730	CLEMENT XII, (Lorenzo Corsini), a Florentine, buried in S. John Lateran.
1740	BENEDICT XIV, (Prospero Lambertini), a Bolognese, buried in S. Peter's.
1758	CLEMENT XIII, (Carlo Rezzonico), born at Venice, buried in S. Peter's.
1769	CLEMENT XIV, (Giovanni-Vincenzio-Lorenzo Ganganelli), born at S. Angelo in Vado near Rimini, buried in the church of the SS. Apostoli.
1775	PIUS VI, (Giovanni-Angelo Braschi), born at Cesena, buried at Valence, in Dauphiné, afterwards removed to S. Peter's.
1800	PIUS VII, (Barnabò Chiaramonti), born at Cesena, buried in S. Peter's.
1823	LEO XII, (Annibale della Genga Sermattei), born at La Genga, buried in S. Peter's.
1829	PIUS VIII, (Francesco-Xavier Castiglioni), born at Cingoli, buried in S. Peter's.
1830	GREGORY XVI, (Maur Capellani), born at Belluno, buried in S. Peter's.
1846	PIUS IX, (Giovanni-Maria Mastai Ferretti), born at Sinigaglia.

CHAPTER I.

*O Roma nobilis, orbis et domina
Cunctarum urbium excellentissima . . .
Salutem dicimus tibi! per omnia
Te benedicimus, salve, per secula!*

Christian Hymn.

FIRST CENTURY.

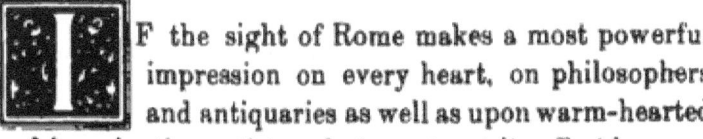F the sight of Rome makes a most powerful impression on every heart, on philosophers and antiquaries as well as upon warm-hearted and imaginative artists, what must not its effect be upon a pilgrim who looks upon this great city as being the capital of the world, the "caput orbis"? Is it not the seat of that undying Church which "has filled the earth with the knowledge of the Lord as the covering water of the sea"; (1) and which, more powerful than either the Republic or the Cæsars, has maintained for eighteen centuries the empire she has won over the universe. The emotion, therefore, felt by a pilgrim on approaching Rome wells forth like a prayer in lamentations unutterable. (2)

(1) Isaias XI, v. 9.
(2) St. Paul, ad Rom., c. VIII. v. 26.

Advancing across a bare deserted land, void alike of houses or trees, here and there he may see herds of buffalo and mares; far beyond, looming through the mist, a great circle of mountains; while before him a vast plain stretches away as far as sight can reach; when suddenly a brightly shining globe comes in view, which is the dome of S. Peter's! Who can then remain unmoved when hastening onwards, eager to reach this city of great memories, it appears far distant for several hours; but, after a while, the graceful form of the dome stands out more and more majestically against the light blue sky, flanked by numerous lesser cupolas and spires, and by lofty square towers built in the middle ages; after which façades of temples, and splendid palaces become more and more visible to the traveller.

The road occasionally passes by ancient tombs, one of which is misnamed the tomb of Nero. Two or three streams cross the path; but, were it not for their gurgling sound as they tumble over the stones, their winding course would pass unnoticed, so hidden is it beneath dwarf laurels and heather. At length the Tiber appears, its tawny waters flowing beneath the arches of a semi-antique bridge; it was just there that Cicero arrested Cataline's messengers; close by to the right, above a little church whose cupola rises behind the pines of the Villa Mellini, tradition says, the luminous cross appeared with the words around it, "In hoc signo vinces". On the very spot where you stand, the armies of Constantine and Maxentius, furious and pitiless, fought that bloody battle immortalised by the genius of Raphael and the glowing brush of Giulio Romano.

On entering the Eternal City one becomes confused by the sound of rushing waters, (1) and the rumbling of ever passing vehicles, from the carriages of Cardinals emblazoned with their arms, and equipages with the smart liveries of nobles, to the light carts of the lower orders.

On every side are churches, statues and graceful fountains; for Rome is indeed a city of masterpieces, contrasts, and of wonders brought from every land; buffalo may be seen chewing the cud as they lazily recline by the columns of the temple of Fortuna Virilis; (2) the Egyptian obelisk rises tall and slender before the temples of Christ, between the works of Phidias and Praxiteles; while instead of resounding to the ancient cry, "Give the Christians to the wild beasts!", the gigantic ruins of the Flavian amphitheatre re-echo with the prayers of monks and peasants invoking divine mercy on the oppressed and their oppressors alike, "pro afflictis et persequentibus eos". (3)

He who sees in the past something more than a mere artistic arrangement of stones, and but

---

(1) "A tous les bruits ordinaires des grandes cités, se mêle ici le bruit des eaux que l'on entend de toutes parts, comme si l'on était auprès des fontaines de Blanduse ou d'Egérie." (Chateaubriand).

(2) These contrasts are common at Rome; the general quarter for oxen is in the ancient Forum, for buffalo the space between the temples of Vesta and Fortuna Virilis.

(3) The Way of the Cross has been set up in the Coliseum.

esteems ancient monuments because they link the history of civilisation with the development of mankind, beholding in the Roman power only a colossus which crushes the world beneath its weight, even refusing to hold out a friendly hand to raise it up, may well exclaim with Tasso:

> "Io non colonne, archi, teatri, e terme
> Omai ricerco in te; ma il sangue e l'ossa
> Per Christo sparte in questa or sacra terra.
> Oh pur, dovunque atra l'involve e serra,
> Lagrime e baci dar cotanti io possa
> Quanti far passi colle membra inferme!"

It is only Christian Rome which is of true value to philosophers. The Rome of Brutus and Cæsar was powerful by her sword; but she corrupted, humbled and enslaved mankind. Christian Rome, without apparent force, consoled, raised up and freed mankind; every wonder of modern civilisation springs from her, and, therefore, to her sacred monuments, her holy relics, are due our homage and respectful admiration.

It is common enough for those who contend for shreds of the curtains from Voltaire's bed at Ferney, who gaze with pious respect upon Jean Jacques Rousseau's handkerchief at l'Ermitage, or who load themselves with bits of marble as relics of heathen fanes, to scoff at the simplicity of Christians who kneel before the richly ornamented shrines which enclose relics of the saints. They ridicule as superstitious Christians who pray before the cradle of the Infant God at S. Maria Maggiore; or by the table of the Last Supper at S. John Lateran; or who mount those steps Jesus Christ ascended during His Passion, on their knees;

who bow at S. Prassede before the column at which He was scourged; at S. Croce before the true Cross; or at the soil sprinkled with His blood in S. Maria in Campo-Santo. The condition of the poor was deplorable in Roman times. "As a slave or a gladiator he either served or died for the amusement of the rich!" Philosophers applauded, declaring that slaves were of a different order of being to freedmen!

The law of Jesus Christ was first preached in Rome by S. PETER in the year of our Lord 42. (1) According to tradition, the holy Apostle dwelt in the Vicus Patricius, between the Esquiline and Viminal Hills, in the house of the Senator Pudens, who, with his family, was among the first to abjure the worship of idols. On the site of this house the little church of S. Pudentiana arose later on, with its tall Byzantine belfry. (2) S. PETER's preaching had the same success at Rome as it had before at Jerusalem and Antioch, and the number of the faithful was already counted

---

(1) S. PETER's coming to Rome has been denied by some Protestants; but all their arguments are powerless against the authority of S. Jerome, "Catalogus scriptorum ecclesiasticorum, in Petro"; of Tertullian, "de Prescriptionibus," c. XXXVI; and of Eusebius, "Historia ecclesiastica," lib. II cap. XIV.

(2) Martial, who lived near the Vicus Patricius, in many of his epigrams mentions his friend Pudens, and his marriage with the Bretonne Claudia, whom the Romans claimed for Rome, and the Athenians for Athens. It is remarkable that the names Pudens and Claudia are quoted by S. PAUL in his second epistle to Timothy, which was certainly written from Rome : "Salutant te Eubulus et Pudens, et Linus, et Claudia." Camden also recognises a Bretonne in the wife of S. PETER's host. But Martial, born A. D. 40, only came to Rome in 63,

by thousands when a persecution directed against the Jews obliged the Chief of the flock to leave Italy. (1) The charge of the infant Church was then confided to Andronicus, to Urban, and to the other beloved children of the Apostle. (2) This Church increased silently from day to day; its "faith is spoken of in the whole world", and S. Paul had a fervent desire to bestow upon her that "spiritual grace" of which God had appointed him the administrator and dispenser. (3)

It was about the year 58 when he addressed his dogmatical letter to the Romans, and thenceforward he speaks to them as if they were old converts. He proclaims to this proud nation the weakness and insufficiency of reason, he declares that her philosophers "became vain in their thoughts and their foolish heart was darkened. For professing themselves to be wise they became fools". (4) He recalls their crimes, their countless vices, their sins against nature, their pride and perfidy; raising himself far above the

which leaves the question any way doubtful. On the other hand some very distinguished writers state that Priscilla was the wife of Pudens; but as Priscilla was the mother of S. Pudentiana, who was only sixteen when she died, towards the middle of the second century, it is difficult to count less than two generations between Pudens and Pudentiana. On this matter it is best to consult the Bollandists, 19th May.

(1) Acts XVIII.

(2) Ad Rom. XVI.

(3) Fides vestra annuntiatur in universo mundo ... desidero videre vos ut aliquid impertiar vobis gratiæ spiritualis, ad confirmandos vos. Ad Rom., cap. I.

(4) Ad Rom. I.

tainted remains of the world, he preaches to the new world humility and submission to teaching; for there is no salvation without faith in Jesus Christ, and faith cannot be gained by the unaided force of intellect, it must be learnt. "Fides ex auditu".

S. Paul was then going to Jerusalem; we know how he was imprisoned and threatened with death in that town, and that Christ appeared to him, and sustained his courage saying to him, "Be constant, for as thou hast testified of me in Jerusalem so must thou bear witness also at Rome". (1) Shortly afterwards, in fact, S. Paul was sent to Rome under strict guard. Disembarking at Puteoli he there met some Christians with whom he stayed seven days, after which he resumed his journey. The Roman converts went forth to meet him at the Forum of Appius and the Three Taverns now called Casarillo di S. Maria et Cisterna. S. Paul praised God when he beheld them, and entered the Eternal City with them; where he was joined by S. Peter, who, however, was at liberty, while a soldier guarded S. Paul, and doubtless he was kept in chains after Roman custom. For in writing to Philemon S. Paul only styles himself the captive of Jesus Christ, "vinctus Jesu Christi". Otherwise he was allowed to lodge where he pleased, and to receive all who came to visit him. The Apostle's room is still shown in the substructure of the church of S. Maria in Via Lata at the foot of the Capitol, with the column and chain to which he was attached. Upon the column were inscribed the celebrated words

(1) Acts XXIII.

he wrote to Timothy: "The Word of God is not bound". "Sed verbum Dei non est alligatum". Fancy loves to recall, when beneath these dark vaults, the various acts of S. Paul's apostleship during his two years' imprisonment. It was then he converted Onesimus, and Epaphroditus brought him presents from the Phillipians; then he wrote to Philemon, Titus, to the inhabitants of Philippi and Colossæ; and then he preached "the foolishness of the cross" (1) with that impetuous ardour and abrupt eloquence which were customary with him.

S. Peter especially addressed the circumcised, S. Paul the Gentiles; (2) he attacked their science to confound it, their understanding to humble it. He had already converted the Proconsul Sergius Paulus, and Dionysius the Areopagite. At Rome his words were not less powerful; some of Nero's courtiers, and probably some of his kindred, yielded to God's will, who revealed Himself in the teachings of His minister. (3). A group of ardent disciples gathered around the Apostle; Onesiphorus of Ephesus, of whom S. Paul says, "he hath often refreshed me and hath not been ashamed of my chains;" (4) Epaphras of Colossæ, "his fellow prisoner in Jesus Christ;" (5) Timothy, whose every thought was his

---

(1) I Cor. I, v. 18.
(2) Gal. II, v. 7.
(3) "Salutant vos omnes sancti, maxime autem qui de Cæsaris domo sunt". Phil. IV, v. 22.
(4) II Timothy, I, v. 16.
(5) Ad Philem. XXIII.

master's and who loved him as a son, "sicut patri filius;" (1) Hermas to whom an angel appeared in the form of a shepherd and revealed the deep mysteries of Christian ethics; Aristarchus, Mark, Demas and Luke the physician, the faithful companion of the Apostle, his beloved disciple, "Lucas medicus charissimus". (2)

After sojourning two years in Rome S. PAUL left it and visited Italy; he then returned into Asia, Ephesus and Crete, only coming back to Rome about the year 64. The success of the Gospel was beginning to disturb the augurs. Simon the magician, a bitter enemy of the Apostles, had endeavoured to oppose them in the Imperial City, and Tertullian states that the Romans raised a statue to him upon an island in the Tiber bearing the inscription "To the holy God". (3)

"Simon called himself the Christ", as we read in one of S. Augustine's homilies, and pretended he could fly to God who was his father. "It is a fact

---

(1) Ad Philippenses II, v. 22.

(2) Ad Colos. IV, v. 14. It is generally believed that S. Luke wrote a great part of the Acts of the Apostles in the dungeon of the Via Lata.

(3) Baronius believes and his opinion is generally followed that Tertullian was mistaken. As a fact, an inscription bearing the words "Semoni Sanco" consecrated to the Sabine God "Sancus", who became celebrated through an elegy written by Propertius, has been discovered precisely on an island of the Tiber. It is, however, strange that Tertullian should have made this error, seeing that he lived less than two hundred years after Simon, and was addressing pagans.

that he did suddenly rise in the air by virtue of his magic power", continues the great Bishop of Hippo, "but Peter knelt down and prayed to the Lord, and the Apostle's prayer immediately checked the magician's flight; Simon fell as if he were fettered, breaking his legs in the fall". (1)

According to Catholic tradition Simon's attempt was made in the Forum, and two stones are preserved at "S. Francesca Romana" bearing the impression of the Apostle's knees.

These wonders, and the daily increasing influence of the new law, stirred up all the evil passions fermenting in the old leaven of paganism. Persecution became imminent; S. PETER had already become an object of pursuit when the faithful begged him to withdraw for a while, "ut paulisper cederet;" and, "although he desired only to suffer", says S. Ambrose, out of respect to the people's entreaties that he should save himself in order that he might continue to instruct and confirm them in the faith, he yielded to their wishes. When night fell, PETER left Rome; but he had not proceeded far along the Appian way when, according to a holy tradition, he met Jesus

---

(1) S. Augus., Sermo III, de Petro et Paulo. Arnobius, a third century writer relates the same incident, which, he says, led to numerous conversions. (Adv. gentes, lib. II, p. 50, Leyden edition.) Suetonius speaks, from his point of view, of a new Icarus who raised himself in the air in the presence of Nero, and who fell close by the Emperor's seat, sprinkling him with blood. Juvenal makes allusion to a similar fact attributing it to a Greek. The magic flight and subsequent fall are therefore actually chronicled by pagans.

Christ bearing His cross. "Lord, whither goest Thou?" he asked. "I am returning to Calvary to be crucified again", replied the Son of Man. S. PETER understood the meaning of his divine Master, and returned courageously to face martyrdom. A small chapel now marks the spot where they met; it is called, "Domine, quo vadis?"

About this time Rome was devastated by a terrible fire which filled the cruel heart of Nero with delight. To this monster steeped in blood, like a beast of prey, it produced the effect of a novel form of amusement. "Now the rumour went abroad", says Tacitus, "that, at the very moment the town broke out in flames, Nero ascended to the theatre of his palace, and sang the destruction of Troy . . . But nothing could stop the hateful report that he himself had caused this conflagration; so in order to stifle this rumour the Emperor sought for victims . . ." and Christians were seized. They were brought to Nero's gardens, which extended from the Tiber to the actual site of S. Peter's, and confined in the Circus, a part of which space is now occupied by the Vatican church; some covered by the skins of wild beasts were torn in pieces by dogs, others were burnt or crucified; while many, steeped in pitch, served for torches to light up the entertainments of the Prince by night. (1) He organised games in the Circus, mingling with the crowd dressed as a charioteer, or driving a chariot.

---

(1) Tacitus I. XV.

Yet in spite of the very strong prejudices of the Romans against Christians, they began to pity them, — "miseratio oriebatur", says Tacitus — people realised they were not being punished for public good, but simply for the amusement of a savage, "sævitiam unius."

Shortly after these shocking scenes PETER and PAUL were placed in chains in the Mamertine prison. This gaol, now S. Pietro in Carcere, had been built by Ancus Martius and Tullius Hostilius in the centre of the town above the Forum. (1) It consisted of numerous dungeons and deep underground vaults which still exist. In these vaults there was a precipice over which criminals were hurled; sometimes they were strangled in prison and their bodies flung on to the steps which led to it, known as the Gemonian Stairs.

The sufferings which awaited the Apostles in this ghastly place could no more lessen their faith, than slacken their zeal. PETER continued to preach, converting the gaolers Processus and Martinianus, and forty-seven prisoners who all embraced the Christian faith. A spring miraculously welled up from the ground for their baptism. That fervent Apostle, S. PAUL, upheld the rights of conscience and of God's justice to Nero; and then joyfully pronounced these last words to Timothy his son and disciple:— "For God hath not given us the spirit of fear, but of power, and of love, and of sobriety. Be not thou therefore

---

(2) Carcer ad terrorem excrescentis audaciæ, media urbe, imminens Foro ædificatur. (Livy.)

ashamed of the testimony of our Lord ... for which cause I also suffer these things; but I am not ashamed ... I charge thee before God and Jesus Christ, who shall judge the living and the dead, by his coming, and his kingdom: Preach the word: be instant in season, out of season: reprove, entreat, rebuke in all patience and doctrine ... But be thou vigilant, labour in all things, do the work of an evangelist, fulfil thy ministry. Be sober, ... I have fought a good fight, I have finished my course, I have kept the faith ....." (1)

PETER's farewell, addressed to those who like him had received the precious gift of faith, was not less touching or dignified:— "Being assured that the laying away of my earthly tabernacle is at hand, according as our Lord Jesus Christ also hath signified to me. And I will do my endeavour, that after my decease also, you may often have whereby you may keep a memory of these things ... But we look for a new heavens and a new earth according to his promises in which justice dwelleth." (Petri Epist. sec.)

The day indeed approached when the two Apostles were to receive the "crown of justice" reserved for them. They were brought from prison on the 29th of June 67 and taken first to the Comitia in the Forum to be scourged. The two columns to which they were bound have been carried to the church of S. Maria Traspontina. Then the mournful procession continued on its way to the great circus. It was in the poor quarter of the town, where doubtless many

(1) II Timothy, I and IV.

Christians resided. We find several monuments on the Ostian and Appian ways, roads followed by the executioners and their victims. On the road to Ostia stands the small chapel of the Separation, (1) one mile from Rome, where the two Apostles parted; on the Appian way there is the church of La Fasciola (of the Bandage) built, according to tradition, on the spot where one of the linen wraps fell from the wounds of S. PETER. The church of La Fasciola, since dedicated to SS. Nereus and Achilleus, is built in the ancient valley of Egeria, occupied, in the time of the Emperors, by unfortunate Jews, whose only wealth consisted of a little matting and hay; they had to pay for everything, says Juvenal, even for the shade cast by old trees. (2) It was doubtless to make them witnesses of their countryman's humiliation that S. PETER's last journey was so much prolonged. (3) The Apostle was finally led to the right bank of the Tiber, also inhabited by Jews, and there he suffered the death of the cross on the summit of a hillock overlooking Nero's gardens, perhaps even in those very gardens already hallowed by the blood of ten

---

(1) This small, church is known as SS. Pietro e Paolo qui separati.

(2)   Nunc sacri fontis nemus, et delubra locantur
       Judæis quorum cophinus fœnumque supellex.
       Omnis enim populo mercedem pendere jussa est
       Arbor . . . .   (Juv., Sat, 3.)

(3) In no other way can we explain the circuitous road S. PETER was taken. It might be, however, prior to this, and when the Apostle fled from Rome by the Appian way, that he let the bandage fall.

thousand martyrs. (1) Either for the purpose of adding to the ignominy of his death or to concede to his last wish, the executioners crucified him head downwards. If we are to credit the words of S. Augustine and S. Ambrose, the great Apostle protested that he was unworthy to be raised in the same manner as his Master Jesus Christ; (2) "indignum se vociferans ut Dominum exultari".

Thus he died, blessing and praising God in the presence of his executioners, and of some good women who had come thither, veiled, to witness his holy death and perhaps be able to rescue his dead body. Two of them, named Basilissa and Anastasia, were seized while collecting the Apostle's blood and were immediately beheaded.

S. PAUL had followed the Ostian way: at a spot where the church of S. Salvatore now stands, he met a lady named Plautilla from whom he borrowed a handkerchief for the purpose of binding his eyes, promising at the same time to return it. Plautilla handed him her handkerchief, and the following night the saint appeared and restored it. His guard led him to a charming valley called Ad Aquas Salvias, three miles from Rome, and there he was

(1) The church of S. Pietro in Montario now stands on this hillock, and the great Basilica di Pietro Vaticano rises in Nero's gardens. The writers who think S. PETER was crucified on the hillock are Baronius, Pancirole, Martinelli and Porzio. Those who differ and think he was martyred at the Vatican are Mallio, Comestore, Biondo, Affaranno, Panvinio and Anastasius the Librarian.

(2) — See, among others, Greg. Tur. "de Gloria martyrum," c. XXV.

secured to a column and beheaded. It is said that his head bounded three times from the ground, while a spring welled up from each spot. S. Peter's body was laid to rest in the Vatican, a spot which was to become for ever celebrated by the great church built to his memory. A Roman lady, named Lucina, buried S. Paul's body in her own grounds near Ad Aquas Salvias, and in the fourth century the Basilica known by his name was built over the place.

Magnificent churches now honour the different places made holy by the presence of the two Apostles. Even in the first century S. Anacletus, third Bishop of Rome, contrived an underground chapel at the Vatican to receive S. Peter's relics. In the fourth century a part of Janiculum, held by many to be the spot where the saint was crucified, was crowned with the beautiful church of S. Pietro in Montorio. In the fifth century the Empress Eudoxia had constructed the handsome Basilica dedicated to S. Peter's Chains, behind the Baths of Titus, in order to preserve and exhibit the chains which had fettered the Apostle both in Jerusalem and at Rome for veneration. The Mamertine prison then became a place of prayer and pilgrimage. The table, upon which the first Vicar of Christ used to consecrate the bread and wine, became the high altar of S. John Lateran. Lastly the Aquas Salvias were hallowed by a chapel in which the white marble column, on which S. Paul was beheaded, was venerated, and within its walls may be seen the three fountains, silent witnesses to his martyrdom.

But all this pious homage of Christian faith to the glorious preachers of the word of Christ did not suffice; temples, pictures, masterpieces of Christian art and civilisation, were not enough to honour those who had planted the germs of those arts and civilisation in Roman soil; it was necessary also that pagan monuments should be humbled before those whom paganism had humbled, oppressed and slain; and that these monuments should become supports to lift up the memory of their triumph. So, instead of the statues of Roman Emperors, we behold those of the fisherman of Tiberias and of the tent maker of Cilicia rising gloriously above two of the most beautiful works of ancient art, the Columns of Trajan and Antoninus. (1)

S. PETER's successors in the government of the Church in the first century were SS. LINUS, ANACLETUS, CLEMENT and EVARISTUS. SS. LINUS and CLEMENT were *disciples* of the Apostles, and had preached the Gospel *with them.* (2) From the pontificate of S. LINUS, no woman might enter a church unless she were veiled. The institution of ecclesiastical notaries, whose duty it was to find out and record the acts of the martyrs, is attributed to S. CLEMENT. (3)

Now, in spite of persecution, the number of Christians steadily multiplied. They used to meet for

---

(1) Their statues were thus placed by SIXTUS V. The Acts of the Apostles say, speaking of SS. Paul and Aquila, "erant autem scenofactoriæ artis."

(2) Ad Philipp. IV, v. 3; et ad Timoth. IV, v. 21.

(3) Hic fecit septem regiones et dividit notariis fidelibus Ecclesiæ, qui gesta martyrum sollicite et curiose unusquisque per regionem suam diligenter perquireret. (Catalogue of Felix, IV.)

prayer in private houses. Priests and Bishops read the Scriptures, consecrated, and administered the Eucharist; and afterwards partook of a meal, for which they thanked God. Above all they preferred the places where martyrs had dwelt for these religious meetings. For instance S. Peter's house at the foot of the Esquiline, and afterwards S. Valentine's near the Flaminian Circus, S. Clement's above Vespasian's amphitheatre, S. Sabina's on the Aventine, and that of S. Pancratius on the Aurelian way were all converted into chapels, within which everything that had belonged to the saints was carefully preserved in order to keep up the memory of their noble virtues and great courage. When it was safe to assemble near the tombs of the martyrs, they did so with great rejoicing. I have spoken of the oratory excavated at the Vatican by S. ANACLETUS; but it was necessary to keep this a profound secret, for a strict watch was kept on all places of execution in order to prevent the Christians from approaching them. But some courageous women devoted themselves to the task of carrying away the remains of saints, hiding them in some cavern or well, near which they could pray. Thus, inside the church of S. Praxedes, there is a well in which this holy woman stowed away the bones of those martyrs which she had succeeded in rescuing from the executioners.

Quiet intrepidity in women is always remarkable; but in these Roman ladies it was especially so, for, about this time, Juvenal describes them as "having courage only to brazen out their shame." We have seen S. Lucina burying S. PAUL; SS. Basilissa and

Anastasia losing their lives in their effort to secure
S. Peter's blood, and these were not isolated cases.

Whenever the Christian assembly could meet at
the tomb of some saint, the sacrifice was offered up
upon it, this altar being then called the "Confession".
Hence the tombs placed beneath altars of the great
Basilicas are called even now the "Confession of
S. Peter", the "Confession of S. Laurence," the "Confession of S. Sebastian", etc. In fact within these
tombs the mortal remains of those martyrs lay who
had confessed their faith in Christ by death as well
as by every action of their lives. During periods of
persecution the faithful prayed with increased fervour
and without fear, remembering the words of S. Paul,
"If God be for us, who is against us?" (Si Deus pro
nobis, quis contra nos?) (1)

After Nero's death the persecution, which had
been terrible during his reign, ceased to be public.
Everyone knows how Nero, steeped in blood and
excesses, miserably took his own life in the house
of one of his freedmen on hearing of the revolt of
his guards. He was buried near the Flaminian way
until his ashes were scattered to the winds, in order
to make way for a church of that religion he had
sought to crush, but which had multiplied by his
cruelties. This is the church of S. Maria del Popolo,
the first church one sees on entering Rome by the
Florentine road. It is adorned with paintings by
Pinturrichio, bas-reliefs by Contucci, marbles and
rich cenotaphs; the sweet name it bears is a symbol

---

(1) Ad Rom. VIII, v. 31.

of that reign of peace and justice which protects the weakest, after having destroyed ancient tyranny for ever.

Under Vespasian the anathemas pronounced by the prophets against that "sinful nation, a people laden with iniquity", (1) who had not feared to let the blood of the Just One be upon their heads, were fulfilled. Jerusalem was carried by assault, the temple destroyed, not one stone being left upon another, and the Jews, dragged in the wake of the Roman cohorts, served to adorn their triumph. As Josephus relates, (2) "So when notice had been given beforehand, of the day appointed for this pompous solemnity to be made, on account of their victories not one of the immense multitude was left in the city, but every body went out so far as to gain only a station where they might stand, and left only such a passage as was necessary for those that were to be seen to go along it.

"Now all the soldiery marched out beforehand by companies, and in their several ranks, under their several commanders, in the night time, and were about the gates, not of the upper palaces, but near the temple of Isis; for there it was that the Emperors had rested the foregoing night. And as soon as ever it was day, Vespasian and Titus came out crowned with laurel, and clothed in those ancient purple habits which were proper to their family, and then went as far as Octavian's walk; for there it was that the senate, and the principal rulers, and those that had

---

(1) Isaias I, v. 4.
(2) From W. Whiston's translation of Flavius Josephus, Book VII, chap. V.

been recorded as of the equestrian order, waited for them. Now a tribunal had been erected before the cloisters, and ivory chairs had been set upon it, when they came and sat down upon them. Whereupon the soldiery made an acclamation of joy to them immediately, and all gave them attestations of their valour; while they were themselves without their arms, and only in their silken garments, and crowned with laurel: then Vespasian accepted of these shouts of theirs; but while they were still disposed to go on in such acclamations, he gave them a signal of silence. And when every body entirely held their peace, he stood up, and covering the greatest part of his head with his cloak, he put up the accustomed solemn prayers; the like prayers did Titus put up also; after which prayers Vespasian made a short speech to all the people, and then sent away the soldiers to a dinner prepared for them by the Emperors. Then did he retire to that gate which was called the gate of the pomp, because pompous shows do always go through that gate; there it was that they tasted some food, and when they had put on their triumphal garments, and had offered sacrifices to the gods that were placed at the gate, they sent the triumph forward, and marched through the theatres that they might be the more easily seen by the multitudes.

"Now it is impossible to describe the multitude of the shows as they deserve, . . . one might see that even the great number of the captives was not unadorned, while the variety that was in their garments, and their fine texture, concealed from the sight the deformity of their bodies. But what afforded the greatest surprise of all, was the structure of the pageants that were borne along . . . for many of them were so made, that they were on three or even four stories, one above another . . . For there was to be seen a happy country laid waste, and entire squadrons of enemies slain . . . cities upon the tops of hills seized on, and an army pouring itself within the walls; as also every place full of slaughter, and supplications of the enemies, when they were no longer able to lift up their hands in way of opposition. Fire also sent upon temples was here represented, and houses overthrown, and falling upon their owners .·. . for the Jews related that such a thing they had undergone during this war . . . Moreover, there followed those pageants a great number of ships; and for the other spoils they were carried in great plenty. But for those that were taken in the temple of Jerusalem, they made the greatest figure of them all; that is, the golden table, of the weight of many talents: the candlestick, also, that was made of gold, though its construction was now changed from that which we made use of: for its middle shaft was fixed upon a basis, and the small branches were produced out of it to a great length, having the likeness of a trident in their position, and had everyone a socket made of brass for a lamp at the tops of them . . . and the last of all the spoils, was carried the law of the Jews . . .

"Now the last part of this pompous show was at the temple of Jupiter Capitolinus, whither when they were come, they stood still: for it was the Romans' ancient custom to stay till somebody brought the news, that the general of the enemy was slain. This general was Simon, the son of Gioras, who had been led in this triumph among the captives; a rope had also been put upon his head, and he had been drawn into a proper place in the forum, and had withal been tormented by those that drew him along; and the law of the Romans required, that malefactors, condemned to die, should be slain there. Accordingly, when it was related that there was an end of him, and all the people had set up a shout for joy, they then began to offer those sacrifices which they had consecrated ... which when they had finished, they went away to the palace."

Such were the triumphs of Rome! To immortalise the memory of this one, an arch was raised in honour of Titus at the end of the Via Sacra nearest the Forum. Upon the inside of the piers may still be seen, sculptured in relief, the seven branched candlestick, the table of the loaves of proposition and the trumpets of the Jubilee, borne by Roman soldiers with the other spoils taken from the vanquished. These spoils were deposited in the temple of Peace, excepting only the tables of the law, and the purple veils of the Holy Place, which were used for decorating the imperial palace. It is said that Jewish slaves were employed to build the triumphal arch of their conqueror, and to construct an immense amphitheatre (the Coliseum), in which the disciples of Christ were to suffer.

Towards the close of Domitian's reign, "that other half of Nero", as Tertullian calls him, "portio Neronis", persecution was again raging. Flavius Clemens, the

Emperor's cousin, was the first to fall victim to the fury of that despot. Flavia Domitilla, his wife, and another Flavia Domitilla, his niece, were afterwards banished to desert islands; two eunuchs in the service of the latter lady, Nereus and Achilleus, after enduring cruel torments, received the crown of martyrdom, as did also their mistress. Their bodies buried by the deacon Cæsarius, in a vault on the Via Ardeatina, now rest in the ancient and venerable church which bears their name.

It was also in Domitian's reign (A. D. 95) that S. JOHN was brought to Rome from Ephesus, to which place, after the separation of the Apostles, he had retired with the Blessed Virgin, and from whence he governed the churches of Asia. As everyone knows, S. JOHN was the Apostle whom "Jesus loved", a man of gentleness and heavenly grace, who, in his old age, was fond of repeating, "My little children love one another", and whose Gospel is redolent with divine love. But even this inoffensive priest, this man of peace, whose lips spoke no words but charity and goodwill, gave umbrage to the hateful and cowardly policy of the tyrant. He considered that it was a crime to preach a doctrine which enchanted the people, and prevailed against gods and proconsuls, or to attack those vices in which the Emperor was steeped. S. JOHN was therefore doomed to frightful tortures; he was led to the Via Latina, and, after his hair had been cut off, he was plunged into burning oil. In vain the executioners stirred the fire, and that the oil seethed in the caldron; S. JOHN remained uninjured. The executioners, wearied out, gave way before God's power, and the saint came forth from the ordeal unscathed, and was banished to the island of Patmos. The saint's hair and the instruments of his torture were carefully preserved by the Christians; they afterwards became the most precious relics of the little chapel, called S. Giovanni-in-Oleo, which was built on the spot sanctified by this miracle. This chapel stands close to the church of S. Giovanni-ante-Portam-Latinam, and was restored with true Italian splendour in the seventeenth century.

Thus ended the century which began with the birth of the Son of Man in the manger at Bethlehem. What events, what changes, had it not witnessed! As yet the heathens did not realise them; they still swore by Hercules, applauded at the gladiatorial fights, abandoned themselves to obscene pleasures in honour of the goddess Flora, and considered that the disciples of the Cross were merely a handful of fanatics who deserved to be flogged like slaves.

But Christians were to be found everywhere; unseen, they gradually spread into every grade of society, influencing its life. Each new excess, each fresh outburst of paganism, exhausted the world already wasted and old; but new blood was suddenly being infused into its veins, to restore the vitality it had lost, and the youth which had faded.

CHAPTER II.

> Beati estis, cum maledixerint vobis,
> et persecuti vos fuerint ... Gaudete,
> et exultate, quoniam merces vestra
> copiosa est in cælis.
> *Ev. Matt. V, v. 11—12.*

SECOND CENTURY.

DURING the second century the position of the Church became modified. She no longer merely required Apostles to preach good tidings to just and simple hearted men, or martyrs to be her witnesses in the amphitheatre; but it became absolutely necessary that she should have orators, philosophers and sages ready to cope with the philosophy and science which were beginning to notice her; capable dialecticians to unravel truth from the subtle quibbles of heretics. The dawn of this century beheld the deaths of the last companions of the Apostles; its evening the brilliant apparitions of Tertullian and Origen. Throughout this period, paganism was quiescent. The Emperors were mostly men of prepossessing manners who were gentle rulers, and heathen philosophy could boast of several distinguished men of genius. At that period there were two distinct parties in pagan society; one of them composed of materialists, men addicted to sensual pleasures of the grossest character, infidels, impious, believing in nothing but luxury; these predominated under Nero and his successors up to the reign of Antoninus: the other consisted of serious men with noble hearts and upright minds, who understood what humiliation there is in leading a brutal life, and sought refuge, from the whirlpool into which the world was sinking, in austere principles which at that time were not tolerated. These men were Antoninus, Marcus Aurelius, and a small band of philosophers. Although they sacrificed to idols they already disbelieved in paganism; probably their much vaunted morality came from something they had heard about the Gospels, which were already reaching family circles even to that of the Emperor. This reaction was, however, short lived. Strict principles could accomplish very little when nothing guaranteed their fulfilment. Morality is a mere dream, a word without any meaning, when separated from dogma. Therefore paganism collapsed after this invasion of philosophy, and opposed the progress of Christianity by brute force and outbursts of cruelty.

Suffering Christianity waited and prayed apart from the feverish activity of a dying religion. Philosophy was not more indulgent towards the new faith than debauchery had been; quite the contrary, persecution was renewed and instruments of torture multiplied.

One of the first Christians to suffer martyrdom at Rome was an old man named Ignatius, Bishop of

Antioch, much beloved by his flock for his piety and goodness. When Trajan condemned him to death for the entertainment of the Romans, he replied, "I thank Thee, O my God, for this mark of Thy love, inasmuch as I shall be fettered like Thy Apostle Paul." The noble captive was dragged in his chains through towns and villages, from Antioch to Seleucia and Smyrna, being met in each place by Bishops, deacons, and the faithful, who were sent by the Churches to encourage and assist him. The saintly priest continued to teach, strengthen the weak, and console the wretched; being wholly taken up with the sufferings of others, oblivious only of his own.

When the Roman Christians heard that he was approaching the city gates, they hastened to meet him; they endeavoured to obtain mercy from the populace, but the saint objected saying, "Let me fall a prey to lions and bears, it will be a very short road to heaven. I am the wheat of the Lord; it is fitting that I should be well kneaded, before becoming bread fit to be offered to Jesus Christ. Rather encourage the beasts to devour me so completely that nothing may remain to give my friends any trouble. Pray to the Lord that I may be received as a worthy sacrifice. I hope that my death may be speedy, and shall encourage the beasts myself, either by endearments or threats. Whether I die by fire, by a slow lingering death on the cross, or that I am devoured by furious tigers or famished lions, no matter what may happen to my body, or whatever rage demons may expend upon it, I shall die happily if only God will receive my soul."

Ignatius was led out, probably to the Flavian amphitheatre, that vast Coliseum used on great occasions by this sovereign people; the authorities showing him no mercy. He advanced with calm and stately bearing, heeding neither the acclamations and stamping which greeted him, nor the fierce yelling of the wild beasts. But quietly kneeling down, two lions, on being released from their dens, rushed furiously at him, and all was over in a minute: some broken hearted men withdrew as quickly as possible from the amphitheatre, with its deafening noise; and on returning home they recorded this tragedy for the benefit of Christians and the edification of the Church.

"After having been witnesses of this murder, which caused us such terrible grief, we remained at home all night in vigil and prayer, entreating the Lord to send us consolation, and some token whereby we should know that this death had been followed by glory. After this shock a few of us had fallen asleep, and dreamt that S. Ignatius came in and embraced us; to others he appeared praying and blessing; while the rest thought he seemed to be bathed in sweat, as a man would be after a deadly and exhausting combat, standing before the Lord in perfect confidence, his countenance being stamped with ineffable joy . . . We have noted down the day, and the hour of his death, in order that we may annually assemble to honour his martyrdom, hoping thereby to participate in the victory gained by this courageous athlete of Jesus Christ." (1)

(1) Acta Sanctorum; Sanctus Ignatius Theophorus.

Under Hadrian and Antoninus blood continued to flow, and twice was repeated the terrible sacrifice of the Maccabees and their mother. Hadrian had built a palace, at the foot of the Tibur Hill, which was an epitome of all he had seen and most admired in art; replicas of Greek and Egyptian monuments, the aspect of countries he had visited, were reproduced in the greatest perfection; all the decorations of the building were carried out in a style worthy of so great and proud a monarch. On its completion, oracles were consulted and priests summoned for its dedication. The oracles replied:— "The widow Symphorosa and her seven sons distract us daily, by invoking their God." Symphorosa was the widow of a tribune who had suffered death rather than kneel before idols. She lived a retired life at Tibur, instructing her children in virtue and fortitude. Symphorosa was summoned before the Emperor, who commanded her to offer incense to the gods. Her only answer was, "Getulius, my husband, and his brother Amantius, your former tribunes, suffered cruel torments for the name of Jesus Christ, and they conquered your demons by death. They were crowned with disgrace before men; but now they rejoice in everlasting life." She answered nothing to the Emperor's threats, so they led her to the temple of Hercules, a stately and magnificent pile which rose in the centre of the town, where she was suspended by her hair and scourged; tortures, however, proving as powerless as threats, this noble Christian was hurled into the Anio, below the temple of the Sybil. Symphorosa's seven sons were then brought before

Hadrian; but they showed as much fortitude as their mother; the executioners bound them to stakes placed around the temple of Hercules, and they were torn asunder by pulleys. (1)

At Tibur to-day the Madonna Quintiliolo alone has profited by Quintilius Varus's heritage; the temple of Hercules has left scarcely a trace behind; while Hadrian's palace, with its porches, temples, and baths, lies hidden beneath bushes or buried under grass, its ruined remains being the sole reward of scientific research; even these would have disappeared long ago, had they not been protected by a few priests who have there succeeded to Roman Emperors. (2)

Under the Antonines a self-immolation, similar to that of Symphorosa, brought about the martyrdom of S. Felicitas, a Roman lady, and her seven sons. It was in the "Campus Martius" that this noble dame, accompanied by her sons, appeared before the judges, and resisted both their promises and their anger. They were all put to death; some being beheaded, others scourged with weighted thongs, while the remainder were flogged to death with rods. (3) The bodies of

---

(1) We may mention the names of these young martyrs, they were:— Crescentius, Julian, Nemesian, Primitivus, Justinian, Stateus, and Eugenius. They were buried on the road to Rome, eight miles from that city, and subsequently a church was built over their remains, under their invocation.

(2) The Jesuits of Roccabruna. The Villa once dwelt in by Horace has, after many centuries, become a monastery dedicated to S. Anthony.

(3) Their names were Januarius, Felix, Philip, Sylvanus, Alexander, Vitalis, and Martial.

these brave martyrs were buried near the Salarian Bridge, in a crypt which soon afterwards was turned into an oratory under the invocation of S. Felicitas. This oratory was circular in shape, and each body reposed in an apse scooped out of the thickness of tufa.

We must not forget to mention the martyrdom of S. Eustachius, a general of the Roman legions, of his wife Theopista, and their two sons, Agapetus and Theopistus. Eustachius was a veteran officer who had greatly distinguished himself when commanding the cavalry at the siege of Jerusalem. Trajan raised him to the highest honours, and Hadrian appointed him commander in chief over his armies. One day on returning a victor to Rome, he refused to thank the gods at the Capitol, whereupon Hadrian gave orders that he and his wife, with their two sons, should be cast into a red hot bronze image of a bull. Subsequently his house, near the Baths of Nero, became a meeting place for Christians where they used to celebrate their rites. It is now called S. Eustachio-in-Thermis.

Mde. de Staël has said that pagans had deified life, while Christians deified death.

We are not unacquainted with the constancy of the saintly Popes ALEXANDER, SIXTUS, TELESPHORUS, VICTOR, and of S. PAUL's convert, Onesimus of Ephesus, who returned to Rome for a martyr's palm. Lyons could boast of two young men, SS. Alexander and Epipodius, martyrs for the faith; Autun of S. Symphorian; while in Asia S. Polycarp received his crown.

The reign of Marcus Aurelius began under favourable auspices; this prince not only set Christians free but allowed them to bring actions against their accusers. Followers of the Gospel no longer feared to appear in public; they walked about openly in the towns, and entered the army. One legion was entirely composed of Christians — the Thundering Legion — whose prayers triumphed over the Marcomanni in bloody battle. Probably no historical fact is supported on better evidence. Christians, pagans, historians, poets and sculptors have vied with one another in describing it. Claudian exclaims, "This time the glory does not belong to generals, for a tempest accompanied by lightning descended upon the enemy whose trembling chargers fled before the flames. Helmets sparkled, swords liquified; it was no longer men who upheld the fight, it was heaven itself." The pagan poet then asks how to account for this prodigy. "Is it some Chaldean magician, or the prayers of Pontiffs that thus armed the gods? Or is it not rather, as I believe, on account of the virtues of Marcus Aurelius?"

The Senate gave the credit of this victory to Jupiter Pluvialis. The god was represented upon the marble bas-reliefs of the Antonine column annihilating the barbarians by pouring down rain and hurling thunderbolts. No one was, however, deceived; and Tertullian when he mentioned this German campaign, and the heavy rains obtained by the prayers of Christian soldiers, addressed the pagans as follows, "Who does not know that drought will yield to fasting and prayer? People sing praises to the God of gods, the Almighty, under the name of Jupiter;

but it is our God to whom, in reality, they render homage." (Ad Scapul. 10.)

This new glory for the Christians, combined with the philosophic pretensions of the Emperor, ought to have assured complete liberty of conscience to the faithful; but the pagans became alarmed, they circumvented Marcus Aurelius and blood began to flow once more. S. Ptolemy was slain because he endeavoured to save a woman from the impurities with which pagan licence sullied marriage. Two Christians who untertook his defence shared his fate. During the reign of Commodus a Senator, Apollonius, also suffered martyrdom. It was not only poor people who faced the torture; but the great and powerful of the world: S. Eustachius, who died a martyr in Trajan's time, was, as we know, a general; S. Sabina and S. Serapia, who were martyred under Hadrian, belonged to the Roman nobility; and S. Hermes was prefect of the prætorium.

Persecutions and tortures did not greatly affect the Church; what did so was the number of schisms which were already springing up in her midst. In our century many philosophers refuse to argue upon any particular dogma, being satisfied with the contemplation of God's goodness. Yet every definition of God, discussed as a merely human command, is a dogma. In the second and succeeding centuries religion was considered from quite a different aspect: it was regarded as a divine revelation, every word of which was sacred; as a vast symbol, of which every part corresponded with the other, and from which not a syllable could be removed. Hence arose the prayers of the faithful and the solicitude of Bishops, when any profane persons dared to touch the sacred ark. The carnal-minded Gnostics considered Gospel morality too severe, so they fashioned a lax and easy code to suit themselves. Montanus, on the contrary, preached more absolute abnegation than the Gospel commanded. Marcion renewed the error of the two principles. In order to answer these simultaneous attacks, the heads of the Church met together several times, notably at Rome in A. D. 192. These were the first Councils after that of Jerusalem. Their decrees were promptly published and diffused by prelates and doctors who undertook the defence of the Catholic Faith in distant lands; in Gaul this was done by S. Irenæus; at Alexandria, by S. Clement; at Rome, by S. Justin. As many as eight Christian apologies were published in this Century, as much against the calumnious imputations of idolators as against the subtle quibbles of heretics: these are the Apologies of S. Quadratus and S. Aristides, presented to Hadrian; two of S. Justin; that of Melito, Bishop of Sardis, addressed to Marcus Aurelius; and those of Athenagoras, Miltiades, and S. Apollinaris of Hierapolis. S. Justin had a school in Rome where, in the guise of a philosopher, and adopting the forms of discussion habitual to scientific study, he taught Christian dogmas. He would say to his students, "Receive a divine doctrine which does not create poets and orators, but holy men; it will obtain immortality for you; and give a kind of sanctity which detaches the soul from earthly things, and raises it towards heaven, heals passions, and reforms the heart.

It is this doctrine which changed me: therefore come and learn what I have learnt, and, as I have been what you are, do not despair of becoming what I am." (1)

S. Justin suffered martyrdom when he was sixty-four years of age, with Charito, Hierax, Evelpistus, Liberius, and a woman named Charitana, all of whom were his disciples. He was noble, courageous, independent, and spoke his mind to the Emperors, "We only worship one God; but in all other things we are ready to give you willing obedience, recognising you as our rulers, and masters of the world. We constantly ask God that you may not only have power, but also a just spirit and upright conduct. If you refuse to notice our remonstrance we shall lose nothing; being convinced that everybody will suffer punishment for his crimes in eternal flames, and that God will require from every man an account of how he has used that power entrusted to him." (2)

S. Justin tells us, when he was interrogated by the prefect Rusticus, where he dwelt in Rome. "Up to the present I have resided near the house of one Marcius at the baths of Timiotinum." These baths of Timiotinum, Timothy or Novatus, recall one of the holiest spots of ancient Christian Rome; some remains of them are still to be seen in the church of S. Pudentiana. They formed an appendage to the palace in which the Senator Pudens had received S. Peter, and which had since remained open to the Christians, especially

(1) S. Justin; "Exhortatio ad gentes."
(2) S. Justin; "Apol. prima."

those coming from the East. Pudens was followed by his son Punicus, whose wife Priscilla obtained the bodies of martyrs and buried them in a Catacomb still bearing her name. Punicus and Priscilla had a son named Pudens after his grandfather; he married a girl called Sabinella. From this union sprang four children: Novatus, Timotheus, Praxedes, and Pudentiana. (1) The history of Praxedes and Pudentiana has been handed down to us by a priest, calling himself Pastor, who lived with this chosen family on terms of intimacy. His letter is adressed to Timotheus, and runs as follows; — "Pastor, priest, to Timotheus his brother, salutation. Pudens was admirable in zeal and hospitality to strangers. Having lost his wife Sabinella, and his parents, Punicus and Priscilla, who had given her to him in marriage, he henceforth disdained the goods of this world and gave himself up to the study of God's precepts. Sabinella left him two daughters, Praxedes and Pudentiana, whom he brought up chaste and well taught, both in the divine law and to love Christ with boundless love. So, finding himself deprived of his wife, Pudens by the advice of the saintly Bishop Pius, wished to turn his house into a church; and this was done for the benefit of us sinners. In that very spot is the title raised in our name in the place called Vicus patricii." (This relates to the title, or celebrated church, of Pastor.)

"Now Pudens died, leaving his daughters chaste and learned in the divine law. They sold all their

---

(1) Such appears to be the genealogy of the Pudens family as taken from monuments and dates. Beyond this it is impossible to affirm anything.

possessions and gave the proceeds to the poor, always persevering in the love of Christ, keeping their virginity intact, glorying only in watchings, fastings and prayer. They earnestly desired to have a baptistery within their dwelling, to which the holy Pius not only consented but traced the plan for the fountain with his own hand. Then summoning all their slaves, those in the town and on their estates, these two virgins liberated all those who were Christians, and exhorted the remainder to accept the faith. Following the saintly Pius's advice this enfranchisement took place in the oratory built by Pudens, and was performed with ancient ceremonies: at Eastertide ninety-six neophytes were baptised; and from that period they assembled within this oratory, which resounded night and day with their hymns of praise. Many pagans came hither to join the faith, and joyfully received baptism.

"Tidings of these doings were brought to the Emperor Antoninus, who issued an edict commanding Christians to remain quietly within their own homes; they were not to meddle with other people, or make purchases in public, neither were they to frequent the Baths, etc. Hereupon Praxedes und Pudentiana assembled all their converts, and keeping them within their house fed them for several days, all the time watching and praying. Good Bishop Pius often visited us with joy and offered up the holy sacrifice for our benefit.

"Now, Pudentiana, being only sixteen years old, was called to God. Her sister and I wrapped her in spices and kept her hidden in the oratory; when, after the lapse of twenty-eight days, we carried her to the cemetery of Priscilla, near her father Pudens.

"Eleven months later Novatus also died. He bequeathed all his wealth to Praxedes; and she besought S. Pius to erect a title (a church) in the Baths of the said Novatus, now disused, and which contained a large and spacious hall. The Bishop dedicated it under the name of the holy virgin Pudentiana, and he honoured another church with the name of the holy virgin Praxedes (1) in the street called Lateran, and a Roman title was established there. In the same place he consecrated a baptistery.

"Now, after two years, a great persecution was raised against the Christians, and many among them received a martyr's crown. Praxedes concealed many of them in her oratory, and fed them with both earthly food and the word of God. But the Emperor Antoninus, having heard of these meetings in the title of Praxedes, had the place surrounded, many Christians were taken, particulary the priest Simetrius and twenty-four others. Antoninus ordered them all to be put to death by the sword without a trial. And the blessed Praxedes collected their bodies during the night, and buried them in the cemetery of Priscilla, on the seventh day of the Kalends of June. After which, this maiden of the Lord, overcome with grief, asked for nothing but death. Her prayers and sighs were accepted by heaven, and fifty-four days after her brethren were slain she was

---

(1) As Praxedes was still alive, this does not signify that it was under her invocation, but merely that the church was known by her name.

taken home to God. And I, Pastor, the priest, buried her body beside her father Pudens." (1)

In the church of S. Pudentiana the chapel of Pastor may still be seen; it was the ancient home of the Pudens family, and consequently that of S. Peter. The table upon which that Apostle offered the holy sacrifice has been religiously preserved within it. The inscription it bore was:— "In hoc altare S. Petrus, pro vivis et defunctis, ad augendam fidelium multitudinem, corpus et sanguinem Domini offerebat." "Upon this altar S. Peter offered up the body and the blood of the Lord for the living and the dead, so as to increase the number of the faithful."

The other portion of the church of S. Pudentiana recalls the oratory instituted by S. Pius in the great hall of the Baths of Novatus. Their ruins are still visible; but that which most attracts attention and respect is the well in which the two saints placed the bodies of the martyrs. (2) The church of S. Praxedes also possesses a well with a similar tradition. Praxedes and Pudentiana used to recover the blood of these athletes of Jesus Christ by means of sponges. Some of these when found were still

---

(1) See the Bollandists for May 19.
(2) The Roman martyrology thus speaks of S. Pudentiana, "After many conflicts, after having gathered up the bodies of many martyrs . . . she left earth for heaven." Generally Praxedes and Pudentiana carried the bodies to the cemetery of Priscilla by night; but this was not always possible, and we have seen that the remains of S. Pudentiana herself had to remain concealed in her oratory for twenty-eight days before they could be borne to her family burial place.

red, and one is preserved in the church of S. Pudentiana. Such are the relics of the first Christian family in Rome. Their home was that of S. Peter and of S. Justin; the meeting place of the first faithful, and there, for the first time, courage, devotion, chastity, humility, charity and prayer were found united in a Roman palace. Here slaves were first freed; and only a few steps beyond Seneca's gardens, who was called by Juvenal, "Senecæ prædivitis," the treasures of Consuls and Senators were bestowed upon the poor. S. Pius I, who was the mainstay and support of Praxedes and Pudentiana, occupied the pontifical throne towards the middle of the second century; Rome being at that time universally considered the centre of Catholic unity. S. Irenæus says, "She was the greatest and most ancient Church known to all, and, being the head, all Christians were expected to belong to her." Consequently the most influential and noted Bishops came to consult the sovereign Pontiff upon matters of faith and discipline at Rome. History cites, among others, S. Polycarp and S. Hegesippus. S. Polycarp, Bishop of Smyrna, was one of the most respected Bishops in Asia; S. Hegesippus had foresworn Judaism, and had devoted himself to the collection of apostolic traditions in order to hand them down to the faithful. It is to be regretted that these visits to Rome left us no memorial. But the disciples of the new law had either fled or were in concealment; scarcely daring to meet by day, they were generally obliged to shut themselves up in the Catacombs, in order to hide the relics of the saints and the mysteries of their sacrifice from the vigilant eyes of their enemies. (1) These vaults, hollowed out of tufa, formed an inextricable labyrinth beneath the Roman Campagna, and afforded a safe refuge to the banished. Imagine thousands of narrow, low, tortuous passages crossing each other in every direction; frightful solitudes of eternal gloom, in which torchlight is dim, as though stifled by the damp miasmas that arise. At nightfall the Christians glided through them like spectres; scooping oblong niches in the walls, one above the other, within which they placed coffins containing their dead, after which they re-closed the opening. If the occupant had been fortunate enough to die for Jesus Christ, a sealed up phial of his blood was placed at his head. Sometimes names were engraved on the stones as well as the Saviour's monogram, or some emblem, a palm, a dove, or a crown. In the crossways of this labyrinth of death divine service was held, the worshippers prayed among themselves, every trace of destruction disappearing beneath the symbols of hope.

---

(1) It is known from Commendatore di Rossi's scientific researches that the Catacombs were not, in the beginning, secret and hidden places. Opened on private properties, they were protected by respect for private right, and reverence for the tomb. But, when they became the property and place of refuge for Christians, the pagans were aroused and these venerated retreats occasionally became a theatre for massacres. Thereupon the Christians concealed the entrances, apertures for giving light were done away with, and nothing but fear and mystery reigned in these underground dwellings. The changes referred to were completed in the third century.

CHAPTER II.—SECOND CENTURY.

Nearly sixty Catacombs surround Rome, and their passages, one above another, extend in all to the enormous figure of 361 miles, (1) or the length of Italy, according to the statement of a very learned man. They were called cemeteries from the Greek word for sleep, κοιμαω. The easiest to visit are those of S. Sebastian on the Appian way, S. Cyriaca on the road to Tivoli, S. Calepodius on the Aurelian way, S. Zeno ad Aquas Salvias, SS. Tiburtius and Marcellinus ad duas Lauros, S. Agnes on the Via Nomentana, S. Priscilla on the Via Salaria, in which were buried S. Praxedes and S. Pudentiana, and the greatest of all containing the largest number of bodies is the Catacomb of S. Calixtus. S. Gregory of Tours relates that, towards the end of the third century, the concourse of Christians was particularly large in the Catacomb where the bodies of SS. Chrysanthus and Daria were buried. The pagans put many Christians to death there by blocking up the exits, which were only reopened long after Constantine's time. (2)

The cemetery of Calixtus is particularly noted for containing S. Cæcilia's tomb, and those of eleven Popes belonging to the second Century. Three of these Popes, SS. STEPHEN, SIXTUS II, and CAIUS, were actually martyred there. This cemetery occupies the right side of the Appian way half a league before

---

(1) The Commendatore di Rossi.—"Rome dans sa grandeur," ch. On the Catacombs. Sometimes there were four and five stages of galleries one above the other, and it has been calculated that in a space of 125 Roman feet there were not less than 7 to 800 metres of galleries.

(2) This event belongs to the reign of Numerian, A. D. 283.

reaching S. Sebastian's, which Catacomb, ever famous for having been a resting place for the bodies of the Apostles, was long mistaken for it. The appellation Catacomb was first given to the cemetery of S. Sebastian, because it was near the tombs of S. Peter and S. Paul, κατακυμβα; this venerated name finally was given to all Christian burial places. The following passage from S. Jerome may be read on the entrance door to S. Sebastian's:— "When I devoted myself to study as a youth in Rome I used to visit the tombs of the Apostles and martyrs with my fellow students on Sundays. We often traversed these underground vaults, the sides of which, both right and left, are peopled by the dead. These vaults are so dark that the Prophet's threat seems to be realised, 'Those that descend into the pit...' (1) Occasionally a glimmer of light, coming through a narrow opening, softens the silent horrors of darkness; but, if you go further on, you plunge once more into profound night, recalling Virgil's verse, 'Horror seizes upon the soul in every place, and silence itself affrights.'" (2)

(1) Ezechiel c. XXVI, v. 20.

(2) "Dum essem Romæ puer et liberalibus studiis erudirer, solebam cum cæteris ejusdem ætatis et propositi, diebus dominicis, sepulchra apostolorum et martyrum circuire, crebroque cryptas ingredi, quæ in terrarum profunda defossæ, ex utraque parte ingredientium, per parietes habent corpora sepultorum; et ita obscura sunt omnia ut propemodum illud propheticum compleatur, 'descendant ad infernum viventes' et raro desuper lumen admissum horrorem temperat tenebrarum, ut non tam fenestra quam foramen demissi luminis patet; rursumque pedetentim acceditur, et cæca nocte circumdatis illud Virgilianum proponitur:
 'Horror ubique animos, simul ipsa silentia terrent.'"
(Comment. "in Ezechiel".)

CHAPTER II.—SECOND CENTURY.

Most of the objects which remain belonging to the early Church have been found in the Catacombs; (1) such as, chalices, glass patens, eucharistic spoons, "ministeria sacrata", which might only be touched by officiating ministers of the altar, and instruments of torture used in the martyrdom of saints. There were small chalices for the priests, and very large ones from which the faithful drew sacred wine by means of tubes, fistulae, arundines. The lamps were often dove-shaped, a mystical union of the two symbols peculiar to that "spirit of truth" which Jesus Christ sent into the world to shed perpetual light, ut maneat vobis in æternum. Diptycha of metal or ivory, inscribed with the names of saints, and engraved with some touching scene from Holy Writ, were exposed upon the altars. They were called diptycha as they folded in two, thus enabling them to be more easily concealed in times of persecution.

It is pleasant to find a record of some of our pious customs in the catacombs. S. Sixtus I gave orders that the "Sanctus, Sanctus, Sanctus, Dominus Deus sabaoth", should be sung during the Holy Sacrifice. S. Telesphorus desired that Christmas night should be sanctified by Midnight Mass, and that the first greeting of Christians on that day should be those words of the angels: "Gloria in excelsis Deo et in terra pax hominibus." In each house there was to be water for sprinkling — "aqua sparsionis" — it was mixed with salt and blest. S. Hyginus de-

(1) Traces of the Catacombs had almost disappeared in the middle ages, and were only completely rediscovered by Bosio, in 1567.

termined the various grades of the hierarchy with greater precision .. S. ANICETUS forbade the clergy to wear long hair like the pagans. PIUS and VICTOR decided that Easter should be kept on a Sunday. When Christians met in the Catacombs, the altars were covered with candles to light them up; and fresh paintings representing Christian hope and faith, although not perhaps very artistically executed, might be perceived on the walls.

Christianity had found the arts on the decline; the poor workmen in the Catacombs were at first unable to give them new life; although they consecrated them to God at a time when men's passions were turning them to evil account elsewhere. Thus they painted or sculptured the anchor of faith, the palm of victory, the dove of sweetness and innocence, the phœnix of the resurrection, the fish, mysterious symbol of that One who had suffered all sorrows without complaining, the seven-branched candlestick expressive of divine light, and the monogram of Christ recalling both the name of the Saviour and, by its shape, the instrument of His Passion.

Sometimes the lately converted borrowed illustrations for their new thoughts from fable. They particularly delighted in reproducing Orpheus, whose sweet music animated trees and tamed tigers, intending thereby to allude to Him whose gentle voice had changed the world. As exiles on earth, fleeing death which pursued them, sighing after the repose of a better life, they loved to represent themselves as the fugitive "hart who seeketh the waterfalls." Destined to martyrdom, they painted, peacefully and boldly, Daniel in the lion's den, and the Three Children in the fiery furnace. Saved from the deluge of evil passions and the dangers of life, they recorded their gratitude in representations of Noah's Ark, Jonah, or the Passage of the Red Sea; but more particularly they painted the God Shepherd bearing the lost sheep upon His shoulders. This design is also found on sacred vases. We may also mention S. Peter's bark, the temptation of Adam and Eve, Moses striking the Rock, the miracle of the loaves and fishes, etc. The heads of the Apostles are often reproduced, and are always stamped with traditional traits. There is a painting of the Blessed Virgin in the catacomb of S. Agnes dating from the second century. Mary, richly attired, with the child Jesus on her lap, stretches out her arms in an attitude of prayer. Jesus Christ is generally represented in the full glory of his sweet youth; (1) but sometimes the artist contented himself with painting Him as a lamb bearing a cross.

Statuary, during the first three centuries, produced very few works, probably out of fear that it might restore the worship of idols. In the fourth century chisellings were replaced by bas-reliefs, particularly in the decoration of sarcophagi, which did not represent joyful scenes, or profane jesting upon death, so often to be seen on ancient monuments; but they encouraged thoughts of hope and peace, expressed

---

(1) M. Louis Perret in his work (Les Catacombes de Rome) particularly mentions a head of Christ which is considered, by one of the greatest French painters, to be the most beautiful in existence. It may be seen in the crypt of the Apostles.

with touching poetical feeling, as in the resurrection of Lazarus; Elijah being borne to Heaven in a fiery chariot, etc. The inscriptions which accompany them spoke of life not death. "Marzia, thou livest in peace;" "Dioscorus, live eternally;" "Laurence has withdrawn from the world;" "Severus has been taken away by angels" (accersitus ab angelis).

Art remains mute, effacing itself, before the piety of the first ages; before that lively faith, and burning love, before those last marks of respect offered to men who were crushed by power, denied by the world, who were true to their calling and passed away doing good. Religion was then in her militant stage; it was necessary for her to lay the foundations of the edifice, spread her doctrines, making them the basis of her laws and customs, and to overthrow the various creeds of nations in order to rebuild them. During this period the arts were abandoned to humble, but pious, workmen. But when religion, strong and dominant, had accomplished her task, when she had solidified society, then her branches spread abroad and increased; she fertilised human intelligence, spurring it onward in every direction, and illuminating its latest discoveries with her flaming torch.

CHAPTER III.

> Hesterni sumus et vestra omnia implevimus, urbes, insulas, castella, municipia, conciliabula, castra ipsa, tribus, decurias, palatium, senatum, forum; sola vobis relinquimus templa.
>
> *Tertullian.*

THIRD CENTURY.

THE first years of the third century witnessed the appearance of two works which make an epoch in ecclesiastical history, Tertullian's "Apologia" and his "De præscriptione Hereticorum." They form the defence of Christianity against the calumnies of pagans and the arguments of heretics, and are written with the greatest eloquence and acumen. To this pitch "these men without knowledge of the arts, and without the polish of letters, the dregs of the people", had risen, as Cæcilius relates in the dialogue of Minutius Felix. In the first century God calls, for choice, the simple minded and humble of heart; in the second SS. Justin and Clement of Alexandria lay down their philosophic pride at the foot of the cross; but, in the third, the Christian Propaganda takes possession of all the greatest, noblest, and most powerful intellects. In the second century the heathen still gloried in Epictetus, Favorinus, Celsus and Plutarch; but in the third they only produced some obscure historians, a few soulless poets, and philosophers without credit, like Plotinus and Porphyrius. Complete decay had set in; society having helplessly sunk into gross debauchery. At that period it was useless to expect anything from it which demanded force and character; the only strength which remained to it was spent in riotous living, the only enthusiasm left was to cry out, "The Christians to the lions!" On the other hand, the Christian family increased and became more prominent, among whom were Tertullian, Origen, S. Hippolytus, S. Dionysius of Alexandria, S. Gregory Thaumaturgus, and, above all, S. Cyprian. In them we find enthusiasm united to science, and the highest faculties of the mind united with never failing humility. S. Cyprian exemplified the words of the Psalmist, "The zeal of thy house hath eaten me up." (1)

It does not appear that S. Cyprian ever went to Rome; but he wrote to the clergy of that city, and to the sovereign Pontiff several times. Tertullian and Origen likewise remained faithful to Africa; the correspondence of the former with Rome, however, had sad consequences, if, as S. Jerome affirms, the envy and unkindness of Roman scholars drove him into heresy. But, if human passions occasionally checked the fervour of the Roman clergy, they did not reach the throne of S. Peter's successor. The papacy was

(1) Psalm LXVIII, v. 10.

the first step taken towards the scaffold, and the courageous fulfilment of its duties was only a holy preparation for martyrdom. Pope S. CORNELIUS wrote, "A Bishop devoted to the Gospel may be killed, but not conquered;" and proofs of this were to be seen everywhere at this period. S. CALIXTUS, S. URBAN, S. PONTANUS, S. ANTHERUS, S. FABIAN, S. STEPHEN, S. FELIX boldly proclaimed the Gospel during torture; S. CORNELIUS was beheaded near the temple of Mars; S. LUCIUS was exiled and afterwards beheaded; S. SIXTUS II was arrested just when he was celebrating Mass in the cemetery of Calixtus, and slain with five deacons; S. CAIUS only escaped from the satellites of Diocletian for a brief period by taking refuge in the Catacombs; S. MARCELLINUS sealed his faith with his blood. According to S. Cyprian the Emperors were more tolerant — multo patientius et tolerabilius — about rivals or tumults, than when they heard that a Bishop of God was established at Rome — "quem constitui Roma Dei sacerdotem. (Epis. ad Anton.)" Yet the building of the first churches dates back to this period. Till then, Christians assembled in private houses, or in the Catacombs; and the oratory constructed by S. ANACLETUS at the Vatican was in reality only a crypt in which they met for prayer. But the peace which the disciples of the new law enjoyed, in the latter portion of the second century, their increasing numbers, which already included Senators, magistrates and consuls, and, also, their faith, and confidence in the future, gave them courage to raise Basilicas openly before all, where they could offer up their sacrifices. Thus we learn from the writings of Origen that during the persecution of Maximin, in 236, several Basilicas were burned. In the reign of Alexander Severus no fewer than twenty-five churches existed in Rome, and the Pope, URBAN, was able to give a silver paten to each one. The most ancient of these churches is S. Maria-Trans-Tiberim built in 224 by Pope S. CALIXTUS upon the site and probably on the abandoned locality of the "Taberna meritoria", a hospital for wounded Roman soldiers. A religious tradition is attached to this place. It is said that, at the moment of Christ's birth, a spring of oil gushed forth, and flowed for a whole day into the Tiber. (1) The Christians obtained possession of this honoured ground and dedicated it to the Mother of God. This annoyed the Roman publicans who complained to the Emperor. Alexander Severus answered them, "I prefer that God should be honoured there, under any name, sooner than that it should be handed over to wine merchants." The church of S. Maria-Trans-Tiberim was rebuilt in the fourth century from ruins. Pope S. JULIUS there united some columns and capitals which were unfortunately neither of like proportions nor style, although their arrangement was grand and majestic. This church was restored in 1139, and was subsequently enriched with curious mosaics, paintings by Domenichino, and a fine portico like the other Roman churches; it is still very bright and sumptuous. What is most interesting, however, is that this church was

---

(1) This fact is affirmed by Dion Cassius, a pagan historian of the third century. Eusebius, S. Prosper and Orosius also mention it.

the first house of prayer dedicated to Mary at Rome by Christians of the old ages; the holy church in which S. Cæcilia and S. Frances loved to kneel at the feet of her who elevated womanhood, leaving an example of her own pure and loving life.

Near this church is another one, dedicated to the founder of S. Maria, Pope S. CALIXTUS. It had been the house of a Roman soldier, in which the Pontiff took refuge during the persecution of Alexander Severus. The well is still shown into which he was thrown by his pursuers.

Several other Roman churches date from this period: S. Cæcilia-in-Trastevere, consecrated by URBAN I in 230; S. Pancrazio, built in 270 by Pope FELIX, and perhaps also S. Prisca on the Aventine.

S. Cæcilia lived at the beginning of the third century. She belonged to a family whose name was associated with the most glorious memories of Rome, from the time of Caia Cæcilia Tauaquil, the distinguished wife of the first Tarquin, down to those Cæcilius Metellus, who had gained the titles of Macedonicus, Balearicus, Creticus and Numidicus. Converted to Christianity, but dwelling in a pagan household, Cæcilia went by night to Christian meetings, and devoted her days to praising God in solitude. A small chapel has been built in the quarter called Campus Martius on the spot where her childhood was passed. It bears the following inscription: "Hæc est domus in qua orabat Sancta Cæcilia." (This is the house within which S. Cæcilia used to pray.) It is commonly known by the name of "Divine Love," (Il Divino Amore.)

In spite of her conversion Cæcilia's father determined that she should be given in marriage. The wedding therefore took place amid great rejoicings, Cæcilia allowing herself to be conducted, sad and silent, "like a lamb without voice before his shearers, so openeth he not his mouth." (1) Having faith in Him who never abandons his faithful children she resolved to obey her parents, whatever risk there might be to her modesty.

It would be difficult to describe the touching scene between the timid bride, strong and gentle as she was, pure and innocent, and her ardent bridegroom. The young lover must indeed have been amazed at the girl's strange request, when she begged him to respect a life dedicated to God, and live with her as angels do in that intimacy and mutual confidence born of true virtue. At first Valerianus rebelled and reproached her; but at length he was touched, the voice of his bride charmed and conquered him, for she trusted in and was watched over by her guardian angel. He then asked her, "Show me this spirit who protects you." Cæcilia replied, "There is an old man who purifies men, and makes them worthy of beholding God's angel." "Where shall I find him?" asked Valerianus. "Leave the town by the Appian way, and go as far as the third stone; you will meet some beggars in whom I am greatly interested, they are in possession of my secret. Greet them from me, and say, 'Cæcilia has sent me so that you may lead me to the holy man Urban.' When you are in his

---

(1) Acts VIII, v. 32.

presence, repeat my words to him; he will then cleanse and clothe you in new white garments. When thus attired, rejoin me in this room, you shall see the Angel who protects me; and he will then become your friend also, and grant you whatever you may desire."

The Appian way led to the Catacombs. Within those vaults the Pontiffs of the third century most frequently withdrew, to instruct and baptise the catechumens. Valerianus obeyed Cæcilia; and the prayers of the Pontiff transformed him "from an impetuous lion to the gentlest of lambs." Arrayed in white the neophyte soon returned to the nuptial chamber. There he beheld Cæcilia on her knees, while an angel hovered over her, holding two crowns of lilies and roses, the colours of chastity and martyrdom. One crown was for him, the other for her. Valerianus's brother, Tiburtius, entering the room, exclaimed, "What may this be? This room is filled with the perfume of flowers, though the season is still cold, and nature has not yet put forth her buds! Whence comes this sweet fragrance?" Hereupon Valerianus related what had occurred, and Tiburtius at once abjured the worship of idols. The two converts henceforth dwelt as brothers with Cæcilia, praying and doing good, until they were called to heaven by the bloody road of martyrdom.

Cæcilia outlived them by only a few days. During that brief period her house had become the very centre of Christian Rome. Pope URBAN made it his residence, and baptised four hundred neophytes within its walls. The prefect Almachius ordered her to be suffocated in a steam bath at her own house. She endured this torture without its proving fatal for three days. Almachius in disgust gave orders that she should be beheaded; but, even after three attempts to do so, the executioners failed to kill her, although she lay bathed in her blood. The lictor fled; but the faithful gathered respectfully around her. Pope URBAN soon followed, and found her looking lovingly at the poor and at the neophytes; addressing the Pope she said, "I have entreated the Lord for a delay of three days, in order that I might transmit to your Holiness these poor whom I have fed, and this house in which I have dwelt, so that it may be consecrated as a church for ever." (1)

The church of S. Cæcilia was rebuilt in 818 by S. PASCHAL, when the bodies of these three blessed martyrs were transferred to it from the Catacomb of S. Calixtus. This church is extremely handsome and of noble proportions; it has a beautiful portico; the mortal remains of S. Cæcilia repose in a rich silver shrine; the pavement is alabaster; the decorations are jasper, agate, and precious stones, while ninety lamps are always burning before her shrine. All this pomp is of small moment compared with the pious memories connected with this hallowed spot. Close by the first chapel to the right, the bath-room in which Cæcilia underwent martyrdom is still to be seen. The leaden pipe which conveyed

---

(1) The authenticity of S. Cæcilia's Acts has been questioned, but has been admirably proved by Dom Guéranger in the interesting history of this saint's life which he has published.

the water, and the earthenware pipes, which diffused the scalding vapour into the room, still exist. These interesting antiquities bring deeds of virtue and courage before us; others only recall scenes of debasing pleasure, or ostentatious pomp.

S. Pancras was a young Roman who at the early age of fourteen confessed the faith and suffered martyrdom. The spot on which he was beheaded was, towards the end of the third century, consecrated by a church which was first dedicated to S. Calepodius, and afterwards placed under his invocation. The present church still retains some of the arrangements which existed in the ancient building, namely, the two porphyry pulpits or amboes used in the first centuries for reading the epistle and the Gospel. An underground chapel was constructed on the spot where the saint was martyred, and a dark, winding staircase leads to the cemetery of S. Calepodius close by. (1)

Holy Scripture mentions a Jew and a Jewess, Aquila and Priscilla his wife, among the first disciples of the Gospel; S. Paul calls them his helpers in Jesus Christ, (2) — "adjutores meos", — and adds, "who have for my life laid down their own necks," — "qui pro animâ meâ suas cervices supposuerunt" —; he worked hard with them at tent-making when they were exiled from Rome. Aquila and Priscilla resided on Mt. Aventine; S. Peter often visited them, and

---

(1) The existing church of S. Pancras only dates from 1609. It was restored in 1814.

(2) Ad Rom. XVI, v. 3—4.

there he baptised S. Prisca, a young girl of thirteen, who was subsequently scourged, exposed to the lions, and beheaded under Claudius. This holy abode became a church under Pope S. EUTYCHIAN, who consecrated it in 280. It was dedicated to this virgin martyr. The vase used by S. PETER to administer baptism is shown in the crypt. Hard by was the temple of Diana, celebrated as the centre of the Latin confederation, and also the Fountain of the Fauns, the den of Cacus, and the infamous place consecrated to the Bona Dea. Towards the Palatine, three gaping arches remain, the site of that great circus of which only the dungeons are left; other majestic and interesting ruins lie scattered about in all directions. The little church alone knows no age; fervent piety is always renewing and restoring it; and the older it gets the more art endeavours to preserve its youth. (3)

We must not omit to mention the church of S. Suzanna on the Quirinal. S. Suzanna belonged to a noble Roman family. Maximian Augustus asked her in marriage, but she refused this persecutor of the Christians, so he condemned her to death. Her throat was cut in her own house, by some of Diocletian's satellites, after which her uncle Pope S. CAIUS turned her residence into a church, and consecrated the room in which she was martyred, by offering up the Holy Sacrifice for the repose of her soul.

---

(3) S. Prisca was restored in the 8th, 15th, and 17th centuries. Since 1814 it has been greatly repaired.

Building these churches during times of persecution proves that divine virtue quickened Christianity. It is well known what struggles there were, and what attacks to surmount, from the period beginning with Caracalla and ending with Diocletian. Heresy and schism somehow allied themselves with paganism in endeavouring to stamp out a religion which threatened to carry all before it. Novatus sowed discord in the churches by preaching tolerance at Carthage, and severity at Rome; later on NOVATIAN insisted upon being elected Pope by three unscrupulous Bishops, during the lifetime of S. CORNELIUS; then came Sabellius, Hierax, Paul of Samosata, and Manes who diffused their poisonous errors throughout Christendom. One acknowledged only one Person in the Godhead, another condemned marriage, a third disbelieved in our Lord's divinity, a fourth taught the existence of two rival principles, the one good, the other evil, as with the ancient Persians.

Meanwhile the Church remained steadfast. Other troubles also afflicted her; loss of zeal, indifference which proceeded from want of faith and weakness of character; persons hesitating between belief and the opinion of the world; all this rendered men capable of good deeds without virtue, and evil deeds without vice. Public prayer was less practised, and even confessors of the faith often led dissipated lives, and were too much attached to their possessions, thereby setting very unfortunate examples. (1) Finally during the persecutions of Alexander Severus, Maximin,

---

(1) S. Cyprian, "de Lapsis".

Decius, and Diocletian, there were a number of most painful apostasies. Then the Church had to institute very severe penances for crimes, hitherto almost unknown, and the Councils of Carthage and Rome, held in 251, drew up a new code of penitential canons. Those who wished to do penance presented themselves on Ash Wednesday at the church door, clad in poor and ragged clothes; the priest sprinkled them with ashes and gave them haircloth to wear, after which the church was closed. They had to pass their days in lamentations and tears, excepting on holidays, when they were permitted to enter the church, and listen to sermons and discourses; leaving, however, before prayers. After several years of penance they might again pray with the faithful; with heads bowed down, but they were obliged to go out before the sacrifice; later on they were allowed to pray standing; but had to withdraw at the offertory. When their penance was finally accomplished, or lessened by the acts of the martyrs, confessors or Bishops, they presented themselves in the garb of suppliants, received solemn absolution and were then allowed to mingle with the brethren. (1)

Penances for crimes were as follows:— two years for theft, eleven for perjury, fifteen for adultery, twenty for homicide, and a lifetime for apostasy. In some churches punishment for homicide and adultery was also for a lifetime. The Holy Eucharist was refused to apostates even in the hour of death;

---

(1) All these penitential degrees are found recorded in the celebrated canonical Epistle of S. Gregory Thaumaturgus.

CHAPTER III.—THIRD CENTURY.

but the Councils of Carthage and Rome relaxed this stern discipline, and the consolations of religion were no longer denied to the repentant and moribund.

In spite of a few lapses, conversions grew more numerous, and "the blood of the martyrs was the seed of Christians," according to a beautiful liturgical expression. (1) Even the Imperial family was reached by the faith. We have heard S. PAUL, in the first century, speak of those Christians, "especially they that are of Cæsar's household." (2) S. Chrysostom mentions a cup-bearer and a concubine of the Emperor who were converted by the great Apostle, this being one reason why S. PAUL was put to death. The Acts of the Martyrs name S. Tropez and S. Evellius as having filled confidential posts in Nero's palace. But, after twenty years had gone by, it was not only slaves and officials at the Emperor's court who yielded to grace, but Flavius Clemens, Domitian's cousin, and two ladies known as Flavia Domitilla who were nearly related to him. A century later Septimus Severus received Proculus, a Christian, at his palace, who had cured him of a "dangerous illness by anointing him with holy oil." (3) Mammæa, the mother of Alexander Severus, was supposed to have been a Christian; so was Serena Augusta, the wife of Diocletian; she, like Lucina, Praxedes, and Plautilla, piously collected the relics of the martyrs. Thus

---

(1) Taken from Tertullian. Op. t. I, p. 46.—Fususque sanguis Christianos seminat.—Hymn to S. Peter in the Paris Breviary.

(2) Ad Philipp. IV, v. 22.

(3) Tertullian, ad Scapulam, IV.

when Suzanna was put to death, Serena, according to the Acts, "went during the night filled with joy to the place of execution. She carried away the inanimate body, and dipped her veil in the blood spilt upon the ground. After placing the veil in the silver casket, she was in the habit of praying before it secretly day and night. As to the maiden's body, Serena embalmed it herself with spices, enveloped it in linen, and laid it in the cemetery of Alexander."

While Serena was fulfilling these pious offices of Christian charity, her terrible husband, Diocletian, was triumphantly dictating inscriptions in which he boasted of having "abolished the superstition of Christ everywhere and promulgated the worship of the Gods." (1)

In 250 there were forty-six priests, seven deacons, seven sub-deacons, forty-two acolytes, and fifty-two exorcists, readers, and porters at Rome. There were also fifteen hundred persons relieved by the Church: widows, paupers, and the sick. It was more particularly a deacon's duty to visit and console these unfortunate people, and give an account of them to priests. When a Bishop or priest was imprisoned, money was freely given to the jailors to obtain leave to enter the jail, in order to serve at his Mass, and to carry home the Eucharist. Then, for want of a table, the priest would consecrate the elements upon the hands of a deacon. But those priests who were free visited their flocks, prayed with them, and took every precaution that they should not be without

---

(1) J.-P. Gruter, p. 280.

the bread of the strong. At the worst period of Valerian's persecution, and on the very day following that on which Pope S. STEPHEN had been beheaded in his pontifical chair, in the cemetery of Calixtus, an acolyte, named Tarcisius, quietly left the Catacomb to take the Holy Eucharist to the Christians in Rome. Just as he reached the Porta Capena, some soldiers stopped him, demanding what he carried. Rather than discover the sacred mysteries, Tarcisius refused to answer, preferring to be beaten to death. The soldiers afterwards vainly searched his clothes; they found nothing. However, they perceived a great number of persons gliding furtively into the underground vaults of the neighbourhood; these were Christians who were going to attend the funeral solemnities of Pope STEPHEN. The soldiers reported this to the Emperor, and Valerian gave orders that henceforth no one should be allowed to enter the cemeteries.

Some Persian strangers came to Rome to assist the confessors of the faith; and therefore deserve to share in their triumph. (1) The deacon Cyriacus, after casting a devil out of Diocletian's daughter, was beheaded in the gardens of Sallust; the deacon Cæsarius was flung into the sea at Terracina, for trying to prevent a human sacrifice which the inhabitants were about to offer to Apollo; the priest Marcellinus and the exorcist Peter were also beheaded in a dark forest some few miles from Rome. The pagans hoped that their burial place would not be

---

(1) SS. Marius, Martha, Audifax, and Abachum.

discovered; but the spot was revealed to a holy woman, who collected their bones, and deposited them in the Catacomb inter duas lauros, on the Via Labicana. An oratory was raised over this Catacomb in their honour, and, as years rolled by, the scene of their martyrdom became a town and an episcopal see under the name of Silva Candida (White Wood).

At this period, under the tribuneship of Claudius, a youthful couple was residing at Rome, Chrysanthus and Daria, whose fervent teaching drew a crowd of pagans around them. Chrysanthus addressed the men, Daria the women. When seized by the lictors, divine protection prevented their persecutors from destroying them for a long time. The chains, with which Chrysanthus was bound, fell to pieces, the place of evil repute to which Daria was taken changed into a house of prayer. When cast into a dark dungeon a celestial light lit up its gloom. At length God permitted his servants to win the martyr's palm, and, like S. Stephen, they were stoned to death. Primus and Felicianus were freed from their irons by an angel; but, on being recaptured, they were led to the amphitheatre; the lions, however, came and licked their feet. Under the reign of Diocletian, several Christians found refuge in the imperial palace, in the apartments of Castulus who had charge of the Emperor's bedchamber and stoves; but at length they were betrayed and most of them put to death. Among those then martyred were SS. Mark and Marcellinus, whose names are recorded in a Catacomb on the Via Ardeatina; S. Tranquillinus, S. Castulus, S. Tiburtius, and S. Chromatis who had been Prefect of

Rome. He was converted by the untiring charity of
S. Sebastian. Women were nobly represented in these
bloody hecatombs by SS. Candida and Paulina who
were cast alive into the deserted crypts of the Via
Aurelia; by S. Sotera, aunt to S. Ambrose, a
very beautiful girl—(valde decora),—who offered her
cheeks to be buffeted, and her neck to the axe; by
SS. Rufina and Secunda, sisters, two maidens, who
preferred death to brilliant alliances. At first the
prefect appeared inclined to spare the younger of
the two, but Secunda cried out, "Why do you grant
honour to my sister, and thrust ignominy on me?
We have confessed Christ together; let us die together." S. Zoë was slain, having been surprised
when praying before the tombs of the Apostles; for
six days she was kept without food, and then suspended by her feet over a smouldering fire of wet
straw. S. Eugenia was accused of having advocated
virginity to her companions; and this pagan world,
which had no word of condemnation for infanticide,
this Rome of the consuls, which daily witnessed the
ghastly spectacle of new born babes being cast into
the Velabrum, became alarmed at the number of
girls who refused to marry! S. Eugenia used to say,
"Now is the time of the vintage; now shall the good
grapes be gathered, and separated from the vinebranches; then shall the juice be pressed for everlasting drink." She was crushed to death. Eugenia
owned on the Latin Way a garden and vault in
which she had buried a great many martyrs with
her own hands, and her mother Claudia laid her
beside them. One day, while Claudia was praying

beside her daughter's grave, Eugenia appeared to her in glory, saying, she had met her father in heaven, and had now come to make an appointment for her mother and brothers to join them there. The body of S. Eugenia is now venerated in the church of the holy Apostles.

We must not omit to mention the humble and courageous deaconess Martina. Eugenia was the daughter of an Egyptian prefect, Martina's father was a consul, and she was endowed with every attraction; but she dedicated her beauty to God, her goods to the poor, and her heart to those who lived in sorrow or affliction. Such examples were living sermons which terrified paganism. Martina was seized and scourged, her flesh was torn with iron hooks, and then, covered with blood, she was driven into the amphitheatre, where the lions crouched down and licked her feet. After this she was tied to a stake, but the flames would not consume her. The executioners being amazed were converted, and martyred in their turn. Finally Martina died by the sword, and the Acts of the Martyrs record that, "the city shook, and many idolators believed in Jesus Christ." The church of S. Martina, which was rebuilt with great taste by URBAN VIII, where the temple of Mars had stood at the foot of the Capitol, is now, according to Padre Ventura, the richest and most sumptuous of all those dedicated to the saintly women martyrs. Among the most celebrated martyrs of the third century are Laurence, a deacon, the learned Bishop S. Hippolytus, and S. Sebastian, commander of the first company of prætorian guards.

When Pope SIXTUS II was arrested with some of his clergy, Laurence approached him, saying, "Father, whither goest thou without thy son? In what have I displeased thee? Thou art not accustomed to offer up sacrifice without thy deacon." The Pontiff replied, "My son, a greater combat is reserved for thee; in three days thou shalt follow me." Now it happened that the Roman prefect coveted the imaginary wealth of the Christians, so he sent for Laurence, the principal deacon, and said, "Show me the treasures of your church, the golden vases and silver cups used for receiving the victim's blood, and the magnificent candlesticks which light up your midnight rites." "I will", replied Laurence, "for it is true that our church possesses vast treasures, greater than those which belong to the Emperor, and thou shalt see them." Then Laurence summoned the poor who were the recipients of alms given by Christians, namely the blind, the lame, and the sick. Turning his radiant face towards the pagan, he said, "Behold God's riches." The prefect flew into a violent rage, but Laurence made answer, "Are not these afflicted ones who are relieved by the benevolent, and enlightened from above, worth more than gold. Profit by these treasures, for Rome, for the Emperor, and for yourself."

Then the cruel drama, immortalised by the Acts of the Saints and the masterpieces of artists, commenced; if we credit tradition, the torture took place in a dungeon on the summit of the Viminal Hill, where the church of S. Lorenzo-in-Panisperna now stands. The martyr's body was lacerated by scourging, and afterwards placed upon a red-hot gridiron. But, while his flesh roasted, his countenance shone with joy, the place of execution was filled with a sweet perfume, and he continued praying for the conversion and welfare of Rome until the end. He was martyred on the 10$\underline{\text{th}}$ of August 258. The Christians collected his relics and bore them out of the city, where they were buried, on the road to Tibur, in a crypt belonging to a holy woman named Cyriaca. It is over this vault, in a little valley surrounded by hills, known as the Ager Veranus, that the patriarchal Basilica of S. Laurence was raised in the fourth century. (1) S. Cyriaca, who buried S. Laurence, was a pious widow who had for some time devoted her life to deeds of Christian charity. She dwelt on that part of the Cælian Hill on which stands the church of S. Maria-in-Dominicâ; and from her house, on the eve of his martyrdom, S. Laurence distributed alms to the poor of Rome.

S. Cyriaca closely followed S. Laurence, by the cruel path of martyrdom, to the crypt in the Ager Veranus; and was succeeded by quite a legion of others. Pilgrims came from all parts to this funeral

---

(1) There are six churches in Rome dedicated to S. Laurence: S. Lorenzo-fuori-le-mura, which is one of the seven great Roman Basilicas; S. Lorenzo-in-Damaso, close to the palazzo della Cancelleria; S. Lorenzo-in-Lucina, near the Corso, where the gridiron on which the saint suffered is preserved; S. Lorenzo-in-Miranda, behind the columns of the temple of Antoninus and Faustina; S. Lorenzo-in-Fonte, on the Viminal Hill, built upon the spot where the holy deacon baptised his jailor, S. Hippolytus, with all his household; and S. Lorenzo-in-Panisperna, where he suffered death.

CHAPTER III.—THIRD CENTURY.

vault, which, although its entrance was wide — "ampla fauce", — was, owing to the crowds, not large enough; Prudentius says:—

"Angustum totis illud specus esse catervis."

Among the many martyrs buried here, history mentions S. Hippolytus, Bishop of Porto, a very learned man, pupil of Irenæus, and master of Origen. His ardent faith caused his death; after being bound hand and foot he was cast into a whirlpool on the 22$^{\underline{nd}}$ of August, 269. Some years before this, in 255, another aged priest named Hippolytus was tied by the feet to wild horses, in commemoration of the death of the son of Theseus.

S. Hippolytus of Porto composed a paschal cycle which became famous. This cycle having been lost for a long time was rediscovered in 1551, as also the statue of the saint, concealed beneath the ruins of an oratory which had been built over his grave. It was engraved in Greek characters upon the pontifical chair in which the venerable Bishop was represented as sitting. This cycle had a period of sixteen years beginning from the first year of Alexander Severus's reign. On one side it determined the moons of March; on the other, the Sundays of Easter. Repeated seven times, his calculations embraced a period of one hundred and twelve years. The statue of S. Hippolytus with his cycle, a curious memento of the primitive Church, may now be seen in the Vatican Library. (1)

Every age, every condition of life found words of consolation and encouragement in holy archives.

---

(1) It is opposite the statue of Aristides of Smyrna.

The story of that young martyr who was led, by the order of Decius, into a beautiful garden, and delivered over, bound hand and foot, to the blandishments of a courtesan, was related as a caution to youth. The lad bit off his tongue and spat it in her face.

The soldiers and veterans of the Roman legions were reminded of the example of S. Maurice and his companions, and of S. Sebastian, who bore an apostle's heart beneath the cuirass of the Pretorian guard. He devoted himself for a long time to visiting prisons, helping confessors, and converting their jailors. In one day S. Sebastian presented sixty-eight persons for baptism. All these conversions, taking place in Diocletian's palace and tribunals, could not fail to betray the work and the name of the young Pretorian captain. Diocletian accused him of ingratitude. "I have learnt", replied Sebastian, "what folly it was to pray to stones; both night and day I have prayed to Christ, the God who is in heaven, for your welfare and for that of the Empire." Diocletian thereupon handed him over to the Mauritanian archers, who bound him to a column and transfixed him with arrows.

Sebastian still breathed when he was succoured by Irene, the pious widow of Castulus, the Emperor's steward, whose quarters had often given refuge to Christians, and who was afterwards buried alive as a reward for his courage. Irene stanched the martyr's wounds and restored him to life. Sebastian again presented himself before Diocletian, and endeavoured to make him feel the injustice of his decrees against the unfortunate Christians, who were always praying for him. Diocletian's only reply was to have him massacred in the hippodrome: and, in order that no vestige of his body might remain, he gave orders that it should be cast into a sewer. Nevertheless S. Lucina recovered it, and caused it to be conveyed to the Catacombs in 288.

Two churches were consecrated to the memory of S. Sebastian at Rome. S. Sebastiano-alla-Polveriera marks the spot on which he suffered, and S. Sebastiano-alle-Catacombe, on the Ostian way, the place of his burial.

Looking back into the bosom of Christian society we shall find that, besides these great examples which appealed to the strong, there were others no less great, which appealed to weak and languid souls, who regretted the seductive pleasures of their past lives, and who almost disbelieved in divine grace. The examples of Aglais and Boniface may be quoted. Aglais was a great lady — (mulier magna), possessing palaces, country seats, with seventy-four stewards to manage her estates; in her grandeur she had thrice given public shows to the populace. Aglais, beautiful and admired, valued life only for its pleasures; although occasionally she feared a future life. Boniface, her chief steward, the companion of her pleasures, was also not destitute of good qualities; he neither lacked hospitality, generosity nor charity. He always welcomed strangers, and sometimes he wandered through the streets and by-ways of Rome, by night, to rescue the unfortunate.

One day Aglais observed to Boniface, "Thou knowest into what shame we have sunk, forgetting that God sees us, and that hereafter we shall have to give an account to Him for the evil we have done in this world. But I have heard Christians say that those, who do honour to the martyrs of Jesus Christ, shall one day share in their glory. Therefore take gold and spices, and bring me back some of their relics." Boniface said, "If instead of their relics mine be brought to you, promise me that you will receive them." Aglais replied to the ironical remark of her servant with sarcasm, and Boniface went on his way. But grace entered his heart, and confessing God he died for Him in 290. A voice from heaven revealed this to Aglais, who thereupon summoned some priests, and, walking respectfully with them, while they sang hymns, she went forth to meet the sanctified body which was being brought back to her. (1) She met it five stadia from Rome on the Latin way, (2) and it was placed in a crypt, over which she built an oratory worthy of his martyrdom—"dignum passionis ejus." (3) Then Aglais renounced her worldly goods, her palaces, her jewels. She enfranchised her slaves, and divided her treasures among the poor; so this pleasure loving daughter of the Roman proconsul Arsaces became a humble servant of Jesus Christ. She lived thus for thirteen years, after which she died full of divine grace. Maidens and children had noble examples in S. Pancras and S. Agnes. Agnes, a young girl, was led to

(1) "Angelicatus homo" are the words of an inscription to be found in the church of SS. Boniface and Alexis.
(2) A stadium is equal to 125 paces or 625 Roman feet.
(3) The body of S. Boniface was afterwards removed to Mt. Aventine. He is still honoured in the church of S. Alexis.

the circus Agonalis, now Piazza Navona, to be menaced, insulted, and outraged. Nothing could disturb the serenity of her countenance nor her calm demeanour: she was conducted to a haunt of vice, beneath the arcades of the circus; but being so chaste she had no fears for her modesty. The vaults to which S. Agnes was taken are of ancient masonry, on which old mosaics recall the scene far more vividly than do the bas-reliefs of Algarde over the altar. The sweet girl was led thither by two soldiers. The occupants of this place of evil repute received her with disgusting jeers, looking with surprise and disdain upon her modest demeanour. They tore off her clothes; but her hair grew miraculously, and concealed her body from their vulgar gaze. The son of the prefect of Rome, daring to look insolently at her, was immediately struck down dead. Then the prefect, who was her persecutor and executioner, fell upon his knees, and implored her to give him back his son, and in her charity Agnes prayed and the youth was restored to life. The saint had striven long enough; she pined for her heavenly crown, which a stroke from a sharp sword obtained for her by the mercy of God. (1)

Agnes's relations took possession of her body, as her Acts relate, with great joy —(cum omni gaudio)—,

---

(1) There are two churches at Rome dedicated to S. Agnes; S. Agnese-di-piazza-Navona, where the evil den into which she was thrust is shown, and S. Agnese-fuori-le-mura built over her tomb. S. Agnes suffered martyrdom on the 21st January 304. With her the account of Diocletian's persecutions is completed.

and buried it on an estate which they owned on the Via Nomentana. A foster-sister of Agnes, called Emerentiana, who had never received baptism, was discovered at her sister's grave by the pagans, who tried to persuade her to deny God, and being unsuccessful they stoned her to death on the spot.

Christians must be struck when reading this history of the weak overcoming the strong; it ought to raise their hearts and courage and strengthen their good resolutions. Paganism, with its brutish pleasures, its sensuality, and its effeminacy, disappeared in its shame from a society that despised it.

CHAPTER IV.

Exurge, veritas et erumpe.
Tertullian.

FOURTH CENTURY.

E have now reached the time when Christian monuments rapidly multiplied at Rome and throughout the empire. But, before days of peace dawned upon the Christians, more martyrs had to suffer under Maxentius. Pope MARCELLUS was condemned to take charge of wild beasts kept for public sports, and during nine months he lived in their stables. Some young students then contrived his escape, concealing him in the house where S. Lucina used to live near the Via Lata, and which had long been a refuge for the sick and the poor. This house had become an oratory in which Christians assembled to hear the pious exhortations of the Pontiff. Maxentius, on hearing this, gave orders that the oratory should be turned into a stable, and that MARCELLUS should be degraded a second time to look after the animals. The Pontiff soon sank beneath the weight of these fresh sufferings, and the place, which had been sanctified by his death, became a church once more and

was placed under his invocation. It is still called S. Marcello-al-Corso.

Meanwhile Constantine had been proclaimed Emperor in 306, and in 312 he decided to march towards Italy. On the 27th of October of that year he boldly pitched his camp with forty thousand soldiers on the banks of the Tiber, in the face of one hundred and seventy thousand men under the command of Maxentius. The Milvian Bridge, now Ponte Molle, separated the two camps; but on the following day the army of Maxentius, trusting in their numbers, crossed the river; the Emperor put himself at their head, as much to disprove a charge of cowardice, which the Romans had brought against him, as because he imagined that victory was foretold by some ambiguous words in the Sybil's books. On the other side a new ensign floated over the legions of Constantine, the Labarum, which bore both the sign of Calvary and the promise of victory. Constantine felt within him not only the power of genius, but a divine impulse — instinctu divinitatis, mentis magnitudine. (1)

The battle was bloody and decisive. Maxentius, in his foolish confidence, had destroyed the Milvian Bridge; thus his retreat was cut off, and he, with a great part of his army, was drowned in the Tiber. But a few hours before this event which changed the history of the world, Constantine, walking at sunset in the country, beheld a luminous cross in the heavens with the celebrated words, "In hoc signo vinces". During the middle ages a church was built on Monte

---

(1) Inscription on the Arch of Constantine.

Mario at the spot where, according to tradition, this vision appeared to the Emperor.

Then the gates of the Eternal City opened before the Cross, and the Senate and the people raised a triumphal Arch in Constantine's honour; in order to adorn it worthily the choicest marbles were collected, the greatest artists sent for, and they even went so far as to plunder the bas-reliefs from a triumphal arch that had been raised in honour of Trajan. Constantine's Arch remains entire to this day, with its statues of renown, its three arcades, and its tall columns of giallo antico. It stands at the end of the Via Sacra, near the Vespasian amphitheatre, in the direction of the Ostian way. Several inscriptions are graven upon it, among them is:— „Liberatori urbis, fundatori quietis." "To the Deliverer of the city and the Founder of peace."

Once master of the capital of the world, the first thought of the catechumen Constantine was to introduce the civilisation of the Gospel in every place. The infamous orgies of the heathen were forbidden under severe penalties. To prevent the murder of infants, a common practice among the Romans, the Emperor gave orders that all children of the poor should be brought up at the expense of the public treasury. The enfranchisement of slaves was encouraged, and blessed by a religious ceremony; divorce, if not absolutely abolished, was rendered more difficult; confiscation of the property of criminals ceased to affect that of their wives and children; prisoners were not to be kept in dungeons or fetters, widows and orphans might always appeal to the Emperor, a privilege denied to their adversaries.

The first Christian monument constructed by Constantine in Rome was a baptistery, under the invocation of S. John. It was in the old gardens of Plautius Lateranus, where the palace of the Empress Fausta stood, that, during Sylvester's pontificate, the magnificent baptistery was erected, which still invites the piety of the faithful, and the curiosity of artists, to S. John Lateran. There is no better example of the style of building peculiar to the early Church, and of the ceremonies which were observed in the administration of the first Christian Sacrament. The basalt urn containing holy water was placed in the centre of a vast laver into which the neophytes descended. This urn had been decorated by Constantine with silver plates weighing 3,000 pounds. It was filled with water issuing from a golden lamb and seven silver stags. Near the lamb were two silver statues five feet high; one representing the Saviour; the other, S. John the Baptist bearing a scroll with the inscription: — "Ecce agnus Dei qui tollit peccata mundi." Lastly, from the centre of this basin rose a porphyry column supporting a gold vase of 52 pounds weight, in which annually, at Easter, 200 pounds of balsam with wicks of amianthus were burnt. (1)

The building still remains; its form is octagonal, this shape being repeated within, by the disposition of

(1) Anastasius tells us that the golden lamb weighed 30 pounds; each silver stag, 80 pounds; the statue of our Lord, 170 pounds; that of S. John, 100 pounds.

the columns which surround the font. These porphyry columns support a frieze, above which rise white marble pillars upholding the lantern-tower, through which light penetrates into the sanctuary.

Formerly, on the morning of Holy Saturday, the Pope went in solemn state to the Baptistery of Constantine. Before entering he turned to the Cardinals, and, blessing them, said, "Go therefore and teach ye all nations: baptizing them in the Name of the Father, and of the Son, and of the Holy Ghost." Then the Cardinals, mounting their horses, rode to the churches from which they took their titles, in order to sprinkle the catechumens with holy water. The Pope himself performed the same service to three neophytes. This ancient ceremony has been discontinued; yet every year, on Holy Saturday, baptism is still solemnly administered to converts in the basalt basin formerly used by S. Sylvester.

Constantine annexed to his baptistery a great Basilica dedicated first to the Saviour and, at a later period, to the two saints John: John the Precursor, and John the Beloved. This is that Lateran Basilica, "the Mother and Head of all the Churches of the City and the World" (1) as the inscription on the façade states. It is the most celebrated of all the churches on account of its ancient baptistery, and

---

(1)   "Dogmate papali datur ac simul imperiali
         Quod sim cunctarum mater caput ecclesiarum..."
S. John Lateran is generally known by the name of the Basilica of the Saviour or the Constantine Basilica in the old Acts. It was only after the 10th century that it began to be called after S. John.

its papal palace, where the Pontiffs dwelt for ten centuries; and also on account of the five Ecumenical Councils which assembled within its walls. This venerable Basilica was consecrated by Pope S. SYLVESTER on the 9th of November (5 Id.) 324, and the commemoration of its dedication has become a festival throughout Christendom.

Old historians frequently speak of the Lateran church as the golden Basilica — basilica aurea — on account of its splendour. The façade which faced the east was composed of a portico in Parian marble, projecting from the building, and a gable-end adorned in its upper part with a mosaic representing the Saviour of mankind. Six columns supported the portico, at the back of which were the five entrances into the church. These were never closed by doors; the mother church remained always open to shelter the destitute and comfort all who prayed. On lifting the curtain which covered the entrance, the magnificence of the five naves was truly striking, more especially the grandeur of the centre nave from which the beautiful sanctuary and paintings in the tribune could be seen. This centre nave was upheld by thirty columns and four pilasters. The lateral naves, less high, rested upon forty-five marble columns of verde antico. All the naves were lighted by a hundred and ten silver lamps.

The high altar stood in the centre of the transept, having the Confession beneath it and a rich baldacchino above. Four angels, the twelve Apostles and Jesus Christ enthroned, surrounded it. The baldacchino and the statues were all silver; and the cornice which supported them was of chased silver. The tabernacle was pure gold, and nard oil was alone consumed in the lamps which burned before it.

The Canons' choir, an enclosure formed of Parian marble, was before the high altar; behind this came the tribune with the pontifical chair raised upon six steps, the upper one being ornamented with sculptured representations of an asp, a lion, a dragon, and a basilisk. This was to recall the words of the prophet: Super aspidem, et basiliscum ambulabis: et conculcabis leonem, et draconem. (1)

Finally, the walls of the Basilica were covered with paintings; the face of the Redeemer prominent among them may still be seen. The head is surrounded by a golden halo, the expression of the Saviour being singularly grave and majestic. According to a pious tradition this painting miraculously appeared during the consecration of the Basilica.

The Lateran church formerly possessed certain liturgical customs peculiar to it. Being dedicated to the Saviour, the Lord's Prayer was usually the only one permitted in the services. Panvinius says, "The Supreme church might easily be recognised by this almost exclusive use of the supreme prayer". The same author informs us that the bells of the Basilica never rang except for joy — "festivo more pulsantur" —, because it represented the Church of Heaven more than any other sanctuary. Neither did they end the

---

(1) Psalm XC, 13.

"Agnus Dei" with, "dona nobis pacem", peace in heaven being eternal. (1)

S. John Lateran has been sacked and ruined several times; it was almost destroyed by fire at the beginning of the fourteenth century, on which occasion Petrarch, broken-hearted, wrote to Pope URBAN:—"Merciful Father, how can you have the heart to pass your time in sleep on the banks of the Rhone, in your gilded apartments, while the Lateran is crumbling to pieces, and the mother of all the churches is roofless and a mere temple of the winds and storms?" The actual Basilica only dates from 1360, the façade being constructed by Alessandro Galilei as late as the last century. It is a vast and noble edifice, where unfortunately Borromini has hidden the columns of breccia, serpentine and brocatel, belonging to the ancient church, beneath massive pillars. Gigantic statues of the twelve Apostles, standing in the thickness of the pillars, majestically remind one of the Council of Jerusalem, which was followed by so many others at the Lateran. Above the Apostles are statues of the prophets; above these last a very striking painting exemplifies the promises of the old law on one side, while, on the other, a still more remarkable painting points out their accomplishment in the Gospel. In the Lateran church is shown the table, now encased in gold, which was used by Our Lord for His last Supper; and the columns, moulded by order of Augustus from bronze beaks torn from ships taken at Actium, support the architrave of the altar.

(1) For these details see "Les sept Basiliques de Rome," by M. le Baron de Bussières.

CHAPTER IV. — FOURTH CENTURY.

Several other Roman Basilicas owe their origin to Constantine: namely, S. Peter's, S. Paolo-fuori-le mura, S. Croce-in-Gerusalemme, and S. Lorenzo.

We have already stated that the first Roman Christians suffered martyrdom, and that the Prince of the Apostles was buried, in the gardens and circus of Nero, at the foot of the Vatican Hill. Since that time this spot was considered holy, being held in great respect. The pagans looked upon the Vatican as the hill of oracles (Vaticinia). These oracles were believed to emanate from the temple of Apollo. Not far from this temple stood an old oak, which, according to Pliny, was even more ancient than Rome — vetustior urbe --, it had always been worshipped from Etruscan times. (1) Otherwise the Vatican Hill was only frequented by potters who came thither to manufacture the brittle vases mentioned by Juvenal, — Vaticano fragiles de Monte patellas. (2) The atmosphere of this place was so unhealthy that Tacitus, remembering the frequent epidemics occasioned by it, calls the spot infamous, -- infamibus Vaticanis locis. (3) In consequence of this the Christians, in spite of its being near Nero's circus and gardens, found the place convenient for their meetings and mysteries. In fact we learn from the Acts of S. Martial that it was there S. Peter taught "great crowds of people". These meetings were probably held in excavations made by these potters, and it is probable that the

---

(1) Pliny, B. XIII, c. 7.
(2) Sat. VI, v. 343.
(3) Hist. II, 93.

bodies of the Apostle and the first martyrs were buried there also.

ANACLETUS established an oratory in honour of Blessed Peter on that spot; S. SYLVESTER afterwards, aided by imperial munificence, built there a glorious church, the foundation stone of which was laid by Constantine.

The mighty Emperor went to the Vatican, surrounded by bishops and clergy singing praises to God, and followed by a large concourse of the faithful. On his arrival the Emperor took off his crown, prostrated himself and confessed his sins aloud, shedding many tears. Taking up a pickaxe, he broke up the ground, and carried away on his shoulders twelve loads of earth in honour of the twelve Apostles. The Basilica rose with such remarkable rapidity that it was consecrated on the 18th of November of the same year, very few days after the church of the Saviour had been consecrated.

The Basilica of S. Peter stood on the slope of the Vatican, and partly rested on the walls of Nero's Circus. It was reached by a staircase composed of thirty-five marble steps, divided by five landings. In front of the façade was a portico, pierced by three windows and three doors, opening between columns of Egyptian granite. To the right, and standing apart, a square shaped and lofty belfry of Byzantine architecture was subsequently erected. The entrances to the portico were closed by bronze doors affixed to a marble framework. The visitor, after passing through them, entered a large rectangular court, resembling by its gallery, columns,

and central fountain a Roman atrium or forecourt.
This court was subsequently paved with white marble
by Pope Donus, and called Paradise. (1) As early
as the fourth century S. Paulinus speaks of it as
dazzling, — nitens. He tells us also that its fountain
was shaded by a bronze dome, and that its waters
gushed forth amidst four columns placed there,
with some mystic significance, "non sine specie
mystica." For S. Paulinus saw in it an emblem of
that stream of grace which flows towards a blessed
eternity, amid the pillars of life. Above the gallery,
and facing the east, rose the church's blue tinted
frontal — "fronte cærulea." This grand church was
possessed of five doorways, five naves, and a hundred
columns. The length of the naves alone measured
400 Roman palms; the central nave was 170 palms
high, the two next were 82, and the outermost 62. (2)

Each door in S. Peter's church has its name in
history. The central door, called the Silver Door, — argentea —, was generally kept closed. It was covered
with silver plates by S. Gregory I, Honorius I and
Leo IV. To the left was the Ravennate Door, named
from the Trastevere, which was sometimes called the
Ravenna quarter: this door was used by men. On
the other side was the Porta Romana, used by women.
The door named Guidonea came next, it was only

---

(1) This name was subsequently used to describe the atrium
of a church. In French it has been corrupted into parvis,
the square in front of a cathedral.

(2) According to Murray a Roman palm equalled $8^{8}/_{10}$ inches.

opened for pilgrims; while, at the other end, was the Door of Judgment, which only opened to admit the dead.

On entering the Basilica right and left of the main entrance were two columns reputed to be the finest in the world. They were of African marble, and, according to Severani, commemorated the two pillars of the church, S. PETER and S. PAUL. But the chief objects of admiration were the principal nave with its grand arch, cast like an aerial bridge, facing the high altar; and the resplendent throne of the Apostle,—"coruscans"—, behind the tribune. S. Paulinus said that this view dazzled him and rejoiced his heart, — "lumina stringit et corda lætificat."

The triumphal arch is still to be found in several Roman Basilicas. In the Vatican it supported the Cross of the Labarum, and S. Peter's Keys. On great feasts, the Sacra Culcitra was also exposed here. This was the bloody shroud highly venerated which had been used by the early Christians to carry the bodies of the martyrs to the Catacombs. Beyond this arch, a twisted white marble column, sculptured with vine leaves, was an object of great devotion; for, according to tradition, Our Lord leaned against it while preaching in the temple. This column and eleven others similar to it, reported to have once belonged to Solomon's temple, stood before the altar. It would be impossible to describe the wealth of gold, silver, and precious stones lavished upon the altar by the Emperor's munificence. Let it suffice to mention that the altar was constructed of the finest marbles, and was overshadowed by a vermilion baldacchino or canopy, upheld by four porphyry columns. Beneath was the Confession or Tomb of the Apostle: this arrangement was intended to recall the Catacombs as well as the Apocalypse, for S. JOHN says:— "I saw under the altar the souls of them that were slain for the word of God, and for the testimony which they held." (1) The body of S. PETER had been enclosed by S. SYLVESTER in a silver case which was placed in a gilt bronze shrine, surmounted by a gold cross weighing one hundred and fifty pounds. The holy deposit was laid in a vault at the Vatican, beneath the oratory of S. ANACLETUS. This oratory in reality formed an intermediate story between the high altar of the Basilica and the tomb of this first Pontiff. It also possessed its altar and its crypt. The latter could only be seen from a small window, and S. Gregory of Tours relates that the pilgrims used to thrust their heads through it in order to pray before the holy relics.

The number of these pilgrims was immense. Sometimes they were seen swarming in the streets of Rome "like clouds of ants and bees;" even Princes, Kings, and Emperors, bowed and humbled themselves at the feet of the Fisherman of Tiberias. History cites Totila as being one of these. Charlemagne would not venture to ascend the steps of the sanctuary until he had kissed them one by one. Fulrad, Abbot of S. Denis, placed upon S. Peter's tomb a deed of gift of those towns and provinces which Pepin offered as a homage to the Apostle's successor.

---

(1) Apoc. Chap. VI, v. 9.

Many Emperors were crowned and saints canonized in this church. Very few Bishops, in the early ages, failed to visit it, at least once in their lives, to pray for themselves and their flocks. GREGORY VII wrote as follows to the Archbishop of Rouen: — "What work, what difficulty, has led you to neglect Blessed Peter, when the furthest nations of the world, even those lately converted, both men and women, make a point of coming every year?" "Quum ab ipsius mundi finibus, etiam gentes noviter ad fidem conversæ, studeant annue tam mulieres quam viri ad eum venire". (1)

On leaving the Vatican, pilgrims flocked along the Ostian way to S. Paul's tomb. That was in fact the second compulsory station for every pilgrimage. The faithful did not come for the sole purpose of praying beside S. Peter's tomb; they came, according to the well known expression, to the tombs of the Apostles, ad limina Apostolorum. The day after S. Zoë was burnt over a slow fire, for praying near S. Peter's tomb, S. Tranquillinus was stoned to death on being discovered praying near that of S. Paul. Both these honoured sepulchres were sometimes known as "trophies". In the second century a priest named Caius wrote, "I can point out to you the 'trophies' of the Apostles who founded this church. Whether you go to the Vatican, or whether you go along the Ostian way, you will meet with them."

The body of S. PAUL had been buried, after his martyrdom, in a field belonging to a holy woman

---

(1) We shall only speak of the actual church of S. Peter from the time of its construction, the sixteenth century.

called Lucina. Her name frequently occurs, in the history of devotion and charity, in the first ages of the Roman church. On this spot S. ANACLETUS consecrated an oratory, as he had done at the Vatican, and Constantine transformed it into a Basilica in the year 324. This church of S. Paul, confined as it was between the Ostian way and the Tiber, lacked the size and grandeur of those of the Saviour and of S. Peter. But the crowds who came to it were so great that the Emperors Valentinian, Theodosius, and Arcadius, determined to give it new proportions and splendour, "ornare, amplificare, attollere." They even proposed to turn the ancient road, should such be the pleasure of the Senate and people; "si placuerit tam populo quam Senatui." The Basilica was then built just as it remained until the disastrous fire in 1823.

Prudentius enthusiastically sang its praises; "Everything here is royal, 'regia pompa loci est'; an excellent prince dedicated this monument, and made its interior resplendent with a thousand gifts. The beams are gilt, in order that the light may only be reflected in golden rays . . . columns of Parian marble support the tawny panelling, 'fulvis laquearibus', while the arches are adorned with beautiful glass, (1) which recalls the variety and the splendour of spring flowers."

S. Paul's church, like that of S. Peter, possessed an atrium surrounded by porticoes, and it had also a long covered gallery which extended to the gates of the town. Both atrium and gallery have long since dis-

---

(1) A reference probably to mosaics.

appeared. A narrow portico, built by Benedict XIII, and a square belfry, said to be the oldest in Rome, rise alone in front of the Basilica. (1) But the Basilica itself had outlived revolutions and centuries, remaining the most ancient and venerable of all the Christian buildings in Rome. There was an apse, a triumphal arch, the Confession of the Apostle beneath the Altar, and five naves supported by a forest of columns. The finest of these columns had been brought by Constantine either from Hadrian's Tomb, or the Æmilian Basilica. They were of violet brescia, and fluted. Formerly there were twenty-four of these columns, but in 1823 their beautiful shafts might have been seen lying on the grass, calcined and broken, after the conflagration, amidst the ruins of the splendid church whose cornice they had supported for so long a period. The remaining columns less beautiful were of Parian marble.

Natives of other countries can form no idea of the effect produced by these long rows of columns, through which every part of the edifice was visible; they seemed placed there more as ornaments, than to support heavy buildings. There might perhaps have been faults of proportion or of harmony between these slender supports and the height of the massive walls above them in these ancient Basilicas. At S. Peter's, these walls rested upon an entablature; at S. Paul's, high arches united them to the columns. Above these ar-

---

(1) At the time this book was written, efforts were being made to discover traces of the old portico, and to restore and embellish the façade.

cades was a cornice over which were portraits of the Popes, in couples, from S. PETER to PIUS VIII. This unique collection was commenced by S. LEO. Arabesques in stucco and ancient frescoes, representing subjects from the Bible and the new law, covered the walls to the height of the windows. The framework topped all, without being hidden by either vault or ceiling; the gilt was effaced from the beams; while the dust of centuries had darkened the fawn coloured panelling; all that met the eye was a commonplace assemblage of rafters and supports intermingling above the graceful arches.

After the conflagration of 1823, nothing remained of S. Paul's but the façade, with its curious mosaics, the apse, the triumphal arch and the high altar. Since then its reconstruction was carried on with activity; and now the old Basilica has arisen from its ashes. Although the new edifice resembles the old one as closely as possible, it cannot bring back the glamour of antiquity which clung to the ancient fane. Amid its new columns of Corsican granite and Egyptian marble, we regret the beautiful full veined marbles of Paros, the porphyry, the cipolin and the violet breccia, spoils from the heathen temples which had adorned the Basilica of the great Apostle.

Over the Catacomb of S. Cyriaca, for ever renowned as the burial place of S. Laurence, Constantine, ever ready to carry out the pious behests of S. SYL-VESTER, raised the Basilica of S. Lorenzo-fuori-le-mura. The church was small, but richly ornamented; silver and porphyry decorated the walls of the tribune; over the high altar there was a representation of the death of the saint worked in silver; before this, day and night three lamps, one of which was of gold with ten burners, consumed the most costly perfumes. Very important works were carried out at S. Lorenzo by Pope PELAGIUS II, towards the end of the sixth century. Even then a neighbouring hill was levelled to give more space for the building. From various writings we learn that the primitive church was not demolished, for annalists recognise two; one of which they describe as major, and was the older; the other as speciosior, and nova, which had evidently been built by PELAGIUS II. These two churches were distinct, only just touching at their apses. HONORIUS III joined them together, and their union produced the present church. It is, however, still possible to distinguish between the major and the nova churches. The two buildings are not on the same level and the style is different. The major church is the first one sees; the nova church is that portion which takes in the triumphal arch and the presbyterium. (1)

All through the middle ages a covered portico united S. Lorenzo with the Tiburtine Gate; it may be remembered that a similar portico existed between the church of S. Paul and the Ostian Gate. Bologna to this day boasts a covered way of six hundred and thirty-five arches, uniting the town to La Madonna di S. Luca, situated on the Monte della Guardia. These monumental avenues show what enormous

---

(1) See Commendatore di Rossi's "Bulletino di Archeologia Cristiana anno secundo," p. 33.

crowds of pilgrims used to come thither, and how generous devotion made the people. (1)

S. Lorenzo has been restored several times, notably in the fifteenth, sixteenth, and seventeenth centuries, and again in the present century by Pius IX, who is there buried. A portico composed of six ancient columns with fresco paintings indicates its position on the road to Tivoli. This is preceeded by a red granite monolith on a white marble pedestal, bearing, at the height of thirty-two feet ten inches, a bronze statue of the holy deacon in the act of distributing alms to the poor. Twenty-two columns of oriental granite divide the Basilica into three naves. It still contains the marble pulpits or amboes formerly used for reading the Epistles and Gospels; a pontifical throne, ornamented with mosaics, and the bodies of S. Laurence and S. Stephen which are there venerated. (2)

Since Constantine had become master of the world, his pious mother had turned her thoughts to the Holy Land; and, although eighty years of age, she

---

(1) The portico of S. Paolo was about a mile and a quarter long; that of S. Lorenzo rather less; that of Bologna nearly two miles.

(2) In the volute of the eighth column of the central nave are sculptured a lizard and a frog, recalling Pliny's story about the Spartan architects of the Octavian Portico, Sauros and Batrachos. They had devoted large sums of money to building and embellishing this Portico, asking, as their only reward, that they might be allowed to inscribe their names on their work. This being refused, they sculptured a lizard and a frog on the capital of this pillar, thus introducing their names figuratively into the ornamentation in order to immortalise them. (Hist. nat., l. XXXVI.)

went thither to tear down the statue of Venus from the temple which Hadrian had raised in her honour on Calvary. It is well known how, on digging up the foundations of that temple, three crosses with several instruments of torture were discovered. A miracle revealed the Cross which had been sanctified by the death of Jesus Christ; and Helena, having left one portion of it at Jerusalem, and despatched another piece to Constantinople, ordered a Basilica to be erected at Rome to receive the remainder. This was the origin of S. Croce-in-Gerusalemme. It now occupies the site of the Sessorian Palace and of the Horti Variani, splendid gardens that were sullied by the infamous debaucheries of Heliogabalus. Since then the palace had been inhabited by Alexander Severus, and in the fourth century the pious widow of Constantius Chlorus lived there. It was therefore in her own home that Helena contrived a sanctuary for the Cross, thus imitating her son's example, who had converted his palace at the Lateran into the church of the Saviour. The Basilica of S. Croce possessed an atrium with marble seats. Since the time of BENEDICT XIV, this atrium has given way to a covered vestibule, or narthex, surmounted by a cupola. The interior of the church was divided into three naves by columns of oriental granite; while, at the extreme end, a low chapel was built upon earth brought by S. Helena from Calvary. This chapel has ever been an object of the deepest veneration. Its principal altar is dedicated to S. Helena, and only the Pope and the titular Cardinals may officiate at it. Among the decorations of this sanctuary are some ancient mosaics in the vaulted ceiling, dating from the reign of Valentinian III; the central one representing the Saviour blessing the world, surrounded by angels and cherubim, and holding in his left hand a book on which is written:— "Ego sum lux mundi." In the surrounding compartments the Evangelists are represented, and also various scenes depicting the finding of the Cross. An inscription, placed in the lobby of the chapel, forbids women to enter it except once a year on the 20$\underline{\text{th}}$ of March, the day of its dedication.

But there is another chapel which must not be forgotten when visiting S. Croce, the chapel of the Relics. It is close by, and communicates with the church by a rich marble balcony intended for the exposition of its precious treasures. The most remarkable of these relics were three fragments of the true Cross, the title of the Cross, one of the nails which had pierced the Divine Limbs, and two of the thorns out of the crown, still bearing traces of blood. Several of the words which composed the title can still be deciphered. The nail is triangular in shape, with a round head, its length being between five and six inches; but the point is gone. It is this portion which, according to Theodoret, was placed by S. Helena in her son's helmet as a safeguard against danger; it now forms the circle of the famous iron crown preserved at Monza. S. Croce has been restored and embellished at different times; but the original building still exists. On its façade, which dates from the last century, are statues of the four Evangelists, Constantine, and his mother; but unfortunately Helena's statue alone remains at S. Croce, for the porphyry urn beneath the altar no longer contains her ashes. (1) We know that S. Helena's body was placed in the Catacomb inter duas lauros on the Labican way; a Catacomb famous for being the burial place of SS. Marcellinus and Peter, and over which the Emperor raised a church under their invocation. This church, built out of love for his mother and respect for the saints, "pró amore matris et veneratione sanctorum," has long since disappeared; although it was thought that some few vestiges had been discovered among the ruins of the Tor Pignatara. Constantine had endowed it with the revenues of three islands, one of which was Sardinia.

All the buildings erected by the Emperor's piety were richly endowed by him. In addition to patens, gold chalices, silver beacons, brass jars enumerated by Anastasius, he settled important domains upon them, as stated above. The total amount of these gifts reached to 27,729 golden "soldi", half of which sum was assigned to the Lateran church alone. The property thus bestowed was generally the confiscated possessions of martyrs, whose heirs were unknown. The Basilica of S. Peter possessed property at Tyre, Alexandria, Antioch, and on the banks of the Euphrates; the proceeds from which, not only contributed towards paying for the services of the church, but also provided all the perfumes mentioned in Holy Writ; balm, nard, cinnamon, saffron, storax, and cloves, which were used in sacred rites.

(1) This urn, ornamented with four lions' heads, holds the bodies of S. Cæsarius and S. Anastasius.

In this manner the pious generosity of the Imperial court was made known to the world. It would be monotonous and wearisome to describe all the churches which are, rightly or wrongly, ascribed to Constantine. The only churches authentically attributed to him are the Lateran, S. Peter's on the Vatican, S. Paul's on the Ostian way, S. Lorenzo fuori-le-mura, S. Croce-in-Gerusalemme, the church of SS. Marcellinus and Peter which was destroyed, and S. Agnes, on the Via Nomentana.

The last named church was, at the request of his daughter Constantia, built by Constantine on the spot where the young martyr of the Circus Agonalis was buried; since then it has remained intact amid all revolutions and pillages, and is the oldest existing Christian edifice in Rome. It is necessary to descend forty-five marble steps to reach it; its most singular feature is a double portico, one above the other, supported by columns of antique breccia and by porta-santa. (1) S. Agnes's statue is composed of an antique torso of oriental alabaster, with modern bronze gilt head, feet and hands. Her relics lie beneath the altar, which is resplendent with precious stones; the side walls are covered with ancient sepulchral inscriptions. Another church close by, of elliptical form, was long considered to be an ancient temple dedicated to Bacchus, because the vaulted ceiling was decorated with children gathering grapes. According to Ana-

---

(1) The Italians give this name to a species of breccia used for the framework of the Holy Door — porta santa — at S. Peter's.

stasius the Librarian, this graceful monument was built by Constantine, for the baptism of his sister and daughter, who were also buried here.

We must now bestow a pious thought upon an older, and more humble, building; S. Sylvester's oratory, and probably his first cathedral. Anastasius thus speaks of it:— "Sylvester built a church in the centre of Rome, on property belonging to a priest called Equitius, close to the Baths of Diocletian, and made it one of the titles (1) of the town." This church is now a dependence of S. Martino de'Monti; there are still some ancient paintings to be seen though unfortunately much effaced: one represents S. SYLVESTER at Mary's feet; another the Virgin between two saints; elsewhere Jesus Christ is depicted with S. Peter and S. Paul on either side, while the Lamb of God stands between the two Saints John. Nothing can equal the desolate appearance of this chilly, deserted, sanctuary, green from damp and age; yet, as one treads the ancient pavement of small squares in black and white, we must remember that S. SYLVESTER prayed there, and that his feet and those of the fathers of two Councils passed over it. It was in this very church that two solemn assemblies met, in 324 and 325, which confirmed the faith of Nicæa and condemned Arius afresh. The first of these assemblies numbered 284 bishops. Among the treasures of this church is shown the back of S. SYLVESTER's pontifical chair, as well as his green silk brocade mitre. (2)

(1) Title may be taken to mean a parish.
(2) "In sacristia monstrant S. Sylvestri stolam atque mitram." Montfaucon, (Diarium Italicum, I. IX.) Nevertheless on this

Some historians attribute the church of SS. Apostoli at the foot of the Quirinal to Constantine; but this is as doubtful as the opinion which classes S. Sebastiano-alle-Catacombe, S. Pietro-in-Montorio and S. Crysogno-in-Trastevere as having been built by that Emperor, although it may be affirmed that their consecration dates from remote antiquity. It is, for instance, quite impossible to doubt that, from the fourth century, the faithful had public oratories in the catacombs of Calixtus, and in that of the Janiculum. When the dwelling places, blood, and relics of martyrs were objects of veneration, it was unlikely that the hill on which S. PETER had suffered, and the hallowed crypt which, for more than a hundred years, had been the burial place of saints, and the metropolis of Christianity, should be ignored.

S. SYLVESTER's successor, S. MARK, founded S. Balbina on the Cælian Hill and S. Marco at the foot of the Capitol. The Christian faith, hitherto violently repressed by the Emperors, henceforth spread rapidly through society. In the second century Tertullian thus addressed the Romans:— "If the multitude of Christians had left you, to withdraw into some far distant land, the loss alone of so many citizens of every rank would have punished you sufficiently. You would have been afraid of your solitude, of the silence, of the astonishment of the world which would have appeared as it were dead." (Apol. 37.)

---

mitre the words "Ave Maria" are inscribed in Gothic characters, which fact has led Mgr. Gerbet to suppose that more probably it belonged to SYLVESTER II.

If at that early period Catholicism was so powerful, what must it not have become after Constantine's time! A large portion of the population had remained idolators; heathen temples still continued to receive offerings, and to be defiled with the blood of victims down to the reign of Theodosius: but in time the Christian churches could not contain the crowds which flocked to them, and gradually pagan fanes were forsaken and closed for want of worshippers.

Alas! this era of prosperity and splendour had unfortunately its days of affliction and trial; for nothing could have been more grievous than the bitter quarrels of Arianism. It was no longer open warfare as in times of persecution; but a strife of captious words, quibbling, and equivocal phrases. Arianism distracted the Roman Empire for nearly a hundred years; but it was chiefly at Constantinople and Alexandria that hatreds and contentions reached their highest pitch. At Alexandria the great S. Athanasius, who appeared to be the genius of Catholicism in this century, strove for fifty years against the riotous passions of men, against calumnies, and against the Emperors. Driven four times from his See, he returned triumphantly four times to retake possession of it; always remaining steadfast, amidst a persecution which spread like leprosy and tainted even those who were most holy. S. Athanasius continued to be as formidable, and terrible to his opponents, from the remotest corner of Gaul or the deserts of Egypt, as he had been from his pulpit at home; he was a strong man, one supported by God, one who hoped against all hope. His enemies, driven to acknowledge his influence and the inspired prudence of his actions, were incited by hatred and spite to accuse him of magic.

S. Athanasius came twice to Rome: first, when the Arians cited him to appear before the Pope; and again, when the intrusion of Bishop Gregory drove him from Alexandria. He was accompanied by some Egyptian monks, with whom he continued to live at Rome, observing the same rules and penances as were practised in the Thebaïd. The introduction of monastic life into Rome may therefore be attributed to S. Athanasius. At Rome he also distributed his book upon the life of S. Anthony, the first hermit; and he inspired S. Marcella with that love of meditation and retreat which, at a later period, induced her and her daughter to adopt a life of retirement and prayer.

The illustrious patriarch informs us that he was received and lodged in Rome by some members of the family of Constantius, who was the protector of his enemies. He says that his hosts lavished honours upon him, serving him with wonderful charity, "mirificæ charitatis obsequia." According to Baronius, they were Eutropia, Constantine the Great's sister, and her son Nepotian, who became Emperor for a brief space at a later date. It may therefore have been at the Palatine, once the home of Augustus and Nero, that Athanasius was thus honourably received. We can imagine him going from this palace daily, for several years, to celebrate Mass in the great Basilicas of Rome, and to attend the meetings of the faithful. "Multum eram in synaxibus celebrandis."

When he was summoned before Pope S. Julius, the only answer he made to his accusers was to recite the sacred Symbol. His first visit to Rome was in 340, his second in 342, when he remained there three years. Speaking about one of these journeys he said:—"I went to Rome in order to seek her Church and Bishop." "Romam ascendi, Ecclesiam et episcopum aditurus." (Bar., an. 349.)

S. Athanasius was the forerunner of that long line of great and noble men of genius who shed lustre on the Church in the fourth century. S. Ambrose, who belonged to a Roman family, followed him shortly. Born at Trèves, while his father was Prefect of the Gauls, he was soon afterwards brought to Rome, where he passed his childhood in his father's house which stood on the spot that is now the site of S. Ambrogio-della-Messima. It was there that this happy child, into whose mouth bees flew and deposited honey as they had formerly done to Plato, used to present his hand to his mother and sister to be kissed, saying playfully, "I shall be a Bishop." His dearly loved sister, Marcellina, devoted herself to both his religious and moral instruction. Marcellina subsequently received the veil from Pope Liberius, (1) in the Vatican Basilica, and Ambrose left Rome to become Governor of Liguria. It is well known how a child's voice proclaiming him Bishop was looked upon by the Milanese as being the voice of God;

---

(1) S. Ambrose has, in the third book of his treatise on Virginity, recorded Liberius's discourse at this ceremony: "Bonas, filia, nuptias desiderasti," etc.

and to what devices he had recourse, some even
imprudent ones, in order to escape from the honours
which were being thrust upon him. His virtues,
courage, and firmness throughout his episcopate, are
all known to fame; as well as his unchanging sweetness, and the eloquence of his writings, which stirred
up feelings superior to those aroused by the master
pieces of Rome and Greece.

The name most intimately connected with that of
S. Ambrose in history is that of S. Augustine. When
Augustine came to Rome, he arrived straight from
Carthage, where his soul had been completely demoralised. This unfortunate young man, weary of
pleasure, finding science powerless to fill the aching
void in his heart, cast hither and thither by the
breath of every new doctrine, used to teach other
young men as ardent, voluptuous and unsettled as himself,
who were most probably also seeking to find a refuge
from the anxieties which oppressed them. S. Augustine's school, to which crowds flocked, was on the
spot where the tall tower of S. Maria-in-Cosmedino
now rises above the ruins of the temple of Pudicitia,
close by the existing temple of Vesta. (1) It was
not until 384 that he left Rome for Milan, where
he met S. Ambrose, and was joined by his saintly
mother, who had followed him thither like his good
angel, and had the happiness of witnessing his conversion in the year 387. Being thus freed from all
anxiety on his account, she determined to return

(1) Even in S. Augustine's time, an oratory must have
existed on this spot founded by Pope S. DIONYSIUS, in the
third century.

home to Africa, and Augustine set out with her on the journey. Having reached Ostia, while waiting for the ship to sail, they were one day leaning against the window of their lodgings, dreaming of the mysteries of a future life in heaven. At length Monica addressed Augustine:— "My son, I must own to you that now there is nothing left to give me pleasure in this world, and I no longer know what I do in it, nor why I linger, having nothing further to hope for. The one thing which made me cling to life was to see you a Christian and a Catholic before I died. God has exceeded my desire, for He has granted that I should see you not only converted, but become entirely His servant, in that you despise all worldly things for love of Him. What need is there, then, that I should tarry here any longer?"

Five days after this conversation she was attacked by a violent fever, and sending for her son she acquainted him with her last wishes, "Bury your mother here, and remember her at God's altar wherever you go." (1) Ostia is now a deserted unhealthy swamp; only a few light boats can enter the sandblocked port; its monuments are in ruins, its boundaries narrowed; just a few fever-stricken peasants wander like spectres through the streets. But the room in which S. Augustine prayed, and where S. Monica breathed her last, is preserved intact. S. Augustine returned once more to Rome, where he composed his treatises, "De Moribus Ecclesiæ Catholicæ," "De Quantitate

---

(1) S. Augustine, Confess., Book IX, chap. X and XI.

Animæ," and "De Libero Arbitro." His after life in Africa belongs more particularly to the general history of Catholicism. Catholicism has considered him to be one of the most intrepid defenders of truth, if not indeed the greatest; for, among the distinguished intellects of that date, no one understood better than he did the harmony of religious dogmas; wherefore he was enabled to inculcate truth more forcibly, and with greater lucidity than many others could do.

S. Jerome and S. Paulinus of Nola were in all probability at Rome about the same time as S. Augustine. It was at Rome that the impetuous Dalmatian passed his stormy, restless, youth, giving himself up to both study and pleasure, with all the zest which afterwards drew him to Palestine, and inspired his eloquence. "How often when in the heart of the desert, in those vast solitudes dried up by the solar heat, have I not dreamt over the delights of Rome! I was seated alone in my retreat, alone, because my soul was filled with bitterness, disfigured, wasted, with a face as dark as an Ethiopian's, and my limbs dried up beneath hideous sackcloth. Every day I shed tears and groaned; I cried to the Lord, I prayed; and when, overcome by slumber against which I fought in vain, sleep came, my exhausted body sank down on the bare ground. I had condemned myself to these tortures in order to escape hell fire. Well! in these joyless wastes, surrounded by tigers and serpents, in fancy I saw myself again among the dances of the Roman maidens. Though my face was wasted by penance, my heart burnt with desire; in an emaciated body, in flesh dead to sense, the flames of passion were rekindled. Then I besought the Lord; I bathed His feet with my tears; both by day and by night I cried out, striking my breast, and ceasing not to petition God until he restored calm to my soul. I remember passing whole weeks without food, dreading even to enter the cell where I had entertained such wicked thoughts; seeking deep valleys, rugged rocks, high mountains, in order to find a fitting place for prayer and mortification . . . . . . There, God is my witness, after torrents of tears, with eyes ever fixed on heaven, at last I raised my soul triumphantly towards the angels, and, in the ecstasy of a heavenly vision, I sang with the Psalmist, 'Trahe me: post te curremus in odorem unguentorum tuorum.' (1) (Draw me: we will run after thee to the odour of thy ointments. Cant. 1—3.)"

S. Jerome returned to Rome, in 384, as secretary to Pope DAMASUS, whose ardent faith, and austere life, bore a singular analogy to his own. He lodged in the house of S. Paula, one of those saintly widows with whom he corresponded from his cell at Bethlehem. S. Paula's home was near the circus of Flora, where the church of S. Girolamo-della-Carità was subsequently built, for which Dominichino painted his famous picture, "The last Communion of S. Jerome." Within that house Marcella, Asella, Albina, Lea, Blesilla, Fabiola, Eustochia used often to meet, and also other devout women whose memory history has immortalised. S. Epiphanus of Salamis spent the winter

(1) S. Hieronym., "De Virginitate ad Eustochiam."

of 382 in this house in the company of this privileged community. S. Jerome remained there three years; but the calumnies with which he was assailed made him return to Palestine. But before sailing from Ostia he poured forth his sorrow by thus writing to S. Asella from the vessel:— "They call me infamous, a knave, a liar, and a magician; yet they kissed my hands while they pitilessly blackened my reputation ... Now, has anyone ever seen me enter the house of a bad woman? Have I ever been given to wear magnificent attire, or paint my face, or indulge in the glitter of gems and gold? I have been several times in the company of maidens; I have constantly explained the Holy Scripture to them to the best of my ability. This study necessitated our being often together; our diligence gave rise to friendship, our friendship led to confidence; but let them say whether they have ever remarked anything unbefitting a Christian in my conduct, anything doubtful in my speech, or passionate in my looks. Before I met with S. Paula all Rome esteemed me, and praised my virtue. I was considered by everybody to be worthy of sacerdotal honours ... Was it only a penitent and mortified woman who could affect me; a woman attenuated by continual fasting, simple to plainness in her dress, almost blind from weeping, and who spent whole nights in prayer? A woman whose only song was the psalms, whose only conversation was the Gospel, whose only pleasure was continence, and only food, fasting? Once more was this one the only woman in Rome who could attract me? Touched by her marvellous chastity, scarcely have I begun to see and offer her marks of my respect, when immediately my merit has disappeared, and all my virtues have vanished! Oh, envy! which begins by tearing itself to pieces! ... I was truly insane to wish to sing the songs of the Lord in a strange land, and to forsake the mountains of Sinaï in order to beg alms for Egypt." (1)

After S. Jerome had departed, S. Marcella and her daughter, S. Principia, retired to a country house near Rome; S. Paula and S. Eustochia visited the Holy Land, and founded a monastery at Bethlehem; S. Asella and S. Fabiola continued to live in the heart of Rome practising the most austere virtues.

The following description of Bethlehem and Rome gathered from letters which passed between members of this scattered band cannot be read without interest. "Doubtless the Church of Rome is holy; she possesses trophies of the Apostles and Martyrs; at Rome they preached the Gospel; there they confessed Jesus Christ, and there the name of Christian daily diffused itself amid the ruins of paganism. But the very magnificence, pomp, and grandeur of Rome, the need felt in her to see and be seen, to salute and be saluted, to praise and blame, to speak or to listen; the crowds and noise, all are opposed to a peaceful existence, or to a religious vocation ... At Bethlehem, on the contrary, what strikes one from the very first is the simplicity of country life, and the silence only broken by prayer. Wheresoever you go in this land of Christ, you hear the peasant's Alleluias, and may observe the

---

(1) Hieronym., Epist., "ad Asellam"; from the French of M. Benoist de Matougues.

hard working reaper varying his toil by psalmody, while the vine-dresser repeats the songs of David, when pruning his vines. Such are the melodies of this land, such its love-songs." (1)

It was in the midst of this society abounding in contrasts, where the vices of idolatry struggled with the severe principles of Catholicism, that Pontius Meropius Paulinus, a Gaul by birth, passed his early years. Paulinus was scarcely a youth when he left Bordeaux for Rome. A graceful poet, an eloquent and stirring orator, he shone at the bar and at the schools. Subsequently he became consul, and married a beautiful, rich, Spanish lady, who bore him a son. When, however, this child, on whom all their hopes were centred, died, they renounced their conjugal life; Therasia entered a convent, and Paulinus, first a priest and afterwards a Bishop, became celebrated as S. Paulinus of Nola.

Ausonius, the poet, was also born in the neighbourhood of Bordeaux. He had been master to S. Paulinus, and always remained a friend. But, being pagan in imagination and deeply impressed with Grecian mythology, he could not understand how his young and gifted pupil could bring himself to abandon Apollo and the Muses. "What a change in your principles," he exclaimed, "oh, sweetest friend!" Then he lays the blame on Paulinus's wife, calling her Tanaquil. "If thou fearest treachery," he says, "or that our friendship should be considered a crime, hide it from your Tanaquil." Paulinus replied, "My

---

(1) Hieronym. Op., t. IV, p. 351.

wife is no Tanaquil; she is a Lucretia." Then, full of tender memories, he adds, "Yes, I am indebted to you for learning and character; also for the glory of knowledge and eloquence; the honours of the toga, the lustre of fame; but why, oh father, recall the Muses whom I have forsaken? When a heart is given to Christ, it has no room for either the Muses or Apollo. Nothing, however, can ever efface you from my memory; my heart will behold you, my thoughts piously surround you; you will be always present to my mind. The soul can no more forget than it can die. Perennè vivax et memor."

But, although Paulinus forsook the Muses, he did not on that account abstain from poetic flights; only he ceased to find his inspirations in Helicon, obtaining them now from heaven alone. Every year Paulinus made a pilgrimage to Rome, for the purpose of praying at the tombs of the Apostles on their festival day. On one occasion he was received by Pope S. ANASTASIUS (398—402) with great kindness and honour, "Tam blandè quam honorificè." Another time a work was sent him to Rome from S. Augustine; but he found no time to read it during his stay in the city, so great was the crush, "tantæ illuc turbæ erant!" Thus he excused himself to S. Augustine. In one of his letters the great Bishop of Hippo refers to this yearly pilgrimage of Paulinus di Nola. He asks, "How is one to live with mankind? If you become enlightened on this subject, I beg of you to acquaint me with the method; or else consult some gentle doctor of hearts, 'mansueto cordis medico,' if such there be, either in your own home or at

Rome during your annual visit. Then write and tell me what God has revealed to him and you, in your mutual conversations."

It is certainly edifying to see what elevation of thought, dignity of conduct, and power of eloquence animated the bishops of this great century. The continual struggles they had to maintain against the deep rooted influence of paganism, and the hypocritical fervour of heresies, increased their talents, and purified their characters. At Rome all the Popes were saints: there were S. MARCELLUS, S. EUSEBIUS, S. MELCHIADES, under whose pontificate Constantine defeated Maxentius; S. SYLVESTER, who powerfully aided him in his work of organisation; S. MARK, S. JULIUS, whose letters form one of the most remarkable monuments of ecclesiastical antiquity; S. DAMASUS, a man of such austere piety and chastity that he was called the Virgin-Doctor; S. SERICIUS, and that LIBERIUS whose name is not written in all the martyrologies, but who ended his long and stormy life in a no less saintly manner. (1)

During the pontificate of LIBERIUS, Arian persecutions against the Catholics reached to the highest degree of frenzy; the Pope himself, having proved inflexible in his confession of faith, was seized by order of the Emperor Constantius. A feeling of alarm had previously been spread throughout Rome, lest the populace might interfere in the Pontiff's

---

(1) Several ancient martyrologies contain the name of Liberius; and Ennodius, Bishop of Pavia in the fifth century, stated in a Council at Rome that up till then all the successors of S. PETER had been saints.

favour. False charges, and being threatened with death, had caused many families to flee; the gates, as well as the course of the Tiber, were closely watched, and LIBERIUS was smuggled out of the city by night, and conducted before the Emperor at Milan. There he was subjected to a long examination, during which he was "the admired of all," according to Theodoret. Constantius reproached him with being the only man in the world who upheld Athanasius. He replied, "Though I should stand alone, the cause of the faith would not be vanquished on that account." "I desire," said Constantius, "that you should embrace the communion of the Churches and then you shall return to Rome." "I have already taken leave of my friends at Rome," answered the Pontiff; "it is better not to dwell in Rome, than to give up the laws of the Church. Send me therefore whither you please." LIBERIUS was exiled to Berœa in Thrace; his chair being filled by FELIX, Archdeacon of the Roman Church, who was elected Pope in the Emperor's palace by three eunuchs and three Bishops. FELIX did at least remain faithful to the Nicæan faith; but his usurpation condemned him to isolation. (1) The clergy avoided him; the people ceased to frequent the churches. Constantius having come to Rome in the April of 357, the Roman ladies earnestly entreated him to recall LIBERIUS. "But you have another pastor," said the prince. "No one enters the church

---

(1) He even condemned Arianism, as the inscription on his tombstone in the church of SS. Cosmo e Damiano records. FELIX is honoured as a martyr in the Roman Church.

when he presents himself," replied the noble ladies. Shortly afterwards the Emperor announced the recall of LIBERIUS by letters patent, on condition that he would govern jointly with FELIX. The people were in the circus when these letters were read out to them. They cried aloud, "There is but one God, one Christ, one Bishop!" So FELIX was forced to resign. The excitement became so great in the city that, at last, Constantius was forced to consent to the return of LIBERIUS "much against his own will," as Socrates states. The holy Pontiff re-entered Rome in triumph; his last years were devoted to endeavouring, by sermons and gentle persuasion, to bring back to the fold those Christians whom Arius had led astray. (1)

In the fourth century we observe for the first time a papal election giving rise to scenes of violence: it occurred on the death of Liberius. There was then in the Roman Church a deacon called Ursinus; his jealous ambition led him to contest the election of S. DAMASUS made by both clergy and people. Writing on this matter, the pagan writer Ammianus Marcellinus says:— "When I contemplate the splendour of Rome, I cannot wonder that those who seek to become her Bishops should exert every effort to attain their object." Again Prætextatus, an eminent Senator, is reported to have said to S. DAMASUS, "Make me Bishop of Rome, and I will become a Christian to-morrow." After having roused dis-

---

(1) As to the reputed fall of LIBERIUS, consult Newman's "Arians". Bossuet ended by retracting everything he had said on the subject in "La Défense de la Déclaration".

content in some few minds, Ursinus managed to be ordained by the Bishop of Tibur, and sustained throughout the whole of the 26th of October, 366, a siege in the Basilica of S. Maria-ad-Nives. The doors of the Basilica were broken, the roof demolished, the church itself only just escaped the flames, and a hundred and thirty-seven corpses remained on the spot.

Fortunately, characters like Ursinus were rare; although whole families of elect were frequently to be met with. S. Augustine was S. Monica's son; S. Ambrose S. Marcellina's brother, and nephew to S. Sotera; the great S. Basil's mother was S. Emmelia; his brothers were S. Gregory of Nissa and S. Peter of Sebaste; his sister was S. Macrina. The two saints Gregory, father and son, succeeded to the see of Nazianzen; the mother of the more distinguished of these was S. Nonna; his brother and sister were S. Cæsarius and S. Gorgonia. S. Therasia was the wife of S. Paulinus of Nola. The statue of S. Benedict (by Bernini) may still be seen at Monte Cassino between those of his mother S. Abondanza and his sister S. Scholastica. In days of trial, families then kept together like a phalanx; the paternal hearth was a sanctuary. Then, too, Christianity produced among her saints and defenders the greatest intellects of the time. The still barbarous Gauls possessed S. Paulinus and S. Hilary; Spain, the great Hosius; Africa, the bright and civilised, was proud of S. Augustine and Lactantius; the East owned S. Basil, S. Gregory of Nazianzen, S. John Chrysostom, Eusebius of Cæsarea, and S. Athanasius. It appeared as though the Church had absorbed all the vigour and life of human intellect. Julian thought he might change this by forbidding Christians the right to study letters; but Julian passed away like a bloody shade, and shortly nothing was left to record his reign but a few martyrs whose festivals were annually honoured. Two brothers, John and Paul, were among those who suffered at Rome during the persecution by the Apostate. Their residence, in which they were beheaded, was near the Palatine, on the slope of the Cælian Hill. That house was shortly afterwards transformed into a church, and may still be seen near the Arch of Dolabella, with its ancient mosaic pavement, its paintings by Pomarancio, its porphyry lions, granite columns, and the stone upon which the heads of the two saints were struck off. From the death of Constantine until the end of the fourth century the number of religious foundations sensibly diminished; for the necessary requirements for worship had been provided, and it was only requisite to raise fresh churches in proportion to the spreading of the Gospel. S. DAMASUS consecrated the church dedicated to S. Rufina, raised over the place of her burial; he also rebuilt with great splendour the church of S. Lorenzo, which to this day is called "in-Damaso". The Pope's father had been attached to this church, and, having himself been brought up there, he ornamented it with rich paintings, endowed it with large revenues, and presented it with eighty pounds weight of silver in patens, chalices, chased amphoræ and coronæ for holding lights.

Anastasius also mentions a church called S. Pietro e Paolo-alle-catacombe built by this holy Pope. It is now the celebrated Basilica of S. Sebastiano. He collected the water which constantly dripped into the Vatican vaults, turning it into a fountain to be used for baptising. This inscription was placed on it:— "It is neither with the treasures of the world nor by the power of art that Damasus, the Bishop of Christ, has accomplished this work; but it was with the help of Peter to whom was confided the gate of heaven. Alone the seat of Peter, alone this bath of life, knows neither fetters nor trammels. Vincula nulla tenent."

Prudentius has also left us a brilliant description of the Vatican fountains. He describes the source as falling in murmuring cascades over beautiful marbles into a deep pond, whose transparent waters reflect a thousand colours from the paintings surrounding it. He says, "Gold itself takes the tint of grass, the blue of the water blends with the brightness of purple; you would think that the very roof trembled as you gaze on its reflection in the waves."

Anastasius relates that on Holy Saturday of 383, at the moment when the crowd was pressing forward to receive baptism, a child fell into the source. Great alarm ensued; but DAMASUS prayed to God, and after an hour the child was restored to perfect health, "vivumque sanumque". "Then," continues the historian, "the people praised the might of God, and the holiness of Damasus."

DAMASUS was buried in a Catacomb on the Via Ardeatina near to his mother and sister. One reads with some emotion the lines in which he unites his thoughts and hopes with this beloved sister:— "Beneath this tomb rest limbs hallowed to God; *she is the sister of Damasus, and was known by the name of Irene; in life she vowed herself to Christ, seeking merit in the holy chastity of virgins* ...... He who walked over the waters of the sea, who gives life to inactive seed, who broke the bonds of death for Lazarus, and, after the lapse of three days, recalled him from the darkness, in order to restore a brother to a sister, will, I know, also raise Damasus from amidst these ashes."

We have mentioned some of the churches which belong to the second half of the fourth century; but we must not omit S. Eusebius on the Esquiline, and S. Maria Maggiore.

Everyone has heard of the miracle which led to the foundation of this last Basilica. The Patrician John, (Giovanni Patrizio) (1), and his wife, being childless, made a vow to devote their fortune to some work which should be agreeable to the Mother of God, and they prayed daily that the Virgin would reveal her wishes to them. On the 5th of August snow suddenly covered a part of Mt. Esquiline. At the same time the Virgin appeared to Patrizio and to Pope LIBERIUS. On the following day the Pope and Patrizio went in state to the Esquiline, and laid the foundations of a church which was to cover all the space whitened with snow. This church, which was the largest dedicated to Mary in Rome, was called S. Maria-ad-Nives, but was afterwards called S. Maria

---

(1) The Patrician John or Giovanni Patrizio. The illustrious Roman family of the Patrizi traces back its origin to the founder of S. Maria Maggiore.

Maggiore. (1) It is one of the seven great Roman Basilicas. The general effect of S. Maria Maggiore does not now present an appearance of antiquity; nevertheless it still possesses the beautiful white marble columns, taken from the temple of Juno Lucina, which divide its three naves. Its gilt panelled ceiling and its façade, pierced by high windows, have neither the grandeur nor majesty of our ancient Christian monuments, nevertheless it remains a rich, harmonious, and beautiful church. The magnificence of its chapel of the Blessed Sacrament, and also that of the Virgin, is unequalled. Jesus Christ's cradle, the hay, and the swaddling clothes are all preserved in this Basilica. Tasso has sung its praises, and S. Charles Borromeo, escaping by night from the splendours of his palace, used to mount the Esquiline upon his knees to pray within its walls.

(1) In ancient Acts it is also sometimes called the Liberian Basilica, in memory of the Pope who consecrated it; and the church of the cradle — il Presepio — after Christ's cradle which was presented to it by Pope LIBERIUS.

CHAPTER V.

> Proh nefas! orbis terrarum ruit; nulla est regio quæ exules Romanos non habeat.
> *S. Jerome.*
>
> Ut nunc omni decore nudata, prostrata jacet, instar giganti cadaveris corrupti atque undique exesi!
> *Poggio.*

FIFTH CENTURY.

THE temporal greatness of Rome had vanished; yet, even to pagan eyes, she remained imposing: she commanded respect by her riches, which still recalled the last days of the Republic; by the majesty of her monuments, which time and changes had respected; and by the titles of her magistrates, those titles of consuls, tribunes, ediles, which always kept fresh the memory of Rome's old power and glory.

On witnessing the extravagance and wastefulness of the aristocracy at this period, it might have been thought that the age of Lucullus was returning. Symmachus spent two millions of gold scudi on celebrating his son's appointment to the office of prætor; on a similar occasion Maximus flung away four millions. All those who had not undergone regeneration through the new faith, which was then spreading over the world, were shamefully steeped in pleasure, or else disputed with the imperial power for some filthy remnants of heathen customs. The temples of the gods, it is true, were closed; "spolia opima" were no longer hung from the arches of the Capitol; neither were statues of Venus crowned with garlands of myrtle and roses; but the amphitheatre still claimed its hecatombs, and the blood of gladiators atoned for the absence of the gods.

One day a Christian recluse from the East determined to assist at the combats of these victims. He took his stand upon the steps, while the victims advanced amid the cheers of the populace; but scarcely had the fight begun, when the stranger leapt into the arena, crying out with all the energy of his soul, and appealing to both combatants and spectators, "Away with these impious sacrifices; away with these idolatrous superstitions!" For a moment the astonished people paused, but, recovering their brutal passions, they unanimously flung themselves upon the saint, who perished beneath their blows. (1)

In the following year, 404, Honorius by law forbade the combats of gladiators. Thus the last blood which flowed in Vespasian's amphitheatre was that of a martyr. Yet it took nearly a century before the Lupercalia were comparatively abolished; these impure

---

(1) This saint is honoured by the Church under the name of Almachus or S. Telemachus. His feast falls on the first of January.

festivals were celebrated by young men running naked through the streets.

> Tertia post idus nudos aurora Lupercos
> Adspicit . . . . . (1)

Turning from these degrading pictures, let us take a glance at those Christian families in whose bosom seeds of the faith were wonderfully developing. From his cell at Bethlehem, S. Jerome exclaimed to the Romans, "Among Greeks, Rome means strength, among Hebrews, sublimity; be therefore strong and sublime; virtue will raise you; in pleasures you will find only shame." (2)

There were some privileged souls who always heard his voice. S. Paula and S. Melania had followed him to Palestine, but Pammachius, Marcella, Principia, and Fabiola remained at Rome. Fabiola had been separated from a vicious husband while very young, and had remarried in ignorance of the prohibition of the Gospel. Becoming a widow, she did penance publicly for this second marriage. In the first days of her mourning she covered herself with sackcloth, and in the sight of all Rome, before Easter Day, she placed herself in the ranks of penitents in the Lateran Basilica. The Pontiff, the priests, the people melted into tears with her. But Fabiola, nobly descended from the Fabii, allied to the greatest families of the Roman aristocracy, sought out the poor and infirm,

---

(1) Ovid, Fasti: Book II.
(2) "Ρώμη ait fortitudo apud Græcos, sublimitas apud Hebræos. Serva quod diceris; virtus te excelsam faciat, sed voluptas humilem". (Advers. Jovin., l. II, in fine.)

founding a refuge for them which became the first hospital of Christian Rome; she nursed them herself, no matter how loathsome were their diseases. Pammachius did not consider it beneath the dignity of a Senator and Proconsul to follow her noble example. S. Jerome when speaking of them said: — "Rome seemed to be too small to receive all the effects of such bountiful charity."

At the same time, the house of S. Melania became like a sanctuary, so greatly was it respected by the populace. Among the members of this family were Publicola, who attained the dignity of a prætor, and his son-in-law, Pinian, was the son of the Governor of Rome. Now Pinian's wife, who was also called Melania, having lost her two children, desired to sanctify her afflicted life by continence. When S. Melania, her grandmother, who was then at Jerusalem, heard of her resolution, she set out at once to join her, in order to confirm it. This form of self-sacrifice was indeed common among the early Christians. In those days the name of sister was not separated from that of wife, and this sign of chaste fraternity moderated passion, and dignified it. Thus when, in search of perfection, conjugal rights were renounced, union of souls remained unbroken, in sweet relationship; "soror mea sponsa." (1)

S. Melania, the Elder, as hagiographers term her in order to distinguish her from her granddaughter, landed at Naples in 403, and went in the first instance to Naples to see the holy Bishop Paulinus. She was

---

(1) Cantic. IV, 9.

humbly clad and mounted on a small horse, surrounded by her children and grandchildren, whose immense suite and gilded chariots blocked up the Appian way. Paulinus only possessed one room and a few cells devoted to visitors; these he placed at the disposal of his guests, and gave up several hours to religious conversation with the holy widow, reading to her the life of S. Martin, just written by Sulpicius Severus, while admiring her virtues. From Nola, Melania came to Rome with the same pomp, and accompanied by the same suite, composed of the most distinguished persons in the Empire. It might have been mistaken for a triumph, had not the central figure been so lowly, and that the poverty of her garb contrasted so strangely with the purple and silk tunics of her retinue. This was no ovation of olden days, when golden crowns were proudly worn; but a Christian triumph, a joyful meeting of parted brethren, a simple expression of a common hope, and a devout respect for virtue.

During her stay in Rome, Melania converted her nephew Apronian, who was of the "Clarissimus" rank, and Albina, the wife of her son Publicola, to the Christian faith.

Meanwhile S. Jerome declared that the Empire was shaken, "orbis terrarum ruit;" the barbarians threatened the capital, and many of the Romans, selling their property, forsook a city which appeared cursed. Among those who fled before the storm were Proba, Juliana, and Demetriades, holy women, who corresponded with S. Augustine, S. Jerome, and S. Paulinus of Nola; the two Melanias following their example. They first retired to Sicily, and afterwards joined S. Augustine and S. Alypius in Africa; some time later S. Melania the Elder returned to die at Jerusalem.

For eleven hundred and sixty years, as Paulus Orosius has remarked, Rome had pursued her career of conquest and glory. Babylon had held sway for a like period. (1) The moment was approaching when the city of Cæsar might be devastated in the same manner as was the city of Semiramis, "they shall make them captains that had taken them, and shall subdue their oppressors." (2)

The Roman Empire had in fact been breaking up since the death of Theodosius, and Goths, Huns, and Vandals were now hastening to share the spoils. Alaric led on the Goths; first as an ally of Theodosius, and marching under his orders; but he subsequently revolted from his feeble successors, ravaged Greece, seized on Illyria, and swept like a torrent over the Italian provinces. Checked for a moment by Stilicho's bravery, he soon resumed his onward course. "I hear a voice," he exclaimed, "bidding me destroy Rome." So Rome was invested, her gates blockaded, the Tiber closed, while the besieged were condemned to famine and disease. Then their excitement and despondency turned to madness. Stilicho had been assassinated at Ravenna on suspicion of communicating with the Barbarians; his wife Serena, a niece of Theodosius the great, was

---

(1) Orosius B. II; 3, VII.
(2) Isaias XIV, 2.

also murdered at Rome; after which the pagans clamoured for the gods of the Empire, the gods of Cæsar and Tiberius! At this price Tuscan soothsayers promised safety for the city; if Narni, they said, was spared by the Goths, it was because Narni had reopened the temples of the gods, and had sacrificed to them once more.

Hereupon Pompeianus, Governor of Rome, with a party of Senators, ascended the Capitol to revive pagan rites: but the crowd fled in horror from their ceremonies; they avoided them in the streets and public squares; and presently the populace gave up all the riches they could obtain from heathen temples to Alaric, hoping thereby to obtain peace. This peace was bought at the price of five thousand pounds weight of gold, thirty thousand of silver, four thousand silk robes, three thousand pieces of scarlet cloth and three thousand pounds of pepper. Pope INNOCENT immediately went to Ravenna to obtain the Emperor's consent to the treaty. Alaric followed him as far as Rimini; but, disgusted with the many delays of Honorius, he suddenly returned to Rome, besieged it again, and forced the Romans to acknowledge Attalus, whose proclivities were for paganism, for their Emperor.

Meanwhile famine raged in the town, and the frenzy of the people was so great that they urgently demanded, during an entertainment in the circus, that human flesh should be sold, and its price taxed. Attalus was then in Alaric's camp, and asked leave to return to Rome; but Alaric relieved him of his diadem, and the terrible chief of the Goths led his legions against the Eternal City for the third time.

It was by the Collina Gate, already celebrated for having opened to Brennus and his Gauls, that Alaric penetrated into Rome on the 25th of August, 410. The first thing that met his gaze were Sallust's gardens, a memory of pride and luxury, which the historical moralist had laid out on returning from his African proconsulship. It comprised a palace, a circus, a temple of Venus, and a portico adorned by a thousand columns, beneath which colonnade Aurelian used to delight to weary out his horses in racing. The gardens extended from the crest of the Quirinal to the summit of the Pincio. Nero had dwelt there; Vespasian preferred this residence to the imperial palace; Nerva died there; Alaric destroyed it by fire.

Pillage began forthwith; the churches of S. Peter and S. Paul were the only ones spared: the Goths, spreading throughout the city, sacked palaces, slew all the men who resisted, and dishonoured the women. They entered S. Marcella's house, clamouring for gold. Marcella's only reply was to point to her mean attire. Then the Barbarians scourged her unmercifully, because they insisted on having gold, and believed her seeming poverty to be only a subterfuge. Marcella appeared insensible to pain; but she fell on her knees, and implored them, with tears, not to separate her from her adopted daughter, Principia, whose youth offered her no protection from insult. Her motherly entreaties touched the hearts of these men of blood; they protected the two women, from their house at Mt. Aventine, to the Basilica of S. Paul, where they would be safe. Only a few days later, as S. Jerome tells us, "Marcella slept the sleep of the righteous; giving up her spirit, her lips smiling, and consoled by the kisses and embraces of her daughter; the remembrance of her life could only bring calm to her conscience, and her soul was happy in anticipation of the approaching joys of heaven."

But the soldiery, keen after booty, also entered the house of another holy maiden. To their demands she replied:— "Yes, I have treasures; these belong to the Apostle S. Peter: take them if you dare; you shall answer for it." She then showed them some priceless golden vessels. Alaric, hearing of this, gave orders that the treasures should be immediately restored to the Basilica to which they belonged, and that the maiden should be conducted in safety to the same spot, with all other Christians who desired to follow her. The soldiers then, bearing the sacred vessels upon their heads, were followed by a great crowd of men and women, who came from their hiding places to follow these emblems of safety and peace, thanking S. Peter as they went along for his protection. Even pagans joined the throng; glad, by these means, to escape death and dishonour.

S. Augustine exclaimed, "Was such a thing ever seen in pagan times? Priam was slaughtered at the feet of his household gods; but, at Rome, barbarians were seen selecting the largest churches to protect victims from their own cruelty, giving orders that no one should be slain or dragged out of them; indeed they even conducted these refugees thither in order to spare their lives. All this is to be attributed to the power of Jesus Christ's name, and to its being a period favourable to Christianity." (1)

The sack of Rome lasted three days, after which Alaric directed his course towards the Campagna; but the consternation occasioned by the devastation of Rome was a world wide topic for conversation. In this disaster the prophecies of the Apocalypse against the "great harlot" were fulfilled, "with whom the kings of the earth have committed fornication: . . . sitting upon a scarlet covered beast, . . clothed round about with purple and scarlet, . . . drunk with the blood of the saints, and with the blood of the martyrs of Jesus," (2) whose name was "Mystery".

S. Augustine wrote his book "De Civitate Dei" in answer to the reproaches of pagans, who attributed all their misfortunes and the decay of the Empire to the spreading of the faith; and, from the neighbourhood of Jeremias's cave, S. Jerome poured forth fresh lamentations. He was preparing his commentary on Ezechiel when the news of the fall of Rome stayed his pen.

He exclaimed, "Lo, all at once I am told of the deaths of Marcella, and of Pammachius, of the taking of Rome, and of the eternal slumber of many of our brothers and sisters. I felt so dismayed and astonished that, night and day, I could do nothing but think about the welfare of all; I felt that I also was a captive among saints; I did not dare to speak, until I should get more certain confirmation of the news.

(1) See the first chapter of "De Civitate Dei."
(1) Rev. XVII, 1 - 2 - 3 - 4 - 6.

Meanwhile I wavered between hope and despair; bitterly feeling for the misfortunes of my brethren! When the brightest light of the world was extinguished, and that I beheld the head of the Roman Empire struck down, or, rather, the entire universe succumbing after the death of a single city, I became mute, and humbled myself, remaining silent, far from the rich; and, like the prophet, my heart leapt in my bosom, and I was consumed by many flames during my meditations." (1)

Thousands of Romans, fleeing from captivity, were scattered over the world; many came to Palestine, and "obscure Bethlehem saw illustrious beggars at her gates, who had formerly been very wealthy." (2) This deep, widespread, distress, the forerunner of utter ruin, gave another motive to S. Jerome for urging maidens to remain unmarried. "Whom would you marry?" he cries to them; "those who flee from danger, or those who remain to fight? Beware lest a shrill trumpet should sound in your ears, instead of a bridal song; beware lest Mourners take the place of Matrons in conducting you to the nuptial bed!" (3)

The last blow had been given to the political system of which Rome was the centre. Rome was not to rule by force any longer; nevertheless she was still to govern, although only in the names of

---

(1) These are the first words of the Commentary on Ezechiel addressed to the virgin Eustochia.
(2) Hieron., Epist. "ad Gaudentium."
(3) Hieron., "ad Ageruchiam."

justice and truth. It seemed as though it were granted to her to rise above empires, and always march on in advance of nations.

> "Terrarum dea gentiumque Roma
> Cui par est nihil et nihil secundum." (1)

There can certainly be no doubt that Rome had maintained all her prestige. When Theodosius came to Rome, in 389, a Gallic orator, Latinus Pacatus, thus addressed the Senate, "Happy am I that I have come from such a distance! Oh, blessed fatigue! What happiness I owe to it! What joys are mine! What joys shall I not relate when I return to Gaul! How I shall be courted and admired when I say:— I have seen Rome, I have seen Theodosius!"

Popes INNOCENT, ZOZIMUS, BONIFACE, CELESTINE and SIXTUS endeavoured to heal the bleeding wounds caused by Alaric's invasion; and, on the morrow of the ruin which had threatened to overwhelm them, they already planned the spiritual conquest of the most distant nations. CELESTINE sent Palladius, a deacon of the Roman church, to evangelise Scotland; SIXTUS III consigned Ireland to the apostleship of S. Patrick. Thus had religion remained safe beneath the wreckage of the empire; no shock being able to destroy it. Yet her enemies, often more dangerous than the hordes of Alaric, multiplied around her. After Arius, Nestorius, Eutyches and Pelagius appeared. It was in Rome herself that Pelagius dared to strive against the Church. Coming from Great Britain to Rome, he devoted himself to a monastic life; but, unfortunately being led away by his headstrong nature, he ex-

(1) Martial, Epigramm. XII, 8.

aggerated man's powers, not understanding the need of divine grace to sustain him during the perils which beset him from the cradle to the tomb. He left Rome, accompanied by his disciple Celestius, at the approach of the Goths, and went to Africa. There, however, pious energetic bishops were guarding the faith. The doctrine taught by Pelagius raised up opponents in every place; it was condemned at Diospolis, Carthage, and Mileva, and Pope INNOCENT confirmed the anathema of the Councils by his own. Pelagius thereupon concealed his opinions by captious revocations. He sent Celestius to Rome, and entreated ZOZIMUS, INNOCENT'S successor, to examine his creed, and remove the decree of excommunication against him. ZOZIMUS ordered Celestius to appear before him in the Church of S. Clement on the Cælian Hill. The heretic came once; but never reappeared, and before the second appointment he had fled from Rome.

The church of S. Clement still exists, and is, after S. Agnese on the Via Nomentana, the most ancient Christian Basilica in Rome. The Atrium is shown where the Catechumens assembled, also the choir surrounded by a marble balustrade, the three amboes used when reading the lesson, epistle, and Gospel; one faces the congregation, the others the altar. Behind the choir rise the altar steps, beneath which is the Confession containing the bodies of martyrs, while above the altar stands the "ciborium," overshadowing it like a diadem, "umbraculum altaris." The apse contained stalls for the clergy, and the bishop's chair was placed at the back, an antique marble seat which is possibly the one in which ZOZIMUS sat.

The Roman liturgy was drawn up in the fifth century much as it has come down to us. The oldest sacramentary known is attributed to S. Gelasius, who ascended the throne in 492; although everyone of his predecessors had partaken in the arrangement of some of our ceremonies. Zozimus ordered that deacons should wear linen bands on the left arm; these were subsequently called "maniples": blessing the paschal candle is also attributed to him; the number of the epact, (1) was stamped upon this candle, and also that of the indiction, (2) and the year of the Incarnation. Celestine I introduced the custom of chanting the Psalms of David before the Sacrifice of the Mass; whereas previously they were only sung at the offertory and communion. Simplicius established weekly priests at S. Peter's, S. Paul's and S. Laurence's, for the administration of the Sacraments at all hours of the day and night. Then Gelasius composed prayers, hymns and prefaces, and replaced the impure festival of the Lupercalia by the holy feast of the Purification of the Blessed Virgin.

Among the pontiffs of this period, so remarkable for their virtues that all appeared worthy of being called saints, one, in particular, left a great name in ecclesiastical history. S. Leo the Great, so styled by the

---

(1) The epact means the excess of the solar over the lunar year, being eleven days.

(2) The indiction was a cycle of fifteen years instituted by Constantine the Great for purposes of taxation. It began on the 1st January 313. The Council of Nice decreed, in honour of the battle at the Milvian Bridge, that it should be used for chronological purposes in lieu of the Olympiads.

Church and the world, was a Tuscan, and was fulfilling a mission in Gaul when elected to succeed Sixtus III in 440. The Romans preferred to remain without a pastor for two months, rather than elect anyone else. Leo's elocution was both graceful and easy, and recalled, if not exactly that irresistible force by which Tertullian and S. Jerome electrified their congregations, at least the impressive and brilliant sermons of S. Augustine. Leo never neglected an opportunity of instructing the Romans, and encouraging them to seek consolation, for all the calamities which befell them, in the mysteries of their faith. When Attila, driven from Gaul, descended on Italy, universal terror reigned among the people. Aquileia was given over to fire and sword; Milan, Verona, Piacenza, were cruelly sacked, and their charred remains shortly afterwards marked the conqueror's route. The inhabitants fled before him, imploring the sea to give them a sand bank which could not be attacked by the Scourge of God.

S. Leo then appeared as the protector of the helpless; he advanced as an ambassador from heaven, making use of promises and threats; Attila withdrew before him as though his strength had withered; henceforth his glory faded, and, a short distance from their meeting place, death awaited him during his wedding festivities.

Genseric succeeded him in his mission of vengeance. Rome had been stained with horrid crimes. The foolish Valentinian III was reigning in Cæsar's palace, consoling himself for the loss of his provinces in a whirl of pleasure, and leaving the honour of the

Empire to the care of Aetius. One day Aetius, being falsely denounced by the patrician Maximus, was murdered in the palace by Valentinian, who afterwards violated the accuser's wife, and rested in security beneath the vaulted roofs which had shrouded the orgies of Tiberius, and the bloody revelries of Nero.

Maximus, however, looked on, hatred rankling in his heart; soon he summoned his partisans, hired assassins, and, on the 17th of March 455, the Emperor fell a victim to his vengeance while taking the air in the Campus Martius.

More horrors followed: Eudoxia, Valentinian's widow, had been forced to wed his murderer Maximus, who admitted his crime to her; whereupon she revolted and summoned to her assistance that King of the Vandals who has said that the prow of his bark was always directed "towards those whom God wished to punish."

Genseric landed on the shores of Italy in June 455. His approach signalised the death of Maximus, who was assassinated and flung into the Tiber; this victim, however, did not suffice to save Rome from her fate. She was too rich a spoil not to tempt the cupidity of these great ravagers. Genseric continued his march on the city and Eudoxia began to tremble. S. Leo set forth to the Vandal's camp to promote peace; but this time his prayers only obtained the safety of the inhabitants, and that of the three principal churches; the rest of Rome was abandoned to pillage during fourteen days. It was then that the gold and silver vases of the temple of Jerusalem disappeared (1), and that the gilt bronze roof of the temple of Jupiter Capitolinus was borne away, as well as the remaining wealth of the city. Thousands of captives were taken on board the barbarians' ships, also Grecian statues and the treasures from the Basilicas: Valentinian's widow, with her two daughters, Eudoxia and Placidia, was sent to atone in bondage for the cruel joy she had experienced in the fulfilment of her vengeance.

Amid all this ruin and shame, the only hopeful feature to be found is in contemplating the dignity, prudence, and power of the Pontiff who reigned at Rome. Leo then saved the world from heresy which was prevailing at Ephesus, and did what he could against the Barbarians. When all was crumbling around him, he did not despair, but considered the future, and paved the way for it by his sermons, laws, and by wise and noble actions.

It is not worth while to follow, through all its phases, the frightful anarchy into which the Empire was steadily sinking. The youthful Emperor Majorian raised a brief hope that he would prove himself a worthy foe to Genseric. Noble, resolute, and brave, every step he took was marked by success. But this budding glory alarmed Ricimer, the Suevian, who commanded under his orders, therefore Majorian was murdered. Severus was proclaimed in his stead, only to be poisoned by Ricimer. Anthemius, who followed,

---

(1) Belisarius retook these vases from the Vandals, and gave them to the Patriarch of Jerusalem. It was not until the holy city was taken that they finally disappeared.

thought to secure Ricimer's protection by giving him his daughter in marriage, but at the end of five years the Suevian besieged him in Rome; and, after sacking that unfortunate city, sealed his crimes by putting his father-in-law to death. Obscurities like Olympius, Glycerius, Nepos, Augustulus, then disputed among themselves for the tattered remnants of the imperial purple; but, suddenly, Odoacer appeared, and the last of the Cæsars faded away, like a phantom, before him.

During this period of turmoil the religious movement continued; it even progressed, for, as the heathen temples were demolished by the Barbarians, Christian churches took their place. The most ancient endowment of the fifth century was S. Maria-in-Aquiro, near the Pantheon. It was erected by Pope S. ANASTASIUS on the site of the temple of Jupiter, and took its name from the Equiria, (1) horse-races in the Campus Martius in honour of Mars, a name which has descended through the ages united to the sweet name of Mary. In our day it is also called S. Maria-degl'-Orfanelli, a touching appellation which it owes to the hospital S. Ignatius built close to it.

The church, dedicated to S. Vitalis and his two sons SS. Gervasius and Protasius, was built in 416, during the pontificate of INNOCENT I, with money given for that purpose by a noble lady named Vestina.

(1) Altera gramineo spectabis Equiria campo,
Quem Tiberis curvis in latus urget aquis.
Ovid, Fasti.
The church of S. Maria-in-Aquiro was rebuilt by Cardinal Salviati in 1590.

Among the treasures with which it was endowed from the beginning were a tower, in which the Holy Eucharist was kept, and a gold dove. This church afterwards became a Cardinal's title; among others who have borne it are Jean du Bellay, and the Blessed Fisher, Bishop of Rochester, the pious friend of Blessed Thomas More; his nomination to the Cardinalate was, however, his death warrant. Restored at various periods, the church of S. Vitalis still stands in the valley which separates the Quirinal from the Vatican, and is near the spot were a temple of Romulus once stood.

During the pontificate of INNOCENT I, S. Alexis lived and died unknown in his father's house on Mt. Aventine. If we believe his legend, S. Alexis fled from the nuptial chamber wishing to preserve his chastity, his parents having insisted on his marriage. For seventeen years he wandered about in distant places, after which he presented himself at his father's house, was received as an unknown beggar, and allowed to lodge under the stairs. There he dwelt for a long time, forgotten by men, but praying to God. The body of the saint, being recognised after his death, was buried by his father, Euphemius, in the church of S. Boniface; this church Euphemius also rebuilt, turning his house, which adjoined it, into a monastery. The convent of S. Alexis is one of the most celebrated Abbeys in Rome; the Emperor Otho III used to pray there constantly, and Christian travellers have always been in the habit of visiting, with veneration, the staircase under which S. Alexis dwelt.

The church of S. Sabina stands not far off; it also dates from the fifth century. It was an Illyrian priest, "rich for the poor, and poor for himself," as an old stone inscription says, "pauperibus locuples, sibi pauper", who dedicated this monument to S. Sabina on the very spot where she had dwelt. The station for Ash Wednesday was held here as far back as the sixth century, and S. GREGORY pronounced several of his homilies in it. Bestowed by HONORIUS III on the Preaching Friars, it has witnessed, praying beneath its roof, and beside its columns of Parian marble, S. Dominic, S. Francis, S. Thomas, S. Catherine of Siena, and S. PIUS V; while Conclaves have been held in the adjoining convent.

A feeling of devotion arises on beholding these spots, which in the past have often witnessed the display of Christian virtue. But the mind is then also carried further back; and, as we gaze from the Aventine over the whole extent of Rome, including the Vatican and Capitol, we ask ourselves, who were the inhabitants that dwelt here before the Christian heroes. On the top of the Aventine, close by the church of S. Sabina, the temple of Juno-Regina formerly stood, built by Camillus after the fall of Veii. Sister and spouse of Jupiter, Juno presided over marriages; her worship in Rome may be imagined from Juvenal's remark, "In five autumns the women could reckon up eight husbands!" The present site of S. Prisca was once that of the temple of Diana, built by the co-operation of the towns of the Latin Confederation. It was surrounded by a dark wood, watered by the fountains of the Fauns; Propertius recommended his Phyllis never to enter it. Then comes the abominable sanctuary of the Bona Dea, now covered by the church of S. Maria Aventina; all that is holy taking the place of everything that was most shameful! Elsewhere are the Baths of Decius, and, on the slope of the hill, the den of Cacus, with an altar dedicated to his sister, Caca, who betrayed him to Hercules. This altar was under the care of the Vestals. In the distance may be seen the slave-market, adjoining the meat and vegetable markets; as well as the ruins of altars on which human blood has been shed; for it was not till the 683rd year from its foundation, in the consulship of Cornelius Lentulus and Licinius Crassus, as Pliny informs us, that human sacrifices were prohibited in Rome. (1)

We have seen that the Basilica of S. Maria Maggiore was founded by Pope LIBERIUS in the fourth century; it was enlarged, and the existing arrangement was completed, under SIXTUS III, in 434. The mosaics above the triumphal arch and the columns of the central nave, representing several subjects from the Old Testament, and the life of the Virgin, date from this time, and offer a curious instance of the condition of the arts in the primitive Church. They moreover remind us of one of the most memorable events in Church history; the condemnation of Nestorius by the Council of Ephesus in 431. Nestorius denied that Christ

---

(1) It must be stated, however, that in spite of this prohibition, human sacrifices occasionally took place at Rome, even during the rule of Cæsar and down to the reign of Hadrian.

became man; according to him, Christ had merely united himself to man; a theory which denied at once the mystery of the Incarnation and the divine maternity. "Let no one call Mary Mother of God," said he, "she was a woman, and it is impossible that God should be born of woman." It was therefore for the glorification of Mary's divine maternity that Sixtus III called in the assistance of genius and art, dedicating this work to "God's people," (Xistus episcopus plebi Dei).

We proceed to a description of this work. On the top of the triumphal arch are representations of an altar and of a throne; upon the altar lies the book sealed with seven seals, being the symbol of mysteries; right and left are subjects taken from the Gospels bearing upon the divinity of Jesus Christ: the Annunciation, the Presentation, the Adoration of the Magi, the Massacre of the Innocents, Jesus preaching in the Temple, the death of John the Baptist. In the picture of the Annunciation, the entrance to her chamber is secured by a gate, the "shut gate" of Ezechiel, -- Porta haec clausa erit. (1) As for Mary, she remains seated before the Angel, while the Holy Ghost hovers above her head in the form of a dove. In the Adoration of the Magi, the new born infant is not lying down, as though he were the child of man, but seated on a throne by his own power. In the picture of the preaching in the Temple, Jesus is crowned with a diadem upon which are two crosses,

---

(1) Ezechiel XLIV, 2.

a small one, doubtless typical of his human nature, and a large one as a mark of his Divinity. (1)

Beneath these paintings on either side are represented Jerusalem and Bethlehem, and, still lower, there are groups of lambs, — pasce agnos meos.

Such was the chief work undertaken by SIXTUS III; but on the walls of the same nave, above the frieze which surmounts the columns, are mosaics executed by order of the same Pontiff, forming a magnificent vista to the triumphal arch. They represent subjects from the Old Testament; Abraham, Jacob, Moses, Josue, quoted by the Council of Ephesus as prophetic types of the Saviour. SIXTUS III, moreover, presented S. Maria Maggiore with a silver altar weighing three hundred pounds, a gold vase of fifty pounds weight, several silver vases, a silver hart as a fountain for the baptistery, and a revenue from lands and houses valuing 729 gold pennies.

At the same time this generous Pontiff sumptuously decorated the Confession of S. Peter; he encircled that of S. Laurence with silver and porphyry columns, and placed a marble architrave to the baptistery of the Lateran, upon which were inscribed verses descriptive of the virtues of baptism, and belief in original sin. Some of these were as follows:—

"This fountain is life; it flows from the wound of Christ, and purifies the world. Dive, O sinner, into this holy stream; it will wash away your sins and transform old into new. O! if thou seekest

---

(1) Several of these explanations are borrowed from Mgr. Gerbet's beautiful work.

innocence thou shalt find it in this bath, even shouldest thou be burdened with Adam's sin or thine own. No distance can afterwards separate those who have been regenerated; henceforth they become one through the action of one source, one spirit, one faith. Let not the number and character of thy crimes alarm thee. He who seeks life in this stream shall be made more holy."

To the Pontiff's gifts, the Emperor Valentinian III added his own. He placed a gold monument, which was ornamented with precious stones, twelve doors, the figures of the twelve Apostles, and the image of the Saviour, upon S. Peter's tomb. He also replaced the silver pediment, carried off from S. John Lateran by the Barbarians, with one that was equally rich.

S. Leo also endeavoured to restore the dignity of worship which had been destroyed by the Vandals. In the treasury of the Roman Church were six large silver vases weighing one hundred pounds, each a gift from Constantine. Leo melted them down, thus renovating the plate belonging to the Basilicas. The Lateran church was also beholden to him for the circular portico which may still be seen behind the tribune; S. Peter's owes to him the regular organisation of a body of chamberlains, or guardians of the Confession of S. Peter. S. Paul's Basilica had been struck by lightning: Leo restored it at great expense, and, at the cost of the Empress Galla Placidia, embellished it with that striking mosaic on a gold ground, representing Jesus Christ and the twenty four old men, which has survived centuries, and the conflagration, and which still decorates the great arch of the apse.

To S. Hilary, Leo's successor, is attributed the foundation of the pontifical library, now the most ancient of existing libraries. It appears strange to find a man, in the midst of this social upheaval which threatened universal destruction, who did not despair of society even when society despaired of itself; and who carefully preserved her archives. This man was S. Hilary, he never separated science from religion, the daughter from the mother! This library, or, to speak the language of the chroniclers, "these cupboards of books," were deposited in S. John Lateran by S. Hilary. The same Pope ordered the construction of a monastery with baths attached to it, near the Basilica of S. Laurence, an evidence that old Roman customs were not quite lost.

An interesting fact about the church of S. Agatha-in-Suburra is that this ancient oratory was handed over by Ricimer to Arian priests, and embellished by him with a view to its becoming his place of sepulture. Towards the end of the sixth century it was purified, and restored to Catholic worship, by S. Gregory the Great. Ciampini mentions that an image of S. Peter, with three tonsures or clerical crowns, had formerly existed in this church. The relics of S. Sebastian and S. Agatha are still venerated there.

The rich Basilica of S. Pietro-in-Vincoli was founded, in 442, by the Empress Eudoxia, Valentinian III wife, in order to preserve the chains which bound S. Peter in the prisons of Jerusalem and Rome. (1) "And when Herod would have brought him forth, the same night Peter was sleeping between two soldiers, bound with chains; and the keepers before the door kept the prison. And behold an Angel of the Lord stood by him: and a light shined in the room: and he striking Peter on the side raised him up, saying: Arise quickly. And the chains fell from off his hands." (2)

It was on the Esquiline, that hill formerly inhabited by Mæcenas, Horace, and other voluptuaries of the Augustan age, near the Via Suburra, where the courtesans were in the habit of walking, just above the Vicus Sceleratus where Tullia urged on her startled horses, "consternatos equos", over the bleeding body of her father, that the fane rose which was destined to immortalise the memory of these obstacles placed by the rich and the pleasure loving in the way of S. PETER's mission. The church of S. Pietro-in-Vincoli, rebuilt by ADRIAN I, richly decorated by JULIUS II, is now one of the most remarkable of the Roman Basilicas. The white marble pillars which divide the nave from the aisles are ancient columns; several pictures by Guercino adorn the altars; it possesses Domenichino's "Deliverance of S. Peter," and the famous "Moses" of Michael Angelo stands in the transept.

At the other extremity of the Esquiline, Pope SIMPLICIUS consecrated the church which a Roman lady,

(1) The first chains had been sent to the Empress by her mother Eudocia, on her return from Jerusalem; the second chains were given by S. Leo the Great.
(2) Acta Apost., XII, 6—7.

called Olympia, had built on the spot where S. Bibiana had lived and was buried. Bibiana was martyred in the reign of Julian the Apostate. She was a pious maiden like Agatha, Agnes and Lucy, whose purity withstood all temptations, threats and violence; divine spirits who only appear on earth as angels of mercy and grace, whose every thought is given to heaven. The body of S. Bibiana was exposed to dogs during two days in the Bull's Forum — "Forum boarium" — in the Velabrum. It remained untouched, and a priest named John, having carried the remains away by night, buried them near the palace of Licinius, in a spot where her sister, S. Demetria, and her mother S. Dafrosa already lay, who had both suffered martyrdom before her. (1) The relics of these three saints are enclosed in an ancient urn of Eastern alabaster, beneath the high altar of this church. Above the altar is Bernini's statue of S. Bibiana, one of the most graceful works of sculpture in Rome.

The church of S. Susanna on Mount Quirinal, and those of S. Stefano-Rotonda and of the Four-Crowned Saints on the Cælian Hill, date from the same period as S. Bibiana. The church of S. Stefano-Rotonda, so called from its circular shape, was built by Pope SIMPLICIUS. Several antiquaries have mistaken it for an ancient temple of Bacchus or Faunus; but it was more probably always a church, although ancient ruins have been used in its construction. Restored by NICHOLAS V, who closed up the inter-

---

(1) See the legend of this saint in the Roman Breviary, 2nd December.

columniation of the first peristyle, the walls of this small building are covered with frescoes by Pomarancio and Tempesta which reproduce with painful truthfulness every detail of the martyrdom of the saints.

The part of the Cælian Hill, on which S. Stefano-Rotonda now stands, was anciently known as "caput Africæ", from a statue which was found there of a woman bearing an elephant's trunk on her head as an ornament. S. Bibiana's quarter was known as "Ad ursum pileatum" (the capped bear), a curious appellation derived from a sculptured bear. The names of great men only remained on record in connection with the buildings they raised.

The great arches of Nero's aqueduct, like a triumphal gate, crown the road to S. Stefano-Rotonda, S. Maria-in-Domenica, S. Maria-Imperatrice, an old church formerly known as S. Gregorio-in-Marzio, and the no less ancient church of the Four-Crowned-Saints. These four saints, Severus, Severianus, Carpophorus, and Victorinus, were brothers, and were reckoned among the bravest soldiers in the Roman army. Having in Diocletian's reign refused to sacrifice to idols, spiked crowns were forced upon their heads, and they were beaten to death with loaded thongs. Their bodies were buried in the Via Labicana, three miles from Rome, in a cemetery within which the remains of several other martyrs had been collected who had suffered in the same persecution. Among these martyrs were five sculptors who refused to model idols. Their names were Claudius, Nicostratus, Symphorianus, Castorius and Simplicius. After suffering cruel torture they were thrust into leaden cases and flung into the Tiber. The remains of all these valiant athletes of the faith, soldiers and artists, were towards the end of the fifth century borne to a small church built for their reception on the Cælian Hill. It is still known as the church of the Four-Crowned-Saints, "Sanctorum quatuor Coronatorum Martyrum," and was restored under PASCHAL II.

Such is the description of the principal foundations established at Rome during the fifth century; and one delights to find traces of them amid the wonders of modern Rome. Most of the churches just mentioned are seldom referred to in guide books, and several of them are rarely opened; yet it is in these places, sanctified by the deaths or lives of martyrs, beneath the roofs which echoed with the hymns first sung by Christians, that we can best understand the saintly piety of the first ages of Christianity.

The election of Popes seldom gave rise to differences at that period. They were elected by the bishops of neighbouring towns (finitimarum urbium), the clergy, and the faithful. Votes were given viva voce, and the Pontiff was usually proclaimed by acclamation. But, from the reign of Constantine, the imperial rulers claimed the right to exercise some influence over the nominations, under pretext of avoiding disturbances among the people. This pretension was finally more or less admitted, each party desiring to rest on the imperial authority. Thus, when in 418 the archdeacon Eulalius managed to be elected in the Lateran Basilica, while the greater part of the clergy and faithful selected BONIFACE in the church of S. Marcello, the two competitors referred the dispute to Honorius, in order to avoid a schism. Eighty years later, Symmachus and Laurence having been elected Popes at the same time, Symmachus at S. John Lateran, Laurence in S. Maria-ad-Nives, remitted the decision to Theodoric, although this prince was an Arian. Theodoric declared that right was on the side of him who had obtained the larger number of votes, therefore Symmachus's claim was acknowledged. SYMMACHUS profited by this occasion to assemble a Council at S. Peter's in order to settle what were the proper regulations for a papal election. He then addressed the assembled Bishops:— "I have summoned you in spite of this rigorous winter in order that we may determine what method will be best to put a stop to the disputes among the clergy, and rioting among the populace, such as took place on the occasion of my election. Let us therefore consider what shall be done when a Bishop of Rome is elected." All present exclaimed, "Jesus Christ, hear us; long live Symmachus."

Decrees were at once drawn up, punishing all intrigues very severely, and the following rider was added, "Should a Pope die suddenly without being able to make arrangements for the election of his successor, he who obtains the suffrages of all the clergy or of the majority shall be consecrated bishop."

This was one of the last acts of the fifth century, which had not been inglorious for Catholicism, for it had produced S. Cyril, S. Prosper, S. Hilary of Arles, Remigius, Clovis, and S. Clotilda; this century also listened to the voices of the last Fathers of the church. Theodoric came to Rome in 500; S. Fulgentius assisted at his triumphal entry; but the display of pomp, and human greatness in its most attractive form, only brought him a supreme contempt for the world. The King of the Goths stayed but a short time in the ancient capital of the empire; Odoacer also only remained a short while in 467, immediately returning to Ravenna; it almost seemed as though this widow of nations were too majestic, even in her ruined condition, for these brave chieftains, who could neither boast ancestry nor recall glorious deeds. They required a new capital; Rome, left to herself, saw the papal power increase daily; the only power, in fact, which could henceforth suit her fallen grandeur, because it united both the past and the future.

CHAPTER VI.

Oblectat me, Roma, tuas spectare ruinas!
Æneas Sylvius.

SIXTH CENTURY.

THE reign of Theodoric was a boon to Italy after the troubles that land had experienced. He was a Prince of worth, who united to the vigour of his race a wise forbearance and a great esteem for talents and virtue in whatever rank they were to be found. Instead of strewing his path with ruins, as Alaric, Attila, and Genseric had done, he raised fresh monuments and protected the arts. Cassiodorus, in his pompous Latinity, has left us unimpeachable testimony as to the admiration the wonders of Rome excited in the King of the Goths: "Quæ tantum visentibus conferunt stuporem ut aliarum civitatum possint miracula superari."

Although Theodoric was an Arian he respected the Catholic churches; moreover he upheld the ancient laws, and forsook barbarian armour for the Roman toga. His entry into Rome, in 500, was therefore marked by the universal applause of the population. It was on this occasion that he met Boethius whom he attached to his services, as he subsequently did Cassiodorus.

Anicius Maulius Torquatus Boethius claimed descent from the ancient families whose names he bore. His youth had been spent in Athens, where, even then, he drew attention to himself by learned Latin translations of Plato, Aristotle, Archimedes and Euclid. Returning to Rome, his native land, he was elected consul in 485, at the age of thirty-two. In 500 his two sons were consuls at the same time, and he was chosen to address Theodoric in the Senate. These glorious memories solaced his prison life, twenty-five years later. When, bowed down beneath the weight of woe, complaints escaped from his lips, he seemed to hear Fortune saying to him, "Can any event, however sad, make you forget that happy glorious day, when your two sons, elected Consuls at the same time, were conducted to your house surrounded by Senators, amid a thousand cries of joy; that day, when seated in the best places the Senators heard you pronounce the King's panegyric with an eloquence that aroused the flattering yet well deserved applause of your audience? . . . Then you had just cause to praise Fortune, for she had marked you as her favourite, by granting you an honour which no other man had hitherto obtained. Are you therefore justified in dealing severely with her?" (1)

Boethius was a theologian, philosopher, mathematician and distinguished musician. He was considered the most remarkable man in Rome: when

---

(1) De Consolatione Philosophiæ, lib. II.

Gundobald, King of the Burgundians, desired to visit the ancient capital, Boethius was charged by Theodoric to act as his guide. Gundobald was apparently struck by only two of the curiosities he beheld. These were two clocks; on one, "the needle marked the time of day, the hours being indicated by a light shadow;" in the other, "not to be beholden to the stars, they had obtained a record of the movements of the heavens from hydraulics." (1) Gundobald requested Theodoric to make similar clocks for him, so Theodoric wrote to Boethius; "Your acquaintance with the four branches of mathematics has qualified you to enter the most unknown paths of mechanical science. Nothing can resist mechanical power; it makes miracles appear natural, and simplifies things considered as impossible by many who are even doubtful when they witness them. Mechanical science can make water rise and fall; it measures and directs the action of fire; organs are filled with wind to make them produce musical harmony . . . brazen bulls bellow, serpents hiss, and birds sing naturally, charming everyone with their melody. You have, as we are aware, studied all these things with great care. Therefore make these two clocks for us, as quickly as possible, in order that your fame may reach where you cannot go yourself. Let nations learn through you that we possess nobles who equal in merit the most distinguished inventors! How often will these people refuse to believe in the reality of what lies before their eyes? How often

---

(1) Cassiodori variarum lib. I, ep. 45.

will they mistake these actual things for the vain fancies of a dream? But, when at last they recover their senses, how will they ever again dare to consider themselves as equal to us, when they remember that wise men capable of such works are among us?"

This emphatic letter points out to what importance Boethius had attained by his talent and character. The austerity of his life was like that of an ancient Roman and devout Christian. He was the son-in-law of Symmachus, a man of consular rank, as much respected for his own worth as for the duties he had fulfilled; indeed every virtue seemed united in this family. Proba, one of the daughters of Symmachus, had taken a vow of chastity, and was in constant correspondence with S. Fulgentius; Galla, another of his daughters, daily entertained twelve paupers at her table, and devoted her fortune to the endowment of a church and hospital. The first wife of Boethius, Elpis, had been celebrated for beauty, piety, and poetic talent: the hymns for the festival of SS. Peter and Paul are attributed to her. His second wife, Rusticiana, a daughter of Symmachus, distributed all her possessions among the poor, during the siege of Rome by Totila, and was reduced to begging her own bread. As to Boethius, while amply fulfilling all his political duties, he was to be seen commenting on the Categories of Aristotle, and defending the purity of Catholic dogma against Nestorius, Eutyches and Arius. His work on the Trinity coincided with the measures taken by the Emperor Justin I against heretics, which measures greatly vexed Theodoric, himself an Arian, and the natural protector of his co-religionists. It may even be surmised that the publication of this work led to the catastrophe which befell Boethius; however he was already in prison when he wrote it, having been accused of high treason by some courtiers, who had accused him of being the cause of the public misfortunes. Symmachus, his distinguished father-in-law, was likewise thrown into a dungeon, on the empty pretext of desiring to maintain the pretentions of the Senate against Theodoric's authority. It was then, when in the presence of death, that Boethius wrote his beautiful work "The Consolation of Philosophy". He looked upon philosophy merely as the dawn of the real light, "veri præviam luminis"; and was about to describe what rewards were reserved to the elect when he was cut short by the arrival of his executioners. The last words he wrote were, "O men, flee from vice, and practise virtue."

S. Boethius was strangled at Pavia in 524 in the seventieth year of his age; Symmachus was also put to death the following year. Meanwhile Theodoric had sent Pope JOHN to Constantinople to obtain the revocation of the edicts against heretics from the Emperor. "I do not promise to do what you demand of me," the Pontiff had replied, "nor to be your interpreter." Nevertheless Theodoric induced him by threats to take ship for Alexandria. The edicts were not revoked, and Pope JOHN, having been imprisoned on his return to Ravenna, died of hunger and thirst in his dungeon on the 27th May 526.

Thus Theodoric, having become restless and suspicious in his old age, tarnished the splendour of a beautiful life by this heinous crime, and was beset by deep remorse. One day he fancied that the gory head of Symmachus had been served at table instead of a fish; consequently he was so terror stricken that his death shortly followed those of his victims. (1)

The church built by Galla, the daughter of Symmachus, still exists in Rome; it was long known under the name of S. Maria-in-Porticu, on account of its vicinity to Octavia's portico. It now bears the name of its foundress. (2) Formerly a miraculous painting of the Virgin was honoured here, having, according to S. Gregory, been given to S. Galla by Angels. It has since been removed to S. Maria-in-Campitelli. The church of S. Galla stands on the site of her home, where also Symmachus, and probably Boethius, lived.

The Theatre of Marcellus has now become a princely palace; the portico of Octavia, stripped of its altars, statues, its beautiful Venus and its citharean Apollo, is now a shelter for fishmongers; but Galla's and Symmachus's home has been transformed into a church and hospital. Pagan Rome only considered the enjoyment of the rich; Christian Rome, on the contrary, wished to alleviate the miseries of the poor.

Theodoric's death replunged the Italian provinces into anarchy. For several years his daughter Amalasontha worthily filled his place; but, Theodatus,

---

(1) Amalasontha, Theodoric's daughter, built a tomb for him near Ravenna. It was circular, and a small imitation of Hadrian's Mole. Theodoric's ashes were placed within it, enclosed in a porphyry sarcophagus.

(2) The S. Galla Hospital has been greatly enlarged and endowed by the Odescalchi family.

jealous of power, ordered that she should be strangled on a charge of adultery. This dreadful tragedy was carried out on an island in Lake Bolsena. Some years later Theodatus in his turn was deposed and slain as a coward. After this Vitiges and Totila struggled with Belisarius for the country which formerly had been conquered by the Goths.

During this ever increasing disorganisation all social ties were at length severed. Rights were no longer respected, no prerogatives were fixed; the awe which formerly enveloped power vanished from the people; and, had it not been for religion, which still drew souls together by a common faith and hope, the world would have consisted of isolated beings, generally at feud with one another, and would have ceased to be a united society.

It is therefore not astonishing that during these years of trial, in the sixth century, monastic institutions began to flourish in the west.

S. Benedict, whose rule has always been a model for all communities, was born in 480 in the neighbourhood of Norcia, in the province of Spoleto. His first years were spent in Rome where his father filled a high position. In Mabillon's time some remains of the house he occupied were still pointed out near S. Benedetto-in-Piscinula. S. Benedict's impression of Rome, with its many pleasures and corrupt youth, was quite different from that produced on S. Jerome, or that which S. Augustine had experienced in Carthage. He did not feel their seductive force, but they disgusted him. While still quite young he fled from the city, and escaped from his nurse who was aware of his design; and wandering alone he looked about for a silent retreat, far away from the noise of the world. Twenty miles from Tibur a hill rises, beneath which the Anio widens into a lake; it is covered with brushwood, quite deserted, and on its summit a low narrow cave opens from the steep side of the rock. Such was the spot S. Benedict chose for his home; and there he dwelt for several years, clad in wild beast's skins, dependent upon God for his safety and food. Some may ask, with scorn, what manner of life this was; whether it arose from a weak brain or fanatical excitement, "deridetur justi simplicitas." (1) It was this very simplicity which won admiration and respect for Benedict; every man who is master of himself can control others; and meditations and trials are necessary for those who wish to attain superior wisdom.

Crowds therefore flocked to Sublacum, and surrounded Benedict's sacred grotto; Equitius and Tertullus, both Roman senators, gave him the charge of their sons, Maurus and Placidus; and it became necessary to build twelve monasteries (2) to receive the world-weary men who wished to place themselves

---

(1) Sanct. Gregor., cap. XII, in Job.
(2) The twelve monasteries founded by S. Benedict at Sublacum were: 1st The Holy Grotto; 2nd SS. Cosmo and Damian, now S. Scholastica; 3rd S. Angelo, after the lake; 4th S. Maria, afterwards S. Lorenzo; 5th S. Girolamo; 6th S. Giovanni Battista; 7th S. Clemente; 8th S. Biagio, since S. Romano; 9th S. Michaele, above the Grotto; 10th S. Vittoriano, at the foot of Mt. Porcarius; 11th S. Andrea; 12th La Vita Æterna, now the Val-Santo. The greater part of these monasteries no longer exist.

under his direction. From Sublacum Benedict went to Monte Cassino, whence he promulgated that admirable rule which has survived the laws of empires, has peopled Europe with religious orders, husbandmen, men of letters, doctors, and scholars, and which has most powerfully aided in civilizing the world.

Towards the close of the sixth century another simple-minded good man, a believer in supernatural visions, in revelations, and in miracles, Gregory the Great, walking through the Roman slave market saw there several youths of remarkable appearance waiting to be purchased. He asked whence they came, and was told "From the Island of Britain." Asking further what was their religion he was informed that they were pagans. Being filled with burning charity, Gregory selected certain monks and sent them to bear the Gospel to Britain. These monks set out on their mission; the language of the people they had been sent to convert was unknown to them; in fact, they could scarcely determine the geographical position of that remote island. They only knew it was at the end of the world, "ad finis terræ"; but they went forward as though guided by a star. Two years after their departure England was gained over to the Christian faith. Such are the labours of the simple-minded and the just!

The traces left of S. Benedict and S. Gregory are too deeply impressed upon the world not to excite keen curiosity in searching for them. Memories of them still live in Rome, Subiaco, Vicovario, where S. Benedict vainly endeavoured to reform a monastery, and also at Monte Cassino.

At Vicovario may still be seen the cells hollowed out of the rock, and the refectory within which the poisoned cup, which some wicked monks offered to the Saint, broke of itself. At Subiaco, the ancient Sublacum, out of the twelve monasteries built by S. Benedict only two remain; The Sacro-Speco and S. Scholastica. The hill, constantly visited by pilgrims, no longer offers that difficulty of access which led to its selection by the pious anchorite. A pathway traced across rocks and verdure, along which may be heard the roaring cascades of the Anio, leads first to S. Scholastica, a curious monument with ogive cloisters and several varieties of architecture, then, ascending still further, the majestic monastery Il Sacro Speco appears above. It was built by S. Benedict in front of the grotto sanctified by him. Mabillon rejoiced when he first saw this dwelling-place of the founder of his order. "*Non sine gestientis animi gaudio tritam a beatissimo patre atque sanctis hominibus viam incessimus.*" (1)

At Subiaco everything speaks of S. Benedict. The grotto he dwelt in, "as long as man's stature but rather less high," (2) still opens behind the altar of a small underground chapel. A few steps beyond it is the field of thorns upon which he rolled to quell his fiery passions. Above the rock was the monastery of Romanus, the monk who daily lowered a small

---
(1) Mabillon, "Museum italicum." It was in the month of December 1685 that this pious and learned Benedictine accomplished the pilgrimage to Subiaco.
(2) "Staturâ hominis non longior, paulò minùs alta," are Mabillon's words.

portion of bread to S. Benedict, by means of a cord and bell. It is said that on the opposite bank of the Anio some vestiges remain of the house of the wicked priest Florentius, who used to send unchaste women to tempt the virtue of the young monks. It was the hatred of this priest which led S. Benedict to forsake Subiaco, and seek a refuge on another mountain above the little village of Cassinum. On the summit of this mountain formerly stood a temple of Apollo within a wood to which the people came for their sacrifice. S. Benedict destroyed both the temple and wood; he built two oratories, one dedicated to S. Martin, the other to S. John on the place formerly occupied by the altars of pagan idols. The tower, which he built, and the two rooms occupied by him still exist at the entrance to the monastery. (1)

In 542, Totila paid a visit to S. Benedict, who predicted his conquests and death. In the same monastery, we must remember, Carloman, Charles Martel's son, lived and died; and Ratchis, King of the Lombards, took religious vows at the hands of Pope ZACHARY, while his wife and daughter withdrew to the convent near Piombarole.

(1) Some authors believe, however, that the tower and two chambers, supposed to have been inhabited by S. Benedict, are ruins of buildings raised by the Abbot Petronax in the eighth century. In any case they have been built on the same spot where the saint had dwelt. The following inscription may be read in the larger chamber:— "Pars superior antiquissimæ turris in quâ S. P. Benedictus cœlestibus visionibus illustratus, dùm viveret, habitabat; et in eâ angelorum concentus, odoris fragrantiam ac lucis immensitatem ab antiquis viris in præcipuis festivitatibus audiri et videri solitum fuit."

The two principal Abbeys of the Benedictines at Rome are S. Paolo fuori-le-mura, and S. Callisto. Science and virtue are stamped upon the children of S. Benedict in an especially modest and gentle manner; wherever you may chance to meet them they will greet you as old friends, their conversation partaking, according to Mabillon, of a sweet familiarity and outspoken simplicity, "familiaritate dulces et simplicitate aperti."

When Totila came to Cassino he had not yet wrested Rome from the armies of the Eastern Emperor. Rome, helpless herself, abandoned by the Cæsars, and demoralised by servitude, passed from one yoke to another; her blood and treasure were nearly exhausted in satisfying the greed of her conquerors. Taken by Belisarius in 536, she afterwards saw herself besieged by Vitiges and the Gothic army. It was then observed how much the Goths respected sacred things. The two churches of S. Peter and S. Paul, although standing outside the walls, were left untouched, and the sacred offices were continued in them without interruption. The siege, however, was long and cruel, aqueducts were broken, Rome suffered from dearth, and the inhabitants were reduced to the painful necessity of embarking their women and children on the Tiber. At length Vitiges was vanquished, and Belisarius left Italy. Then Totila appeared. His first exploit was the conquest of Naples, and he then advanced on Rome, which had to undergo a new siege and famine. The Romans clamoured for bread to the Imperial generals, saying, "If you cannot give us food, open the gates, or at least kill us." The generals answered, "To give you food is impossible; to let you depart would be dangerous, and to kill you would be wicked." When things were at this pass, one day three children were seen clinging to their father, whose only answer to their famished cries was the hopelessness of despair. Suddenly he cried, "Follow me," and the children did so in gladness and hope. Arrived on one of the bridges of the Tiber, the wretched father wrapped his cloak about his head and flung himself into the river. After this, the people were allowed to quit the city, or rather permission was sold to them to do so.

But it was not long before Rome was delivered up to the enemy through the treachery of some Isaurian soldiers who had charge of the Porta Asinaria, near S. John Lateran, on the 17th December, 546. Totila entered the city by night and ordered his trumpets to sound, in order that the inhabitants might take refuge in the churches. He none the less allowed pillage, and the people, turned out of their dwellings, were forced to leave the city. Totila desired to make Rome into a field of pasture; and that city, "the mistress of nations," became then "solitary and widowed" as Jerusalem had been before her.

But scarcely had Totila departed when Belisarius returned, and restored those portions of the walls which had been destroyed. The wall raised by Belisarius still exists at the foot of the Aventine, and on the Cælian Hill; but we must go back to the time of Honorius and Aurelian to account for the origin of the rest of the enclosure.

Justinian's general having withdrawn a second time, Totila again appeared before the capital, re-entered the town through the treason of the Isaurians who admitted him by the Porta S. Paolo; after which a terrible massacre took place of all the Greeks found within the city.

It was reserved for the eunuch Narses to put an end to the dominion of the Goths in Italy. Twice he defeated Totila in 552, who died of his wounds after the second battle; and Rome, having again become a vassal of the Eastern Empire, was forced to submit to viceroys, who, under the title of Exarchs, ruled at Ravenna. The bridge across the Anio, at the foot of Monte Sacro, is a monument of the visit of Narses to Rome.

We shall not trace the history of the Exarchate of Ravenna, which, after all, would be little more than a relation of the weakness and incapacity of some nonentities, amid one of the most violent crises which ever afflicted humanity. To Huns, Vandals and Goths, succeeded the Lombards, an impious and sacrilegious race, who did not even spare holy places, but who filled heaven with martyrs and "depopulated the earth." (1) "What is left in the world to make us happy"? exclaimed S. Gregory. "We only see sadness, and hear lamentations; cities are destroyed, fortresses ruined, fields laid waste; the earth has become a solitude, and what does remain of the human race is being continually crushed by the flail of God. Some

---

(1) "Depopulati sunt agri, in solitudinem terra redacta est" (S. Greg. papa, hom. VI, l. II.)

are carried away into captivity, others mutilated, and some slain. We can see to what extremities Rome, once the mistress of the world, is reduced: oppressed by griefs, forsaken by her citizens, insulted by her foes, filled with ruins! Where is the Senate? Where the people? what say we, where are there men? Buildings are crumbling away; and walls are falling. Where are they who once rejoiced in her glory? Where their pomp and their pride? Formerly her princes and chieftains went forth to conquer; youths flocked to her from all parts to seek advancement; while now she is deserted and ruined no one approaches her; she has no warriors left capable of valorous deeds."

The holy Pontiff could only explain so great a decay by thinking that the end of the world was at hand. So the voice of his sorrow unceasingly resounded in the Roman churches, like the voice of those prophets who called out "Woe! Woe!" round the walls of Jerusalem. He exclaimed:— "God has already overthrown the glory of the world, and these accumulating ruins foretell the day of his wrath and justice. (1) Let us therefore despise the world with our whole hearts, particularly now when it is perishing." (2)

S. Gregory had the happiness of saving Rome from a fresh catastrophe by obtaining a promise from Agilulphus, King of the Lombards, not to enter the city. Shortly afterwards Agilulphus embraced the Catholic faith, to which his great and noble wife Theodelinda

---

(1) "districti sui judicii diem propinquantem denuntiant".
(2) Hom. XVIII "in Ezechiel," et Hom. V "in Isai."

already belonged. Thus Christian influence acted upon the conquerors and sowed seeds of civilization among them, just when it seemed about to be destroyed.

At this period Catholic work was very conciliatory and persuasive. It no more attached itself to what little remained of the Imperial purple than it did to sheep-skins worn by the Barbarians; for, like the Apostle, no difference was made between Jew, Greek, freeman or slave; all were "brethren in Jesus Christ." Besides which relief of misfortune, and the right of opposition to violent and iniquitous measures, belonged to the clergy. From this epoch the people began to recognize, with respect and confidence, that Catholicism held important social jurisdiction over a renovated world, a jurisdiction which increased and strengthened as centuries rolled by.

Observe also what progress was made in the world, through Catholicism, in the principle of Christian equality, at the very moment when the entire universe appeared to be subjected to a despotic system. Under paganism, Jupiter was supposed to deprive those whom he destined to slavery of half their intellect. Homer says this. Pagans not only considered that slavery was not contrary to the primordial laws of humanity, but they asserted that it was actually right in the due order of nature. Aristotle demonstrated this fact in syllogisms which do not admit of any answer. Finally, lest any remorse might trouble the conscience of society they declared that no good could lodge in the soul of a slave; and this doctrine had received the applauses of the wealthy. Countless nations and generations have passed away since those degrading principles were the laws of the world. A century after our Lord's birth, Hermes, a Roman prefect, enfranchised twelve hundred and fifty slaves on the day of his conversion to Catholicism. Under Diocletian, Chromatius, another Roman prefect, freed fourteen hundred slaves who were baptised with him. "Those who became children of God", he said, "may not be slaves of man." We know that the two holy virgins Praxedes and Pudentiana were of this opinion in days gone by. Pagans smiled with scorn; and accused Christians of admitting into their company abject and ignoble souls. "Are there not among you" said they, "rich and poor, masters and slaves." "No", replied Lactantius, "because we consider ourselves to be equals and brothers. If our conditions differ, this does not mean we are to have slaves; and, from a religious point of view, we are all servants of God." (1)

In the fifth century S. Chrysostom issued a proclamation at Constantinople to those powerful nations who, being governed by Roman laws, considered they had the right of life and death over their slaves, to the effect that if the slave were not well treated by his master he was not bound to serve him. (2) The rough usage by the Vandals and Lombards only forwarded these charitable ideas, which henceforth appeared to be the only safeguard of society from barbarism; and the conquerors were soon reduced to conceal, by milder forms of servitude, the power they claimed over the vanquished.

(1) "Instit. divin"., lib. I. cap. XVI.
(2) Hom. XI, "in Ep. I ad Corinthios."

It is not to be wondered at, on beholding what power religion obtained, that great men, nobles, emperors and kings, should endeavour to take some of her bold independence from the Church in order to make her subservient to their policy. Thus, after Constantine, the successors of the Cæsars arrogated to themselves some influence over the election of the Roman Pontiffs. At first this influence was merely indirect; but under Justinian it became patent, and even claimed its exercise as a right. The Pope was then named, after three days of fasting and prayer, by the clergy, nobility, people, and soldiers, (clerus, optimates, populus et milites). The nomination was then submitted to the Emperor for his approval. In Constantinople the Court considered its strength superior to that of the Pontiffs, and desired to dispose of pontifical power accordingly. Two courtesans, Theodora and Antonina, one being the Emperor's consort, the other being married to the greatest general in the Empire, actually tried to sell the Popedom for gold at the sacrifice of faith. Pope SYLVERIUS, in their opinion, was too strict in maintaining the purity of Catholic dogma; so they ordered Belisarius to depose him, under pretext of his corresponding with the Goths. Belisarius summoned SYLVERIUS to the palace; when both general and courtesan flattered, threatened, and ordered him to give a written agreement with heretical belief, under pain of abdication. The worthy old man remained unmoved, and retired to S. Sabina. Twice he was invited to return to the palace, and twice he complied, but on the last occasion his followers were refused admittance, and he himself was seen there no more. On the following day Belisarius ordered the election of a new pontiff; and, in spite of the hesitation of many Romans, he succeeded in securing the election of the deacon Vigilius, a confidant of Theodora. SYLVERIUS was first banished to Patara, then to the island of Palmaria, where he died of misery and want on the 20th of July 538.

As for Belisarius he soon repented of his crime, and even endeavoured to expiate it by building a church, which remained a lasting memento of his grief. It still stands near the Fontana di Trevi, and is known as S. Maria-in-Fornica. An old stone bears the following inscription:— "The patrician Belisarius, a friend to this city, founded this church to obtain forgiveness for his sin (ob culpæ veniam), do ye, who set foot in this holy place, often pray God to have pity upon him."

The death of SYLVERIUS alone could legalize the election of VIGILIUS; but, by one of those remarkable judgments of God, which can turn a worldly wise man's act against himself, VIGILIUS became the steadfast champion of orthodoxy. He even dared to excommunicate the Empress who had manœuvred for his election. But the fate of his predecessor became his own. Theodora wrote to the Governor of Rome, "Arrest him anywhere, whether in the Lateran Basilica, or elsewhere, except in S. Peter's. Bring him before me, or, if you do not, I swear by God the Eternal, I shall have you flayed alive (excoriari te faciam)." VIGILIUS spent several years in captivity at Constantinople, but his spirit remained unbroken: he said,

"Although you hold me captive, you do not hold S. Peter."

It was to VIGILIUS that Aratore, a sub-deacon of the Roman Church, dedicated his poem, "The Acts of the Apostles," written in hexameters and divided into two books. (1) He presented it to him at a meeting of the greater portion of the clergy "in the presbytery, before the Confession of S. Peter," and, as the most distinguished persons in Rome had requested that the work might be read publicly, the Pope gave orders that this should be done in the Basilica of S. Pietro-in-Vincoli. Aratore read his own poem; but so great was the applause, and so frequently did the populace, who crowded the Basilica, demand the re-reading of certain passages, that it took him four days to complete the task.

During the pontificate of PELAGIUS II, Rome suffered by an inundation of the Tiber; and when the waters subsided they left such tainted miasmas in the houses that the plague ensued. This plague was terrible; people died sneezing and yawning; even the Pope was carried off by the contagion. "Death does not wait for sickness," exclaimed S. GREGORY, "it carries

---

(1) Aratore was one of the most distinguished men of the sixth century. Theodoric confided several important missions to him, and Athalaric named him Count of the Servants. In the letter in which Cassiodorus informed him of this last mentioned favour, he congratulates himself on the fact that "Liguria also has her Cicero." Aratore gave up the world, joined the priesthood, and thenceforth devoted his talents to religion. His poem "The Acts of the Apostles" is to be found in the collection of the Latin ecclesiastical poets, Fabricius's edition.

off sinners before they can dream of doing penance; it is not only a few who perish, all fall together, and the houses remain empty!"

GREGORY, who was at that time PELAGIUS's secretary, had assembled the people in the church of S. Sabina; he proposed that next day, the Feast of the Resurrection, they should go in procession, in seven different bands starting from seven different churches, to S. Maria Maggiore. Hence comes the name of the "Septiform Litany." "The clergy's litany," says Gregory, "shall start from the church of Blessed John Baptist; that of men from the church of the Blessed Martyr Marcellus; that of monks from the church of the Martyrs John and Paul; that of the handmaidens of God from the church of the Blessed Martyrs Cosmo and Damian; that of married women from the church of the Blessed First Martyr S. Stephen; that of widows from the church of the Blessed Martyr Vitalis; and, finally, the litany of the poor and the children from the church of the Blessed Martyr Cæcilia." (1)

(1) Gregory of Tours mentions a different order, taken from a sermon by S. GREGORY, which leads Baronius to suppose that there were more than one "Septiform Litany." The following is the order given by Gregory of Tours. The high clergy at SS. Cosmo and Damian, with the priests of the sixth district; the nuns at SS. Marcellinus and Peter, with the priests of the first district; the children at SS. John and Paul, with the priests of the second district; the widows at S. Euphemia, with the priests of the fifth district; laymen at S. Stephen, with the priests of the seventh district; and married women at S. Clement with the priests of the third district.

This procession was renewed every year from this period under the name of "Great Litany", without being subdivided into companies as in those days of sorrow, when the whole population wished to unite in public prayer. Towards the end of the seventh century the Great Litany was fixed for the 25<u>th</u> of April, on which day it is still held.

Meanwhile GREGORY was chosen to succeed PELAGIUS; but this humble Christian, once the danger was passed, only sought obscurity, and refused the proffered title. At first he begged the Emperor Maurice not to confirm his election; when he did so, Gregory disguised and concealed himself, being carried out of Rome among some bales of goods; thus he escaped to the woods in search of peace and solitude. Meanwhile, at Rome, people fasted and prayed to God for the restoration of their Bishop. Their prayers were heard; Gregory's retreat was discovered, and he was solemnly consecrated on the 3<u>rd</u> of September 590.

GREGORY belonged to the illustrious family of the Gordians. He was born at Rome on that slope of the Cælian Hill which faces the Palatine, and was known in ancient times as Clivus Scauri. His mother was S. Sylvia, his aunts S. Trasilla and S. Emiliana; among his ancestry he reckoned Pope FELIX IV. In his youth he was in the civil service, and was appointed Prefect of Rome in 573; but, being soon weary of grandeur, he renounced the world, and turned the paternal residence into a monastery under the invocation of S. Andrew, living there with some monks under the severest discipline. BENEDICT I named him one of the seven deacons of Rome. Being sent on an embassy to Constantinople he was conspicuous for his dignity and saintly independence, which were ever after distinctive qualities of his character. His pontificate is one of those which have left a deep mark in the history of the Church. The acts which have rendered Gregory the Great famous among men, and holy before God, were his efforts to reform the morals of the clergy by giving them an example of self-denial and economy; to convert Jews and heretics by persuasion and gentleness; to send missionaries abroad to preach the faith; to maintain the integrity of Catholic dogma and the authority of the Holy See, as firmly as was consistent with his benevolent courtesy, and, lastly, by speaking to his people as their confidant in all their joys and sorrows.

It was he who, when the patriarchs of Constantinople claimed the title of "Universal Bishop," preferred being called the "Servant of the Servants of God," a noble title, and one which remains the most beautiful appellation of his successors. It was Gregory, also, who endowed the Roman Liturgy with majestic grandeur in its chants and ritual. (1) He was accused of having set on fire and destroyed the Palatine library founded by Augustus; but whether there is

---

(1) "Je n'ai jamais entendu ce chant grave et pathétique entonné par les prêtres et répondu affectueusement par une infinité de voix d'hommes, de femmes, de jeunes filles et d'enfants, sans que mes entrailles ne s'en soient émues, n'en aient tressailli, et que les larmes ne m'en soient venues aux yeux." (Diderot, "Essai sur la peinture".)

any truth in this statement or not, I cannot say, the fact was only mentioned by an historian more than 500 years after his death. (1)

From this epoch, that is to say from the Sixth Century, the supreme pontificate assumed nearly all the duties of royalty; and Gregory, in spite of infirmities which made his life one long martyrdom, occupied himself no less with the defence of Italy than with the salvation of the world. Gibbon remarks, "The misfortunes of Rome involved the apostolic pastor in the business of peace and war ... Gregory awakened the emperor from a long slumber, exposed the guilt or incapacity of the exarch and his inferior ministers ... encouraged the Italians to guard their cities and altars; and condescended, in the crisis of danger, to name the tribunes, and to direct the operations, of the provincial troops ... he presumed to save his country without the consent of the emperor or exarch .... in the attachment of a grateful people, he found the purest reward of a citizen, and the best right of a sovereign." (2)

The paternal residence of S. Gregory is now occupied by the Camaldolesi, whose monastery he

---

(1) John of Salisbury, Bishop of Chartres in the latter half of the twelfth century, first makes mention of the matter in his "Polycraticus". S. Gregory died in 604. Thus, for more than five centuries, an event of this importance had been ignored, although at Rome it must have caused the greater interest inasmuch as the Pope must have trenched upon the rights of the Emperors, to whom belonged the sovereignty of the city and the ownership of its monuments.

(2) History of the Decline, etc. Vol. VIII, Chap. XLV.

founded there under the invocation of S. Andrew; it is now the famous Abbey of S. Gregorio-Magno. The small chapel is still shown in which S. Gregory preached his homilies, the chamber where he slept, the marble table at which he daily entertained twelve poor pilgrims, and at which one day an angel became his guest. One of the first Priors of this monastery was S. Augustine, the Apostle of England; one of the last was the humble Cardinal Capellari, who reigned as Gregory XVI.

The church of S. Gregorio-Magno, built soon after the death of its saintly patron, has, at different periods, been restored and renovated. Michael Angelo, Guido, Domenichino, Annibale Caracci, Carlo Maratti have beautified it with their works. It is one of the places in modern Rome most frequented by pilgrims and artists; there is no other spot whence a more beautiful view of the ruins of ancient Rome can be obtained.

When S. Gregory transformed the family dwelling into a monastery, S. Sylvia withdrew to a neighbouring spot known as New-Cell, now covered by the old church of S. Sabas.

The memory of S. Gregory lingers around many of the monuments of Rome. We know that he held several Councils before the Confession of S. Peter, and that there he delivered eleven of his homilies. He preached three homilies at S. Maria Maggiore; others at S. Lorenzo, S. Clemente, S. Stefano-Rotondo, S. Sabina, SS. Nereo-ed-Achilleo, and, above all, at the Lateran, where he lived. In the apse at SS. Nereo-ed-Achilleo stands S. Gregory's marble pulpit. Part of the twenty-eighth homily, which was spoken "near to the tomb" of these Saints, is engraved on the back of the pulpit. The greater number of the Churches, in which the stations were then held, most probably heard his voice, for the sermons which have come down to us embrace every period of the year.

It will now be fitting to speak of the Roman Liturgy as it was finally fixed by this holy Pontiff; but first we had better glance at the principal foundations of the sixth century, and at those whose uncertain origin dates undoubtedly prior to S. GREGORY.

Pope S. SYMMACHUS raised above the church of S. Martino, once the venerable cathedral of S. Sylvester, a new and larger church which he dedicated jointly to the great "Thaumaturgus" of the Gauls and to the powerful ally of Constantine. The greater number of pilgrims used to ascend the flight of thirty-five steps leading to S. Peter's on their knees, therefore, in order to facilitate this act of piety in bad weather, SYMMACHUS constructed two covered staircases one to the right, the other to the left. By his orders, two episcopal residences (episcopia) were erected on either side of the portico; new sanctuaries were created within the Vatican Basilica, among others that of S. Andrea, now S. Giovanni-Battista-in-fonte, which was most richly decorated. S. Paolo-fuori-le-mura and S. Pancrazio also benefited by the Pontiff's generosity; he annexed a convent for women to S. Paul's (matroneum), and he reconstructed S. Pancrazio from top to bottom. Anastasius informs us that SYMMACHUS established fountains and baths in the forecourts of several churches. The fountain in the atrium of S. Peter's certainly dated from his pontificate. Anastasius undoubtedly refers to a vast laver (cantharum), and several ornaments, such as crosses and palms, which were placed there. This famous fountain was formed by the ancient fir-cone now to be seen in the Belvedere Gardens, and which was compared by Dante to a giant's head. (1) The water gushed from the top, and fell in little cascades; above it rose a pavilion, adorned with palm leaves and gilt crosses, and upheld by eight porphyry columns. Above this pavilion dolphins and peacocks, with golden plumage, cast forth streams of water into the large basin of SYMMACHUS: the topmost point of the structure was crowned by Constantine's Labarum. Among the numerous gifts SYMMACHUS bestowed on the Roman churches, mention is made of the ciboria and richly sculptured baldacchini.

During the Pontificate of HORMISDAS, Theodoric offered two silver candlesticks weighing seventy pounds to S. Peter's; FELIX III built the church of SS. Cosmo and Damian on the Via Sacra, close by the temple of Venus and Roma, utilising the apse of the temple of Romulus and Remus as a vestibule. This small church has been successively restored by S. GREGORY, ADRIAN I, and URBAN VIII. A curious mosaic, by the first Christian artists, and an antique bronze door are to be seen in it. The plan of Rome,

---

(1)   La faccia sua mi parea lunga e grossa
             Come la pina di San-Pietro a Roma.
                     (Inferno Can. XXXI, v. 58.)

now in the Capitol, was found at SS. Cosmo and Damian.

"Everything at Rome bears the stamp of dominion and continuity; I have seen the map of the Eternal City which is engraved on the marble rock at the Capitol, in order that its picture might never be effaced." (1)

PELAGIUS I began building a church, under the invocation of SS. James and Philip, which was completed by his successor JOHN III; it was richly adorned with paintings and mosaics. PELAGIUS II completely restored the church of S. Lorenzo-fuori-le-mura, which was falling into ruins. The triumphal arch of the Basilica was decorated on its eastern façade with a mosaic of which only traces remain. It represented our Saviour seated on a globe, in the act of blessing; to His right were S. Peter, S. Laurence, and Pelagius, to His left S. Paul, S. Stephen and S. Hippolytus. Bethlehem was above on one side, while doubtless Jerusalem was on the other as at S. Maria Maggiore.

Near S. Lorenzo there existed a hospital for poor people and pilgrims, founded by S. SYMMACHUS. Similar charitable institutions were attached to the greater number of Basilicas.

Under the Pontificate of PELAGIUS II, in 580, Monte Cassino was ruined by the Lombards. The monks came in their distress to seek refuge at Rome, bringing with them only a few books, with the copy of their rule written by S. Benedict himself, the bread-weight

---

(1) Chateaubriand, "Martyres."

and the measure for wine. PELAGIUS gave them leave to build a monastery near S. John Lateran, so the Benedictine order was established there during its exile, which lasted one hundred and fifty years.

May be S. GREGORY did not build new Churches; but he restored and carefully maintained those which existed in his time; particularly S. Cæcilia-trans-Tiberim, and S. Agatha-in-Suburra which he reconsecrated and enriched with paintings and mosaics. According to Anastasius he presented a silver baldacchino supported by columns to S. Peter's Basilica: this reminds us that the Silver Gate (Porta Argentea), by which name the principal entrance to that Basilica is known in history, is partly due to him, because he was the first person to ornament it with plates or bas-reliefs of silver. S. GREGORY relates that, in his time, in the vestibule of S. Clemente, a poor paralytic was often seen praying and asking for alms, but never complaining, in spite of acute sufferings. Everyone gave him alms; these the paralytic at once distributed among the poor. After his death his remains were laid near those of Pope S. CLEMENT and S. Ignatius, Bishop of Antioch; his name was also inscribed in the martyrology. He is venerated by the church under the name of S. Servulus. (1)

About the same time three virtuous women, Romula, Redempta, and Herondina, lived very secluded near S. Maria Maggiore. Herondina had passed part of her life in solitude on the hills of Præneste. These women occupied their time in prayers and good works;

---

(1) His feast falls on the 23rd of December.

Romula was paralysed for many years, her resignation to God's will being most edifying. These poor maidens, unknown to the world, are now reckoned among the Saints. (1)

Among the monuments of the sixth century, we must not, in conclusion, omit to mention S. Cæsario-in-Palatio, alluded to by S. GREGORY. This church, being situated in the neighbourhood of the baths or palace of Caracalla, bears the designation "in Palatio"; it possesses some columns, precious spoils from some pagan monument. Near S. Cæsario the celebrated temple of Mars-extra-muros had formerly stood, which could boast of a hundred columns, and of the dripping stone (lapis manalis) placed outside the walls, but which was solemnly brought into the city when rain was wanted. S. Adriano-in-campo-Vaccino was considered from the year 600 to be one of the most ancient deaconries of Rome. The great brick wall which forms its façade is ancient; it was formerly covered with stucco, and probably belonged to the Emiliana Basilica. The beautiful bronze door now admired at S. John Lateran once adorned S. Adriano.

S. Georgio-in-Velabro, near the arch of Janus, was one of the churches in which the stations were held in the time of Gregory the Great.

Among the other Station-churches may be noticed S. Nicholas-in-Carcere; the station was held there on the fifth Saturday of Lent. This church owed its name either to an old prison for debtors, on the site of which it is said to stand, or to the neighbourhood

---

(1) Their feast falls on the 23rd of July.

of the famous prison of the Decemvirs, which was changed by the Republic into a temple of Pity. Pliny's story is well known: "A poor young woman of low degree, and consequently ignoble (et ideo ignobilis), had obtained permission to visit her mother who had been condemned to die of hunger in this gaol. The warder kept strict watch that she brought no food to the prisoner. But one day he surprised her giving the breast to her mother and this marvel of filial piety obtained her mother's pardon. A competence was moreover granted them for life; and a temple consecrated to Pity was raised on the very site of the prison, where now the theatre of Marcellus stands."

Does not the name of S. Nicholas, the patron "and liberator of prisoners", as S. John Damascene calls him, lend itself well to this memory? Similar affinities are to be met with at every turn in Rome. Thus, for example, at the foot of the Palatine, facing the fictitious lake which swallowed up Curtius to save Rome, the devotion of the early ages has raised a small church to the Saviour of the world under the name of S. Salvatore-in-lacu. Afterwards this church was called S. Maria liberatrice dall'Inferno. (1)

Churches were distinguished at Rome by the different appellations of Patriarchates, Basilicas, Titles, Deaconries and Oratories. Patriarchal churches depended more especially on the Pope; they were like cathedrals all over the world, and from them Popes always dated their Bulls and Decretals. S. John Lateran, generally known in history as the Basilica

(1) The following is the invocation of this church:— "Sancta Maria libera nos a pœnis inferni et libera nos a peste."

of the Saviour, was the first of the patriarchal churches; then followed S. Pietro del Vaticano, S. Maria Maggiore, S. Paolo on the Ostian Way, and S. Lorenzo-fuori-le-mura. They represented the union of the four patriarchates of Constantinople, Alexandria, Antioch, and Jerusalem, under the supremacy of the great and universal patriarchate of Rome.

There are now thirteen Basilicas, the number of the Apostles after the accession of S. Matthias and S. Paul. First among them come the seven great Roman Basilicas, the obligatory goal of all pilgrims. These churches are the five patriarchal churches and with them S. Croce-in-Gerusalemme and S. Sebastiano-alle-Catacombe.

The titular churches, or cardinalates, were the parish churches of the city; they numbered already thirty in the time of Pope SYMMACHUS.

The deaconries were intended for hospitals or dispensaries, and, governed by a deacon, were always attached to a church. Originally there were seven local deacons; S. GREGORY the Great increased the number to fourteen, and, later, GREGORY III to eighteen. The most ancient deaconries in Rome were: S. Maria-in-Dominica, S. Maria-in-Cosmedin, SS. Cosimo-e-Damiano, S. Pietro-in-Montorio, S. Maria-in-Aquiro, S. Agatha-in-Suburra, and S. Adriano. S. Maria-in-Dominica was, and still is, the first of the deaconries, in memory of the great archdeacon S. Laurence, who distributed alms to the poor in the house of S. Cyriaca.

Oratories were not permitted to have either public services or officiating priests. There was an oratory in each cemetery, and often in private dwellings. Mass might be celebrated in them only by a Bishop's special permission.

As regards the order for solemnities in the Roman Church, it was first settled by S. GELASIUS, and finally by S. GREGORY. The Christians had preserved the heathen names for the days of the week, excepting for Sunday, and perhaps for Saturday. They had also kept to the division of days for holidays and festivals, but with a different meaning to that formerly attached to the expressions. "All our days, even the most ordinary, are consecrated," says Tertullian; (nobis omnis dies etiam vulgata consecratione celebratur). (1) The consecration of Sunday was distinguished from all other days by compulsory attendance at Mass, and by abstaining from all work, fasting, and genuflection. Tertullian says, "We consider it unbecoming to fast and to pray to God kneeling on Sundays;" (2) and S. Peter of Alexandria supplies the reason, "For it is with us a day of rejoicing." (3) Fasting and genuflections were also omitted during Paschal time, as we learn from the Council of Nicæa. (4) Every Sunday, at Rome, the Pope sent some leaven by his acolytes to all the cardinal-priests in the city, that, being a portion of the Eucharist, they might add it, as a sign of union, to the sacrifice they were about to offer. On Wednesday and Friday the faithful fasted until the hour for Nones; for it was on a Wednesday that the Jews "consulted together,

(1) De Jejun., 14.
(2) De Corona.
(3) Ep. canon.
(4) Can. 20.

that by subtility they might apprehend Jesus, and put him to death;" (1) and it was on a Friday that the Son of Man bore the cross for the salvation of mankind. There were, in fact, but few days not marked by some station in one of the churches. (2) The origin of the stations goes back to the earliest period of the Christian era. The name was taken from a military term; it was like a halt under arms in the cemeteries on the festivals of martyrs; later on, this took place in certain churches which consequently were known as stational churches. There were also stational crosses, those of S. John, S. Peter, and S. Maria Maggiore, which alone might precede the faithful bound to a station. The meeting place was some church previously selected by the archdeacon; they then began by singing Psalms, this was called the collect or gathering; after which they marched onwards singing "Kyrie eleison". The celebrant, who was often the Pope, advanced barefoot. Having reached the stational church, he delivered a homily, offered up the Holy Sacrifice of the Mass, and administered Holy Communion to the people. S. GREGORY the Great seldom missed going to the stations; thus establishing their definite organisation. Ash Wednesday station took place at S. Sabina; those of Passion Sunday at S. Peter's; Palm Sunday at S. John Lateran;

---

(1) S. Matth. XXVI, v. 4.
(2) The stations dropped out of use during the residence of the Popes at Avignon, and were never revived. Nevertheless the ancient stational churches are to this day objects of pious pilgrimages on the anniversary of the station.

Holy Tuesday at S. Paolo-fuori-le-mura; Good Friday at S. Croce-in-Gerusalemme; and the station for the Shepherd's Mass on Christmas Day at S. Anastasia.

The ceremonies of the Mass were almost identical with those of the present day. After the Gloria in excelsis, only sung at episcopal Masses, and not permitted otherwise except at Easter when any priest might sing it, the officiating priests went round to collect the offerings of the congregation, first from men, who sat on the north side of the church, then from women who occupied the south side. (1) These offerings were bread in the shape of crowns for use at the communion.

S. Gregory compiled a Sacramentary and Antiphonary in order that these offices might be perfectly arranged; and, being anxious to increase the grandeur of worship, he instituted a school for singers, giving them two houses, one near S. Peter's, the other near S. John Lateran. He presided at these lessons, holding a baton, which was long preserved at S. John Lateran as well as the famous Antiphonary in his own hand-writing. The Gregorian chant after the lapse of twelve hundred years is still greatly admired in our churches.

When a new Pontiff took possession of S. Peter's chair he sent deacons to convey letters of communion to all the Bishops; who on their side kept up this union by their synodical acts, by having recourse to

---

(1) The only church that, to my knowledge, retains this custom is S. Ambrogio at Milan, where the men and women are separated by curtains.

Rome in all the difficulties of their administration, and by frequent pilgrimages which they made from all parts of Christendom. In the fifth century, to speak only of Gaul, we see S. Vitricius of Rouen, S. Germanus of Auxerre, S. Hilarius of Arles, and S. Prosper coming to kiss the steps of the Basilicas of the Apostles (apostolorum et martyrum ut exoscularentur limina). In the sixth century, S. Cæsarius of Arles received the pallium at the hands of Pope SYMMACHUS, and S. Gregory of Tours was honoured with a golden chain from GREGORY the Great, on the occasion of his bringing the homage of his church to the Confession of S. Peter. Then envoys from all parts of the world conferred with the Supreme Head upon the requirements of Spain, Gaul, Greece or Palestine. Unity was thus maintained unbroken, and established itself more and more both in liturgy and discipline. Everywhere provincial councils, the only legislative assemblies of the period, proclaimed the same civil laws, the same principles of order; this happened at Alexandria and Carthage, at Orleans and at Toledo; and, as the civilising movement came from heaven, it worked efficaciously throughout the known world.

CHAPTER VII.

Ingens ara fuit.

Virgil.

Le seul talent digne de Rome est de conquérir le monde, et d'y faire régner la vertu.

J.-J. Rousseau.

SEVENTH CENTURY.

FOR about three hundred years paganism had ceased to preside over the destinies of the Empire; its temples had been closed at the end of the fourth century, and were it not for the protection of Honorius, who was an admirer of the beauty and splendour of pagan art, they would all have fallen beneath the religious movement which accompanied and followed the reign of Theodosius. So these ancient buildings still stood, but were empty, forsaken, and as melancholy looking as ruins. They might be compared to vast quarries of bronze and marble, whence the Barbarians drew brazen tiles, and the Christians columns of breccia and brocatelle for their Basilicas; for the Augurs were silent, and the Books of the Sibyl lay sleeping in the Capitol.

Many of these sanctuaries of mythology were renowned, one was especially so: it had been built by Agrippa in honour of Augustus, and consecrated to Jupiter the Avenger, to Venus, and Mars. The attributes of these three divinities, who united among them authority, beauty and force, or, perhaps, as Pliny states, the convex form of the roof of this temple, made to represent the sky, had in antiquity gained for it the name of Pantheon. (1)

The Pantheon, built at a period when the fine arts had attained their zenith, was remarkable for the purity and majesty of its architecture, while the temple of Jupiter Capitolinus chiefly owed its fame to its columns brought from Olympia, and to its statue of the god, fashioned from the brass of the Samnites' helmets. It frequently happened, indeed, that the buildings of the Republic contained nothing of merit but the decorations of their interiors. It was the statue of the sitting Mars and the Venus of Scopas which people went to see in the temple of Brutus Callaicus, and the Niobe group which was to be admired in the temple of the Apollo Sosianus.

But, under the Emperors, the genius of art asserted itself, even amidst the preoccupations of war, and the Pantheon appears to be an inspiration of the glorious days of Greece. Augustus's wealthy favourite spared nothing to unite dazzling decoration with beauty of form in this structure. Granite columns all of one piece, fifty-six palms high, were transported from the Thebaid to support the pediment. At the back of the peristyle there were wondrous statues of Agrippa and Augustus, with graceful bas-reliefs representing

---

(1) "Quod formâ convexâ fastigiatum cœli similitudinem acceperat."

the sacrificial vessels. The interior of the temple, which was round, received light from a circular opening in the centre of the cupola; an arrangement which prevented light from entering the god's temple, except from the top. The pavement was of granite and porphyry; a coating of marble concealed the walls, while panels of silver and gilt bronze enriched the ceiling.

The Pantheon was restored several times by pagan Emperors, for it was destroyed by conflagrations more than once, and age had injured the building according to an inscription graven on its architrave by Septimus Severus, "Pantheum vetustate corruptum." The Temple had existed for two hundred and twenty four years when the inscription was placed there, it has now stood for eighteen hundred years without showing signs of decay.

At the beginning of the seventh century Pope BONIFACE IV requested the Emperor Phocas to allow the Pantheon to be consecrated to the worship of the true God; this permission having been granted, the bronze portal of the temple of Jupiter the Avenger swung open to receive the bones of martyrs collected from every cemetery of the town. These bones filled thirty-two chariots, which brought them in state to their new resting place on the 13th May 610. "I behold", wrote de Maistre, "Christ entering the Pantheon, followed by His Evangelists, Apostles, Doctors, Martyrs, and Confessors, as a conquering King enters the capital of his vanquished enemy, accompanied by all the great men of his empire. At His sight all these god-men vanish before the Man-God. He sanctifies the Pantheon by His presence.

and fills it with His Majesty. The deed is done: all the virtues have taken the place of all the vices. Error and falsehood have fled before indivisible truth. God reigns in His sanctuary, as He reigns in heaven, amid all His saints." (1)

The pediment of the Pantheon formerly represented Jupiter hurling the Titans to the ground. Never probably was this allegory more striking than on that memorable day when the temple of demons was placed under the invocation of martyrs and of the Virgin. That day the Pantheon became S. Maria-ad-Martyres.

About the same time another ancient monument, situated at the foot of the Palatine, and which several scientists hold to have been the temple of Vesta, in which the Palladium was preserved, was similarly transformed into a church, and dedicated to S. Theodorus of Amasia, a martyr of Pontus. (2) The Lupercal cave dedicated to Pan by Evander was near it. The Lupercalia were abolished, and the crowds instead of going to Pan's cavern visited the church of S. Theodorus. Children suffering from scrofula were brought there, so this impure pagan festival was transformed into a pious pilgrimage. The church of S. Theodorus has undergone several restorations, first in 774 under

---

(1) "Du Pape."

(2) According to M. Ampère, the temple of Vesta stood on the site of the actual church of S. Maria Liberatrice. S. Teodoro, according to the learned Academician, had in fact never been anything but a church, only it was constructed over the ruins of an ancient temple. (See "l'Histoire Romaine à Rome", t. I, p. 147 and 360.)

Adrian I; and again in 1674 under Clement X; but the ancient form and arrangement have been faithfully preserved.

Meanwhile Rome remained subject to the Eastern Emperors; and, at the beginning of this century, a monument in honour of the Emperor Phocas was erected in the Forum; a distinction very rare since the time of Constantine. It was not the Senate or people who had decreed that Phocas should see his golden statue placed on a high marble column in that celebrated spot. The Senate and people had long been dumb, and their silence was better than the base flatteries with which they formerly associated themselves to the crimes of Nero and Heliogabalus. The column and statue of Phocas were marks of homage from the Frank Smaragdus "to the clement Emperor", for "the innumerable benefits" he had granted Italy, "for the peace he had procured her, and her liberty, which he had preserved." Within two years, after his sublime virtues had been thus recorded on stone, the clement Emperor was dragged from his palace, deprived of the purple and crown, tortured and beheaded.

> "Et de tant de soldats qui lui servaient d'appui,
> Phocas, après sa mort, n'en eut un pour lui." (1)

The reign of Phocas was only noted for its assassinations and despicable iniquities. That of Heraclius, his successor, at first appeared to promise a new era of good fortune to the Empire; but the tide soon turned, and it was indeed under this Prince that the imperial crown was deprived of its brightest gems.

---

(1) "Heraclius," Act V, sc. VI.

Then, in an obscure town of Arabia, that camel-driver appeared who was to found a religion and a nation whom the tribes of the desert hailed as "the glorified one, el Mahammed."

The Roman Empire had already experienced the ravages of the Barbarians from the North, those from the South were reserving the final blow. These Arabs were the descendants of Ishmael and were to accomplish the prophecy of the angel. "He shall be a wild man: his hand will be against all men, and all men's hands against him, and he shall pitch his tents over against all his brethren." (1)

The Arabs, scattered over the wastes of Asia, without other tie than those of tribe and family, no laws but tradition, and no fatherland, for they had neither fixed home nor records, with imaginations quick to grasp every fleeting idea, only needed a commander and discipline to become a conquering and mighty nation. Mahomet was the lawgiver to this wild race: he spoke to them as a prophet, in order that he might more easily obtain dominion over their mystery-loving minds; his illnesses, the events of his wandering life, everything was turned to account by this impostor, in order to give a supernatural aspect to his mission. Precepts fell from his lips interlarded with vulgar stories which please the mob, and coloured with imaginative pictures which appeared to these Eastern minds like reflections from heaven. (2)

---

(1) Genesis, XVI, 12.
(2) The idea of the Koran being a religious work makes one repeat with Voltaire:— "c'est un livre inintelligible, qui fait frémir le sens commun à chaque page."

A life at once hard and easy, sober as becomes warriors, voluptuous as warriors love life to be, such, was the double principle of his religion: by means of it he at the same time secured their support and preserved some of their primitive simplicity to these uncivilized men, thus preventing them from changing their habits and manners when they came in contact with other nations. Among them he introduced numerous practices and frequently repeated prayers, thereby binding together this race which only needed union in order to become great. However degrading to humanity may be a doctrine which reconstituted slavery and offered sensual pleasures as the chief aim of life, it became none the less a terrible and all-powerful weapon in the hands of soldiers inured to fatigue.

In 635 Damascus fell before Omar; in 636, after a siege of two years, Jerusalem was taken; Antioch fell the same year, and, in 640, the Empire lost Alexandria, the spoil of Actium.

The Emperor was at this moment drawing up an "Ecthesis" in favour of the Monothelites; while all the subtle intellects of Greece were employed in wrangling! No one can tell the suffering endured at these tidings by the successors of S. Peter in the Lateran! The Empire of Christ diminishing; the churches of Basil, Cyril, and Athanasius, whose light had shone so brilliantly at the dawn of Christianity, were about to be profaned by sacrilegious hands! This torrent of invasion had to be kept in check. All material force was at Constantinople; the only influence at the Lateran was that of virtue and prayer. But prayer is efficacious with God: the Eastern provinces lost to the Church were replaced by new ones in the West, won over by the labours of zealous missionaries. S. Birinus bore the faith to the Western Saxons; others evangelized the Frisians, others the tribes between the Rhine and the Elbe. At the same time the Lombards, abjuring Arianism, were received into the Church.

Several princes of these newly converted nations came during the seventh century to confess their faith at S. Peter's tomb. Among them history cites Alfred, the son of Oswi, King of Northumbria, and Cædwalla, King of the West Saxons. Bæda has recorded the touching history of Cædwalla. He says:—
'After reigning two years right manfully, 'strenuissime', Cædwalla gave up his kingdom for the sake of God and an eternal kingdom; then he set out for Rome, being desirous of the most rare glory of receiving the baptismal water at the tombs of the Apostles, and in the hope that once cleansed he should be freed from his fleshly trammels, and might pass in all his new purity to the joys of eternity. Now, what he desired, by the aid of God, came to pass. For, having reached Rome during the pontificate of SERGIUS, and received baptism on Saturday, the vigil of Easter, in the year of the Incarnation 690, he was suddenly seized with faintness, while still bearing the white robe of baptism, and was delivered from the bonds of his flesh to be admitted into the fellowship of the blessed in heaven." He was buried in the Vatican; and his tombstone may still be seen there, bearing a long and beautiful epitaph inscribed upon it by order of SERGIUS.

Alfred came to Rome with the indefatigable Benedict Biscop. Benedict, or Bennet, was one of England's most energetic apostles at this time; difficulties and distances vanished before his zeal; he came five times from England to Rome, and took back with him to England, in addition to the Liturgy and Roman discipline, a considerable library with which he enriched his monastery at Wearmouth. Other apostles, S. Amandus of Maestricht, S. Humbert of Marolles, also made the pilgrimage to Rome; S. Wilfred, Bishop of York, actually made the journey three times, and carried back to his diocese relics of saints, rich purple-stuffs and silks for the adornment of his churches.

Rome was becoming daily more and more the centre of the world. If the temporal power no longer resided on the Palatine, at the Lateran was another power towards which all eyes were directed. Moreover, Rome had preserved sufficient of her ancient splendour to be able, even as regards the arts and sciences, to march at the head of civilisation, a privilege she has never yielded. The Popes rapidly followed one another during the seventh century. SABINIAN, BONIFACE III, BONIFACE IV, and DEODATUS reigned only a short time. SABINIAN introduced the use of clocks in churches; an idea happily described by Chateaubriand:— "Une idée qui trouvait le moyen, par un seul coup de marteau, de faire naître, à la même minute, un même sentiment dans mille cœurs divers, et forçait les vents et les nuages à se charger des pensées des hommes." (1)

(1) "Génie du Christianisme."

Honorius transformed his paternal house near the Lateran into a monastery, of which the cloister, reconstructed in the thirteenth century, is now one of the most curious appendages of the Basilica. The same Pontiff covered the central nave of S. Peter's with gilt bronze tiles taken from the temple of Romulus, or, possibly, from that of Jupiter at the Capitol.

Boniface V and Honorius had to contend against the many difficulties raised by the Monothelite heresy, to which adhered the patriarchs of Constantinople and the Emperors. The interference of these Emperors in Papal elections then became a constant source of trouble and discord. The vacancy of the Holy See was indefinitely prolonged, and the Emperors exacted tribute from each new Pontiff, for the cupidity of the Cæsars increased as the Empire decreased under their sway. On the death of Honorius, advantage was taken even to pillage the Lateran Palace. The patriarch Isaac, Archbishop of Ravenna, and Maurice, one of the Emperor's officers, led the troops on this disgraceful expedition. They seized upon money intended for the poor and for ransoming captives, and forwarded a portion of it to Constantinople.

Severinus was proclaimed Pope and died the same year. John IV, his successor, condemned the Ecthesis of Honorius in favour of the Monothelites. In the chapel of S. Maria-ad-fontes, or of S. Venantius at the Lateran, may be seen a mosaic representing, in its upper portion, Our Saviour between two angels, below this, the Virgin between S. Peter, S. Paul, and the two saints John; then Popes John IV and Theo-

DORUS, the saints, whose relics rest beneath the altar, holding triumphal crowns; and, lastly, the two mystic cities, so frequently represented, Bethlehem and Jerusalem. In this picture the Virgin has her arms stretched out, and her heart is pierced by a cross. This curious mosaic was begun by JOHN IV and finished by THEODORUS I.

In addition, THEODORUS reconstructed the church of S. Valentine, founded by JULIUS I on the spot where this holy priest, who suffered martyrdom under Aurelian, was buried.

MARTIN I held a Council at Rome on the ever burning question of Monothelism. Since the days of S. GREGORY Councils had frequently been held at Rome. Through these assemblies faith revived, and more complete unity was established throughout the provinces of the Christian empire. The acts of this Council condemning Monothelism were sent by Martin to every Bishop; he said to them, "Neither imitate nor fear men whose lives pass and fade like grass; none of them has been crucified for us." The Emperor Constans II fell into a violent rage when he was informed of the anathemas pronounced by the Pope. He had already given instructions to Olympius, Exarch of Ravenna, to seize upon Martin. Olympius had come to Rome during the Council; one day, when he was to receive Holy Communion from the Pope at S. Maria Maggiore, a member of his suite was ordered to assassinate the Pontiff; but, when the moment arrived for striking the blow, the assassin was struck blind; Olympius, terrified at this act of God, left Rome, after avowing the wicked orders he had received.

Then Constans sent Calliopas, another Exarch, to Rome, bearing an accusation of high treason against Martin. He was charged with Olympius of plotting the ruin of the Empire and the death of the Emperor. But, when Calliopas beheld the devotion of the people to their bishop, he concealed his real motive, pretending that his only object was to adore the successor of the Apostles. Every day he threw himself at the Pope's feet; but the crowds around the Lateran frightened him. Moreover, having complained to the Pope that stones were probably piled up within, and armed men hidden in the palace, the Pontiff immediately gave orders to open the doors, and led the Exarch's messengers through that home of peace and prayer. This frankness removed the Exarch's fears; he summoned his troops, surrounded the Lateran, and seized Martin, who being ill had been carried into the church. The scandal did not end here; soldiers rushed, with bent bows, into the holy place, overturning candles, and strewing the pavement with wreckage; while the Exarch summoned the clergy to depose the Pope. Only one cry was heard in reply from the assembled clergy, and that was of anathema against Calliopas. Meanwhile Martin was dragged out of the Lateran, and embarked the following night on the Tiber: he was first taken to Calabria, and subsequently to the island of Naxos where he spent a year deprived of all he possessed. Finally, in a dying state, he was taken to Constantinople where a terrible fate awaited him. The noble old man was deprived of the pallium, the straps of his shoes were broken; he was arrayed in a ragged old tunic for his only covering, and, with a halter round his neck, was dragged through the streets. This happened on the 15th December 654. It was not the will of God that he should sink beneath this trial; he was imprisoned with murderers; then exiled to the Chersonese, where his sufferings were shortly ended with his life. The relics of this courageous Pontiff were afterwards brought to Rome, where they now repose under the high altar of the church of S. Martino-del-Monte.

The heretical Constans no doubt rejoiced in his victory; and it was probably to celebrate it that he came to Rome during the pontificate of VITALIANUS. The presence of this man, who never spoke but as a divinity (nostræ divinitatis sanctione), was a curse to the imperial capital; he carried away the bronze decorations on monuments, and stripped the Pantheon of its rich roof. Laden with spoil, like Genseric, Constans, after twelve days pillaging, directed his course towards Sicily. He got no further, for death overtook him there, and the Saracens, whose galleys then swarmed in the Mediterranean, alone profited by the plunder.

Pope EUGENIUS I and Pope VITALIANUS are only famous in history for their goodness and generosity. Some authors date back the introduction of organs into churches to VITALIANUS's pontificate. DEODATUS II and DONUS only reigned a few days. The last named paved the forecourt of S. Peter's with large marble squares; this forecourt, it will be remembered, was then called "Paradise."

Pope AGATHO devoted 2,140 gold pennies to lighting the churches of the Apostles and S. Maria Maggiore. During his pontificate the sixth General Council was held at Constantinople.

The Emperor Constantine IV sent the first locks of hair taken from his two sons Justinian and Heraclius to Pope BENEDICT II, as a mark of their being adopted by the Pope, who thus became a second father to the young princes.

On the death of JOHN V serious divisions took place respecting the choice of a successor. The army, desiring to proclaim the priest Theodorus, closed up the Lateran Basilica to prevent the clergy from entering it; they then proceeded to the church of S. Stefano, where they waited for the people to join them, in order to go on to the election. The clergy, however, penetrated into the pontifical palace, and quickly elected a wise and pious old man, named CONON, as their Bishop. The magistrates and people eagerly acknowledged him, and the army submitted in a few days. But these divisions were only quelled for a time, and broke out with renewed violence on the death of CONON. Before this an archdeacon, called Paschal, had promised to deliver the treasures of the dying Pope to the Exarch of Ravenna, on condition that the Exarch secured his election to the Papal See. This shameful bargain was *struck*, and emissaries hastened from Ravenna to ensure *its* execution. But the partisans of Theodore were not asleep; they determined to make up for their first defeat by a striking victory. So, as soon as the Pope was dead, they seized upon the Lateran Palace. The supporters of Paschal, on the other hand, established themselves both in the Oratory of S. Sylvester and the Basilica of Julius, dependencies of the palace; and a fierce struggle began between the rivals. But the magistrates and greater part of the clergy and people, averse to these violent intrigues, went off to the Baths of Caracalla, and there, amidst the crowd, they elected Sergius, priest of S. Suzanna, and conducted him to the neighbouring church of S. Cæsario-in-Palatio, where they greeted him with acclamations. Sergius at once proceeded to the Lateran Basilica, surrounded by crowds singing his praises. The gates of the Basilica were closed, but the populace broke them open; the two competitors, Theodorus and Paschal, came, of their free will or by force, to kneel at the Pontiff's feet.

History mentions with respect to this election a point which should not be overlooked; the Exarch of Ravenna, John Platys, exacted from Sergius, as being the price of the Emperor's confirmation, the 100 lbs. of gold which the simoniacal Paschal had promised. This is to what the high patronage of the successors of Constantine had sunk! It would not have signified had they confined their demands to gold alone; but they also coveted the repository of faith; and wished to destroy that spiritual power which in the hands of the sovereign pontiffs was a bar to their despotic tyranny.

Sergius had to suffer as Martin and Sylverius had suffered before him. He refused to approve the Council of Constantinople "in Trullo," in spite of the Emperor's threats. Thereupon the Emperor sent Zachary, one of his chamberlains, with orders to arrest the Pontiff; but, at the first rumour of this mission, the people and militia of the Roman territory and of Pentapolis rose in a body and hurried to Rome. Their tumultuous shouts so alarmed Zachary that he fled for protection to the Pontiff's arms, even hiding beneath his bed. Still shouting continued, the anxious crowd clamouring to see their shepherd. SERGIUS ascended his throne, ordered the doors to be thrown open, and then addressing the people succeeded in calming their excitement. Zachary had to quit Rome, or rather was ignominiously driven from it.

From the pontificate of SERGIUS date the processions, or litanies, which were held every year in Rome on the feasts of the Nativity, Purification, Annunciation, and Assumption of the Virgin. The faithful assembled at S. Adriano and proceeded to S. Maria-del-Presepio. (1)

It was also Sergius, according to Anastasius the Librarian, who gave orders that the words used by S. John the Baptist at the sight of Christ, "Ecce Agnus Dei", should be sung during Mass. He also built the church of S. Maria-in-via-Lata on the spot, indicated by tradition, where S. PAUL dwelt on his arrival in Rome. Paul the Deacon mentions, among the many rich gifts he distributed to other churches, a large gold censer, with columns and a lid, in which perfumes were burnt during Mass.

(1) This was the name by which S. Maria Maggiore was then most generally known. The Assumption of the Virgin was called the "slumber" or the "repose"; the Purification, the Festival of S. Simeon.

Thus ended the century which had begun under GREGORY the Great. Several of his works have been mentioned; but others must not be forgotten. During the great Litany, by which Gregory sought to appease the anger heaven was visiting on Rome, by the decimation of her people, the pious Pontiff suddenly saw an angel sheathing his sword above Hadrian's Mole. From that moment the virulence of the plague declined. It was no doubt to perpetuate the memory of this supernatural apparition that BONIFACE IV erected a chapel dedicated to S. Michael, under the title of S. Angelo-inter-nubes over the Roman Emperor's mausoleum. Henceforth the mausoleum lost its ancient name. Turned into a fortress since the Barbarian wars, and placed under the invocation of the heavenly powers, it was no longer called Hadrian's Mole, but the Castle of S. Angelo.

To Pope HONORIUS is due the church of S. Lucia, which afterwards became S. Maddalena-al-Corso, and that of SS. Vincenzo-ed-Anastasio ad aquas Salvias, in which, besides the relics of S. Anastasius, are those of ten thousand martyrs.

The church of SS. Vitus and Modestus, near the Gallienus Arch, certainly existed as a deaconry from the seventh century; this title has since become famous as having been borne by S. Carlo Borromeo. S. Vitus was a child who had been brought up as a Christian by his nurse, Crescentia, and her husband, Modestus. Being threatened by his father with cruel punishments he remained steadfast in the faith. The father delivered him to the judge, who ordered him to be flogged and returned to his father, for lashes had proved as useless as threats. Vitus then fled with Crescentia and Modestus; but, during the persecution of Diocletian, they were taken and flung into a caldron of boiling pitch. But their voices were heard singing the song of the young Hebrews in the furnace:— "Blessed art thou, O Lord the God of our fathers; and worthy to be praised and glorified, and exalted above all for ever." (1) Vitus, Modestus and Crescentia ended their lives on the rack.

It is pleasant to dwell on these touching pictures of Christian virtue while reviewing these sad ages, upon which God's hand lay heavily. The sixth century might still boast a Boethius, an Aratore, a S. Benedict, a S. Gregory the Great. Under the Gothic kings there were still public schools of grammar, rhetoric, and law in Rome. Statues were raised to Theodoric in most of the towns of the peninsula; and the buildings, erected by his orders, reproduced, without great differences, the harmonious forms of ancient architecture. But when the Lombards, accompanied by their wives and children, adoring a goat's head, measuring God's judgment by the might of their arms, dragging their captives along "by the neck as though they were dogs," as S. Gregory remarks, swept down from Pannonia, black night settled over the land. Towns, libraries and monasteries, in which stores of learning were kept, were burnt; the most thickly peopled countries became deserts, (in eremis); arts, sciences, letters were lost at one

---

(1) *Song of the three children*; Daniel III, v. 52. Omitted in Protestant versions of the Holy Scriptures.

stroke. Then it was that man's thought was left alone with itself and God; poetry sought refuge in legends, the simple expressions of a sublime faith; legends which shall always be read and venerated, for "one hears the utterances of holy minds with greater respect than even the voice of genius." (1)

(1) "On prête l'oreille aux sons que rendent les âmes saintes avec plus de respect qu'à la voix du génie." Mgr. Gerbet

CHAPTER VIII.

> Le règne de Charlemagne eut une lueur de politesse qui fut probablement le fruit du voyage de Rome.
> *Voltaire.*

EIGHTH CENTURY.

SINCE the invasion of the Lombards Italy was split up into a number of small principalities, whose only tie with the central government at Pavia was that of vassalage. There were Dukes of Friuli, Benevento, Spoleto, and, at a later period, Dukes of Turin, Brescia, Tuscany, and Naples. The Exarch of Ravenna now only governed Pentapolis; and Rome, encircled by ambitious princes, and reduced to the old boundaries of early Republican days, also formed a Duchy, nominally under the rule of a magistrate sent from Constantinople, but in reality under the authority of the Popes.

Justinian II, descendant of Heraclius, occupied the throne during the second half of the seventh century; but, having treated himself to the sight of Constantinople in flames, he was deposed in 689, by the patrician Leontius, who cut off his nose, and banished him to the Chersonese. Leontius had only reigned a few days when the African legions proclaimed Emperor their own general Apsimar, under the name of Tiberius, and, after undergoing terrible mutilations, Leontius was imprisoned in a monastery. Still Justinian II in his exile dreamt of the throne and meditated fresh crimes. He allied himself with the King of the Bulgarians, came to besiege Constantinople in 705, entered the city by an aqueduct, and regained the power which he had lost for a time. Then ensued a horrible scene. Tiberius and Leontius were dragged to the hippodrome, flung into the arena like animals about to be butchered, and the ruffianly Emperor placed his foot on their throats, while the insensate mob cried out, "You walk on the asp and the basilisk, and tread down the lion and the dragon." The two victims were then beheaded. By the Emperor's orders the eyes of the patriarch Callinicus were gouged out, and blood continued to flow until 711, when Bardanes-Philippicus took Constantinople and cruelly avenged Justinian's victims. Justinian's head was paraded through the cities of the empire, even reaching Rome. Philippicus was a Monothelite, and determined to summon a conventicle with the object of revoking the decisions of the sixth General Council, whereby the heresy of Macarius of Antioch had been condemned.

The Romans were so indignant at this news that they would neither permit the Emperor's picture being carried into the church, nor his name being mentioned in the prayers; they assembled on the Via Sacra, in front of the palace, and assaulted the soldiers of Duke Peter, whom Philippicus had sent to govern Rome. Twenty-five men of the rival parties were slain; the populace gained the day, and Peter

was in great danger of losing his life when Bishops
and priests, sent by the Pope, hurriedly appeared on
the scene, bearing the cross and gospels, and succeeded in their mission of peace by appeasing the
tumult. (1)

Philippicus did not reign long: one night, while
he slept, his eyes were put out, and the crown was
placed on the head of his secretary Artemius, who
took the name of Anastasius. Two years later
Anastasius was shut up in a monastery by Theodosius III, whom the Phœnician army proclaimed
Emperor in his stead. In his turn Theodosius experienced the same fate when Leo, the son of an
Isaurian bootmaker, ascended the throne of the Cæsars
on the 25$\underline{\text{th}}$ March 717. To live and to slaughter
was the sole object of these Emperors of a day.
What mattered Rome to men who did not feel they
were secure even in Constantinople; who saw the
Saracen fleet insolently cast anchor at the entrance
of the Bosphorus; and whose beds and tables might
next day belong to assassins like themselves!

Similar lawlessness was rife among the Lombards;
but with them it was rather the restless energy of
a new people than the result of effeminate decay.
The Dukes quarrelled among themselves for towns
and fortresses, but, none the less, the central power
remained stable, being generally held by firm and
able hands.

---

(1) A few years previous to this Pope JOHN VI had saved
the Exarch Theophylactus who was about to be assassinated
at Rome by the soldiers.

It can easily be understood how difficult the position of Rome and the Popes became, amid all these contending claims. On the one hand, the government of the Eastern Emperors was sometimes oppressive, never protective; on the other, the Lombard sword was never sheathed; but, wielded by such men as Liudprand and Astolphus or Astolf, was a ceaseless menace to the wretched population. In addition to this the inhabitants of the Roman territory were constantly suffering pillage from the troops of the Dukes of Benevento and Spoleto; their flocks were raided, farms belonging to S. Peter were burnt, and fortresses seized; had it not been for the energy of the people who opposed force to force, and the unceasing mediation of the Popes, Rome must soon have fallen completely under the power of the Lombards.

The Popes occupied the first rank in Rome; first on account of the primacy of the Apostolic See, and also because the Popes enjoyed the usufruct of the domains of S. Peter, already very extensive, and of which they were the administrators. These domains, devoted to lighting churches, feeding the poor and pilgrims, and maintaining hospitals, had been formed and enlarged as much by the successive gifts of Emperors as by the generosity of the faithful. Besides the endowments made by Constantine to the Basilicas which he had founded, twenty-three other domains might be counted spread over Italy, Istria, Dalmatia, Illyria, Sardinia, Corsica, and Gaul as early as in S. GREGORY's time. One alone of these comprised the Cottian Alps, with the towns of Aix, Bobbia, Savona, Genoa, etc. At the other end of Italy the Church owned Gallipoli and Otranto. Even **Naples** received a tribune whom the Pope sent to command her troops and defend the city. On the increase of anarchy it became more necessary to have recourse to the only living force remaining in society. As for the Popes, their power naturally increased, by reason of their social and moral duties, "for the welfare of the unhappy people who had no other defender." (1)

"What is really astonishing," says de Maistre, "is to witness the Popes unconsciously becoming sovereigns, and, as it were, in spite of themselves. An unseen law had exalted the See of Rome; and it may be said that the head of the universal Church was born a king. From the martyr's scaffold he ascended a throne, unseen at first, but which, like all great things, insensibly consolidated itself, and, from its earliest age, proclaimed its presence by some nameless atmosphere of surrounding majesty not traceable to any human source. The Roman Pontiff had need of wealth, and treasures were poured into his coffers ... they flowed from the hand of Providence, who stamped them from their origin with the seal of legitimacy. They are seen, and no one knows whence they come; they are seen and no one can raise a complaint against them. It is respect, love, piety, and faith that have amassed them.

"In still pagan Rome, the Roman Pontiff had been a thorn in the side of Cæsar. He was but Cæsar's subject; Cæsar was all powerful against him; he had no power against the Emperors. Yet they

---

(1) Rohrbacher, "Hist. de l'Église", t. IX, p. 409.

found it impossible to live beside him ... a hidden hand drove them from the Eternal City which was surrendered to the head of the Eternal Church." (1)

SERGIUS was still upon the throne at the beginning of the eighth century; he was succeeded in 701 by JOHN VI. It is related of him that he devoted the treasures of the Church to redeeming the captives taken in Campania by Giswulf, Duke of Benevento. This was one of the principal purposes to which the wealth of the Church was applied; sometimes even altar vessels were sold, and Fortunatus, Bishop of Fano in 592, ransomed in this manner a great number of unhappy persons who had been carried off by the Lombards.

But it was not only chains and imprisonment which men had to fear in these disastrous times. The Iconoclast heresy had become fierce and persecuting; not only were statues destroyed, paintings rent asunder, and sanctuaries stripped bare; but Bishops were driven away, and tortures and assassinations were instituted by the Emperor. This Emperor, Leo the Isaurian, having vainly endeavoured to pervert the professors at Constantinople, set fire to the library, thereby destroying thirty thousand volumes, countless paintings and medals, as well as their learned guardians. But such a triumph did not satisfy the Emperor's pride; he further insisted that Italy should be laid waste by fire. It is impossible to conjecture to what lengths the Italians and the Emperor's adherents would have gone, against

---

(1) "Du Pape", l. II, ch. VI.

one another, had it not been for the firmness of GREGORY II.

GREGORY was born at Rome in 669; his youth had been spent in the Lateran Palace where his talents and virtue had developed; the influence he exerted among the lower ranks of the hierarchy naturally pointed him out as being worthy of the Pontificate. From his accession to power in 715 he devoted himself to the duties of sovereign and Bishop. He repaired the Roman walls, he established monasteries near S. Paolo and S. Maria Maggiore for the due observance of divine service in those two Basilicas; and, on the death of his mother Honesta, he turned the family mansion into a monastery near which he erected a church under the invocation of S. Agatha. GREGORY also raised the Abbey of Monte Cassino from its ruins after it had been destroyed by the Lombards, and he sent S. Boniface to the conquest of Thuringia and the whole of the north of Germany. Boniface was a young Englishman whose real name was Winfrith. The monks at his monastery having wished to raise him to the dignities of the order he fled from England and came to Rome, alone, in order to receive instructions and authority from the Pope to labour for the conversion of nations. Whole kingdoms were converted by the preaching of S. Winfrith. GREGORY then recalled him, and he was ordained Bishop, in the Vatican church, on the 30th November 723. Boniface returned to Rome a third time in his old age to pray for the protection of the Apostles; he then went back to Frisia (Friesland) where he was martyred in the seventy-fifth year of his age.

Meanwhile orders were sent to Gregory II to destroy all statues, paintings, and bas-reliefs which represented God or the saints throughout his dominions. Gregory refused to obey, saying, "As Jesus was really born, performed miracles, suffered, rose from the dead, may it please God that heaven, earth, sea, every animal and plant shall proclaim his wonders, by word, by writing, and by painting!"

The eloquent and courageous Pontiff then gave way to his deep feelings, and recalled his impressions on entering S. Peter's:— "Christ is my witness that, when I went into the temple of the Prince of the Apostles, and beheld his image, I felt so overwhelmed with compunction that my tears fell like rain from heaven. Jesus Christ restored sight to the blind," he added, addressing Leo the Isaurian, "and you are blinding those who see best."

The Emperor then sent hirelings to kill him. These assassins were named Basil, Jordanus and Lurion, and were sanctioned and approved of by Marinus, Duke of Rome, who, however, being struck down with paralysis, before the intended crime, it was thereupon abandoned. Paul, Exarch of Ravenna, endeavoured to rekindle the zeal of the assassins; but the Romans rebelled and tore Jordanus and Lurion in pieces. On hearing these tidings Paul assembled his troops, and marched on Rome; but the whole population was in arms, and he was unable to enter the city.

A few days later the streets of Rome resounded with the news of the massacres at Constantinople, the burning of its library, and the outrages committed against the patriarch. The statues of the Emperor were then immediately thrown down, mutilated, trampled under foot, and the people calmly awaited the result of his vengeance. This vengeance might be terrible, for the Exarch of Ravenna had allied himself with Liudprand, King of the Lombards, and their united armies were marching towards Rome. When they arrived at the city gates, GREGORY went out and spoke to Liudprand with such noble animation that he fell on his kness, unbuckled his mantle, shoulder-belt, and sword which was inlaid with gold, and laid them as an offering upon S. Peter's tomb, as well as a gold crown and silver cross. GREGORY then forgave the Exarch, and even assisted him with his influence in maintaining the Imperial power over Tuscany.

However, dissatisfaction was still rife in Italy, when new orders arrived from Constantinople for the destruction of images. Hereupon the whole of Italy rose in rebellion. Paul, Exarch of Ravenna, and Exhilarat, Duke of Naples, who wished to attempt the Pope's life, were massacred; and it was unanimously decided to elect a new Emperor. GREGORY, faithful to his mission of peace, opposed this extreme measure. Everyday he assembled the Romans for processions and prayers, and endeavoured to inspire them, not only with steadfastness under persecution, but with charity and gentleness, which alone can subdue hatred and heal wounds. It was while practising these acts of devotion and piety that he ended his career on the 13th February 731.

Amongst the most honoured existing images of our Saviour is one which, it is said, was brought miraculously from Constantinople to Rome, during the Iconoclast persecution, under Gregory II pontificate. It represents Jesus Christ standing; the figure is life size, and rests upon a shelf of either cedar or olive wood. This statue has always been called "Acheiropoietos," that is to say, "not made by the hand of man". Gregory II placed it in the Lateran Palace, in the chapel of S. Laurence, known to-day under the title of Sancta Sanctorum. For a long period it was never uncovered except on the Feast of the Assumption, and now it may be seen only during Holy Week, the Octave of the Assumption, and on Jubilee years. On the Feast of the Assumption, and whenever misfortune threatened the city, the Popes solemnly carried the "Acheiropoietos" statue from the Sancta Sanctorum to S. Maria-Maggiore.

It is natural that to the memory of this venerated image is united that of the Virgin of S. Maria-in-Cosmedin, which also escaped the Greek persecution, and was brought to Rome during these sad times. The church, in which it is highly prized, is one of those whose internal arrangements best recall its ancient origin. It seems that it replaced an oratory, founded by S. Dionysius in the third century, and the school in which S. Augustine taught. It subsequently became an asylum for those Eastern Catholics who fled before the Iconoclasts, and from that time was known as the School of the Greeks. Finally, rebuilt and decorated by Pope Adrian I, it became solely known by the surname "in-Cosmedin", signifying the adorned or the beautiful. (1)

S. Maria-in-Cosmedin stands on the banks of the Tiber, and on the waste land which stretches from its portico to the temples of Vesta and Fortuna virilis, as a solitary representative of the desolated church of S. Chrysostom. Its belfry is Byzantine, its name Greek, and the Virgin, whose image attracts attention at the back of the high altar, is a pious reminder of the persecutions at Constantinople, besides being one of the most beautiful productions of Eastern art. Its ancient inscription still remains; "Mother of God, ever Maiden," Θεοτοχος αειπαρθενος.

GREGORY III, who succeeded GREGORY II, made use of the same weapons of courage and patience in his dealings with the Emperors. Only a few days after his accession he wrote to Leo, "You think you can terrify us by saying, 'I shall send to Rome and break the image of S. Peter, and Pope Gregory shall be carried off in chains, even as Constans served Martin.' Learn that the Popes are mediators and arbitrators of peace between the East and West ... We do not fear your threats."

He then summoned a Council at which the respect due to images was sanctioned by the authority of 93 Bishops; and at the same time sums of money were distributed to Italian painters and sculptors,

---

(1) From Κοσμος ornament, glory, honour. This church is sometimes called Bocca della verità, from an antique mask forming probably the spout of a gutter; the mouth of this mask, so they say, closed upon the hands of liars.

that they might increase the number of pictures and images in the churches. Leo's anger now reached its height. He despatched a fleet against the Pope; but it was wrecked in the Adriatic, and now Leo beheld himself growing old, excommunicated, and dying without having had his revenge.

The image of S. Peter which the Emperor desired to break is the same which is still venerated at Rome; and speaking of it Maphoeus Veggius said, "With the exception of the high altar there was no spot in the whole Basilica which attracted so many people." Another writer, quoted by Mgr. Gerbet, calls it, "the very ancient statue of S. Peter in bronze, which was formerly that of Jupiter Capitolinus." It appears to be a fact that the Capitoline Jupiter was melted down by orders of S. Leo in order to cast the Apostle's statue. It was intended to be a thank-offering for the deliverance of the city from Attila.

Leo the Isaurian was succeeded by his son Constantine Copronymus, who, if possible, surpassed his father's crimes. Like Nero, he played upon his lyre while the orthodox were being mutilated or slain by his orders. Blood flowed in torrents during his reign; but Italy in reality no longer depended upon Constantinople, and was therefore safe from his fury. Unfortunately internal divisions prevented her from enjoying repose. Liudprand besieged Rome, because Gregory III refused to deliver up the Duke of Spoleto who had sought refuge in that city. The siege was not successful; yet any moment the yoke of the Eastern Emperors might be replaced by that of the Lombards, a restless nation, whose habits had been only partially improved by Catholicism, and who still retained rough and savage energy.

It was not Italy alone, but the whole of Christendom, that was plunged into a state of the deepest suffering. Her enemies were swooping down from all sides. Despoiled of her beautiful Asiatic and African provinces, she could no longer defend herself even in Europe; for the sea had ceased to be a barrier to those terrible swarms of two and three hundred thousand men who, as they passed on, devastated kingdoms, cruel fate driving them forward. During a century the Arabs had divided the world among themselves, swayed as they were by their adventurous spirit, and fanatically influenced by what they considered God's commands. While some went to India and China, (1) others poured into Spain and crossed the Pyrenees; it required all the strength of Charles Martel's military prowess to exterminate these fierce hordes at Poitiers. The victory of Poitiers probably saved European civilisation; it certainly placed Charles Martel, Duke of Austrasia, in the foremost rank of Christian princes. It was therefore not astonishing that Rome, left to her own resources, and powerless to defend herself alone against the enemies which surrounded her, applied through the agency of her Pontiffs to Charles.

GREGORY II was the first who solicited help; GREGORY III also sent him an embassy, in 740, bearing the keys of S. Peter's tomb and a portion of his chains, requesting help against the Lombard Kings. "These Kings," wrote the Pope, "take advantage of

---

(1) Arabs were seen in Canton as early as the eighth century.

our confidence in you to insult you. 'Let this Charles and the Frankish army come, in which we hear he trusts, and let them aid him if they can, let them save him from our hands.'" At the time, however, the friendship of the Lombards was useful to the Duke of Austrasia in his war against the Saracens; so the embassy was of no avail.

A few days after taking this step, which constitutes an epoch in history, GREGORY III died. Among the foundations of his pontificate, history mentions an oratory in the Vatican Basilica, situated near the great arch, on the side for men, and dedicated to S. Maria. In this Oratory GREGORY deposited behind a bronze balustrade a number of relics collected from all the countries of the world. The devotion to saints was attacked; he only replied by greater homage. Monks in neighbouring monasteries were ordered to celebrate in this oratory all vigils of the feasts of those saints whose relics were honoured within it. Anastasius also delights to enumerate the gold vases, hanging crosses, and precious clasps with which the piety of the Pope enriched this sanctuary.

The same Pontiff raised the ancient deaconry of SS. Sergius and Bacchus, which formed part of the dependencies of the Vatican, from its ruins. He placed six twisted columns before the Confession of S. Peter, and adorned them with silver architraves, which represent Jesus with the Apostles, and Mary with the Virgins; he also gave a bas-relief in gold, sprinkled with precious stones, to the Capella del Presepio in S. Maria-Maggiore. This bas-relief represents the Virgin embracing her Son.

The dissensions throughout Italy were prolonged far beyond this time; and the pontificate of Zachary is remarkable for the courageous efforts he made to bring about union among the different princes of the Peninsula. He was, says Anastasius, a man of rare sweetness, and adorned with every virtue. He obtained the restitution of all the towns which had been usurped from the Duchy of Rome and the patrimony of S. Peter from Liudprand, against whose ambition he also defended Ravenna and the Imperial domains; but, while he protected people's rights, he assisted the unfortunate. He redeemed and enfranchised a great number of slaves, whom the Venetian merchants were taking to Africa; he established regular distributions of alms for the poor, pilgrims, and sick of the different quarters of the city in the palace which he completely restored, having found it, says Anastasius, in great penury. Among the apartments he restored was a dining-room, "triclinium", situated in front of the Basilica of Theodosius. Zachary ornamented it with various marbles, glass windows, precious metals, mosaics and paintings; he also ordered several sacred paintings for the oratory of S. Sylvester, and raised a portico and a tower, which afterwards became two of the most remarkable portions of the pontifical residence. The portico served for the entrance, which was surmounted by the tower. In the highest story of this tower was a second triclinium, on the walls of which was a fresco representing the map of the world; Zachary had this made in order that he might never lose sight of the extent and responsibility of his charge, and, doubtless also, that pilgrims on crossing the threshold of the universal Shepherd might remember their native land.

This same Pontiff placed a cloth of gold tissue and precious stones, representing the Nativity of Jesus Christ, upon S. Peter's altar, and enriched that Basilica with all the books required for the recital of the various offices.

It was to Pope ZACHARY that Pepin le Bref, Mayor of the Palace to Childeric III, sent S. Burchard, Bishop of Wurzburg, and Fulrad, Abbot of S. Denis, to consult about his claims to the throne which had long been in his family's power. Zachary only saw, in the advent of this new dynasty, the consolidation of that good order which it had succeeded in establishing in Gaul; and he considered it just that the title of King should be given to him who already had the power of a monarch. Pepin was accordingly consecrated King of the Franks (Francorum rex) by S. Boniface, Archbishop of Mainz: Childeric ended his days in a monastery.

A priest, named Stephen, was chosen to succeed Zachary; he actually took possession of the Lateran: but in three days, even before he was consecrated, he suddenly lost his speech, became unconscious, and died.

Then STEPHEN II was by common consent elected in the church of S. Maria Maggiore. He inaugurated his pontificate by the re-establishment of four ancient hospitals at Rome, and by founding three new ones. Hospitals are one of the noblest institutions of Christianity: in pagan times nothing similar existed: but no sooner had the Gospel been preached than seven deacons were deputed to distribute alms among the needy and sick. The deaconries of Rome were hostelries open to all sufferers, and the treasures of the Church were particularly devoted to the maintenance of houses for the poor. We must notice that two of the hospitals, built by Stephen II, were in the neighbourhood of S. Peter's, probably because pilgrims congregated there. It was also near S. Peter's that Ina, King of Wessex, at the beginning of the eighth century, ordered a spacious building to receive pilgrims from Britain, also a church under the invocation of S. Mary. (1) This church and hospital were destroyed several times but were rebuilt, in the thirteenth century, by INNOCENT III, under the title of S. Spirito-in-Sassia. It is now one of the most magnificent establishments in Rome.

King Ina's hospital was the first of the kind founded by foreigners in the papal city; a fact proving the great concourse of West Saxons to Rome. S. Kilian, S. Ceolfrid, S. Boniface, Kings Ina and Offa, and the celebrated Alcuin, all belonged to the British Isles. "It was then the custom", says Bæda, "of many English clerics and laymen, men and women, to go and end their days near the tombs of the Apostles, in order to be more easily welcomed by them in heaven."

We read that during the eighth century a Bavarian Prince came on a pilgrimage to Rome;

---

(1) Ina imposed a tax of one penny a year upon every house in his kingdom, for the maintenance of this hospital. This tribute was paid every year at Rome, on S. Peter's Day; whence it has since become known as Peter's pence.

and men of all costumes and colours still came to pay their homage to S. Peter.

Astolf, the Lombard King, seized upon the Exarchate of Ravenna, during the pontificate of STEPHEN II; and, thereupon, he determined to add Rome and her territory, the last remnant of the Western Imperial power, to his dominions. In face of this danger, STEPHEN ordered a procession, in which he marched bearing the celebrated Acheiropoietos image of our Saviour upon his shoulders. He walked barefoot and was followed by the people with ashes on their heads, uttering dismal groans and lamentations. The treaty of peace, which had been violated by the Lombards, hung from the arms of the cross.

At the same time STEPHEN requested Constantine Copronymus to assist him; but Constantine returned no answer, so the forsaken Pontiff turned towards Gaul, and, in spite of opposition from his subjects, he left Rome to ask for help from Pepin, chief of the Franks. Pepin made a solemn gift of all the towns seized by Astolf to the Church; and shortly afterwards set forth to reconquer them. The return of Pope STEPHEN was celebrated at Rome by universal rejoicings. The clergy met him at the fields of Nero, carrying the cross and singing hymns, the crowd crying out, "Long live our Father; he is our hope after God!"

Now Astolf submitted to the all-powerful influence of the King of the Franks; although he was not long faithful to the promise he had made him. Pepin's army had hardly recrossed the Alps when the Lombards again marched on Rome. They besieged it for three months; burnt and plundered neighbouring farms; exhumed the bodies of Saints, and defiled the convents of holy nuns with the vilest outrages. STEPHEN then wrote to Pepin and his two sons saying:— "We are plunged into such deep grief, and our anguish and sorrow are so unceasing, that it seems as though we should require help from the elements to describe them. You know that the impious Astolf has broken the peace; he is encamped at our gates ever since the kalends of January. 'Open the Porta Salaria', he said, 'and deliver up your Pope, then I will be merciful to you; but, if you refuse, I will destroy your walls, and put you to the sword, and then who will save you?' His soldiers burn our churches, destroy our images, they place the sacred gifts, that is to say the body of our Lord, into impure receptacles, which they call sacks (folles), and eat them after being replenished with food. Such are the evils they inflict upon us, no pagans did worse, the very stones cry out with us. They have besieged unhappy Rome during fifty-five days; night and day they assault and batter her walls . . . O most Christian Princes, do not withdraw your protection, and God will not abandon you when you have to meet your foes. Hasten, O beloved, to aid and save us, before a dagger is plunged into our heart. We beseech you not to let us perish or permit that nations should say from one end of the world to the other: 'What has become of that confidence which the Romans had placed in the Franks and their Kings, after their trust in the Lord?' every nation which has applied to them for assistance has been saved. How much more necessary it is that you should strive to save God's Holy Church and His people!"

In another letter STEPHEN writes as though from S. Peter:— "I look upon you, O Franks, as my adopted children, and chosen people among nations. The Mother of God, ever virgin, beseeches you as I am doing. She urges and commands you, with all the choirs of heaven, the martyrs and confessors, to have compassion upon the sorrows of Rome. It is a fact that, of all nations under heaven, the Franks have always been the most devoted to me, Peter Apostle . . ."

Pepin at once took the field, out of love for S. Peter, as he said, "nisi pro amore sancti Petri;" and a few days afterwards Fulrad, Abbot of S. Denis, placed the keys of the towns of Pentapolis and Emilia upon the Confession of S. Peter, as well as the deed by which the Frankish chief restored — "restituit, redonavit" — these two provinces to the Roman Church. (1)

STEPHEN, on his side, had conferred the titles of Roman patricians on Pepin and his sons; and the government of Rome became a Republic, of which the Pope was the head and Pepin the protector.

Daunou, a historian above suspicion, remarks that the Romans must have been attached to their

---

(1) The towns given by Pepin numbered twenty-two, namely:— Ravenna, Rimini, Pesaro, Fano, Cesena, Sinigaglia, Jesi, Forlimpopoli, Forli, Castrocaro, Montefeltro, Acceraggio, Monte-Lucari, Serravalle, San-Marino, Bobbio, Urbino, Caglio, Lucoli, Engubbio, Comacchio, and Narni.

Pontiffs, who were nearly all worthy men. Fathers and defenders of the people, mediators with the great, heads of religion, the Popes united in themselves every means of credit and influence which can be obtained from "wealth, good deeds, virtue and from the supreme priesthood."

Sismondi is no less clear. Finally Gibbon declares that "their temporal dominion is now confirmed by the reverence of a thousand years; and their noblest title is the free choice of a people, whom they had redeemed from slavery." (1)

Thus S. Peter's successors were no longer mere holders of an authority which ruled men's consciences, but they became also temporal sovereigns like other princes, with secular power and jurisdiction. No dynasty can claim a nobler origin.

STEPHEN II died in April 757. He founded a monastery at Rome, under the invocation of S. Denis, to receive the relics of that saint which he had brought from Gaul. He bestowed it upon some Greek monks in remembrance of the first country of that Dionysius, the Areopagite, who became the Apostle of the Gauls.

PAUL I was STEPHEN II successor and brother. He reigned eleven years, and his memory was honoured. Anastasius tells us that at night he used to visit the sick, the poor, and prisoners, to whom he took food and spoke words of comfort.

PAUL rebuilt the church of S. Sylvester in the Campus Martius, and he seems to have included his own house in the new buildings. He adorned this

---

(1) "Decline and Fall etc." Book IX, chapter XLIX.

church with marbles and mosaics, and annexed a monastery. But the most precious treasure with which he enriched it was a collection of relics from the Catacombs. Since the siege of Rome by Astolf, the Catacombs had been entirely neglected. The Lombards had pillaged them; for, even though they were at war with the Pope, these barbarians eagerly sought for the bodies of martyrs to place in their churches; and since then the Catacombs had been abandoned; the piety of the people no longer paid them the same respect; and the shepherd of the campagna penned his flocks amid the bones of martyrs.

Among the holy bodies discovered by Paul was that of S. Petronilla, S. Peter's adopted daughter. It was conveyed by his orders to an Oratory situated at the end of the Vatican Basilica to the left, which was for a long time considered to be the ancient temple of Apollo in Nero's circus. This Oratory, which was rotund, was octagonal within, and had six altars. The two other sides were left for doors. Paul I endowed it richly, and this Saint was so much venerated that, eight hundred years later, Paul V placed S. Petronilla's altar among the seven privileged altars of the new Basilica.

The chapel of S. Maria-dei-Cancelli, to the extreme right of S. Peter's, was also enriched by Paul I pious offerings. He placed many relics there, which were protected by bronze balustrades, "cancelli". The chapel was also decorated with mosaics, a silver gilt statue of the Virgin, weighing a hundred pounds, was a gift from the Pontiff. Women were not allowed in this chapel.

By order of the same Pope S. Peter's façade was covered with a mosaic, representing Jesus Christ sitting within a circle of stars, holding a book on which was written:— "Ego sum resurrectio et vita." Five angels surrounded Him, and four saints were offering crowns.

Lastly, the church of SS. Pietro e Paolo in the Via Sacra, afterwards known as S. Maria Nuova, and now called S. Francesca Romana, is attributed to PAUL I. This holy Pope wished to honour the spot where, according to tradition, S. Peter had knelt while Simon the magician was raising himself in the air. The stones bearing the mark made by his knees still form part of the treasure of this church.

PAUL I death was the signal for a schism. The news had scarcely been announced when a Lombard Duke, called Toton, hurried to Rome with his brothers, and followed by a disorderly rabble entered the city by the S. Pancras Gate, and proclaimed his brother Constantine Bishop of Rome, although he had no ecclesiastical order whatever. George, Bishop of Præneste, was seized upon and commanded to confer orders on Constantine. At first he refused; but, on being threatened, the wretched man finally gave way.

Constantine's intrusion lasted a year: at the end of which period a revolt broke out against him, and STEPHEN, priest of S. Cæcilia, was canonically elected Pope. The people, always in extremes, then rushed upon Constantine's partisans tearing out the eyes and tongues of some; Constantine was led to the monastery of Cella Nuova, now called S. Saba's, mounted on a woman's saddle. He was afterwards dragged from this retreat, his eyes put out, and he was left lying helpless on the pavement.

In order to prevent the recurrence of similar excesses, STEPHEN III and the fathers of a Council, which he convoked at Rome, decreed anathema on every layman who took part in the election of a Pope. The election was confined to the Bishops and the clergy, and the elect was only to be acknowledged by the people and militia before taking possession of the patriarchal palace.

STEPHEN III was remarkable for a resolute character (strenuus), and for a deep knowledge of the Scriptures and traditions of the Church. His successor ADRIAN I united similar gifts to those which make ruling easy; namely, noble birth, physical beauty, graceful carriage, firmness, sweetness, and mercy. He showed himself capable and powerful, according to the historians of the time, "in omnibus efficax et idoneus."

It was during his pontificate that the ruin of the Lombard Kingdom was accomplished, after a sway of more than two hundred years. Astolf was succeeded, in 756, by Desiderius, a fierce and ambitious Prince, who trampled all the treaties which bound him to the Church under foot; he seized upon Pentapolis and marched with his armies upon Rome. ADRIAN removed all the relics which were in the Basilicas of SS. Peter and Paul fuori-le-mura, after which he locked up the doors, so that the Lombard King might not enter those holy places, "unless he broke open the doors at the risk of his soul."

At the same time the courageous Pontiff took steps for the defence of the town; he summoned the country militia and determined to hold his own against the bold adventurer. Hereupon Desiderius withdrew to Pavia; but the time had arrived when Charlemagne descended the Alps and very soon took possession of Pavia.

Charlemagne went to Rome for Easter 774. The magistrates and senators received him thirty miles from Rome; the militia and school children met him at a distance of one mile bearing palm and olive branches, singing and cheering; these were followed by people carrying crosses and banners. At the sight of the cross Charlemagne dismounted; devoutly following the clergy as far as S. Peter's, as he mounted the steps he kissed each one, and entered the church with the Pope who had waited for him on the steps. The clergy and people sang, "Benedictus qui venit in nomine Domini."

After having remained prostrated before the Confession of the Apostle for some time, Charlemagne eagerly begged (obnixè) the Pope to allow him to enter Rome in order that he might fulfil his vows in the different churches of that town. The Pope was then solemnly acknowledged to be sovereign of the pontifical city. The Pope and the King proceeded to the Lateran Basilica, where ADRIAN, according to custom on Holy Saturday, baptized the catechumens. Next day, Easter Sunday, Charlemagne assisted at the pontifical Mass in the Basilica of S. Maria-Maggiore; on Monday, in that of S. Peter; on Tuesday, in that of S. Paul. Panegyrics were sung in his honour from the ambo. These consisted of praises, good wishes and prayers, such as, "To the most excellent

Charlemagne, crowned by God, life and victory!" and the people answered, "Saviour of the world, be his aid!"

On Wednesday, the 6<u>th</u> April, Charlemagne placed a deed of gift of some provinces, which he offered as a homage to the Church, over S. Peter's remains. This deed confirmed Pepin's gift, and in addition he gave Venetia, Istria, the duchies of Benevento and Spoleto, Mantua, Parma, the island of Corsica, and extended the papal power as far as the Gulf of Spezzia.

Adrian and Charlemagne were made for understanding one another; and they entered into close bonds of friendship. Adrian celebrated the Emperor's praises in acrostic verse; Charlemagne composed eighteen lines to serve as an epitaph for Adrian. (1) When the Emperor returned to Rome in 781 and 787 ADRIAN I still lived; he baptised the young Carloman, whose name he changed to Pepin, consecrating him King of Italy, and his brother, Louis, King of Aquitaine.

During one of Charlemagne's visits to Rome, a lively quarrel arose between the Frankish and Roman singers, as to the respective beauties of their chants. Rumours of this dispute even reached the Prince's ears, and the Franks were congratulating themselves

---

(1) The following are four lines from this long epitaph:—
"Nomina jungo simul titulis, clarissime, nostra;
Hadrianus, Carolus, rex ego, tuque pater
Quisque legas versus, devoto pectore supplex,
Amborum mitis, dic: miserere, Deus!"

on obtaining his support when the Emperor said to them:— "Which is purest water, from the source or from the stream? Go back to S. GREGORY who is the source, because it is clear that you have corrupted the ecclesiastical chant." He even asked the Pope to send him some singers and professors to teach grammar and mathematics, whom he placed at the head of the Frankish schools. (1)

A contemporary writer observes that the rough throats of the Franks could never quite succeed in rendering certain shakes and delicacies peculiar to Italian singing.

ADRIAN I occupied S. Peter's Chair for twenty-three years; the offerings he made to various Roman churches amounted to 1,384 lbs in gold and 1,773 lbs in silver. The churches of S. Apollinaris and of S. John Lateran were erected by him. He also restored several that were in ruins; among others, S. Marco, an ancient foundation of the fourth century, which was close to his father's house, and in which, while a child, he was accustomed to pray. The church of S. Anastasius was also rebuilt by Adrian; when the edifice was destroyed by fire the Pontiff had hastened to its rescue. Anastasius enumerates fifty-five religious buildings as having been splendidly renovated by Adrian. Chief among these were the Lateran Basilica and Monastery. S. Peter's was

---

(1) The two schools of singing founded by Charlemagne were those of Metz and Soissons; both have attained great renown, more particularly that of Metz. The choristers brought from Rome by Charlemagne instructed the Franks in organ-playing.

indebted to Adrian for the bronze doors of its portico; upon which were inscribed in silver the names of towns which owed allegiance to the Roman Church. In addition, the Pope presented a beacon to this Basilica, in the shape of a cross, capable of bearing 1270 candles; an ornament of gold tissue and precious stones, representing the deliverance of S. Peter; and sixty-five purple curtains to hang across the doorways of the temple and the arches of the nave. He also gave curtains of varying richness to several other sanctuaries; fifty-five to the Lateran, fifteen to S. Maria-Maggiore, forty to S. Maria-dei-Martiri, twenty to S. Stefano, etc. He also endowed the deaconries, and burdened his private fortune with a charge of supplying bread, wine, and soup to one hundred Roman or foreign paupers. This distribution took place at the Lateran; and was represented by a fresco on the walls of the portico. Adrian is credited with repairing ancient aqueducts, restoring the city walls, and displaying, like his predecessors, that magnificence for art, and the pomps of worship, which became a characteristic glory of the papacy. (1)

A pilgrim, who visited Rome in the year 800, made a careful calculation as to the fortifications which then surrounded it, just after being completed by Adrian. He enumerates 383 towers, 7020 bastions, 2066 large and 1981 small loopholes.

When Charlemagne came to Rome he dwelt with the lords of his suite "near S. Peter's", an expression

(1) It should not be forgotten in Adrian's honour that he burnt several Greek ships employed in the slave-trade, in the harbour of Centumcelle (Civita-Vecchia).

doubtless referring to the Vatican Palace, and which therefore proves it to have been even then one of the largest in the city. The founder of this immense palace is doubtful. Some historians trace its origin to Constantine, others to LIBERIUS, others to S. SYMMACHUS. Thus, while the Imperial palace was falling into ruins on the Palatine, that of the Pontiffs was proudly rising on the ancient hill of the Augurs, near the river Tiber which, in the days of antiquity, had also been looked upon as a prophet: "Quinimò vates intelligitur". (1)

The pontificate of LEO III was disturbed by shocking riots. Two of the palace officials, Paschal and Campulus, relatives of Pope ADRIAN, determined to murder LEO, regardless of his gentle habits and pure life. (2) Accordingly one day, on the 23rd April 799, just as the stational litany was going from S. Lorenzo-in-Lucina to S. Georgio-in-Velabro, they fell upon LEO with an armed band, flung him to the ground, rent his garments, and strove to tear out his eyes and tongue. The people who were following the procession fled; and the assassins, on seeing the Pope motionless and speechless, withdrew: but Paschal and Campulus soon returned; they dragged LEO into the neighbouring church of S. Silvestro-in-capite, and there, at the foot of the altar, assaulted him once more until he was covered with blood, after which fearing that he might still be able to speak they made another infuriated attack upon the unfortunate Pontiff. That

(1) Pliny, "Hist. nat." B. III.
(2) They had hoped that one of them might have been elected Pope on ADRIAN's death.

evening Leo was carried to the monastery of S. Erasmus: he still lived, and God permitted him to recover both his sight and his speech. (1)

Meanwhile some of the faithful had carefully followed the conspirators. They succeeded in rescuing the Pope and conducting him to S. Peter's, where he was surrounded by homage; the Duke of Spoleto invited him to his ducal estates, whence Leo set out for Paderborn where Charlemagne was staying.

Charlemagne had just vanquished the Huns, and he sent his son Pepin, at the head of 100,000 victorious troops, to meet the Pope. On seeing him this vast army fell upon their knees, and Leo, lifting up his hands towards heaven, blest the Frankish host. Charlemagne awaited the Pontiff at a short distance from Paderborn with another army composed of men from all nations. The clergy marched in front, forming three distinct choirs bearing banners.

As the Vicar of Jesus Christ approached, Charlemagne formed this immense multitude into a circle, and exclaimed:— "Come, O ye brave, take up the arms you use in battle, and let us hasten to meet the august Pontiff!"

"Pontifici, celeri cursu, occurramus opimo."

Now, as soon as the King who was "the father of Europe", to use the poetic language of a contemporary, had met the "shepherd" who was "the father of the world", priests, soldiers and people, prostrated themselves three times, the Pope blessing them three times and praying for them. Charlemagne then bowed

(1) "Et visum recepit et lingua ad loquendum ei restituta est." (Bar. Ann. ad ann. 799.)

respectfully, after which the Pope and Emperor embraced and proceeded towards the principal church of Paderborn while the Gloria in Excelsis was being chanted. (1)

Meanwhile the step taken by LEO III, and the welcome accorded to him, filled Paschal and his assassins with alarm; they endeavoured to neutralize their effects by impeaching the Pope to Charlemagne of the most criminal charges. Nevertheless the Pope did not delay his return to Rome; he was accompanied by a great number of archbishops, bishops, and nobles, and was received as a martyr in every town and country. The whole Roman population, men, women, priests, nuns, and strangers from all lands, from Frisia, Saxony, and Gaul, came forth with banners to meet him as far as Ponte Molle, and thence conducted him in triumph to S. Peter's, where he celebrated Mass.

Charlemagne had commissioned several Bishops to institute inquiries into the accusations made by Paschal and Campulus against the Pope; but he came himself to Rome in the following year, in order to fulfil his duties as a patrician and protector of the Roman Church. The clergy, nobility, and people were therefore convoked at S. Peter's to attend the solemn inquiry into the calumnies affecting the Sovereign Pontiff.

The Pope and Emperor were already seated side by side, crowds filled the church, when suddenly the bishops and abbots rose in a body protesting their

---

(1) Dom. Bouquet, t. V, p. 394.

unfitness for the task. "No one," they exclaimed, "can have the audacity to accuse the Holy Father; the Apostolic See is now, as it ever has been in the past, the sovereign judge, and therefore may be judged by no man." Leo III thereupon ascended the ambo, and demanded as a favour permission to justify himself publicly; then, laying his hand upon the Gospels, he swore that he had no knowledge of the crimes imputed to him. The vast concourse was filled with enthusiasm at the Pontiff's words, and the canticle of S. Ambrose, "Te Deum laudamus, te Dominum confitemur", was enthusiastically sung by the crowd.

Another solemnity, a month later, brought back the Pope and Emperor to S. Peter's. Charlemagne, with all his suite, wished to be present at the pontifical Mass in the Basilica on Christmas Day. But, when the service had begun, Leo took a crown from the altar, approached the Prince, and placed it on his head, while the people cried out, "Life and victory to Charlemagne, the most pious Augustus, crowned by God, the great and pacific Emperor of the Romans!" The Pope then anointed Charlemagne and his son Pepin with holy oil, making an inclination according to the old custom with regard to the Emperors, (a pontifice, more antiquorum imperatorum, adoratus est). (1)

After this manner the title and prerogatives of the Emperor of the West were restored, 323 years after the fall of Augustulus.

---

(1) According to Eginhart this coronation took Charlemagne by surprise.

Charlemagne took the titles of defender and humble auxiliary of the holy Church of God, "Sanctæ Dei Ecclesiæ defensor humilisque adjutor," and on every occasion he endeavoured to prove himself worthy to bear them.

On either side of the portico of the Vatican Basilica may be seen two equestrian statues which appear to guard the entrance; the one on the right represents Constantine, the other, on the left, Charlemagne.

Before leaving Rome, Charlemagne distributed numerous gifts to the principal sanctuaries; to S. Peter's a silver table, a two-handled chalice, a gold crown set with precious stones to be suspended above the altar, etc.; to the Basilica of S. Salvatore, a stational cross ornamented with hyacinths, and a copy of the Gospels enriched with gold and jewels; and various silver vases to S. Maria Maggiore. He had previously made a present to Pope ADRIAN of spoils recovered from the Huns, the greater part of which had been taken from Rome. Some authors attribute the foundation of the church of S. Michele near the Vatican to him. This church served as the place of sepulture for many persons from Gaul who had been buried in the crypts near Nero's palace. (1)

We must call attention to the fact that the churches dedicated to S. Michael in Rome had increased in number since the fifth century. BONIFACE II

---

(1) "Occasione quorumdam Gallorum qui in bello pro ecclesiâ Romanâ suscepti mortui in cryptâ juxta Neronis palatium sepulti sunt." (Mabillon, "Musæum Italicum".)

had built one, at the beginning of the sixth century, in the Flaminian circus; a second had risen on Adrian's Mole, and, before Charlemagne commemorated by a monument his devotion towards the leader of the heavenly hosts, a third church had been built to replace the chapel of BONIFACE II, which the crumbling walls of the circus had involved in their ruin. This church is S. Angelo-in-pescariâ at Octavia's portico. Near this spot the column once stood from whose summit a lictor used to shoot an arrow in the direction of a nation against which Rome declared war.

"Hic solet hasta manu belli prænuntia mitti
In regem et gentes" . . . . (1)

A matter worthy of remark, during the period we have passed in review, is the spirit of faith and sacrifice which was transmitted through families, in spite of the sanguinary brutality of manners and the licentiousness of the times. The infamous Constantine Copronymus had a daughter who practised the highest virtues. (2) Astolf, King of the Lombards, had a brother-in-law who relinquished the duchy of Friuli, and came to Rome for the purpose of receiving a monastic habit from STEPHEN II; he became famous as S. Anselm. Abdications were not then rare; it seemed as though monarchs found their crowns too heavy to bear.

Ratchis, King of the Lombards, withdrew to Monte-Cassino; S. Ceolwulf, King of Northumbria, preferred a monastic life to a throne; Carloman, brother of Pepin

---

(1) Ovid, "Fasti."
(2) S. Anthasia.

le Bref, abandoned Thuringia, where he had gloriously reigned, in order to take vows of poverty at S. Peter's. The last of his wealth was devoted to presenting a silver bow weighing 105 marks to the Basilica of the Apostle: then, having received his habit from Pope ZACHARY, he built himself an Oratory and cell on Mt. Soracte. Mt. Soracte was on the route to Gaul and Thuringia, and thus many lords of both countries, who were making pilgrimages to Rome, went to visit the hermit. This he endeavoured to avoid, because any homage recalled the grandeur he no longer desired, so he hurried off to conceal his virtues and titles in the solitudes of Monte-Cassino.

Sometimes these sudden retreats from the world were a self-imposed penance; for a whole life of mortification was not then considered too great to atone for abuse of power, unrestrained ambition, or for unjust wars.

Religion was then the only restraint put upon Kings; and it was already beginning to inspire them with respect for the dignity of man.

European civil laws were formulated everywhere through the influence of the Church, whose Councils spread among nations, as from a living source, new principles of order and of social intercourse. Rhotaris and Liudprand gave a code to the Lombards; and, a few days after receiving a collection of the Canons of the Roman church from Pope ADRIAN, Charlemagne published his "Capitularies". The first sentence of this celebrated code is noteworthy. Charlemagne describes himself therein as, "King of the empire of the Franks, rector and pious defender of the Church, and, in all things, the aid and support of the apostolic clergy."

The laws of this period, especially those drawn up by assemblies of Bishops, laid particular stress on three points: 1st Ecclesiastical discipline, because the ministers of a holy religion should likewise be holy; 2nd Restrictions on marriage, under which head were comprised all things bearing upon the constitution of a family. It was, in short, by preventing any causes of disturbance in the sweet familiarity which sometimes originates in the cradle, and nearly always at the paternal hearth, by obtaining confidence, and maintaining purity in domestic intercourse, that the clergy endeavoured to remedy the gross licentiousness of the Barbarians and the depravity of Roman habits. 3rd They endeavoured to destroy, by the increase of charity, that anomaly between rich and poor which must always appear as an insoluble mystery to cultivated minds. Thus the elements of civilisation, which Christian Rome preached and diffused throughout the world, were holiness of worship, family purity and charity to all.

CHAPTER IX.

> Tanta vis admonitionis inest in locis! ... et id quidem in hâc urbe infinitum: quâcumque enim ingredimur, in aliquam historiam vestigium ponimus.
>
> *Cicero.*

NINTH CENTURY.

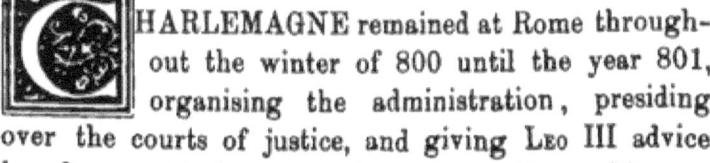HARLEMAGNE remained at Rome throughout the winter of 800 until the year 801, organising the administration, presiding over the courts of justice, and giving Leo III advice based upon his long experience in dealing with men as their ruler.

The empire of this remarkable man had even then exceeded all known limits. He was obeyed from the furthest boundary of Hungary to the Ocean, from the Liris (Garigliano) to the Elbe. Caliphs offered him the sovereignty of the Holy Places, and the Eastern Emperors, whose dominions he had curtailed, solicited his alliance. Wherever the influence of his genius spread, a new life sprang up simultaneously; civilisation was promoted by his laws and schools; letters found a home in the Prince's palace; agriculture was no longer sterile labour; commerce arose, and to facilitate matters the imperial mind was already conceiving an immense thoroughfare, by the junction of the Danube and the Rhine, between Aachen and Constantinople. His armies were always ready; his fleets constantly patrolled the seas, protecting the peaceful development of progress and order against all foreign aggression, and particularly against inroads by the Norsemen, who, descending from the icy North, threatened Europe with fresh and terrible disasters.

Charlemagne lavished benefits on the poor and on the churches, both in Italy, Germany and Gaul. Most of the precious vessels and ornaments, belonging to the Roman churches, were restored by the wealth he bestowed upon Pope Leo III; and doubtless it was from this source, as well as from the offerings made by pilgrims who became daily more numerous in the holy city, that the Pope carried out all that history relates of his bounty. Anastasius mentions silver gilt strainers for purifying the sacrificial wine; a silver lamb, which, from the top of a column, poured water into the baptistery of S. Andrea; and variously stained glass windows at the Lateran Basilica. Leo embellished the pavement round S. Peter's Confession with gold, protecting it by a silver railing; he also erected two large galleries at the patriarchal palace; one destined to receive pilgrims of every rank and from all lands; (1) the

---

(1) Dinner was served there for pilgrims, according to the inscription:— "Deus . . . tua sancta dextera protegat domum istam et omnes fideles convivantes, qui de donis Apostoli tui hic libantur."

other specially intended for the reception of Princes and Emperors. The first was paved with marble, and ornamented with mosaics; in the centre was a fountain whose gushing waters fell into a porphyry basin. The second occupied nearly the whole eastern side of the Lateran, and was the "triclinium majus" or great dining-hall of Leo III. It was supported by columns of Parian marble and of rosso antico, the walls being covered with paintings, mosaics, and very precious marbles. The mosaics which ornamented the principal apse (1), a small portion of which remains, should be specially noticed: one represents S. Peter with three keys, Leo kneels to his right, Charlemagne to his left; the Apostle hands the pallium to the pope, and presents a standard to the Emperor stamped with six roses, and bearing the inscription, "Holy Peter, grant long life to Pope Leo and victory to King Charles."

By his will, Charlemagne bequeathed the money obtained from the sale of his library and part of his furniture to the poor; the remainder of his goods he divided among the twenty metropolitan towns of his Empire; (2) while Rome received a silver table on which a plan of Constantinople was engraved.

---

(1) The structure had three apses, one at the end and one on either side. The mosaics were removed from it and placed behind the Scala Santa by BENEDICT XIV.

(2) These cities were:— Rome, Ravenna, Milan, Friuli, Gratz, Koln, Mainz, Salzburg, Trier, Sens, Besançon, Lyons, Reims, Arles, Vienne, Tarantasia, (3) Embrun, Bordeaux, Tours, and Bourges.

(3) Tarantasia is a district in Savoy. (Note by translator.)

Rome was the capital of the Papacy, and also the principal metropolis of the Empire; she had not been included in the donations made to S. Peter by Pepin and Charlemagne, but probably this was because they considered the rights of the Church were incontestable. Charlemagne, as we know, only entered the city after having obtained the Pope's consent. It has been said that Louis le Débonnaire added Rome and its territory to the previous donations; but Louis had merely guaranteed their possession to Pope Paschal and his successors in the same manner as the preceding Popes had enjoyed them. (Sicut a prædecessoribus vestris usque ad nunc in vestrâ potestate et ditione tenuistis et disposuistis.) This act of confirmation was far from being useless, for Rome was often a prey to popular factions, and the Popes had not always the physical power required to put them down. Thus, even under Paschal, the Lateran palace was polluted by two assassinations. Lothair, who had just been consecrated Emperor by the Pope, sought to vent his anger upon him; but Paschal justified himself with honour, and moreover declined to submit to the Emperor's demands.

S. Paschal is described by a contemporary writer as being a "chaste, pious, innocent, and magnanimous" Pope, gifted with pleasing eloquence, distributing all his goods to the poor, cheerfully and with good judgment. He spent long hours discoursing with the clergy about the proper maintenance of their rules, passing a portion of his nights in prayer, and daily strengthening his humility and chastity by fasting.

The name of this holy Pontiff is closely united in history to several highly venerated Christian monuments in Rome. PASCHAL made it a special object to honour with renewed devotion the most celebrated of those maidens, who, at the dawn of Christianity, were like angels of mercy and grace to pagan Rome; namely, Praxedes, Pudentiana, and Cæcilia. Following the examples of BONIFACE IV and PAUL I, he continued to remove the bodies of martyrs from the abandoned crypts of the Roman campagna, in order to expose them to the veneration of Christians in the churches of the city; a vast undertaking which is still persevered in after the lapse of nine hundred years. (1)

S. Cæcilia's body was long sought for. It was known in what part of the cemetery of Calixtus she had herself placed the remains of Valerianus, Tiburtius, and Maximus, therefore it was surmised that her own grave would be close by. Still the search remained unsuccessful, and, supposing that the remains of the holy maid had been among those carried away by the Lombards, PASCHAL finally ordered it to cease. "But one day, by the mercy of God," says Paschal, "while sitting before the Confession of the Blessed Apostle Peter, listening to the sweet singing which ushered in the dawn of Sunday, our frail body fell into a trance, when there appeared to us a young girl of maidenly appearance and of great beauty, gloriously attired; gazing at us she said, 'We owe thee many acts of charity. But hast thou, on false

---

(1) It has been calculated that Rome alone had two million martyrs. (See Gaume, "Trois Romes", t. IV, p. 592.)

rumours and without good reason, given up the task thou didst undertake on my behalf? Yet hast thou been so near me that we might actually have conversed.'"

Paschal immediately recommenced the search, which resulted in the discovery of the saint's body. It was clothed in gold brocade, while blood-stained linen had been rolled up and placed at her feet. "We have touched them with our own hands," writes this devout Pontiff. Already for some time past Paschal had undertaken to rebuild the Basilica of S. Cæcilia. He caused her relics to be carried thither, together with those of Valerianus, Tiburtius and Maximus, placing them near those of S. Urban, which had also just been discovered in the Catacombs.

From that date the church of S. Cæcilia-trans-Tiberim became one of the richest sanctuaries in Rome. The altar and Confession were covered with silver plates. These were surmounted by a baldacchino of the same metal, weighing five hundred pounds. Four silver statues, among which that of the holy patroness alone weighed ninety-five pounds, surrounded the marble sepulchres within which reposed the bodies of the martyrs. Paschal furthermore gave twenty-six chalices to the Basilica, as well as two lamps, a basin of pure gold, ornaments of brocade and purple with embroideries representing the resurrection of the Saviour, and S. Cæcilia crowned by an Angel, etc. He, moreover, decorated the apse with a mosaic which has outlived revolutions and centuries. It represents Jesus Christ, standing clothed in a golden mantle, while near him are SS. Peter, Paul, Cæcilia, Valerianus, Agatha, and Pope Paschal holding a model of the church. The Lamb of God appears above bearing the monogram of Christ upon his head. The five ancient rivers, symbols of grace, flow at his feet; and twelve lambs, types of the Apostles, come towards him from two cities which are evidently Bethlehem and Jerusalem. There are very few mosaics of that period which do not reproduce these cities, which were considered emblems of hope and life.

There is a detail in this grand composition which must not escape attention; it is the phœnix perching upon a palm, the martyr's tree. "It will be reduced to dust, but will rise again like the phœnix," Tiburtius had said to Maximus, when he wanted him to understand the mystery of a future life; and, after the martyrdom of Maximus, Cæcilia had the phœnix engraved upon his tomb.

The bodies of SS. Praxedes and Pudentiana had been removed from the Catacombs before the ninth century; but S. Paschal surrounded them with fresh honours, reconstructing the Church dedicated to the first of these two virgins, and bringing to it the relics of quite a legion of martyrs, apparently to serve as a triumphal escort to the heroic daughter of Pudens. The number of these martyrs was 2,300; the names of some are known, as for the others, "the Almighty alone knows them", according to the beautiful inscription placed over them:— "Quorum nomina scit Omnipotens". Near these blessed remains may be seen the marble slab upon which Praxedes slept, the well into which she lowered the bodies of martyrs, and, in the neighbouring church of S. Pudentiana, the vases found in the sisters' tombs, vases which, according to tradition, they had used for collecting the blood of our Lord's athletes.

Paschal showered his gifts on the church of S. Praxedes in the same manner as he had done on that of S. Cæcilia: among these were a silver baldacchino, a silver propitiatory, a crown of burnished gold with precious stones (regnum spanoclistum ex auro fulvo ...), an ornament, stitched with gold and jewels, representing with wonderful skill (mirificè) the parable of the wise virgins whose lamps were trimmed, a silver Confession, and a silver statue weighing ninety-five pounds.

The mosaic upon the great arch recalls in many ways that of the trans-Tiberim Basilica. It represents the heavenly Jerusalem towards which numerous pilgrims are wending their way, laden with gifts. An angel is pointing out their path. In the centre of the city appears the Saviour; a hand issuing from the clouds places a crown upon His head, while sheep are lying at His feet. To the right stand S. Paul, clad in a white tunic, S. Praxedes, arrayed in a gold garment studded with gems, and Pope S. Paschal, with a square nimbus, holding a model of the church in his hand. To the left of the Saviour stands S. Peter presenting S. Pudentiana, and further on are to be seen the palm and phœnix.

The place occupied by S. Peter at S. Praxedes's, at S. Cæcilia's, and in most works of art of that period, may occasion some surprise. He is always represented standing on the Saviour's left, while S. Paul occupies the right. This arose from the Greek custom of considering the left side to be the place of honour, as being nearest to the heart. Nearly all workers of mosaic came from Constantinople, and it is difficult to overpraise the number and brilliancy of their labours. Mosaics have the great advantage of withstanding time, and, in those days, now so much depreciated, men did not work for present success, but for after ages.

Paschal annexed a convent to the church of S. Praxedes to receive the numerous religious who fled from Greece, which country was now hopelessly given over to heresy and contention; henceforth Mount Esquiline resounded, both day and night, with praises of God sung in the tongue of Homer and of S. John Chrysostom.

One might suppose that these works would have exhausted S. Paschal's energy and resources; yet he comes before us again, completely rebuilding the church of S. Maria-in-Dominica, and bestowing ninety-two curtains of cloth of gold on S. Peter's, half of which represented scenes of the Passion and Resurrection, and half subjects drawn from the Acts of the Apostles. These curtains formed hangings for the presbyterium when the Pope officiated. Lastly, Paschal entirely renovated the choir of S. Maria-del-Presepio, placing six porphyry columns before the Confession, and enriching the altar with silver arches, upheld by sixteen small columns of the same metal. The precious metals used by the Pope in decorating this Basilica reach the figures of 308 lbs. of gold, 639 lbs. of silver gilt, and 218 lbs. of silver, without taking note of crosses, chalices, patens, lamps, crowns, etc. which he also presented with unequalled generosity. He moreover raised the Apostolic Chair eleven steps; until then it had stood at S. Maria level with the congregation, and so near the women that they might have heard every word pronounced by the Pope even when speaking in his lowest tones.

Eugenius II, archpriest of S. Sabina, succeeded Paschal in 824, Lothair claiming the right to confirm the election before the Pope's consecration. Eugenius was a pious and alms-giving Pontiff. He convoked a Council at Rome in 826 which, among other matters, ordained the establishment of schools for teaching letters, the arts, and Christian doctrine, in every parish both in the country and in towns. One of the canons of this Council forbade the forcible detention of anyone in monasteries, excepting criminals imprisoned by act of justice. Another canon reproved women for the manner in which they kept feast-days, frequently spending them in bathing, dancing, and singing.

Meanwhile the Saracens had taken Sicily, and their incursions brought mourning and sorrow to the shores of the Mediterranean, at the very time that the Normans were devastating the countries bounded by the Ocean and English Channel. Under these circumstances Gregory IV resolved to raise Ostia from its ruins. He surrounded it with a moat and walls, and armed it with mangonels to protect the entrance to the Tiber.

Gregory had ascended the pontifical chair in 828. Historians tell us he was the personification of courage and courtesy, "strenuus ac benignissimus." Although elected unanimously, he only yielded to force; he fled to the church of SS. Cosimo-e-Damiano under which he knew there were some subterranean passages in which he might remain concealed; but he was so closely followed by the people that his efforts were unavailing. He was dragged from his hiding place and conducted to the Lateran Basilica while the multitude sang hymns.

One of the hardest trials he experienced during his pontificate was the unnatural warfare between Louis le Débonnaire and his children. Desiring to bring about peace, Gregory IV even went to Germany to offer his mediation. "Know", he said, "that I have only come to restore that peace which the Saviour recommended so much to you." But his efforts were unable to triumph over implacable hatred, and Gregory, disgusted with men, passed the remainder of his life at the Lateran Palace plunged in grief.

The great mosaic on the façade of the ancient Basilica of S. Peter dated from the reign of this pious Pontiff. Gregory also founded a convent for nuns near S. Maria-trans-Tiberim, in order that the sacred offices might be celebrated there; and he added several apartments to the Lateran, such as baths and dormitories where rest could be taken after matins.

The election of his successor SERGIUS II, priest of S. Silvestro, who was consecrated and enthroned without waiting for imperial confirmation, was very nearly the cause of a collision with the Emperor Louis II, the son of Lothair, who marched with an army on Rome. The Pope sent magistrates, with crosses and banners, to meet him; then having received him on the steps of S. Peter's, he said, "The doors of this Basilica will open, if you come hither to work for the good of the Church and State; if that is not your intention, they will remain closed." Louis protested his devotion and respect for the Prince of the Apostles, and the Pontiff and King went together to kneel before the Confession. Some days later Louis was crowned King of the Lombards, and anointed with holy oil.

During the pontificate of Sergius II the Saracens, advancing up the Tiber, forced their way as far as the gates of Rome. They had already, in 843, ravaged Campania and pillaged Monte-Cassino, (1) but they wanted most to despoil all that was precious from the ancient capital of the world. So they advanced to Rome, in spite of the new fortifications at Ostia; and, failing to enter the city, whose ramparts could have resisted their attacks, they plundered the churches of SS. Peter and Paul, which were outside the walls. The silver altars, gold ornaments, precious stones, were all piled up in their galleys, and they sailed towards Fondi and Gaeta in search of slaves and to desecrate other holy places.

It was under these difficult circumstances that Leo IV ascended the pontifical throne. "He was a born Roman," says an author, "the valour of the first ages of the Republic revived in him, just as one of those beautiful monuments of ancient Rome is occasionally discovered among the ruins of the modern city." Leo IV first care was to repair the damage

---

(1) The Saracens carried off from Monte-Cassino 130 pounds weight of gold, 665 of silver, precious objects and money to the value of 35,000 gold pennies.

done by the Saracens. He restored all the grandeur of divine worship to S. Peter's Basilica; (1) and, in order to place this church beyond the reach of further violence, he determined to surround the Vatican quarter with a wall. From all parts people associated themselves with this great work; the Emperor Lothair sent money, nobles and monasteries despatched workmen, and the Pope, always present either riding or on foot, superintended and animated the men.

One day the Bishops and people, barefoot and with ashes on their heads, assembled and marched round the enclosure, singing psalms in procession, while Leo blessed the walls, gates, and houses of the new city, which henceforth took the name of the "Leonine City".

At the same time that the Pontiff was repairing the ancient Roman fortifications, he closed the entrance to the Tiber by two towers provided with chains. The inhabitants of Centumcelle had been driven to the woods in their dread of the Saracens; Leo built a strongly fortified town for them, which took the name of Leopolis; (2) but, while protecting his people

(1) The gifts S. Leo IV made to the Basilica of S. Peter reached the weight of 5,791 marks of silver. Among them were a breastwork of enamelled gold, containing the portraits of Leo and Lothair, and a gold cross weighing 1000 lbs., sparkling with diamonds, emeralds, and rubies. Forty silver lamps hung around the cross, while 150 candles burned before it by day and 250 by night.

(2) The site of this modern town being less favourable to commerce than the ancient city, Centumcelle re-peopled itself in the end, and in opposition to Leopolis was called Old City, Civita Vecchia.

against their foes, he also beautified the churches, among others that of the Quatro-Santi-Coronati, from which he had formerly taken his title. His own family dwelling he transformed into a church under the invocation of S. Symetrius.

Leo IV had spent his youth in the monastery of S. Martino, near the apse of the ancient Vatican Basilica, the spot being now occupied by one of the pillars of the dome. Leo delighted in beautifying this monastery from a feeling of gratitude. He replaced the gorgeous doors of the Basilica, stolen by the Saracens, with others plated with silver like the old ones, and ornamented with bright and edifying sculptures, (historiis lucifluis salutiferisque). S. Peter's belfry, one of the most ancient in Rome, also dates from his Pontificate, as does the little church of S. Maria-in-Campo-Santo, north of the Vatican. This church, also known as S. Salvatore-de-Ossibus, was within the enclosure of Nero's circus, a spot hallowed by many martyrs, and close by the cemetery to which S. Helena had brought earth from Jerusalem. (1)

The clergy and Roman populace elected Benedict, priest of S. Calixtus, as successor to Leo IV, in spite of the endeavours which he made to escape a burden

---

(1) Leo IV died the 17th July 855, and Benedict III was elected on the 22nd of the same month. It is nevertheless between these two Popes that writers have introduced Pope Joan; "an absurd fable and foolishly imagined, destroyed by actual fact, and which no one now gives himself the trouble of refuting," says President Hénault. Besides which more than three hundred years had elapsed from Leo's death before Richard of Cluny made his marvellous discovery as to this so called female Pope. A century later the story as told by

CHAPTER IX.—NINTH CENTURY. 275

to which he felt himself unequal. In due course legates were sent off to the Emperor to ask for his imperial confirmation.

Meanwhile Arsenius, Bishop of Engubbio, resolved to place Anastasius, priest of S. Marcello, upon the papal throne; he had recently been removed from his charge by Leo IV for non-residence during several years. With this object Arsenius approached the imperial representatives and gained them over to his views, and even succeeded in getting them to lead Anastasius triumphantly to Rome. At their command the clergy, senate, and people, came to meet them at the church of S. Lucius, beyond the Milvian Bridge. Then Anastasius went to S. Peter's, and subsequently seized upon the Lateran Palace, driving out Benedict. The Romans had not expected such violence, and were quickly roused on seeing this scandal. In streets, assemblies, churches, wherever the imperialists showed themselves, the cry was raised, "Give us back our holy Pope BENEDICT!" One Sunday, while the clergy and people were praying in the Eudoxian Basilica (S. Pietro-in-vincoli), an armed force summoned them to acknowledge Anastasius. "Never, never!" was the reply from all. Neither by tricks, nor threats, could

Martin Polonus, Archbishop of Gnesen, attained sufficient celebrity to be taken for granted by a great number of authors. But, with the increase of knowledge and the critical faculty, this ridiculous invention collapsed of itself. Among its refutations may be cited that of David Blondel, a Protestant clergyman at Amsterdam, in 1605. Cardinal Baronius supposes that the weakness of JOHN VIII, who undertook to pay tribute to the Saracens, and received Photius into communion with the Church, may have originated the idea that a woman sat on S. Peter's throne.

18*

the Bishops of Ostia and Albano be induced to impose hands upon the intruder. Then the envoys of the Emperor, discouraged by this unshaken unanimity, resigned themselves to acknowledge Benedict's election.

Thereupon Benedict left the church in which he had been imprisoned, mounted Leo IV horse, and was conducted, amid the shouts and hymns of the populace, first to S. John Lateran, and subsequently to S. Maria-Maggiore. For three days and nights he remained in prayer in this latter church, and on Sunday, 1st September 855, he was solemnly consecrated in S. Peter's.

Anastasius, the Librarian, has described BENEDICT III in a few words. He had a handsome face, a distinguished mind, was gentle and kind in manner, learned in doctrine, wise of speech, compassionate to all misery, and ready to obey rather than command. The memory of this excellent Pontiff remains particularly attached to the church of S. Maria-trans-Tiberim, whose apse he rebuilt, filling the windows with stained glass, a rare luxury in Rome. Among the letters addressed to BENEDICT III is one from Lupus, Abbot of Ferrières, who asks for some books such as "Commentaries of S. Jerome on Jeremias", Cicero's "de Oratore," Quintilian's "Institutions," and Donatus's "Commentary on Terence", books he had sought for in vain beyond the Alps. He promised to return them after they had been copied. Thus was Rome then looked upon as the centre of learning as well as of doctrine.

Ethelwulf, King of England, went to Rome as a pilgrim during Benedict's Pontificate. He offered a golden crown to S. Peter's and made many gifts to the clergy and people. This same prince, by his will, made his kingdom tributary to the Church for the sum of 300 gold marks a year, 100 for S. Peter's, 100 for S. Paul's and 100 for the Pope's private charities.

NICHOLAS I, who succeeded BENEDICT III in 858, like his predecessor only accepted the heavy duties of the pontificate with great reluctance. Historians tell us he was a man of wonderful sweetness, "miræ beatitudinis"; even in childhood there was nothing puerile in him, for his mind was engrossed with heavenly subjects; to those about him he appeared to be almost perfect, "ut a cunctis cerneretur perfectionibus rutilare." (1)

Such was the man whom God formed to meet the trials of the ninth century, and who was to enter the lists both against Photius and Lothair. The schism of Photius belongs to the general history of the Church; but Lothair's bigamy gave rise to scandalous scenes at Rome, actually reaching the Confession of S. Peter, the memory of which is inseparable from the places and monuments to which this work is devoted.

Lothair II, young and masterful, had repudiated Theutberga, daughter of Boso of Burgundy, after five years of marriage, on the charge of having been guilty of incest in her youth, and had replaced her on the throne of Lorraine (Lothringen) by Waldrada,

(1) Among the places in Rome, which more particularly bring Nicholas I to mind, is S. Maria-in-Cosmedin, near to which he built a dwelling for the use of the Popes, "hospitium ad utilitatem pontificum." It even appears that he actually dwelt therein.

his concubine. He even found lax Bishops to sanction his crime, and sent two of them to Rome, Gunther, Archbishop of Köln, and Theutgaud, Archbishop of Trier, to reply to Theutberga's complaints.

Thus the successor of the Apostles was applied to from all parts, and constituted judge of any question which in its moral aspect was necessarily subject to his spiritual authority. We must not forget that, from its earliest days, Christianity had maintained that domestic morality which formed the basis of social order.

The Roman Pontiffs had bravely upheld those pure traditions of ancient Christianity, in spite of the claims which the spirit of licence had endeavoured to oppose to it during nine centuries. They again refused to yield, though polygamy presented itself with a diadem on its head, and supported by the lawlessness of feudal customs. Nicholas deposed the two lax Bishops, thus solemnly reprobating Lothair's second marriage. Gunther and Theutgaud then appealed to Louis II to avenge the royal prerogative, which they alleged had been insulted in the persons of the King's ambassadors. Louis, who was then at Benevento, immediately marched on Rome. He took up his quarters at the Vatican; and, at the moment when the people were ascending the steps of the Basilica in procession, his followers furiously attacked them; banners were upset, priests struck down, and a cross given by S. Helena was broken and cast into the mud. On hearing of these outrages, Nicholas left the Lateran, crossed the Tiber in a boat, and took refuge at the tomb of S. Peter. There he remained for two days; when, being summoned to the Emperor's presence, he spoke with such conscientious freedom that Louis withdrew from Rome and dismissed the Bishops.

It is painful to relate that during Louis II sojourn at Rome his soldiers, accustomed to disorder and want of discipline, pillaged and burnt several houses, ransacked churches, outraged nuns, and gave way to the same excesses as the Saracens had committed, against whom they had been fighting for ten years. Gunther, Archbishop of Köln, sent his brother, Hilduin, to lay a solemn protest on the Confession of S. Peter against the Papal decree which had degraded him. Hilduin, although a priest, entered the Basilica armed and surrounded by assassins; he attacked the guardians of the tomb, slew one, and flung his brother's protest upon the sepulchre, afterwards leaving the church sword in hand.

Meanwhile Waldrada reigned over the Rhenish provinces; but the voice of religion, and the outspoken indignation of the nations, was so great that at length Lothair II was compelled to give way. The crown was restored to Theutberga, and Waldrada followed the Papal legate who was returning to Rome. But one day, on the banks of the Danube, she escaped, and fled towards Provence. It was believed both in France and Germany that she subsequently returned to Lothair and reigned by the side of his neglected wife. Lothair was then excommunicated. This sentence dismayed him, for anathemas pronounced by Popes were as disastrous in their consequences then as those caused by revolutions are now.

Lothair came to Italy when ADRIAN II occupied the Papal chair. They met at Monte-Cassino, and Lothair entreated the Pope to allow him to receive Holy Communion. Adrian promised to grant his request, provided he had forsaken Waldrada since Nicholas had excommunicated him. Lothair swore that he had obeyed his order as though it had been God's command; so he followed Adrian to Rome. Arrived there the Pope celebrated Mass at S. Peter's, and, when Lothair approached to receive the Host, the Pontiff said to him, "If your heart is pure come without fear; but, if you still contemplate adultery, tremble and go hence." Lothair received Communion without hesitation. Several courtiers withdrew from the Holy Table after Adrian had asked each in turn, "Have you approved of your King's conduct?" but the greater number proclaimed their innocence, and communicated.

A month later Lothair left Rome in the highest spirits; but on reaching Lucca a raging fever spread like a contagion among his followers. Many sank beneath the sickness; he himself among the number.

The last thirty years of the ninth century were not less calamitous than those which had preceded them. The Normans threatened Paris from the West; the succession to the various thrones in France and Germany brought about bloody conflicts which exhausted the energy of nations, while it enabled the feudal lords to set up a sort of lawless independence. Then some of the Popes made use of their great influence to nominate Emperors and Kings. They thought that the right conferred by holy unction would prove more sacred to nations than that arising from shedding torrents of blood. Chateaubriand says, "If there existed a tribunal in Europe which could judge nations and monarchs in God's name, and which could prevent wars and revolutions, that tribunal would be a poetical masterpiece, and would attain to the highest degree of social perfection. The Popes, through their influence over the Christian world, had been on the brink of realising this bright dream." (1)

Yet Italy was neither more happy nor more peaceful than the rest of Europe. For a long while past the Saracens had successfully resisted the Imperial forces; Naples, Amalfi, and Gaeta paid them tribute; they advanced into the Sabine country, even at times crossing the Anio, and plundering the churches outside Rome. Under these melancholy circumstances, ADRIAN II could only save the treasures of S. Peter's by transporting them to the Lateran. "He entered S. Peter's house," says Anastasius, "and, having collected all the treasures he could find there, he carried them off to the Lateran; after which he covered Blessed Peter's altar with haircloth, and closed all the doors of the Basilica." Later on the weak Pope, JOHN VIII, made up his mind to buy peace at the price of 25,000 marks a year.

But the Saracens were not the only plague these unhappy provinces endured, for there were also the inroads, freebooting, and rivalries of the Lambertis, Guidos, Berengars and Adalgises, who, from their

---

(1) "Génie du Christianisme", B. VI, ch. XI.

duchies of Spoleto, Friuli, and Benevento, aspired to the royal crown, and too frequently paid no respect either to the Papal tiara or to the Imperial sceptre. Lambert twice entered Rome and delivered it over to pillage. On the death of Charles the Fat, Guido of Spoleto and Arnulf, the illegitimate son of King Carloman of Bavaria, contended for the Empire which of right belonged to Charles the Simple. Arnulf marched into Italy against his competitor. Agiltrude, wife of Guido of Spoleto, immediately took refuge in Rome, and succeeded, in spite of the wishes of Pope Formosus, in making the populace rise in her husband's favour. But Arnulf carried the Leonine city by assault, the rest of the town capitulated, and the conqueror received the Imperial crown at S. Peter's from the Pontiff.

It is remarkable that, in spite of the instability of power existing among the Princes of the Peninsula, the elections to the Apostolic See were rarely disturbed. Adrian II had been unanimously proclaimed, although it had been necessary to drag him from S. Maria Maggiore, where he was at prayer, in order to conduct him to the Lateran Palace. This was the third example of similar disinterestedness during this century, nor was it the last.

Under the Pontificate of John VIII the ancient temple of Fortuna Virilis was transformed into a church. (1) It is well known how Servius Tullius,

(1) M. Ampère maintains that the title Fortuna Virilis does not belong to the temple in question. According to Ovid and Varro, indeed, the temple built by Servius Tullius was in the Trans-Tiberim Region.

the son of a slave, and sixth King of Rome, felt bound in honour to raise a temple to the goddess who had served him so well. After having been destroyed by fire during the Republic, this sanctuary was immediately rebuilt in the strong, severe, style, characteristic of the period. JOHN VIII dedicated it to the Virgin. Since then the Armenians, to whom it was given by PIUS V, have placed it under the invocation of S. Maria Egiziana, their patron saint. The temple of Fortuna Virilis is one of the most valuable and best preserved of any of the monuments which remain of ancient Rome. It still stands with its Ionian columns, and its freize adorned with heads of oxen, and garlands upheld by children. On beholding the cattle belonging to the farmers of the Campagna lying beneath its shade, one is reminded of the days of the consuls, and the time of the "Forum boarium". Close by was the altar raised by Hercules, upon which contracts were entered into, with the solemn oath, "mi Hercule!" In the same neighbourhood were the Palatine Bridge, constructed by Scipio; the Argiletum Way, where dwelt the booksellers, and where Cicero's brother had a house; and the little temple of Pleasure, facing those of "Patrician Chastity", and "Plebeian Chastity", for the Roman had turned everything into gods! Pleasure was represented in her fane, pale and worn, sitting on a throne with the Virtues beneath her feet.

JOHN VIII occupied S. Peter's Chair for ten years, and was followed by MARTIN II, ADRIAN III and STEPHEN V who merely passed by that throne. During the pontificate of ADRIAN III, the Saracens, to whom Docibilis, Governor of Gaeta, had conceded lands near the Garigliano, took Monte-Cassino, in spite of the stout fortifications with which Abbot Bertaire had surrounded it, and destroyed the monastery from top to bottom. The community, decimated by these barbarians, and deprived of their superior whom the Saracens slew before S. Martin's altar, took refuge at Theano. This was the second time that the sons of S. Benedict were driven forth to seek an asylum far from the mountain which they loved as their home.

STEPHEN V only accepted the Pontificate with reluctance. The people collected and broke open his doors, and, in spite of his own and his father's entreaties, dragged him first to the church of Quatro-Santi, of which he was titular, and then to the Lateran Basilica, where he was proclaimed Bishop. He was universally respected as a pious, humble, priest; his days were spent in doing good, and his nights in prayer. Munificent in his works, endowed with an active and prolific genius, his countenance conveyed the idea of pleasant gaiety, while the judicious simplicity of his conversation recalled at once a sovereign and a shepherd.

On reaching the Lateran, STEPHEN saw with regret that the wardrobe and treasury had been plundered. Scarcely any carpets or curtains were left of all the precious stuffs which once constituted its greatest wealth, and all the gold, and silver, with the ornaments belonging to the altar, had entirely disappeared! In vain search was made for a very celebrated gold cross formerly presented by Belisarius to the Prince of the Apostles. Baronius remarks, "The Pontiff was plunged into deep affliction: the granaries and cellars were empty, so that, in the midst of the general scarcity which prevailed, he found himself unable to provide food for the starving, to help the clergy and schools, or to redeem captives. From that time began, alas! that dreadful tendency to plunder the patriarchal palace on the death of a Sovereign Pontiff. In the face of such general difficulties, what could STEPHEN do? He applied to his father, and, taking all the riches belonging to his noble parents (inclyti parentes), he distributed them with a liberal hand to all sufferers."

STEPHEN V, throughout his Pontificate, established a custom of daily entertaining orphans at his table; he also invited the nobility, and, while offering them food for the body, according to Baronius, "he gave spiritual nourishment to their souls."

Baronius also describes him as "a most energetic uprooter of every vice." There is a sermon extant by him in which he eloquently inveighs against "the insolence of the people and their blindness of heart," which leads them to disturb the holy peace in churches by culpable conversations and frivolous discourses.

The memory of this pious Pontiff is particularly attached, in Rome, to the church of Quatro-Santi, of which he was rector, and to which he fled in order to escape the call to the Papacy; also to the Lateran Basilica, which he enriched with a treasury of relics. These relics were the result of excavations in the Catacomb of SS. Chrysanthus and Daria on the Via Salaria. It must be remembered that the Emperor Numerian had walled up the Catacomb while a great number of Christians were praying within it. STEPHEN had the happiness of once more discovering this legion of martyrs, whose bones he collected and solemnly conveyed to the Lateran in 886.

FORMOSUS, Bishop of Porto, succeeded STEPHEN V. This was the first instance of a Bishop being raised to the Apostolic See. According to ancient discipline, a Bishop was compelled to remain united to his church, as a husband should be to his wife, any other desire on his part being looked upon as unfaithful. The election of Formosus was, however, not contested; but, after his death, STEPHEN VI, one of his successors, cited him before a Council, and the body, being exhumed, was stripped of all Pontifical ornaments, the two fingers used in blessing were amputated, and the corpse was cast into the Tiber.

This deplorable scene was followed by a prompt reaction. STEPHEN VI was taken prisoner in a riot and strangled. JOHN IX, later on, solemnly annulled the condemnation of Formosus. It is none the less remarkable that the acts of the Council which reversed the attainder of Formosus maintained ancient discipline in all its severity. The Fathers of the Council said, "Formosus having only been translated from the church of Porto out of necessity, and on account of his merit, to the Apostolic Chair, we forbid anyone whatsoever to take it for a precedent, having regard to the fact that canon law prohibits it, and refuses communion to offenders even were they on their death bed." This same Council also forbade, under severest penalties, all pillage in the patriarchal palace during an interregnum. Whenever a Bishop died robberies took place, and frequently in their excitement thieves did not respect the houses of the dead; palaces, monasteries were ransacked, and depredation spread, like wildfire, throughout the city.

Up to now very few of the monuments, erected at Rome by the Pontiffs of the ninth century, have been mentioned; if they only built a few, they restored many: a considerable number of churches were entirely rebuilt; sanctuaries were beautified, and monasteries endowed with a profusion of treasures, mosaics, marbles, aud precious metals impossible to enumerate. The description of these works of art and offerings made by Adrian alone fill six folio pages in the annals of Baronius. Therein we see catalogued stuffs and ornaments whose very names are lost, for instance, the "stauracinum", and the "quadruplum", which were rich kinds of silks, the "chrysoclavum", the "oloverum", etc. The statues are mostly silver, while the designs on the embroideries are generally enriched with precious stones. Anastasius mentions altar draperies presented by GREGORY IV to S. Maria del Presepio on which were worked pictures of the Nativity, the Presentation, the Baptism and the Resurrection of Our Lord on a ground incrusted with jewels. They contained 381 pearls, 50 hyacinths, 22 topazes, with quite a surrounding of diamonds. Pope LEO III had rebuilt the small church of S. Suzanna, at the Quirinal, in which he had been proclaimed Pontiff, and had decorated the Confession with three silver columns. LEO IV placed, in the gallery above the twisted columns at S. Peter's, silver statues of Our Saviour, two angels, the twelve

Apostles, and twenty other holy personages. Doubtless, too, the creative spirit manifested itself in new foundations. Montfaucon quotes fragments from some anonymous writer of the ninth century, in which occur references to several churches no doubt of different dates, but of which no mention has previously appeared. (1) Among these are SS. Sotera, Sixtus, Antheros, and Miltiades on the Appian Way, S. Eugenia on the Latin Way, and S. Lucia-in-Septizonio, on the Palatine. Several of these ancient Oratories no longer exist; but the others still remain open for the prayers of pious persons.

The monastery of S. Sixtus is specially remarkable for the miracles performed in it by S. Dominic in the thirteenth century. It was in later days turned into a manufactory for stamped paper; though now it has happily reverted to the possession of the Preaching Friars.

S. Lucia-in-Septizonio recalls a saint foreign to Rome. S. Lucy was born at Syracuse; she, at an early age, gave all she possessed to the poor, and, when the day of her martyrdom arrived, her courage did not fail her. "You shall be dragged to a place of evil repute," threatened the judge. Lucy replied, "If my chastity be tarnished against my will, it shall receive a double crown in heaven." In the ninth century there were three churches at Rome under the invocation of S. Lucia. One, built by HONORIUS I, has already been mentioned; another still exists, S. Lucia-in-Silice, near to S. Martino del Monte;

(1) "Iter Italicum."

but the most celebrated of all in ancient Christian days, S. Lucia-in-Septizonio, or "in Septem Soliis", has been completely destroyed.

The Septizonium was situated between the Palatine and the Clivus Scauri, near to the church dedicated to S. Gregory the Great. The use to which this building was put and also its style of architecture are unknown. According to Nibby it served as an entrance to the Imperial Palace; but the anonymous writer, quoted by Montfaucon, states that it was a temple dedicated to the sun and moon; while Baronius says it was raised upon seven orders of columns, and had the appearance of a high tower, "qui celsæ turris speciem exhibebat". The church of S. Lucia was built upon the top of this tower, in the same manner as S. Angelo was erected on Hadrian's Mole. S. Lucia-in-Septem-Soliis was one of the deaconries of Rome. It disappeared after the wars of the eleventh and twelfth centuries, during which the Septizonium was turned into a fortress. Some ruins which still remained of this ancient monument were demolished by SIXTUS V and used in the construction of S. Peter's.

The church of S. Sabbas, on the Pseudo-Aventine, was certainly in existence during the ninth century; in fact an Abbot of S. Sabbas at Rome assisted at the second Council of Nicæa in 787 as legate of Pope ADRIAN I. This church occupied the site of an old temple of Apollo, and more recently of that of the monastery of Cella-Nuova, to which, as already stated, S. Gregory's mother, S. Sylvia, retired.

One melancholy fact is palpable, as one pursues one's way through these early times, called by

Italians "tempi bassi"; it is that, amid all the disorderly government, endless wars, and despotism based upon brutal force, man deteriorated. Then nations left justice to Providence, because they believed more in miracles than they did in man's honesty. (1) Uncertain of the morrow, their only desire was to live, to defend honour, goods, and life; such were the only thoughts which absorbed them all, and thus nations sank into a state of materialism no longer animated by intelligence. Still Christianity had her Apostles. At Rome, SS. Paschal I and Nicholas I, and Adrian III proved themselves worthy successors of S. Peter; and it was in the palace of Leo IV that Alfred the Great acquired those sciences and virtues which made him a model for Kings. (2)

At the same time S. Athanasius shed lustre over the See of Naples, and S. Ignatius over that of Constantinople. In France S. Benedict of Aniane was reforming monasteries; S. Ancharius was converting Sweden and Denmark in the North; the Slaves were listening to the voice of S. Methodius; the Bulgarians were sending to Rome for priests and books, while the blood of martyrs was deluging Spain. But the

---

(1) It is generally believed that judicial duels, and ordeals by iron and water, were introduced by the Lombards. Ordeals were carried out at Rome in the church of S. Pancras. This kind of jurisprudence, then common throughout Europe, was only completely abolished in the thirteenth century by the fourth Lateran Council.

(2) Voltaire says:— "I know not if ever man existed on the earth more worthy the respect of posterity than Alfred the Great."

time was not far distant when, by the help of ignorance and lawlessness, corruption was to enter the holy place; this being, indeed, the most bitter trial which God had reserved for His Church! In charging Peter to "confirm his brethren" in the faith, Jesus Christ had founded the truth upon him as though upon a rock; but Our Lord did not promise either to him or to his successors impeccability which would have made them gods. No one need therefore be surprised that evil passions occasionally crept into the hearts of some of the Pontiffs; for, although they became ministers of Providence, they did not cease to be mortal: it is also fair to acknowledge that divine light was never obscured by their vices, it never failed in their keeping; through generations it has shone brightly above the false glimmer of reason, as clearly as on the day when it first dawned upon the world: "Habitantibus in regione umbræ mortis, lux orta est eis." (1)

(1) Isaias, IX, 2,

CHAPTER X.

Quomodo obscuratum est aurum, mutatis est color optimus?
Jeremias.

Vindicaverat omnia sibi libido, sæculari potentiâ freta, insaniens, castro percita dominandi.
Baronius.

TENTH CENTURY.

O period in the history of Christian Rome is so deeply painful as that between BENEDICT IV and SYLVESTER II. Popes no longer won a martyr's crown, as did those holy Pontiffs under the Roman Emperors; neither were they conspicuous for virtue, as were many who lived during the reigns of the Eastern Emperors, and of Charlemagne and his successors. The Popes were often the sport and nominees of factions, and constantly only representatives of lay power which usurped the holy place. The tenth century shows us what the Church may become, when instead of commanding she obeys, and when Popes instead of being "Priests and Kings" are simply courtiers. Therefore we cannot be surprised that we come across a Pope without holiness, dignity, or power, who

allowed even the government of Rome to fall into the hands of an immoral woman and low men. Yet, in spite of his vices which appeared to belie the divinity of religion, even he upheld the dignity of the church in a manner respected by saints.

The clergy have always promoted civilisation: they opened schools, founded libraries, preserved and copied ancient manuscripts, practised medicine, cultivated waste lands, and became the advocates and protectors of the defenceless. If the morals of the clergy were not always in accordance with the sanctity of their mission, if they occasionally took part in quarrels, they never failed in their duties of instructing the people, who consequently owed them a debt of deep gratitude. If they had vices, they were those of the period; and in no other profession were so many virtues to be found as in the ranks of the clergy.

Leo V and Christopherus occupied the Apostolic Chair but for a brief moment; Sergius III however reigned seven years. He was descended from the Counts of Tusculum, and was placed on the throne by one of the powerful factions who disputed for the sovereignty of the Roman States. A woman of senatorial rank was at the head of this party, indeed she was occasionally called Senatrix. Baronius mentions that she was singularly beautiful, possessing a mind fertile in resources, and that her daring, encouraged by her liaison with Adalbert, Marquess of Tuscany, was unlimited. She had succeeded, by aid of adultery (ex adulterii potentia), in forming a sort of kingdom within the city. Her name was Theodora;

she had two daughters, one called by her own name, Theodora, the other Maria or Mariuccia, more generally known as Marozia. The daughters followed their mother's example, and exercised tyrannical sway based upon intrigue and vice. Possessed of Hadrian's Mole, now the Castle of S. Angelo, this family turned it into an impregnable fortress, and from its height they domineered for more than fifty years both Rome and the Pontiffs.

Liudprand, a writer who is often at fault, says that SERGIUS was abjectly enslaved to every whim and caprice of Theodora; and it must be admitted that his account has generally been accepted by history: but, on the other hand, Flodoard, an old Frankish monk, speaks of Sergius as having been, for more than seven years, a cause of triumph and joy to the Church. All we can do is to record these two adverse opinions. (1)

SERGIUS III rebuilt the Lateran Basilica which had been destroyed by several earthquake shocks, in 896, leaving only the portico and apse standing. Its reconstruction, begun in 905, was completed in two years. The new edifice was adorned with paintings and mosaics, and the memory of its restorer preserved in several inscriptions, in which Sergius is called the pious Pontiff (Pius Papa).

ANASTASIUS III succeeded him in 911 and was remarkable for the gentleness of his government (blando moderamine), according to the words of his

---

(1) Baronius appears to accept the opinion of Liudprand, Muratori that of Flodoard.

epitaph. LANDO, raised to the See in 913, only reigned a few months, after which JOHN X took possession of the Apostolic Chair in 914. Here we again come across Liudprand and his anecdotes. By his account we are to believe that John owed his election entirely to Theodora, in whose vices he shared. Flodoard limits himself to the statement that John, after having wisely ruled over the Church of Ravenna, was called to the government of the mother Church; and that, for fourteen years, he distinguished himself by his zeal in adorning her, and in preserving peace. But the great glory of JOHN X was that he freed Italy from the Saracens, who had carried their advanced posts to the banks of the Garigliano.

Strong in the support of Berengar, King of Northern Italy, whom he had consecrated Emperor on Easter Day, 915, this Pontiff succeeded in forming a strong league which was joined by Berengar, the Greek Emperor, and the Princes of Capua, Salerno, Benevento, and Spoleto. The Pope, placing himself at the head of their troops, annihilated the Saracens in a bloody battle, and re-entered Rome in triumph. There unfortunately he was fated to meet the all-powerful courtesans who were reigning in the Castle of S. Angelo. About this time Theodora died; but Marozia succeeded her. Her first husband was the Marquess Alberic, whom Leo of Ostia styles (doubtless after his marriage to Marozia) consul of the Romans. Towards 925 she married Guido of Tuscany, and they plotted together to slay the Pope.

Muratori writes, "Pope John could not put up with the domineering of Marozia and of Guido, Duke of Tuscany, who continued more and more to usurp the temporal government of Rome. Discord therefore prevailed between them, and no doubt the Pontiff, who was a man of courage (uomo di petto), lost no opportunity of maintaining his rights, and of beating down those disturbers of his lawful authority. A frightful sacrilege put an end to this struggle. Guido and Marozia assembled a body of "sbirri" who one day entered the Lateran Palace and, in the very presence of the Pontiff, assassinated his brother Peter who was particularly obnoxious to the Duke of Tuscany; after which they laid hands on the Pope and cast him into a dungeon. It was not long before the unfortunate John ended his days; whether their natural term was cut short by sorrow or by another crime is unknown. In Liudprand's time a rumour was afloat that he had been smothered."

Leo VI and Stephen VII rapidly succeeded each other upon the throne, which, after them, fell into the hands of Marozia's family. John XI was in reality this woman's son by Alberic, her first husband, and Pope Sergius was not his father, as asserted by Liudprand. Meanwhile Marozia, being a widow for the second time, offered her hand to Hugh of Provence, promising him, as a bait, the lordship of Rome. Hugh accepted, and in 932 took possession of the Castle of S. Angelo. His pride then rose to the pitch of insanity; he even affected to treat the Roman nobility with scorn. Muratori relates, "But, what was worse, Marozia's young son Alberic, by her first busband, having been ordered by his mother to pour out some water, in order that King Hugh might wash his hands, did so with such bad grace that Hugh struck him in the face with the back of his hand. Alberic at once summoned the Roman nobles, and said to them, 'What have we not to fear in the future, after such a beginning, and such insolence!' These words were expressed in accents of hatred towards the Burgundians; anger fermented, the whole populace rose up in arms, closed the gates of the city, and marched off to besiege the Castle of S. Angelo. King Hugh was so terrified that, not considering himself safe in the fortress, he was let down over the wall on the side facing the Campagna, when he hastily rejoined his troops outside the town, then, placing himself at their head, fled, covered with ignominy from the duchy of Rome.

"The Romans, weary of being governed by a woman, took this opportunity of proclaiming Alberic as their Prince and lord; fearing if they re-installed Pope John, as in duty bound, they would in reality be handing it back to his mother Marozia. Alberic, on the other hand, wishing to secure his position, imprisoned his mother Marozia, and placed such a strong guard about the Pope that henceforth he could do nothing without Alberic's knowledge and consent." (1)

Alberic thus remained master of Rome, exercising supreme power in that city, sometimes under the title of Prince, at others as Consul of all the Romans.

---

(1) Annali d'Italia, 932.

Coins still exist bearing his name, conjointly with that of the reigning Pope. Several are mentioned by Coppi of Popes MARINUS and AGAPETUS which have engraved on them the words ALBERICUS or ALBER. PRI. (Albericus Princeps). Alberic died in 954.

His memory and that of Marozia attach themselves not only to S. Angelo, which was their palace and fortress, but also to one of the most sacred and beautifully situated monuments of Rome, the church of S. Maria-Aventina, built by Alberic in the house where he was born. (1) Strange coincidence! Marozia's house was raised over the ruins of the temple of the Bona Dea, and her son transformed it into a monastery under the invocation of the Virgin! The tranquillity of this spot, the beauty of the landscape which takes in the Tiber, Janiculum, S. Peter's, with Rome melting away in the far distance on the right, affords a strange contrast to the memories of tumult, tyranny, and murder which the name of Marozia recalls. It is possible to imagine that woman at Hadrian's Mole, but not at S. Maria-Aventina.

S. Odo, Abbot of Cluny, was summoned to Rome during these sad days by LEO VII, who wished him to mediate for peace between the contending parties. Odo was alike distinguished for his intellectual power and personal holiness. Gifted with exceptional genius, both as a poet and musician, he left the Court of Duke William of Aquitaine, while still very young, to dedicate his life to God's service in the church

---

(1) See Coppi, "Memorie Colonneri", p. 7.

of S. Martin of Tours. He used to sleep on the bare floor, prayed, fasted, almost entirely abstaining from wine, contrary to Frankish habit, "extra naturam Francorum", as an old chronicle expresses it. But these early mortifications did not satisfy his ardent devotion; he therefore set out with a friend, whose views agreed with his own, to look for another monastery in France, where the discipline was more severe, and where human passions would not be recalled; they first stopped at Baume, in Burgundy, after which Odo was elected Abbot of Cluny, and the fame of his virtues spread afar.

When he came to Rome in 936, his humility, learning, and boundless charity, made him an object of universal esteem. He lodged at the monastery of S. Paul, where he restored the ancient severity of its rule; his authority was so greatly respected that he succeeded in stilling hatred, and producing peace among the quarrelling factions.

But, before two years had elapsed, hostilities broke out afresh. Then Odo returned to Rome, and again persuaded the combatants to lay down their arms. In 942 he visited the holy city for the last time, at the request of Pope STEPHEN VIII, and employed himself not only in re-establishing peace, but in the reformation of monastic orders, according to his pious custom. Unfortunately he was attacked by a malignant fever which exhausted his strength. The saint hailed the approach of death with joy; the only favour he asked from heaven was that he might return to the tomb of S. Martin to breathe his last sigh on the spot where, in his youth, he had consecrated his life to God. (1) This prayer was granted: he returned to France to die, and was buried in the church of S. Julian of Tours, which had been raised from its ruins chiefly through his instrumentality.

STEPHEN VIII, MARTIN III, and AGAPETUS II were charitable and devout Popes. According to Baronius, STEPHEN VIII so incurred the hatred of King Otho that he became the victim of a sacrilege. He was cruelly beaten and so terribly disfigured that henceforth he avoided observation, "although surely," proceeds the illustrious historian, "this stigma received from the ministers of Satan, in a righteous cause, is more of an ornament than a shame." Muratori disbelieves in this outrage on the part of a Prince who at that time had no power whatever in Rome.

MARTIN III devoted his pontificate to the reformation of both the regular and secular clergy, to the reestablishment of the Basilicas and to the relief of the needy. Continued disturbances afflicted society; wars raged everywhere, and the Pope, powerless even in Rome, became more energetic in his endeavours to restore peace among Christians. The author of the life of S. Udalric attributes the gift of prophecy to Pope MARTIN.

AGAPETUS, his successor, is described as being most holy "sanctissimus" by contemporary historians.

(1) At this period LEO VII, writing to Hugh the Great, Duke of the French, speaks of the tomb of S. Martin as being, after the tombs of the Apostles, the most famed of all the places visited by pilgrims.

Octavian, a youth of eighteen or nineteen years of age, son of Alberic the patrician, having succeeded to his father's authority at Rome, was elected Pope in 956. Octavian took the name of John XII, being the first Pope who changed his name on ascending the Papal throne. It was the common opinion that he took the name of John in memory of those words of the Gospel; "Fuit homo missus a Deo, cui nomen erat Joannes." (1) His morals and character were such, however, as to make him only worthy of being Marozia's grandson. His chief act as Pope noted in history was that he revived the Imperial title in favour of the German Princes of the Saxon dynasty. The tyranny of the descendants of Theodora at Rome was to be followed by that of the descendants of Henry the Fowler.

Let us take note of the position of Italy at the accession of John XII. She was groaning beneath the heavy oppression of Berengar II and of his son Adalbert, who from the banks of the Po held the whole Peninsula in subjection. It was under these circumstances that John sent legates to Otho the Great imploring his aid. Otho immediately set forth after taking an oath to exalt the Roman church and her rulers to the utmost of his power, to ensure to the Pope "his life, his limbs and his dignity," to take no step at Rome, concerning the Romans, without his participation, and to restore to the Church all the lands of which she had been deprived. He added:—
"He, to whom I shall entrust the kingdom of Italy,

---

(1) S. John I, v. 6.

shall swear to be your support and aid in defending the lands of S. Peter. So may God and the holy Gospels help me!"

The German Prince was received in Rome with confidence and hope. He received the Imperial crown from John XII, and Otho solemnly ratified the donations made by Pepin, Charlemagne, and Louis le Débonnaire. He even added several towns, Rieti and Amiterne, with their fisheries, only reserving for himself the right of suzerainty which the Western Emperors had enjoyed, as well as the right of approving and confirming elections of Popes. The clergy and nobility of Rome then swore fealty to him as defender of the Church, always excepting that fidelity promised to the Apostolic lord, according to the terms of the oath previously agreed upon between EUGENIUS II and Lothair.

But Otho's authority soon showed itself selfish rather than protecting, and John XII summoned Berengar's son to Rome to defend him against the Emperor. On receiving this piece of news, Otho, who had quitted the Peninsula, sent emissaries to Rome to sound the inhabitants as to their views. They were divided in opinion; but many complained of the Pope's immorality, and were consequently inclined to embrace the Imperial cause. They reproached John XII with giving away governments, even crosses, and gold chalices from S. Peter's, to his concubines; of transforming the Lateran, once the abode of saints, into a place of evil repute, and of permitting the Basilicas to fall into ruins, so that the altars were no longer sheltered from rain, and the lives of the faithful were no more in safety. (1)

Encouraged by the support he found among a portion of the population, Otho retraced his steps to Rome, which he entered without difficulty; while John XII and Berengar's son fled with a considerable amount of valuables taken from S. Peter's. The Emperor then assembled a Council, or Conventicle, composed of forty Bishops and fourteen Cardinals. In this Council the most serious charges were brought against John XII who was deposed and Leo VIII was elected in his stead.

However wicked John XII conduct may have been, the right to depose him was very properly denied to this meeting of Bishops. The Romans divided into two parties: a rebellion took place during Otho's sojourn in the town, which he repressed with rigorous severity. But he had scarcely left the Papal States when Leo VIII had to flee, for John XII returned, summoned by the populace, and gave orders that two of the Emperor's partisans should be cruelly mutilated. John XII did not long survive his restoration to the Apostolic See. The circumstances of his death are unknown; for no one is bound to believe, on the isolated word of Liudprand, one of the forty Bishops who deposed him, that the devil first struck the Pontiff on the forehead, and then pushed him, without consolation or the Sacraments, into the tomb.

---

(1) See Liudprand and Baronius.

John XII founded a chapel, beneath the portico of the Lateran church, which he dedicated to S. Thomas. This chapel served as a vestry or secretarium to the Popes. The same Pontiff decorated the eastern portico of the atrium at S. Peter's with a mosaic, representing Our Lord in the act of blessing with one hand, and embracing S. Peter with the other, the saint is represented holding three keys and a cross. To the right of the Saviour, according to Greek custom, stands S. Paul; while above is the inscription: "Tibi, Christe, sit laus, honor et gloria".

The Romans elected Benedict V to succeed him, he was a learned and virtuous priest; but Otho claimed the right of upholding Leo, whom he had proclaimed Pope during the life of John XII. He therefore besieged the city, and permitted no one to leave without undergoing some kind of mutilation (1). Finally the city yielded, and Leo VIII was replaced by Otho upon the Papal throne.

Leo then held a Council in the Lateran Basilica, the Emperor being present as well as the magistrates and people. Benedict V was summoned to appear before it, and came arrayed in full Pontifical vestments. Leo made him sit on the ground, tore off the pallium, stole, and chasuble, and broke his pastoral staff before all the people. Soon afterwards Benedict was carried off to Hamburg by Otho, where he lingered one year, edifying the Saxons by his virtuous example.

After the decease of Benedict V and of Leo VIII, John XIII assumed the Papal tiara, and incurred the

---

(1) Fleury, "Hist. Ecclés."

enmity of the Roman nobility by his haughty manners. One thing is certain, that, during the first year of his reign, he was taken prisoner and confined in the Castle of S. Angelo, and eventually sent to a fortress in Campania; but, after eleven months, the nobles out of fear of the Emperor, who was advancing on Rome, decided on recalling him. Otho, however, severely punished the authors of this revolt, of whom twelve were hanged, and Peter, prefect of the city, was handed over to the Pope who condemned him to exile after being paraded through the streets sitting backwards on an ass.

BENEDICT VI, who succeeded John XIII in 972, only reigned eighteen months. Crescentius, a grandson of the unchaste Theodora, then held absolute sway in the city of Rome. He seized upon Benedict, imprisoned him in the Castle of S. Angelo, and, after having proclaimed Franco the deacon Pope, who took the name of BONIFACE VII, he delivered the legitimate Pope over to his mercy. Franco gave orders to strangle him. This time, however, the guilty one did not profit by his crime, for the indignant Romans drove him out of the city, and he took refuge in Constantinople. Ambition was not, however, dead in the heart of this scheming brigand; he brooded over it during the nine years of his exile, then, in 985, he suddenly reappeared at Rome, during the pontificate of JOHN XIV. (1)

---

(1) Benedict VI was succeeded by DONUS or DOMNUS II, BENEDICT VII, and JOHN XIV. This last was called Peter. He was the second Pope who changed his name, it is thought out of respect for the great Apostle.

He seized the Pontiff and condemned him to be starved to death in S. Angelo, so in this manner he retained his power until his death which occurred some months later. Franco was so detested that the mob seized his corpse, pierced it with lances, and left it exposed in the public square at the foot of Constantine's statue.

It was during Franco's intrusion, and the troubles it caused the Church, that Otho II and his mother, S. Adelaide, offered the Papal throne to S. Mayeul, Abbot of Cluny. S. Mayeul refused, for, being a simple though learned monk, he was averse to grandeur, and had already refused a bishopric. (1) S. Mayeul went twice to Rome: on returning to his monastery the second time he and his companions were captured when crossing the Alps by some Saracens, who had established themselves on the shores of the Mediterranean. Travellers from various lands had followed him, hoping that his sanctity would be their protection. This holiness became an object of respect and veneration even to the infidels, who were kind to their captives until they were ransomed by Princes and religious.

Among other saints who performed the pilgrimage to the tomb of the Apostles during the tenth century, history mentions S. Odo of Canterbury, who made the journey with Duke Athelm; S. Dunstan, to whom John XII gave the pallium; S. Udalric or Ulrich

---

(1) S. Mayeul answered Otho's proposal by saying, first, that the undertaking was beyond his strength; secondly, that the Romans and he differed as much in habits as they did in nationality.

of Augsburg, who dragged himself thither in a dying condition in 972; S. Adalbert of Prague, S. Nilus of Rossano, and S. Romuald; all steadfast and brave warriors of the faith, whose virtues were noble examples to those dissipated men who defiled the dignity of the sacerdotal ministry.

It was during the Pontificate of JOHN XVI that S. Adalbert left his bishopric of Prague where, in spite of all his endeavours, the clergy married, and the laity lived in shameful polygamy, even publicly selling Christian slaves to the Jews. Adalbert, much disheartened, withdrew to the monastery of S. Alexis at Rome on Mt. Aventine, which had been recommended to him by S. Nilus. Twice he was recalled to his diocese, and twice he reluctantly obeyed, quitting with regret that peaceful retreat in which the presence of his fellow men was manifested only by their virtues. (1) Recognising the futility of his labours in Bohemia, Adalbert carried the Gospel to the heathen in Poland where he underwent martyrdom on April 23rd 997.

John XVI was succeeded in 996 by a relative of the Emperor Otho III, named Bruno, who was raised to the throne by imperial influence, and assumed the name of GREGORY V.

Since the time of Otho, or Otto the Great, the German sceptre had remained in the family of Henry the Fowler. Otho the Great was succeeded in 973

---

(1) The monastery of S. Alexis possessed at that time several monks of great virtue, among whom were S. Nilus, and S. Leo of Nonantula.

by his son, Otho the Red, whose ten years' reign was made up of victories and disasters. This Prince aspired to the conquest of Magna Græcia; but, being defeated in a bloody battle, and made prisoner on a galley, from which he escaped by swimming, his only remaining ambition was to obtain the coronation of his son, Otho III, after which he withdrew to Rome, where he died while still a young man. His treasures were divided by his will between churches, the poor, his companions in arms, and his sister Matilda. Otho II was buried on the eastern side of the enclosure in front of S. Peter's. A mosaic on his porphyry tomb represented Jesus Christ, standing between S. Peter and S. Paul, in the act of blessing. The faithful always knelt down before this tomb on entering the church.

During the Pontificate of Gregory V, Otho III came to Rome to receive the Imperial crown. Now, the Romans secretly hated the Germans; and Crescentius, (1) who for thirty years, in spite of the Emperors and Popes, had maintained his power over the city, was still the energetic and intrepid representative of this hatred. S. Angelo was by turns either the centre of his influence or his place of refuge, according to the changes in his fortunes, and was indeed now only known by the name of Camp of Crescentius (castra Crescentii).

During Otho III sojourn at Rome, in 996, he wished to exile this rebel; but Gregory V dissuaded

---

(1) This must be Crescentius the younger, the other Crescentius dying a monk in 984. (Note by translator).

him from doing so. The Pope soon had reason to repent of his generosity; for scarcely had the Emperor returned to Germany than Crescentius contrived that Philagathus, a Greek, should be elected Pope, under the name of JOHN XVI, (1) and Gregory, despoiled of everything, fled. Otho at once returned to Rome, accompanied by Gregory, who had solemnly excommunicated Philagathus at a Council held at Pavia. On their approach Crescentius shut himself up in the Castle of S. Angelo, and the antipope endeavoured to escape; but he was captured by the imperialists, who cut off his nose, and, tearing out his tongue and eyes, cast him thus mutilated into a prison.

S. Nilus, countryman and friend of Philagathus, (2) had often urged him to shun glory and vain honours; so, when he was told of what tortures were inflicted upon the antipope, he was deeply moved and, in spite of his age, and the austerities of Lent, started off at once, hoping to rescue the unfortunate victim. Pope and Emperor went forth to meet him; they took him by the hand and led him to the patriarchal palace, overwhelming him with honours and respect.

(1) Sometimes JOHN XV, who died before consecration, is reckoned as a Pope, sometimes he is not. The John, son of Leo, elected in 985, immediately on the death of John, son of Robert (the John XV who died before consecration), was called by the Romans of that day — John XVI. But when Crescentius obtained the election of Philagathus, in 997, his party reckoned John, son of Leo, as John XV, and consequently called their nominee JOHN XVI (Note by translator).

(2) Previous to his intrusion Philagathus had been Archbishop of Ravenna, and had held high dignities at Rome and in the Imperial Court.

But the holy monk said to them:— "Spare me; I am only a sinner, an old man approaching his end, and totally unworthy; it is more becoming that I should bow down and pay reverence to your high dignities. It is not for glory or wealth that I am here; but to entreat your clemency for one who has served you well, who baptised you both, and whom you have so cruelly deprived of sight and otherwise ill-treated. Give him up to me that we may weep together over our sins." (1)

The Emperor promised to grant S. Nilus his request, provided he would accept the government of a monastery at Rome, and undertake not to leave the city, which would then profit by the wisdom of his counsels, and the example of his virtues. S. Nilus, who loved his peaceful home, and disliked the noisy world, hesitated; but Otho offered him the monastery of S. Athanasius-ad-aquas-Salvias, then occupied by Greeks, and in a most retired position. Whereupon S. Nilus, from desire to save Philagathus, accepted the Imperial proposals. But, at the very time he was thus sacrificing his most cherished desires, Philagathus was being paraded through the streets, clad in ragged sacerdotal robes, seated backwards upon an ass whose tail had been placed in his hands. On learning this, the saintly old man left Rome shocked and broken-hearted.

Meanwhile the Castle of S. Angelo resisted all the battering engines brought against it, and Crescentius appeared likely to resume the Imperial power. According to Italian writers, recourse was then had

(1) Fleury, "Hist. Ecclés."

to treachery; Crescentius was promised his life if he would surrender the fortress. No sooner had he done so than Otho gave orders that his head should be cut off, and flung from the top of the Castle. His body was afterwards hung up by the feet, and, as a last token of victory, the Emperor dishonoured the tribune's widow. (1)

After such scenes it is pleasant to look upon the noble figure of S. Romuald who entered the presence of Otho, like Nathan before David, to demand an account of his perjury; "Quare ergò contempsisti verbum Domini, ut faceres malum in conspectu meo?" (2)

Otho's pride fell before God's minister: he made a pilgrimage barefooted to Monte-Gargano, (3) and passed the Lenten season of 999 in fasting and mortification, at the monastery of S. Apollinaris-in-Classe near Ravenna.

Many writers condemn the anathemas pronounced against some of the sovereigns of the middle ages, and the penances imposed upon them, as being needless humiliations of their royal dignity; as though the reparation could be a greater indignity than the

---

(1) German historians merely state that the Castle was carried by assault and Crescentius beheaded after the victory.

(2) II Kings, XII, 9.

(3) Monte-Gargano rises at the extreme boundary of Puglia (Apulia), above Manfredonia, its appearance is that of a promontory projecting into the sea. On its summit is a vast cavern, which has been transformed into a church dedicated to S. Michael the Archangel. On the 8th May a solemn festival is held there annually to commemorate an apparition of S. Michael. See the legend in the Roman Breviary.

fault. It was on the contrary a great lesson of equality and justice given to Princes and nations. The prophets of the Lord did not spare either Saul or David because they had been anointed with holy oil. It is dangerous to assign inviolable autocracy to monarchs; for in order to be superior to human nature it is necessary to possess superhuman virtues. If religion does not check them, nations become dissatisfied, and great reactions follow, striking at random and often mistaking what is right for wrong, and ending by the complete overthrow of society.

Gregory V died in February 999, and was buried at S. Peter's, near the tomb of his relative Otho II. His epitaph informs us that at Rome he preached in three different languages; in the vulgar tongue, in French and in Latin; and that he distributed clothes to twelve poor persons every Saturday.

His successor was Gerbert, Archbishop of Ravenna, who took the name of SYLVESTER II. Gerbert was born in Auvergne, and was educated in the monastery of Aurillac. Being subsequently attached to the Duke of Barcelona's court, he devoted himself to the study of the exact sciences, which the Spaniards, following the examples of the Arabs, were cultivating with great success. He afterwards accompanied the Duke of Barcelona to Rome, where his remarkable attainments attracted the attention of Pope John XIII, and of the Emperor Otho I who desired to attach him to his person. But love of study drew Gerbert to Reims, where the archdeacon Gérard had acquired a great reputation as a logician. Gerbert attended his classes; but, instead of a scholar, he was soon recognised as a master, and Archbishop Adalbéron was greatly pleased to entrust the metropolitan school to his care. Gerbert taught dialectics, rhetoric, arithmetic, geometry, astronomy, and music. "He was a man of great intellect and eloquence" (magni ingenii ac eloquii), says Richer, one of his pupils, and was the first who made "Gaul shine like a beacon light". Gerbert excelled in making the study of mathematics simple and elementary; he introduced the Arabic figures, endeavoured to diffuse the decimal system, and invented a calculating table which was divided into twenty-seven squares, by means of which multiplication and division could be produced mechanically. Music was scarcely known in France before Gerbert; but then it became quite popular. He arranged the various styles into a harmonical canon, distinguishing concords or symphonies by tones, semi-tones, and sharps. Astronomy had been an abstract science; but he made it live and speak by the invention of a revolving globe, which represented the equator, the poles, degrees and parallels, and the movement of the stars. He also constructed organs worked by hydraulics. This marvellous inventive genius brought him under the suspicion of magic; proofs of this were supposed to be found, not only in the marvellous powers of his intellect, but also in his never failing success, which had led the poor child of Auvergne from the cloister to the palace, and from the palace to the highest dignities, first at Reims, then at Ravenna, and finally at Rome. It is, however, a fact that these absurd calumnies were only uttered long after his death, and were the outcome of superstitious admiration awakened by his good fortune and works.

Gerbert, or rather Sylvester II, was the first Frenchman who occupied the Papal throne; he was also the first Pope who originated the idea of a crusade for the deliverance of the Holy Places; while its fulfilment was to be carried out by URBAN II, another French Pope, on a future occasion. In a letter addressed to Christendom, Sylvester makes Jerusalem speak: "O immaculate Bride of Christ, whilst thou art strong, thou of whom I am a member, great hope dwells within me that I may soon lift up my bruised head! How could I distrust thee, O mistress of the world, whilst thou dost acknowledge me to be as thine own! Rise up, then, O soldier of Christ, unfurl thy standard, take up thy arms! (Enitere ergò, miles Christi! esto signifer et compugnator!")

This eloquent appeal was unheard amidst the din of strife.

Rome enjoyed a span of peace during Sylvester II reign; but the inhabitants of Tibur were in ceaseless rebellion against Imperial authority. S. Romuald succeeded once in quieting them, and appeasing Otho's indignation; but on the second occasion they were obliged to submit to the Pope, who pardoned them. Some of the Romans then rebelled; the Imperialists instantly closed the gates; and Bernward, Bishop of Hildesheim, after confessing and giving Holy Communion to those persons who were in the palace, marched at their head bearing the sacred lance which belonged to the German Emperors. The rebels thereupon threw down their arms, and peace was restored without bloodshed.

About this time Otho III sent for the relics of S. Adalbert from Germany, and placed them beneath the altar of a church he was building on the island in the Tiber. This island, called in antiquity Lychaonia, from the temple of the Lychaonian Jupiter which stood there, had been formed, or at least increased, by the accumulation of sheaves from Tarquin's field, which the Roman used to throw into the river. During the Republic, a temple was built there dedicated to Æsculapius, in which for many centuries the priest had kept a serpent, which had been venerated by the common people as being that sacred serpent brought from Epidaurum. It was upon the site of this ancient temple that Otho raised the new church, and deposited, not only the relics of S. Adalbert, but those of a great many other saints and martyrs taken from the church of SS. Abbundius and Abbundantius near Mt. Soracte, and also the body of S. Bartholomew, which he had entreated the inhabitants of Benevento to give him, when making his pilgrimage to Monte-Gargano. S. Bartolomeo-in-Isola is one of Rome's most interesting monuments. Rebuilt by GELASIUS II in the twelfth century, one may yet see the old granite columns of the temple of Æsculapius, and a few remains of a marble and porphyry pavement, which was probably laid for Otho III Basilica.

Otho III died, on the 28th January, 1002, at Paterno in the Roman Campagna, poisoned according to tradition by the widow of Crescentius, which statement, however, is far from being authentic.

A few years before his death Otho paid a visit to the retreat of S. Nilus; and, on perceiving the low narrow huts which formed the monastery, he exclaimed:— "These are indeed the tents of Israel in the wilderness. Behold the inhabitants of the kingdom of heaven; the earth is not their home, for they are only pilgrims and travellers." Otho offered another monastery to the saint with a sufficient revenue for the maintenance of his monks. The saint replied, "He who has protected them hitherto will not forsake them when I am gone." "Ask me then," said the Emperor, "for anything you may require as though I were your son." S. Nilus, placing his hand upon the Emperor's heart, said, "Think of the salvation of your soul!"

S. Nilus was a Greek, for Calabria, the country of Pythagoras, had always been considered a portion of land belonging to the Hellenes. (1) He was born at the small town of Rossano, not far from Croton, near the shore where Sybaris stood, surrounded by every memento of ancient wisdom and luxury. S. Nilus who aspired to the highest virtues had been a victim to human passion. He had wished in his youth to marry a very beautiful girl, but when his illusions were dispelled he retired to a monastery. He founded successively the monasteries of Val-di-Luce and Val-de-Serperis. In his old age and on

---

(1) The little town of Rossano, where the saint was born, preserved the Greek language until the sixteenth century.

the approach of death he was informed that the Prince of Gaeta contemplated the removal of his remains to the town as holy relics for its protection. Then, infirm as he was, he rode off in search of some country where his name was unknown. The monks mourned his departure. "Console yourselves," said S. Nilus to them, "I am going to prepare a home to which I will summon my scattered sons."

S. Nilus selected a monastery near Tusculum dedicated to S. Agatha, and inhabited by Greek monks. The news of his arrival spread far and wide before he had recovered from the fatigues of his journey. The Roman nobles did their best to induce him to come to the tomb of the Apostles; the Count of Tusculum fell at his feet exclaiming, "I am unworthy of receiving so great a servant of God; but my house and possessions are at your service, do with them as you please." But S. Nilus replied that he had only come there to die.

He did however petition for a retired spot where he might pray in peace, whereupon the Count offered him Cicero's ruined villa in which probably his "Tusculan disputations" were written. The place was called Grotta-Ferrata, (1) and thick brushwood and undergrowth had converted the villa, to which the Roman orator had once invited Atticus and Quintus, into an almost inaccessible grotto.

But the monks whom S. Nilus had quitted set out one day to join their superior, clad in sheepskins

---

(1) Both the Basilians of Grotta-Ferrata and the Jesuits of Ruffinella claim that they occupy the site of Cicero's villa.

and sandals. The saint was overjoyed, and appointed Grotta-Ferrata for their meeting place; but his strength failed him, and he was unable to reach it; he then gave orders that he was to be buried without honours outside the church; after which he became unconscious for three days. Although unable to speak he prayed, and passed away surrounded by the monks of S. Agatha in 1005. His corpse was borne to Grotta-Ferrata, the brethren holding lighted candles and burning incense. The monks of Serperis arrived at the meeting-place in obedience to S. Nilus's command; they had lost their father, but would henceforth be protected by a saint.

Grotta-Ferrata is one of the most celebrated Abbeys in the neighbourhood of Rome: Bessarion dwelt there, and it is still occupied by Greek monks of the order of S. Basil, who preserve to this day the ancient liturgy and psalmody of the East. This venerable abbey stands in the fields between Frascati and Marino; it is approached by long avenues of elms and plane trees; high above the valley, through which a brook slowly winds, probably Cicero's Aqua crabra, splendid views are obtained over the Roman Campagna. The church of Grotta Ferrata is enriched by the frescoes of Annibale Caracci and Domenichino, which have made it famous in the annals of art. One of these represents S. Nilus curing a young epileptic, and another shows S. Nilus receiving the Emperor Otho III. Although they are beautiful and noble works, one cannot help regretting that the artists relied more on their genius than on Christian inspiration.

The sequel of events has carried us beyond the limits of the tenth century. We must return to it to mention that holy sanctuary which replaced the temple of Jupiter on the Capitol. Gibbon writes, "It was at Rome on the 15$\underline{\text{th}}$ October 1764, as I sat musing amidst the ruins of the Capitol while the bare-footed friars were singing Vespers in the temple of Jupiter, that the idea of writing the decline and fall of the city first started to my mind."

The temple of Jupiter Capitolinus was, as it were, the very centre of Roman power. Raised by the two Tarquins, re-built by Sylla, again by Vespasian, and finally by Domitian, each time with renewed magnificence, it responded worthily to its proud title of metropolis of the world. It was the fane of Minerva, goddess of wisdom and war; also of Juno, haughty and jealous, whose emblems were the peacock and owl; but more particularly that of the "very great" and "very good" god, the vanquisher of giants, Leda's swan, Europa's bull, Danae's golden rain, Ganymede's ravisher, Jovi optimo, maximo.

Such was the temple, and its gods, at the period of Rome's greatness! but at its decline the temple was abandoned. Barbarians abstracted the statues, and stripped it of its brazen roof as well as of the marble which had ornamented the portico, leaving only gaping ruins, which gradually vanished also, without leaving any fixed date for their disappearance.

As soon as the temple had ceased to be, a few monks set to work, raised up the fallen columns, one of which had supported the ceiling of the Emperor's bed-chamber, and had been a silent witness of the debaucheries of Nero and Tiberius. (1) In course of time these monks obtained the marbles of the temple of Romulus on the Quirinal as a gift, and utilized them in constructing a staircase of one hundred and twenty steps, which led to the summit of the Capitol. Thus a triumphal approach and splendid decorations for a modest church were formed out of these remains of temples to the gods. This church was named Aracœli and dedicated to the Virgin. The name signifies altar of heaven.

Aracœli recalls an ancient and interesting tradition. At the very time when Virgil was announcing the coming of a Virgin and Child, who should renew the Golden Age — "Jam redit et Virgo, redeunt Saturnia regna . . .;" when the whole world was expecting a Saviour; Augustus consulted the oracle as to the one who should succeed him as master of the world, and he received this reply:— "A Hebrew child, God himself, the Master of the gods, orders me to give up my place to him, and return sorrowfully to hell. Depart, therefore, from my altars, and do not consult me any further." (2)

Apparently Augustus raised an altar on the Capitol bearing the inscription:— "Ara primogeniti

---

(1) This column is the third to the left on entering, and bears the inscription "A cubiculo Augustorum".

(2) "Me puer Hebræus divos deus ipse gubernans
Cedere sede jubet tristemque redire sub Orcum;
Aris ergò dehinc tacitus abscedite nostris."

An excellent dissertation on this subject may be read in the "Annales de Philosophie chrétienne" by M. Bonnetty, Book XIV, p. 62.

Dei"; and another story relates that the Emperor beheld the Mother of God bearing the Infant Jesus in the glory of heaven, after which he never permitted his courtiers to address him by the title of God.

The venerable and ancient altar to which this tradition clings is still preserved at Aracœli. It stands to the left of the sanctuary, and during the seventeenth century a small cupola supported by columns of oriental alabaster was placed above it.

The date of the foundation of Aracœli is uncertain; but there is a distinct reference to it in 985, under the name of S. Mary of the Capitol, and for this reason it has not been mentioned until the tenth century. One fact remains, namely, that from the period when the temple of Jupiter was destroyed, possibly during the Pontificate of GREGORY the Great, an Oratory had existed amongst the ruins. This is at least the opinion of several learned archæologists.

Aracœli possesses, in addition to the antique altar from which it takes its name, a celebrated picture of the Virgin, and a much venerated statue of the Child-God, "il Santissimo Bambino". Every year, during the Christmas festival, this statue is on view, arrayed in silks and embroideries according to Italian custom. Pious exercises accompany this solemnity, and the sermon is preached by a child, Christmas being especially a holiday for children. It is very touching to hear a child expounding the faith as Our Lord Jesus Christ had done in the temple.

Their pure, sweet, voices always express innocence and candour.

> "Du cristal ou de l'or que notre encens émane,
> Le vase le plus pur est le cœur d'un enfant." (1)

The close of the tenth century was expected by the nations with fear and anxiety. They concluded that the end of the world was at hand, and were conjecturing the advent of Antichrist, on account of the invasions of the Huns and Scytho-Russians; their lively imaginations realising thereby the apparition of Gog and Magog, those mysterious people mentioned in the Apocalypse, "the number of whom is as the sand of the sea," (2) and that the devil, after a thousand years, should make war with the saints. They might also have noticed precursory signs of this terrible catastrophe in the utter corruption which was spreading like a hellish legion throughout the world; but man is not permitted to fathom the designs of God. The period which has just elapsed had witnessed the triumph of Christ's religion over reason, and that of truth over human power. Such prodigies of virtue had never previously been witnessed on earth. Religion henceforth possessed power and wealth, so that it was reserved for the following century to complete her work of civilisation, long checked by Barbarians and anarchy, and to stamp art, science, and literature with her own peculiar characteristics, and give them an impetus never experienced before. If the progressive development of

---

(1) Lamartine, "Harmonies."
(2) Apocalypse XX, v. 7.

our faculties was at some future date to embue us with unbounded confidence in our own powers, if every yoke was to become a burden, and laws unbearable, the Church had a duty to perform, in upholding the tottering fabric of society by means of the strong roots she had herself planted in deep soil throughout the world. It was reserved for her to triumph over the exhaustion and chaos produced by free thought, as once before she had prevailed in consequence of the enthusiasm awakened by the authority of the Word.

CHAPTER XI.

> À la cour du pape, se réunissaient tous les hommes sages et vénérables de l'Europe. Tous les trésors affluaient à cette cité sainte; Jérusalem était vengée; et Rome elle-même était devenue Jérusalem, la sainte résidence du gouvernement divin sur la terre.
>
> *Novalis.*

ELEVENTH CENTURY.

THE eleventh century witnessed the beginning of that bitter struggle, between the Church and the Empire, which German Protestant historians have, in late years, depicted with much learning and great impartiality. But, before noticing this duel between two adverse powers who frequently made Rome the centre of their strife, we must glance at the social condition of Europe at this period.

Europe was then almost without political laws; the possession of power, as well as its transmission, was regulated sometimes by force of circumstances, at others by virtue of certain customs, which, owing to their being still under discussion, could not be considered established laws. In France, power was transmitted in the same race, though not always in direct order of succession; (1) for, when the Mayors of the Palace, who were elective, obtained the crown, the elective principle prevailed; and even Charlemagne, when dividing his kingdom among his sons, felt he must ask the consent of the nation: "quem populus eligere velit ut patri suo succedat in regni hæreditate." (2)

In Germany elections were remarkably liberal; sometimes bastards, for instance Arnulf, were elected in preference to legitimate Princes to rule over the land.

This instability and dependence on power induced sovereigns, who were surrounded by ambitious and restless vassals, to obtain solemn and religious consecration, such as God had bestowed on Jewish Kings by the hands of His prophets.

It was a grand and noble idea thus to place the crown under God's protection, publicly acknowledging that Kings had a divine mission to perform during their reigns, which many only considered as a rich inheritance. But obligations were attached to this sacred rite; in exchange for the power and respect bestowed upon Kings at the altar, they were bound to give guarantees for good and just administration. Three things should be noticed in the ancient rite of consecration:— 1st, the monarch was enthroned on a shield and acclaimed by warriors who were asked

---

(1) Among the Franks and most barbarous nations, power was often confined to one family; but no woman might exercise it.

(2) Quoted by Montesquieu, "Esprit des Lois," XXXI, XVI.

by the Bishop, "Do you acknowledge Henry or Charles as your King?" 2nd, the Sovereign took an oath to govern with truth and equity; 3rd, the people, having heard this pledge made before God, then swore to be faithful to him.

It is true that all these obligations were quite independent of consecration; but it stamped them with a solemn character which rendered them more inviolable; and consequently, in the absence of any legal supervision, an imperative duty devolved on the clergy, namely, that of enforcing the performance of a contract, which had passed through their hands. Henceforth holy unction was sought by all Sovereigns, for it inspired nations with respect and loyalty to royal authority, and protected monarchs from incessant strife. Pepin was consecrated twice; first by S. Boniface, and again by Pope STEPHEN II: most Emperors were successively anointed at Aachen or Mainz and Rome. Consecration became a distinctive mark of royalty, Princes often securing it for their children during their own lifetime so as to ensure their succession.

The Church now possessed all powerful influence. First of all her clergy were invested with spiritual authority; her Apostles wandered to and fro from South to North, from West to East, courageously struggling against the last remains of idolatrous superstition. This authority was, however, not all that the clergy possessed; their schools have already been mentioned where they taught letters and sciences as conscientiously as they preached the faith; moreover, they tended the sick in hospitals, fed the poor, defrayed the expenses of travellers and protected the weak; in truth they concentrated in their mission all that constituted civilisation:— schools, hospitals, hostelleries and churches. This influence was all the more respected because it was based upon the services they had rendered; besides which the ranks of the priesthood were open to all; they were the living evidence of Christian equality, at a time when everyone was groaning beneath the weight of frequent and heavy oppression. The populace beheld with joy the monastic belfry rivalling the castle keep in influence and power.

The possessions of the clergy were formed and increased by successive donations, which were often the result of expiation for crimes, too frequent among the barely civilised Northern nations, among whom violence and murder, if bravely done, were considered honourable, in so much that the clergy were obliged to enforce the ancient canonical penances with the greatest severity, in order to counterbalance the debasing influence of these savage customs. Thus the guilty were often condemned to bestow abundant alms, the crime not being washed away thereby, but these alms were considered as a sort of satisfaction to outraged society. None the less, the criminal had to confess and perform the penances enjoined by the Church. If these alms were only made to the clergy, it was because the clergy alone were in possession of all charitable institutions. No doubt abuses crept into this system, that must happen in whatever man has a hand; but the idea of inflicting punishment upon the rich, by depriving them of their riches, gave the clergy the means of compensating the poor for all their privations, and was indeed a noble and saintly inspiration.

In addition to this the gifts bestowed by Christian charity were considerable. Kings were especially generous to the clergy, because the religious foundations were centres of civilisation, or, according to Ancillon, "schools of culture and obedience". Furthermore, the clergy by being made feudatories became an impregnable rampart against the encroachments of the nobles.

The nobles considered themselves, as in Germany, the companions of Princes, "comites"; the very word has been retained, and the *counts*, devoted in the hour of danger, though usually ambitious and stubborn, succeeded eventually in establishing half independent states, which were too often financially supported, in the words of Tacitus, "by war and rapine." From this period war became the normal condition of society; when Prince was not contending with Prince, it was noble against noble, or against pilgrims and merchants, in mountain passes and on the high roads throughout Europe. The Church, after vainly endeavouring to remedy this evil, at length instituted the "Truce of God", (1) and largely increased the number of sanctuaries.

The Truce of God was a sublime idea. It prohibited fighting between Advent and the Octave of the Epiphany, from Septuagesima to the Octave of

---

(1) The Truce of God was first started in France. Afterwards it was extended to the whole of Christendom by the Council of Clermont in 1095.

Pentecost, and on all Thursdays, Fridays, Saturdays, and Sundays throughout the year. Churches and monasteries within a radius of sixty feet were declared inviolable, and crosses were also placed at intervals along the roads to serve as sanctuaries for travellers.

Thus the Church, powerless to root up the evil, endeavoured to lessen it, making use of her spiritual thunders to preserve society from utter ruin. This ruin was imminent. Moral corruption was spreading under cover of anarchy, and assisted by ignorance which followed in its train. Ignorance allies men to beasts, and gives to them their habits. Amidst all this disorder it was impossible to pursue a course of uninterrupted instruction or general teaching. All attempts made by the clergy were powerless; they became evil themselves, neglecting their sacred duties and studies, and submitting to the corrupt and perverting influences which surrounded them. Simony soon aggravated the mischief. Kings asserted that, by virtue of their gifts to the clergy, they had the right of disposing of bishoprics and abbeys as fiefs, and of bestowing investiture of the cross and ring, as though they had spiritual authority. Now it so happened that these investitures were, more often than not, granted in return for money or vile compliance with the royal will; unity of purpose ceased to guide the Church; nobles, who were envious of the authority of Abbots and Bishops, bought nominations favourable to their interests; and, had it not been for the reaction of Christian feeling, everything would have been sold, even to S. Peter's throne.

Such was the state of religion and society in the eleventh century. Ardent faith was undoubtedly required not to despair of both. We cannot therefore wonder at the zeal, even the severity, of some of the Pontiffs, who were courageous enough to apply a red hot iron to the wound which was mortifying. It was no longer a question of the interests or vanity of a few passing men, it had become a question of the present and the future.

SYLVESTER II did not long survive the Emperor Otho III; he was buried in the church of S. John Lateran. When this church was rebuilt, in 1648, the marble tomb in which he lay was opened, and for a moment it seemed as though the onlookers beheld the Pontiff himself, arrayed in his episcopal vestments, with his mitre on his head, his arms crossed upon his breast; but, no sooner were these secrets of the tomb disclosed, than the apparition vanished, leaving nothing else behind but a few ashes, a cross and a pastoral ring!

JOHN XVII, JOHN XVIII and SERGIUS IV reigned peacefully during the years of rest Robert I of France and S. Henry II of Germany procured for the Church. BENEDICT VIII election was contested by a faction; but the antipope, who was set up in opposition to him, was driven out of Rome. He vainly appealed to King Henry, for that monarch set out for Italy and solemnly recognised BENEDICT VIII. The coronation of S. Henry and of his Queen, S. Cunegund, took place on the 22nd February 1014, in the Basilica of S. Peter. Twelve senators stood around the King and Queen; some were clean shaven in Roman fashion, others wore long moustachios like the Germans, and all carried wands. At this ceremony the Imperial globe first made its appearance. Glaber, a monk, tells us that, "The Pope had ordered a golden apple to be made, ornamented by two circles of precious stones, and surmounted by a cross. The apple typified the world; the cross, religion, which the Emperor was bound to protect; the jewels represented virtues he ought to possess." The Emperor said, "This present could not be better bestowed than on those who have trodden under foot all the pomps and vanities of the world, thus enabling them to follow the cross more freely." He therefore sent the gift to the Abbey of Cluny.

Consecrations of Emperors had become frequent since the days of Charlemagne, and the ceremonial was now well defined. Three Bishops used to receive the Emperor at the steps of S. Peter, giving him their benediction; after which they conducted him to the Pope, who awaited him in the little church of S. Maria-in-torre, so called from the tower of the Basilica. The future Emperor and his suite then kissed the feet of him who represented Jesus Christ, and the Emperor took the following oath: "In the name of Our Lord Jesus Christ, I promise and swear, boldly and resolutely, fidelity to God, to Blessed Peter His Apostle, and to the Blessed Vicar of Our Lord, Pope N., as also to his successors, canonically instituted; and I undertake henceforth to be the protector and defender of this Holy Roman Church, of your person and of your successors, according to my knowledge and power, and in good faith, as long as I may be upheld by divine aid. So may God and His holy Apostles help me."

The Sovereign Pontiff then put the following questions to the Emperor:— "Do you wish to live in peace with the Church? Do you wish to become a son of the Church?" On the Emperor answering three times in the affirmative, the Pope said:— "Then we give you peace, even as the Lord gave it to His disciples. We also receive you as a son of the Church." Then he kissed him in the form of a cross, on the forehead, the chin, the cheeks, and the mouth, and, throwing his mantle over him, he led him from the bronze gate across the Atrium to the silver gate, holding him by the right hand. Meanwhile the choir sang, "May the Lord, the God of Israel, be praised and exalted." The Pope then entered the Basilica accompanied by the strains of the antiphon, "Peter, lovest thou me?" When the King was brought in, the Pope asked him, whether he desired to be pious, temperate, unselfish, gentle, and mild, and whether he sincerely accepted all the articles of the Christian faith. Upon the Prince answering in the affirmative, the Bishop of Ostia anointed him on the shoulders and the right arm, after which the Pope placed the Imperial crown upon his head before the Confession of S. Peter. He also gave him the ring, the sword and the sceptre, sometimes also the golden orb filled with ashes; a symbol both of power and of nothingness.

On his part, the newly made Emperor presented the Pope with bread, candles and money; then, after having received the kiss of peace, he partook of Holy Communion. Lastly, on being led to the Oratory of S. Maurice, which opened on to the north transept of the Basilica, he was invested with boots and spurs, after which he left in procession with the Pope.

This solemn consecration therefore constituted the Emperor as "protector and defender of the Church," and it was on this ground that he was permitted to receive the oath of the clergy, who "swore to be faithful to him, saving that fidelity promised to the Apostolic Chair." (1)

S. Henry's sojourn at Rome was marked by an addition to the Roman liturgy. Up to that time the Mother Church, being considered free from heresy, had not been accustomed to proclaim the faith during Mass by chanting the Creed. But, on the request of S. Henry to BENEDICT VIII, this custom was abandoned, and from that time the Symbol was sung in the Roman churches, as well as in all churches throughout Christendom.

S. Henry accompanied by S. Cunegund often went by night to S. Maria Maggiore where he remained in prayer until dawn.

This saint was also a hero; but, although victorious in Flanders, Bohemia, Lombardy, and Calabria, this monarch, whose name was mighty, whose undertakings were always successful even in those disturbed times, aspired only to a life of repose and prayer in the cloister. Ambition and power with all their

---

(1) "Salva fide quam repromisi Domino apostolico." This formula had been agreed upon by Pope EUGENIUS II and the Emperor Lothair. (See Rohrbacher, vol. XI, p. 461.)

fleeting passions wear out a man; but prayer can never exhaust him.

BENEDICT VIII distinguished himself by the vigour with which he repulsed the Saracens, who had already seized upon part of Tuscany. He marched against them at the head of the Bishops and notaries of the churches, defeating the enemy in a bloody battle, and capturing their Queen. Historians observe that this Queen was beheaded, and that the Pope took possession of her golden crown studded with precious stones. The Saracen leader incensed by the death of his consort, and the destruction of his army, sent Benedict a bag filled with chestnuts, informing him that in the following year there would be the same number of soldiers ready to avenge him. Benedict replied with a sack of millet seed, in order to show there would be plenty of men to repulse him. The Saracens however did not return.

Then the Emperors of Constantinople, awaking from their long slumber, made up their minds to reconquer Italy, for they still retained several strongholds in Magna Græcia. Basil's forces therefore left Calabria in 1022, and, marching northwards, took possession of Benevento, even menacing Rome; but the Emperor Henry, appearing suddenly from the Adriatic shore, attacked and defeated them, marching across the ancient Grecian possessions as a conqueror, while the populace asked for mercy in the words "Kyrie eleison." Subsequently the Emperor and Pope visited Monte-Cassino, where the Emperor presented a copy of the Gospels bound in gold, and a gold chalice set with precious stones, as a thankoffering; after which they returned to their respective capitals, both dying shortly afterwards.

Benedict VIII was succeeded by JOHN XIX, his brother, who was (if we may believe Glaber) a layman, and merely elected by bribery. Henceforth simony became general; and, at John's death, Theophylactus, his nephew, a lad scarcely twelve years old, unscrupulously ascended the Apostolic throne, under the title of BENEDICT IX. Like his two predecessors he was related to the all powerful family of the Counts of Tusculum: but God did not permit that he should enjoy the authority procured for him by his father's gold. His vices, extortions, and cruelty, rendered him so obnoxious to the Romans that they drove him out in 1044. Benedict returned to his family and shortly afterwards besieged Rome at the head of a numerous army, even effecting an entrance into the city. But his life still continued to be so great a scandal to the Church that he, who ought to have been surrounded by the veneration of the faithful, merely earned contempt. The archpriest John Gratian at length offered him 1500 pounds provided he would abdicate; he accepted the money and laid down the sceptre.

John Gratian was elected Pope in his stead and became GREGORY VI. He was a humble virtuous man, whose first consideration was to restore order from the chaos which existed at Rome. All the possessions of the Church had been usurped; reckless adventurers infested the roads, and pilgrims were unable to approach the tombs of the Apostles except in large armed bands. At length the city became the theatre of daily recurring robberies and murders; people were assassinated even in the Basilicas; for no sooner was an offering laid upon an altar than bravos fell upon it, disputing for its possession, in order to spend it in rioting and on their concubines. (1)

Gregory first had recourse to exhortations and prayers; but hearts were hardened, and ears no longer heard. He therefore anathematized all who were turning the capital into a den of thieves. The Romans were accustomed to brigandage, so this unusual severity, after twenty-five years of license, drove them to revolt. They accordingly assembled under arms, uttering cries of "Death to the Pope". Gregory, however, was not alarmed, but summoned his troops, took possession of S. Peter's and put to death all sacrilegious plunderers. Despairing of victory, the rebels accused Gregory of simony, on account of those 1500 pounds which he had paid for Benedict's abdication. This money had only been given with the approval of the clergy, in order to put an end to the scandal which afflicted the Church: nevertheless Gregory referred the matter to the decision of a Council, which assembled at Sutri, Henry the Black, the new King of Germany, being present. Opinions were divided; therefore Gregory voluntarily laid aside the emblems of papacy, and withdrew to end his days in peaceful retirement at Cluny.

(1) "Supra sacra altaria gladii nudabantur; et oblationes accedentium vixdùm appositæ de manibus abripiebantur; abreptæ in comessationes et scortorum abusiones consumebantur." (Baron., "Ann. eccles." ad ann. 1044.)

A German, named Suidger, under the name of Clement II, next ascended the Pontifical throne, because, according to contemporary historians, "no one could be found at Rome with the necessary qualifications." That this was a fact is proved by the lamentations of S. Peter Damian and S. Anselm of Lucca.

S. Peter Damian wrote: "Because of our sins, no clergy remain worthy of the episcopate; they desire it well enough, but do nothing to deserve it... Simony is committed, not only by buying and selling Holy Orders, but also by selling synodical decrees; it is not for the purpose of providing what is necessary that men covet riches, but that their table, laden with viands, may exhale an odour of rare Indian spices, and that their honeyed wine may sparkle in crystal goblets; that, wherever they may go, their chambers may be hung with magnificent tapestry, both on walls and ceilings, and that their seats may be covered with rich stuffs ... Their beds are more sumptuously adorned than altars; purple is too simple, they require materials of variegated colours; and, as they despise lambs' wool, sable and ermine are brought from distant lands... No, the time has gone by when humility, mortification, and priestly discipline were exercised." He wrote to the Pope as follows, "When I visit you I hear jesting, witticisms, frivolity; while dissipation prevails to the utter destruction of piety and good example."

Peter Damian, with a few other enthusiastic men lived in the monastery of S. Croce d'Avellano; where, with a view to appease celestial wrath, they practised discipline by flagellation in imitation of what Christ endured before Calvary. Haircloths, or rather sharp pointed cuirasses, made a continual sacrifice of their lives; these apostles of suffering believing that this constant self-inflicted pain was the only remedy against the degrading instincts which ruin man. (1)

CLEMENT II reigned only a short time; at his death the simoniacal Benedict IX, who, in his retirement at Tusculum, still coveted the treasures of S. Peter, returned to Rome, and took possession of the patriarchal palace. He remained there during eight months, after which time, being filled with remorse for his many sins, he retired to Grotta-Ferrata to pray for pardon.

Rome at this time, by her internal disorders and corrupt elections, had so completely lost all respect that, on several occasions, Pontiffs were nominated by the Emperors, without consulting either the clergy or the people. Thus Henry the Black sent DAMASUS II from Brixen; and, after that Pope's death, a Diet held at Worms, presided over by Henry, elected Bruno, Bishop of Toul, to succeed him. Bruno was a holy and austere man. Being closely related to the Emperor might naturally lead him to expect that he would be eligible for ecclesiastical preferment; but his retiring nature made him dread the prospect; so, when the inhabitants of Toul selected him as their Bishop, he readily accepted, hoping that the direction of this small diocese would

---

(1) S. Dominic Loricatus (the breastplated) was a companion of S. Peter Damian.

shelter him from more brilliant responsibilities. With
many virtues he combined charming gifts of nature,
which greatly increased his good influence over others.
Lastly, the respect and holy affection which he inspired
were such that voters at the Diet unanimously proclaimed him Pontiff. Bruno declined; but the King
and nobles insisted. The good Bishop demanded
three days for consideration; during which time he
fasted and prayed, publicly confessed his sins, hoping
that, when his unworthiness became known, the
honours of the Papacy might be conferred on some
one more saintly. But the multitude answered his
humble avowal by affectionate entreaties; so Bruno,
faithful to tradition, acceded to the wishes of the
clergy and Roman populace. He started off in pilgrim's
attire for Rome, and throughout the journey prayers
alone issued from his lips. On passing through
Augsburg a voice addressed him in the words of the
Lord to Jeremias:— "For I know the thoughts that
I think towards you, saith the Lord, thoughts of
peace, and not of affliction, to give you an end and
patience. And you shall call upon me, and you shall
go: and you shall pray to me, and I will hear you". (1)

These words calmed his troubled heart, and gave
him confidence. Pious travellers joined themselves
to his train all through the journey, and the whole
Roman population came forth to meet him in holiday
attire, singing hymns. Bruno walked on barefoot
surrounded by this throng, still petitioning that he
might be spared; "I have come against my will",

---

(1) Jeremias, XXIX, 11 and 12.

he said, "and I should return with pleasure". But there was only one opinion at Rome; so the enthronement of the new Pope took place on the 12th February 1049, Bruno taking the name of Leo IX.

Leo at once began to repress simony with great severity, as well as immorality among the clergy, extortion by nobles, and the shameful vices of the people. He constantly travelled about, and in one year actually held Councils at Reims, Mainz and Rome.

The Council of Rome, in 1050, deposed several simoniacal Bishops. One of these, the Bishop of Sutri, when accused, endeavoured to justify himself on oath; but, while raising his hand, he was struck down like Ananias, and carried out dying from the hall.

Meanwhile the licentious habits of the day afflicted the Church quite as much as did simony; these habits had corrupted the highest ranks, and profaned the sacred ministry. The clergy openly demanded permission to marry; but the Church remained firm throughout these attacks, hoping against hope, and faithfully maintaining, for purer ages, that principle of perfect chastity, which, a pious writer says, is "like the sacred poetry of virtue". (1)

Luden, a Protestant, has said, "It is ecclesiastical celibacy which has made us what we are, and has procured for us what we have, intelligence, culture, progress of the human race: it has essentially contributed towards preserving unity in the Church, and,

---

(1) Mgr. Gerbet. "Dogme générateur de la piété catholique".

through that unity, the vigour required to resist the brutal power of the sword, and to check that inhuman oppression which the feudal system had introduced into social life." (1)

Among the regulations made by Leo IX, to put a stop to the immorality of the clergy, was one which condemned any woman to servitude who had connection with an ecclesiastic, and the same was decreed for any child born from such an union!

Leo IX dominant virtues were chastity, patience, mercy, and that austerity in daily life which welcomes trials. Pope and sovereign, allied to Emperors and to every monarch in Europe, he only allowed himself, amidst the gorgeous splendours of the Lateran palace, a stone for his pillow, and a carpet for his bed. One night, finding a leper at his door, he carried him in his arms to the state couch known as the Pope's bed. Under Leo IX the Lateran became once again a palace devoted to the poor and prayer.

These eminent virtues appeared sublime, surrounded as the Pope was by sorrows caused by the inroads of the Normans on Church territory, and by the Greek schism which had sprung up again under the ambitious patriarch Michael Cærularius. Michael objected to the Roman custom of using unleavened bread for the Eucharist; he said it was a crime on the part of the Roman Church that the Wednesday abstinence was not observed, that priests were allowed to shave, and that Bishops were allowed to wear rings like married persons. Such were the grievances

---

(1) History of the Germans.

which rekindled the forgotten animosity of Photius; or rather, let us say, the Bishops of Constantinople were weary of the yoke of Rome. After a long struggle to assume the title of Œcumenical Patriarch, they were determined to break the bonds which united them to the centre of Christendom; preferring thus to command a dead religion than to owe their faith and spiritual life to obedience.

The Normans dated their first establishment in Italy from the year 1016. Sixteen years before that, forty pilgrims of their race, returning from Jerusalem, went to Monte-Gargano to pray in S. Michael's cave. There they met a rebel whom the Greeks had exiled from Bari, and he invited them to conquer Apulia. Now, the most remarkable undertakings were simple matters to these adventurers who were accustomed to conquer kingdoms; therefore they were easily persuaded, and hurried off to assist Salerno, which was then besieged by the Saracens, and saved it from almost certain destruction. The Italians were amazed at the bravery of these strangers, whose tall figures, and handsome faces, combined with prowess in arms, excited their admiration. The Prince of Salerno endeavoured to retain their services; but the pilgrims, having placed him securely on his throne "for the love of God," returned to their native land.

Then the Prince sent citrons and almonds, costly stuffs and gilt harness, to Normandy in order to tempt the gallant Normans to come and dwell in a country which produced such wonders. A great number did in fact do so: they drove the Greeks from the principality of Benevento, received gifts of lands from the

Emperor S. Henry, and founded that Republic of Apulia which was made illustrious by the government of the four sons of Tancred de Hauteville.

It is easy to see that loving adventure as they did, with spirits both warlike and ambitious of power, the Normans paid slight respect to vested interests, or to the dignity of ancient customs. Leo IX represents them to us as "plundering and burning churches, sparing neither children, women, nor old men," but putting them to death with horrible tortures, and making no difference between what was holy or profane. Leo declared war against them; but the issue was disastrous for him: his army was destroyed, he himself falling into the hands of the Normans. He remained nine months among them in semi-captivity, which was somewhat alleviated by the respect shown to him by his victors. Leo then redoubled his accustomed austerities; but, being attacked by sudden illness, he resolved on returning to Rome, and left Benevento regretted by everybody. Count Humphrey accompanied him with his Normans as far as Capua. The Pope rested there for twelve days, after which he proceeded to Monte-Cassino, and thence to Rome, where he arrived in a state of great fatigue after a month's travelling. Feeling that his end was approaching, he requested to be carried to S. Peter's, where he received the viaticum, and, pointing to the spot he had chosen for his grave, he said, "How small and wretched, dear brethren, is the home which awaits me! Of all my honours, behold what remains to me on earth!" Leo IX died on the 19th April 1054. The Church numbers him among her saints.

The selection of his successor was left to the Emperor by the clergy and Romans, who sent the sub-deacon Hildebrand to help and advise him. An Assembly was convoked at Mainz, and Hildebrand succeeded in making the suffrages turn in favour of Gebhard, Bishop of Eichstadt, who, in spite of his resistance, was proclaimed Pope, and enthroned at Rome, under the name of Victor II.

This is the first time that the great name of the monk Hildebrand appears prominently in history; but, though he was only a sub-deacon, the importance of the mission confided to his care shows the influence he already exerted at Rome. This influence he owed entirely to his own merits, for his family was obscure, his father being reputed a carpenter in the small town of Sovana in Tuscany. Hildebrand was brought up by a maternal uncle, the Abbot of S. Maria Aventino; and it was in this monastery, known in the present day as the Priory of Malta, that this enthusiastic young man submitted to discipline and obedience, which he always considered to be absolutely necessary for the government of human affairs.

The Abbey of Cluny had, at this period, a very high reputation, based upon the erudition and virtue of its monks, more than upon its vast possessions and enormous wealth. S. Odo, S. Mayeul, and S. Odilon had rendered the holiness of this school quite traditional, and in consequence it received pupils from every part of Europe. Hildebrand went there to complete his studies; afterwards he proceeded on a preaching mission throughout Italy and Germany, during which the Emperor, Henry the Black, was greatly struck by his eager zeal and apostolic boldness, which, in those days of neglect and weakness were marked characteristics of his sermons. Shortly afterwards Leo IX, a pious and strict Pontiff, sought out Hildebrand, and confided the monastery of S. Paolo-fuori-le-mura, which had been allowed to fall into a disgraceful state of decay, to his care. S. Paul's, one of the patriarchal churches of Rome, was practically abandoned; the cattle, grazing by the banks of the Tiber, used to rest in its shade during the heat of the day. There were a few monks left in the monastery, however, to watch and pray; but they, regardless of a future life, had brutalized themselves by debauchery. Hildebrand restored this holy place to its former stateliness, placing at its entrance bronze gates cast at Constantinople, and ornamented with tracery; (1) but, above all, he revived the severity of the rule in all its vigour; the nobles who had usurped the possessions of the church were compelled to restore them, and order and decency reappeared where for so long they had been ignored.

Such was Hildebrand, when Victor II ascended the Apostolic Chair. Victor united the humility of a saint with the firmness of an apostle. In his great struggle against simony and concubinage, he depended upon the support of Hildebrand who went to France

---

(1) These gates were ornamented with fifty-four designs separated one from the other by arabesques. The outlines of the figures were in gold, silver, and enamel; an inscription stated that they had been ordered by Hildebrand, under the pontificate of ALEXANDER II, "assisted by the consul Pantaleone", who had given the order, "qui illas fieri jussit".

as his legate, holding Councils at Lyons and Tours for the purpose of reforming abuses.

Subsequently, when Victor II was dead, the clergy and Romans requested Cardinal Frederick, Abbot of Monte-Cassino, to designate a worthy Pope to succeed him; Frederick named five likely men as being equally deserving of their votes, namely, four Bishops and the sub-deacon Hildebrand. (1) However, those who had asked his advice refused to accept any of the candidates he suggested; but they selected himself, conducting him forcibly to S. Pietro-in-vincoli, where Frederick was unanimously proclaimed Pope under the name of STEPHEN IX, in memory of Pope S. Stephen whose festival day it chanced to be. The new Pontiff was brother to Godfrey the Bearded, Duke of Lorraine; but his high birth had in no way affected his pure simplicity as a priest. His first act was to write to the seven Cardinal Bishops complaining of the laxity of discipline. He said, "It appears to us that the episcopacy only consists in luxurious dress, gold, soft furs, smart equipages, and in suites of armed knights; not at all in purity of life, or in the practice of virtue."

Thereupon he recalled S. Peter Damian from his hermitage at Avellano; and, in spite of the saint's determined resistance, he compelled him under obedience to come to Rome, where he was wanted as a

---

(1) The four Bishops were Cardinals Humbert of S. Rufina and John of Velletri, and the Bishops of Perugia and Tusculum.

living example! S. Peter Damian was consecrated by the Pope Bishop of Ostia.

STEPHEN IX reigned barely a year. A few days before his death, he assembled the clergy and people and forbade their proceeding to an election until Hildebrand, who was absent, had returned to Rome. But scarcely had Stephen breathed his last when the faction of the Count of Tusculum elected John, Bishop of Velletri, under the name of BENEDICT X. The Cardinals, with the greater portion of the clergy, opposed this election. Peter Damian, who, as Bishop of Ostia, had the right of consecrating the Pope, refused his ministration to this act of rebellion; so the enthronement took place at night, amidst uproarious crowds of armed men. Meanwhile, at Siena, Hildebrand, being invested with full powers by the best of the clergy and Romans, immediately elected Gérard of Burgundy, Bishop of Florence. Gérard took the name of NICHOLAS II, and advanced towards Rome, accompanied by a great number of Bishops and by Godfrey the Bearded, Duke of Lorraine and Tuscany. On hearing this the antipope Benedict quitted the patriarchal palace, Nicholas taking possession of it amidst popular acclamations.

Some days later, a Council was convened at the Lateran, with the object of preventing the renewal of such disturbances as had broken out after the death of Stephen IX. This Council decided that the Pope's election should be made principally by the Cardinal-Bishops, and subsequently confirmed by the other Cardinals, receiving the assent of the clergy and the approval of the people, "in such a manner that the most religious men should commence the election and that the others should follow". Finally the Emperor's authorization had to be obtained by virtue of the title bestowed upon him of "defender and protector of the Church". S. Peter Damian informs us that, in case of any immediate danger, the enthronement of the new Pontiff should be carried out at once.

The title of Cardinal was already of ancient usage in the Church of Rome. At first it was the distinctive appellation of priests placed at the head of titles or parishes. (1) Leo IV called them "presbyteros sui cardinis", and, in the Council of Rome in 853, the deacons who were attached to the service of hospitals likewise received the title of "Cardinales". The same title was from that time attributed to the seven suffragan Bishops of Rome. Finally, the right of election being reserved to the Cardinals, it placed them, as Peter Damian says, "not only above Bishops, but also above patriarchs and primates." (2)

(1) There were twenty-five parishes at Rome under the pontificate of S. Marcellinus, 308—310 (or 309), twenty-eight under that of S. Leo the Great, (440—461) etc.

(2) Pietri Dam., Ep. XX. Baronius quotes a ritual of 1057, in which the Cardinals are thus apportioned to the patriarchal churches:— The church of S. John Lateran, which is the Metropolitan church of Rome, had for suffragans the seven Cardinal-Bishops, that is to say, the Bishops of Ostia, S. Rufina (united since 1120 to Porto), Porto, Sabina, Præneste, Tusculum, and Albano. These alone might officiate in S. John Lateran in the Pope's absence. The suffragans of S. Maria Maggiore were:— The Cardinal-priests of SS. James

However, the Council convoked at Rome by Nicholas II did not occupy itself solely with the pontifical succession; for it was before this assembly, composed of a hundred and thirteen Bishops, that Bérenger, Archdeacon of Angers, and Scholiast of S. Martin of Tours, was summoned to answer the charge of denying the real presence of the body and blood of Jesus Christ in the Eucharist.

Bérenger placed his signature to a profession of Catholic Faith, and, lighting a fire in the centre of the Lateran church, he cast all his books into it, but, immediately after leaving the Council, he protested against his recantation, and overwhelmed Cardinal Humbert who had drawn it up with abuse. Bérenger's heart was so filled with falsehood that no one has ever been able to say what his last opinions really were. At three different periods he preached heresy; five times he abjured his errors; and a few years after making one of these recantations at Rome, during the pontificate of GREGORY VII, he ended both his inconsistencies and his life in France.

---

and Philip (Holy Apostles), S. Cyriaca, S. Eusebius, S. Pudentiana, S. Vitalis, SS. Peter and Marcellinus, S. Clement. The Basilica of S. Peter had the Cardinal-priest of S. Maria-trans-Tiberim, S. Chrysogonus, S. Cæcilia, S. Anastasia, S. Lorenzo-in-Damaso, S. Marco, and SS. Martino-e-Sylvestro. To the church of S. Paul were attached the Cardinal-priests of S. Sabina, S. Prisca, S. Balbina, SS. Nereus et Achilleus, S. Sixtus, S. Marcellus, and S. Susanna. Finally the Cardinals of S. Lorenzo were the priests of S. Praxedes, S. Pietro-in-Vincoli, S. Lorenzo-in-Lucina, SS. John and Paul, the Four Crowned Saints, S. Stephen on the Cælian Hill, and S. Quiricus. The Cardinal-deacons bore the titles of the

One of the most important acts of Nicholas II pontificate was the grant he made to Richard the Norman of the principality of Capua, and to Robert Wiscard of all the lands he had conquered, that is to say, of Apulia, Calabria, and even Sicily, whence Robert hoped to drive out the Saracens. Robert, on his part, undertook to pay a yearly tribute to the Church of twelve Pavian pennies for every pair of oxen, payable for ever at Easter; he also took the oath of allegiance to the Pope as his Sovereign. Thus arose the vassalage of the Kingdom of Naples to the Holy See.

Nicholas II had not a longer reign than his predecessors (1), and Hildebrand, whose influence continued all powerful at Rome, managed that Anselmo di Lucca should be elected to replace him. He took the name of ALEXANDER II. But the clergy of Lombardy grew weary of seeing the Apostolic Chair filled by austere men, who had no sympathy with

---

chapels attached to their deaconries. At first there were only seven; but later on fourteen were established, one for each quarter of the town, and to these fourteen were added four, called palatines, because they dwelt in the papal palace, and were assistants to the Pope. The eighteen deaconries were: S. Maria-in-Dominica, S. Lucia-in-Circo, S. Maria-Novella, SS. Cosimo-e-Damiano, S. Adriano, SS. Sergio-e-Baccho, S. Teodoro, S. Georgio-in-Velabro, S. Maria-in-Cosmedin, S. Maria-in-Porticu, S. Nicolas-in-Carcere-Tulliano, S. Angelo-in-Pescaria, S. Eustachio, S. Maria-in-Aquiro, S. Maria-in-via-Lata, S. Agatha-in-Equo-marmoreo, S. Maria-in-Silice, SS. Vito-e-Modesto. Leo X created a nineteenth, S. Onofrio.

(1) Every day, or night, according to the leisure he found from business, Nicholas II washed the feet of twelve beggars.

their effeminate style of life. They managed to circumvent the young King, Henry IV, and, authorized by him, elected Cadalous, Bishop of Parma, who was addicted to simony and quite as immoral as they were. Cadalous at once set out for Rome at the head of an army, encamping in the fields of Nero behind the Vatican. He gained some advantage in his first assault; but, in the second, his troops were put to flight, and he himself only escaped by bribery. Yet he was not disheartened, for ambition is rampant in man's heart; so, in spite of being defeated and forsaken by his followers, condemned and deposed by two Councils to which his own partisans adhered, Cadalous none the less put forth his claim to the Papal throne. During the night he burst into the Leonine city, in 1064, and seized S. Peter's; but the crowds, which filled the Basilica next morning, so terrified his accomplices that they took refuge in the neighbouring houses and cellars. Cadalous was received by Cencius, the son of the prefect of Rome, in the Castle of S. Angelo where he remained two years, closely blockaded by the Papal guards. This long confinement exhausted his patience; he took leave of Cencius, who, however, made him pay a ransom of three hundred pounds as if he had been a prisoner; so, poor and destitute, he considered himself fortunate in being able to escape stealthily by night with a band of pilgrims.

During the whole twelve years of his pontificate, Alexander II was remarkable for the purity of his life, and the sweetness of his character. When he died, a three days' fast was proclaimed according to custom, accompanied by processions and prayers, in order to prepare for the nomination of a new Pope. But, at the very moment when Alexander's obsequies were taking place at S. Peter's, a great tumult suddenly arose; Hildebrand was seized upon, and taken to S. Pietro-in-Vincoli, where the Cardinals and clergy proclaimed him Pontiff. The only cries heard were: "S. Peter has elected the Archdeacon Hildebrand! S. Peter has elected Pope Gregory!"

On the following day Hildebrand wrote to inform King Henry of Germany of his election, and to entreat him not to give his consent to it; for, added he, "if I am Pope it will not be possible for me to leave the crimes of which you are charged unpunished". At the same time the Bishops of Lombardy and Germany, nervous on their own account about Hildebrand's severity, aroused the royal susceptibilities against him; so Henry sent Count Eberhard to Rome to complain that this election had taken place without his being consulted. "God is my witness that I have never sought this dignity", replied Hildebrand; "the Romans have chosen me against my will; but they have not succeeded in obtaining my ordination; nor shall they, until I am assured, by a special mission, that the King and nobles of the Teutonic kingdom have consented to my election. Therefore I shall wait until some one comes from the King to inform me of his will."

The noble simplicity of these words, joined to the humble yet frank openness of Hildebrand, determined Henry to confirm the title which had been given to him; the new Pontiff was accordingly consecrated at Rome, on the 30th June 1073, under the name of GREGORY VII. We must here remark that royal confirmation had almost fallen into desuetude. Alexander II, Gregory's immediate predecessor, had not asked for it; and, according to Father Pagi, Gregory VII was the last Pope who applied for it. Doubtless he might have dispensed with it; but his moderation in this case proves that, however masterful his character might be, he never allowed it to have recourse to the subterfuges of common minds.

Henry IV, son of Henry the Black, Emperor of the Romans, for long only bore the title of King, for, according to the custom of the time, he might not assume the loftier title until he had received the Imperial crown from the Pope. (1) He had not yet attained his fifth year when he ascended the throne, and his mother, the Empress Agnes, held the reins of power during his childhood with marked wisdom. But, having attained adolescence, the young Prince desired to reign alone, and gave way to his evil passions. All his noble feelings were extinguished; he became suspicious and cruel; and in order to forestall all opposition, or chance of remonstrance, he made a public sale of ecclesiastical titles. "The Emperors nominated to Bishoprics", says Voltaire,

---

(1) "It seems very reasonable and well established", says a contemporary historian, "for the maintenance of peace, that no prince should take the title of Emperor, unless he be chosen by the Pope, on account of his merits, and has received from him the mark of this dignity". (Glaber, lib. I, Cap. ult.)

"but Henry IV sold them; Gregory VII opposed this abuse". (1)

Now, in the heart of Germany, a violent tempest burst over Henry's head; the Saxons and Thuringians threw off his authority, and threatened to choose another sovereign unless he sent away his advisers and mistresses, returned to his wife, and spent his time equally in the different parts of his dominions. Henry turned to Gregory VII, hoping, by his intervention, to obtain the submission of the rebels.

Gregory sent legates on a mission to pacify the malcontents, and they were accompanied by the Empress Agnes, who, since the disorderly outbreak of her son, had lived the life of a saint in retirement at Rome. The legates were furthermore instructed to hold Councils and depose any Bishops who might be convicted of simony or incontinence; but the clergy opposed the holding of these Councils, concealing, beneath frivolous pretexts, their repugnance to any conscientious inquiry which might prove too severe. In fact the great Episcopal Sees, not only in Germany, but also in France and Italy, had been, so to speak, sold by auction. In France, Philip I traded in ecclesiastical honours as did Henry IV in Germany; indeed, to such a pitch had the insolence

---

(1) "Annales de l'Empire, année 1076." The Bishop of Halberstadt, who was on the spot, thus speaks:— "He (Henry) has sold the Bishoprics of Constance, Bamberg, Mainz, and several others for money; those of Regensburg, Augsburg, and Strasburg for murder; the Abbey of Fulda for an adultery; the bishopric of Munster for a still more detestable crime". See Fleury, "Hist. ecclés."

of the simoniacs attained, a woman, niece to the Archbishop of Milan, gave orders to cut off the ears nose, lips, and hands of the deacon Arialde, and to tear out his eyes and tongue in order to punish him for his evangelistic energy. (1)

So far as morals were concerned, the opposition of the clergy was intensified against all reform, because, in losing their chastity, they had ceased to believe it was a virtue capable of being practised on earth. But, in spite of all opposition, Gregory VII persevered in his undertaking. The Protestant historian Luden writing on this subject says:— "However terrible the struggle may have been, and however uncertain the issue had been for long, the result decided in Gregory's favour, showing that the Pontiff demanded nothing that was not suitable to the conditions of his time, knowing as he did how to express its needs and vivify its spirit by his words." (2)

Even in Henry's complaints we learn that Gregory's energy in purifying the sanctuary had ensured his popularity. "You have", he said, "by your management of them (the simoniacal and immoral clergy), obtained the people's favour."

Gregory held at Rome annual Councils, which sometimes imposed penances, at others commanded the clergy to live in community under regular rule: the canons of these Councils were delivered throughout Europe by his legates. At the same time, in

(1) Arialde died in consequence of this brutal treatment. He is honoured by the Church as a saint.
(2) "Histoire du peuple allemand." Luden published this work in 1833: he has been named "The Father of German History."

order to make Kings cease from using their power for the perversion of God's Church, the zealous Pontiff threatened them, not only with spiritual fulminations, but also with the loss of their temporal dignities. It has been asked whether he possessed the right to do so, or whether oaths taken by monarchs at their consecration were merely empty forms of speech. In those days of anarchy, was nothing sacred left upon the earth but violence and oppression! Disorder reigned everywhere; and such confusion existed in the laws that barbarous customs, such as wreckage and ransom, ended by becoming legal rights: there was not a throne in Europe which rested on accepted principles, or was free from reproach. Amid all this chaos Gregory VII appeared; a man whose spiritual authority gave an entirely new moral and religious direction to society. His right was the only one universally acknowledged and respected; nations had no other bulwark against despotism but in the power of his word; religion had no hope against demoralisation but in the strength of his character. This man recognised, through the whirlwind of human passions, the necessity for certain stringent laws, holiness for the clergy, justice for Princes; and to ensure their execution he only relied upon S. Peter's Chair, which rose high above the constituent portions of Christendom, as though it were the eye of God Himself. (1)

(1) "Le pouvoir papal disposant des couronnes," writes the Protestant divine, Coquerel, "empêchait le despotisme de devenir atroce ... Un Tibère eût été impossible, Rome l'eût écrasé. Les grands despotismes arrivent quand les rois se

Gregory VII excommunicated all the priests and Bishops who disgraced the Church, and solemnly abolished the custom of investiture used by Princes, and which apparently attributed spiritual authority to them. Then a furious storm arose against him on Christmas night 1075, and just as the Pope was celebrating the first Mass at S. Maria Maggiore, in the chapel of the Presepio, Cencius, sword in hand and accompanied by an armed band, invaded the church. They seized the Pope, wounding him on the forehead, striking him down, and, dragging him by the hair, they conveyed him to a tower built by Cencius on S. Peter's Bridge.

At the news of this outrage, the solemn offices of the Nativity were interrupted in all the churches; altars were profaned, bells rung and guards were placed at all the gates of the city to prevent the Pontiff from being taken away, while a tumultuous crowd collected in front of Cencius's tower, with torches and machines of war. Cencius was forced to surrender the Pope, to whose intercession, indeed, he owed his life; because, without Gregory's intervention, nothing but his blood would have satisfied the populace.

With his face still disfigured, Gregory was led back in triumph to S. Maria Maggiore, where he completed the service, and solemnly blessed the people.

History does not record whether this brutal outrage had been contrived with the consent of Henry

persuadent qu'il n'y a rien au-dessus d'eux. C'est alors que l'ivresse d'un pouvoir illimité enfante les plus atroces forfaits." (Essai sur l'Hist. du Christianisme, p. 75.)

of Germany; but, a short while afterwards, Henry, irritated by the Pope's persistent efforts to reform the abuses which disgraced the clergy, obtained his deposition at a Council held at Worms. (1)

The letters from this assembly were brought to Rome, and presented to the Council then sitting there by Roland, a cleric of the Church of Parma. They caused great excitement in the Lateran Basilica; some armed men actually rushed at Roland, and were about to kill him, when Gregory interposed. "My children", said he, "these are the times of danger spoken of in Scripture, when there shall be men full of self-love, avaricious, proud and disobedient. But it is necessary that scandals should come; and God has sent us like sheep in the midst of wolves."

He then opened the letters brought by Roland, and read them with unchanging countenance. They were addressed: "Henry, King, not by usurpation, but by the command of God, to Hildebrand, a false monk and no Pope," and ended with, "I say to thee, together with all our Bishops, Descend! descend!"

Then, and then only, at the request of all the Bishops at the Council, a solemn anathema was pronounced. Gregory spoke as follows:—

---

(1) It is impossible to imagine all the absurd and infamous charges alleged against Gregory VII. It suffices to quote one: he was accused of practising magic, he had been instructed, so it was alleged, in this science by Benedict IX, who had acquired it himself from Sylvester II, the illustrious Gerbert. Gregory, continued the charge, possessed a book on necromancy; and as soon as he had read a few lines demons appeared ready to perform all his wishes.

"S. Peter, Prince of the Apostles, hearken to thy servant, whom thou hast nurtured from childhood, and delivered until this day from the hands of the wicked who hate us because we are faithful to thee. Thou art our witness, thou, and the holy Mother of God, S. Paul, thy brother, and all the saints, that the Roman Church compelled us, against our wish, to undertake its government, and that we would much rather have ended our days in exile than usurped thy seat by human means. But, *being therein* by thy grace, and without any merit *on our own* part, we believe it to be thy will that the Christian world shall obey us, according to the power God has granted to us after thee to bind and to loose on earth. It is with this conviction, for the safety and honour of the Church, and in the name of Almighty God, the Father, the Son, and the Holy Ghost, and by thy authority, that we prohibit Henry, son of the Emperor Henry, who, with unheard of pride, has arisen against thy Church, from governing the Teutonic kingdom and Italy. We absolve all Christians from the oath of allegiance made to him, in the past or in the future, and we forbid all men to serve him as their King . . ." The King thought he could depose the Pope; the Pontiff retaliated by deposing the King.

The impression produced throughout Germany by this anathema was prodigious. The Dukes of Bavaria, Swabia, Carinthia, with a certain number of prelates assembled at Tribur, where, after recapitulating all the acts of injustice and tyranny of which Henry had been guilty, they cited him to appear and justify himself before the Pope at a Diet to be held at Augsburg. Henry, too pleased that by this condescension he might prevent them electing someone to succeed him, willingly consented: but, without waiting for Gregory's arrival, he proceeded to Italy to meet him, hoping that his justification might prove easier at a distance from the theatre of his crimes, and in the absence of his accusers. Gregory was already on the road to Germany when Henry crossed the Alps. Thereupon the Pope withdrew to the fortress of Canossa; where, after many difficulties had been made, Henry obtained permission to visit him.

Gregory VII was an austere monk, equally devoid of the perfidious dissimulation and exquisite politeness of a skilled diplomatist. What chiefly engrossed his thoughts, amidst the general existing confusion, was the necessity of maintaining ancient discipline, and of severely punishing simoniacs, adulterers, and homicides. Now the man, who was to appear before him, was guilty of all these crimes: his accomplices had only received absolution after they had fasted on bread and water in narrow cells; and Gregory held that a crown was no protection against penance. When men wish to enter the temple, they must put aside honours and titles; for in God's house there are no Kings and no subjects; there all are only dust and ashes, "pulvis es et in pulverem reverteris." (1)

(1) It was only the clergy who understood that justice must not be a respecter of persons. This Innocent III nobly expressed in a brief addressed to the French clergy:— "Non

Henry spent three days within the second enclosure of the fortress of Canossa, barefoot and attired in woollen garments; food was only brought to him in the evening, according to custom on fasting days. On the fourth day he was admitted into the presence of the Pope who absolved him, on condition that he appeared before the Diet of Augsburg, and answered the accusations which his subjects alleged against him.

A distinguished Professor of the Protestant University of Halle has said:— "When we study the spectacle given at Canossa, national must yield to intellectual interest; this event is a triumph obtained by that sovereign power of the soul, which creates exterior forces, when they do not already exist, over an effeminate tyrant who however knew how to retain the material force with which he was armed." (1)

Henry was absolved; but no sooner had he left Canossa than he resumed his corrupt habits. The Lombards clung to evil practices more stoutly than any other nation, and the dissatisfaction which arose among them, on account of the King's submission, so alarmed that monarch that he removed the mask sooner perhaps than he had intended. Then a fierce war broke out: the Germans elected Rudolph of Swabia as their King; Henry was again excommuni-

debet esse acceptio personarum ut aliter divitibus et potentibus, aliter de abjectis et pauperibus judicemus; ne sit in manibus nostris iniqua mensura et statera dolosa, si . . . in alicujus personæ favorem injuriam dicamus, aut aliter illis, aliter istis metiamur."

(1) M. Leo in his "Introduction to the History of the Middle Ages", 1830.

cated and deposed; while, on their side, Henry and his partisans once more deposed Gregory and elected Guibert, Archbishop of Ravenna, to replace him.

Throughout these bitter struggles, Gregory always received the most devoted support from Matilda, Countess of Tuscany, the widow of Godfrey the Hunchback, Duke of Lorraine. The Countess had inherited from her father, Boniface III, dominions which comprised, besides Tuscany, Mantua, Parma, Reggio, Piacenza, Ferrara, and Modena, a part of Umbria and the Marches, and the territory of Verona. She constituted a powerful defence to Rome towards the North; but the Pope wished to be equally well protected on the South. Robert Wiscard exercised full power in that quarter; he had incurred excommunication several times by letting his still adventurous spirit lead him into plundering and pillaging; but Gregory promised to remit these censures, provided Robert bound himself to defend the Roman Church and guaranteed to secure the free election of a Pontiff whenever a vacancy should occur. This deed was signed on the 29th June 1080.

Nine months after this, Henry advanced on Rome with the antipope Guibert, and, leaving the fortresses of Countess Matilda behind him, he encamped in the fields of Nero. The Romans received the King and antipope with jeers and insults, and gallantly beat back an assault directed against the Leonine City. This unlooked for resistance disheartened the German Prince; sickness decimated his army, and the Countess might cut off his retreat: these combined reasons induced him to abandon the expedition and return to the North.

But, in the following year, he returned more determined than ever to destroy Gregory; he besieged the city throughout the whole of Lent; it is even said that he set fire to S. Peter's in order to absorb the attention of the Romans; but Gregory was among the first to reach the fire, which the inhabitants succeeded in extinguishing, before it had placed the Basilica in danger. Henry, a second time, retired; but he left Guibert at Tibur with some troops who had orders to pillage the country and weary out the patience of the inhabitants. He also constructed a high tower to command the Leonine City; but the garrison he placed in it perished to a man from sickness and want.

The siege of Rome lasted two years; and before he could obtain possession of it the King had to pour out his gold like water. The populace, won by his bribes, delivered over the Lateran gate and palace to him on the 21st March 1084; Gregory taking refuge in the Castle of S. Angelo, with many of the nobility, while his nephew, Rusticus, defended himself in the Septizonium of Severus.

Guibert was then enthroned as Pope, under the name of CLEMENT III; and, on Easter Day, the 31st March, he bestowed the Imperial crown on Henry. Meanwhile the struggle continued; the Imperialists were unable to penetrate within S. Peter's, while the sieges of S. Angelo and of the Septizonium were prolonged unsuccessfully for a month. After this Henry was informed that Robert Wiscard was advancing to the assistance of the Pope; so, not feeling strong enough to resist him, he left Rome for Lombardy.

Robert entered Rome at the head of 30,000 foot soldiers and 6,000 horse. A portion of the population having opposed him, this fierce conqueror set fire to the city. Thus numbers of monuments were reduced to ashes, especially those in the neighbourhood of S. John Lateran and the Coliseum. The atrocities perpetrated on this occasion by the Normans, on men, women and nuns, the sacrileges and pillage carried out, fully justified the many excommunications pronounced against them by Gregory VII and his predecessors. (1)

Gregory VII did not long survive this sad catastrophe. He remained some time in Rome, endeavouring to repair the evils of war; then, convinced of the futility of his efforts, he withdrew to Monte-Cassino, and thence to Salerno where he died on the 25th May 1085. His last words were:— "I have loved justice and hated iniquity; that is why I die in exile." His name was inscribed in the Roman martyrology by order of Gregory XIII.

If the Kings had left the Roman Pontiffs independent to pursue their work of reformation among

---

(1) Gibbon thus describes Robert Wiscard:— "His boundless ambition was founded on the consciousness of superior worth: in the pursuit of greatness, he was never arrested by scruples of justice, and seldom moved by feelings of humanity ... Robert is praised by the Apulian poet for excelling the cunning of Ulysses and the eloquence of Cicero." "Decline and Fall." Vol. X, Chap. LVI.

the clergy, and had not unceasingly interfered with their spiritual authority, by claiming to dispose of ecclesiastical preferments, doubtless this strife between the two powers would not have arisen, and each might have maintained full liberty of action. It was especially to preserve intact this exercise of his spiritual authority that Gregory VII claimed the right of commanding Kings. His whole life was a proof of the uprightness of his intentions. It was written of him, "Abandoned by fortune, driven from his country, he remained firm and unshaken in his principles, thus sacrificing himself to the one great idea, which was the support of his life and of his heroic perseverance; but, in his last hour, it was given him to discern that his schemes had been based upon justice and truth, facts not understood by many of the intellects of that day." (1)

Another Protestant, Johann von Müller, tersely describes Gregory's character:— "He had the courage of a hero, the prudence of a Senator, the zeal of a prophet; and his morals were pure and austere."

S. Gregory VII pontificate was too stormy to allow of his leaving any durable monuments in Rome. What was, however, much more important was that

---

(1) Henry Steffens, "le Siècle actuel," 1817. On the subject of Gregory VII the "Manuel d'Histoire Ecclésiastique chrétienne," by Dr. Schmid, professor of Protestant theology at Flessen; "l'Histoire d'Allemagne," by Professor Eichhorn; and, above all, Voigt, in his fine work "Hildebrand und sein Zeitalter," translated into French and annotated by the Abbé Jager, may be consulted. Cardinal Wiseman's two interesting articles on Gregory VII have proved very useful to us.

he confirmed the independence of the Church, and reestablishing sanctity in the holy places. At every step taken in Rome his saintly memory and grand presence come before us: at S. Maria Aventino as a child, practising every virtue which gives strength to the soul; at S. Paolo-fuori-le-mura appearing as an active and zealous reformer; at S. Maria del Presepio the Pontiff, enemy to all evil, is torn bleeding from the altar by rebels, to be brought back in triumph by the populace; finally in the Lateran, as father and judge, kneeling for hours in prayer before the Saviour's altar, and then presiding over Councils with marvellous dignity. The hall in which was heard the anathema against King Henry has now disappeared. It was doubtless in the ancient Leonine Basilica at the Lateran, built by Leo III, and in which so many Councils assembled; this Hall occupied that portion of the palace which reverted perpendicularly towards the transept, and communicated with the corresponding right of the Basilica by means of a great staircase.

The pontifical throne remained vacant for nearly two years after Gregory VII death, owing to the determined refusal of Desiderius, Abbot of Monte-Cassino, whom Gregory had designated as his successor, to accept the post. Finally the clergy and Roman populace resolved to overcome his opposition by force. They seized and conducted him to the deaconry of S. Lucia, where he was invested with the mitre and red cope, which were the distinctive marks of papacy. Desiderius submitted to what he could not prevent; but, four days after his election, he left

Rome, and retired to Monte-Cassino, where he resumed the humble habit of a monk.

Guibert took advantage of this interregnum to strengthen his position within Rome. He made himself master of S. Peter's and the Capitol, and made incursions into other parts of the town. Affairs became worse and worse; so fresh overtures were made to Desiderius in a Council held at Capua, when at last he was persuaded to accept the pastoral ring. He at once proceeded to Rome; the Prince of Capua recovered S. Peter's from the antipope, and Desiderius was enthroned, on the $9^{\underline{th}}$ May 1087, under the name of VICTOR III.

The two parts of Rome divided by the Tiber were now subject to two different Popes: the right side, with the island of S. Bartholomew, where Victor dwelt, recognised his authority; the left bank obeyed Guibert, who had established himself at S. Maria-della-Rotonda. Victor III only reigned a few months. He died and was buried at Monte-Cassino, whose church he had restored with great magnificence.

Otho, Bishop of Ostia, succeeded him: he was elected by an assembly of the clergy held at Terracina, and assumed the name of URBAN II. (1) His character inspired the Romans with such confidence that Guibert was ignominiously expelled; although the schism, being under Henry's protection, did not come to an end. Henry even benefited by Gregory VII premature death, and that of Rudolph of Swabia, who had disputed the empire with him, and his par-

---

(1) Urban II was born at Châlons-sur-Marne.

tisans even affected to believe that these events were the result of God's anger. The Bishop of Halberstadt replied:— "You must therefore consider Nero happy to have outlived SS. Peter and Paul, Herod that he survived John, and Pilate Jesus Christ!"

God's hand did indeed weigh heavily on Henry. His sons rose up against him; whole populations forsook his standard; and a day was at hand when this King, who had sold all the preferments of the Church, would, in his misery, solicit a post as chorister in the Cathedral of Spires, saying:— "I have studied and know how to sing." (1)

Meanwhile the antipope Guibert ruled at Rome. Driven out by the inhabitants in 1089, he had managed to re-enter the city in 1091, even obtaining possession of S. Angelo.

Urban's poverty was now extreme; it repelled him to shed blood, and not having the wealth of the Imperialists he could not purchase treason. But Geoffrey, Abbot of La Trinité of Vendôme, hastened from France to help him in his distress. He brought the Pope 100 marks weight of silver, nor did his filial devotion end here; he sold his horses, plate, and carriages, and with the proceeds obtained the surrender of the Lateran palace, where the Apostolic Chair was being profaned by schismatics. Urban created Geoffrey Cardinal-priest of S. Prisca on Mt. Aventine, and for three hundred years the title of Cardinal remained attached to the Abbots of La Trinité of Vendôme.

(1) This is recorded by Helmold and Sigonius.

These alms, which restored both palace and Cathedral to the Pope, continued that tradition of devotion to the Holy See in days of peril which has ever distinguished the French nation. French pilgrims, too, did not cease to flock to the tombs of the Apostles; among these were S. Odilon, S. Hugo, S. Bruno, and good King Robert, all men of note. Robert came on a pilgrimage to Rome in 1016, during the pontificate of Benedict VIII. Instead of gold or silver, he placed on S. Peter's Confession an antiphon written by himself, in which he had poured forth the poetical feelings of a Christian soul.

S. Odilon was the fourth Abbot, and third saint, of Cluny. He ruled over that monastery for fifty-six years, and lived nearly a century. Charity, kindness, and gentleness formed the basis of his character, and such was the purity of his heart that, like Pope Damasus, he was called the "virgin", and, after his death, "virgo centenarius". Odilon came to Rome when over eighty years of age, during the pontificate of CLEMENT II. His biographers say that his greatest wish was that he might die near the tomb of the Apostles; but his weakened constitution suddenly re-established itself, and he was enabled to return to Burgundy. He modestly styled himself, "Brother Odilon, the most wretched of all the poor of Cluny." The memory of S. Odilon lingers on Mt. Aventine, where he is said to have repeated the miracle of Cana.

S. Hugo was S. Odilon's successor; it was while he governed Cluny that that illustrious monastery gave three Popes to the Church: S. GREGORY VII, URBAN II, and PASCHAL II. S. Hugo was present in Rome at the Council which condemned Bérenger; and, throughout all the troubles at the end of the eleventh century, he was one of the most respected advisers of Popes and Kings.

When S. Bruno fulfilled the duties of chancellor of the Church of Reims, URBAN II was one of his disciples. As soon as the disciple became Pope, he summoned his old master from the Grande Chartreuse to aid him with his advice; but Bruno could not find the peace he loved at Rome, so he quitted the city with his monks in search of it, and found it amidst the deserts of Calabria.

We must not omit to mention Halinard, the learned and pious monk of S. Benignus at Dijon, a physician, a geometrician, but, above all, "a powerful preacher, gifted with persuasive eloquence". Raised against his will to the primatial See of Lyons, through the entreaties of the people and by command of the Pope, he would have been elevated to the Chair of S. Peter, on the death of CLEMENT II, had he not fled in order to escape from the demands of the Romans. Yet Halinard loved Rome with a great love; he frequently visited it as a pilgrim, and much desired to end his days in that city. His wish was granted for he died, poisoned through envy, at Rome in 1052. The Roman nobility buried him with great respect in the Basilica of S. Paul.

Another Frenchman, Cardinal Humbert, occupied high positions in the Church about the same time. Summoned to Rome by LEO IX, from the monastery of Moyen-Moutier in the Vosges, he was sent as legate to Constantinople, where he distinguished himself by his theological knowledge and profound acquaintance with Greek literature. After the death of Victor II, Humbert's name headed the list of candidates proposed by Cardinal Frederick, who was himself elected Pope by the clergy and people. Humbert is probably the first Frenchman who attained to the purple.

Among the number of pilgrims from other countries, who visited the Roman Basilicas during the eleventh century, was Canute, King of Denmark, England, Scandinavia and part of Sweden, as he styled himself. He came to Rome in 1027 with a wallet and pilgrim's staff, and assisted at the consecration of the Emperor Conrad. One of his great objects was to obtain from the Emperor and princes "who held the mountain passes greater justice and more safety for his people on their journeys to Rome".

Macbeth, King of Scotland, Duncan's murderer, came to Rome, haunted by remorse:—

"Still it cried, Sleep no more! to all the house:
Glamis hath murdered sleep; and therefore Cawdor
Shall sleep no more, Macbeth shall sleep no more!" (1)

Historians relate that Macbeth was in Rome in 1050; "lavishing abundant alms upon the poor." (2)

Three Archbishops of Canterbury accompanied their Kings from Great Britain; S. Æthelnoth, S. Elfege, and S. Anselm. S. Elfege, or Ælfheah, to give him his old English name, who suffered martyrdom by a Danish axe in 1011, came to Rome early in the

(1) Macbeth, Act II, Sc, II.
(2) Rohrbacher, t. XIII, p. 532.

eleventh century. John XVIII had so great a regard for him that he gave him his own stole, "greatly honouring him before the whole Roman Senate". (1)

Canute said that S. Æthelnoth always made him think of God and influenced him to be merciful and just. It was this saint who induced Canute to make a pilgrimage to Rome, as he had done himself in 1022.

S. Anselm came to Rome towards the end of this century (1097), fleeing out of England on account of the wickedness and injustice of William Rufus, and "because he thought that men in this country did little according to right, and after his instruction". (2) Anselm was received with great honour at the Lateran Palace, where he stayed ten days; but, the climate of Rome not agreeing with him, he retired to the monastery of S. Salvatore. S. Anselm was one of the most eminent men of the eleventh century; succeeding ages, in spite of their pretentiousness and glory, have produced no one who has surpassed the exactness of his knowledge, or the depths of his reasoning.

Among other pilgrims of the eleventh century were S. Simeon of Armenia, S. Alfano of Salerno, S. Bruno of Segni, and the Empress Agnes, the pious mother of Henry IV of Germany. The education of her son having been taken from her she came to Rome in 1062, and made a general confession at S. Peter's before the altar to S. Peter Damian, whom

---

(1) Rohrbacher, t. XIII, p. 349.
(2) Saxon Chronicle, Ann. 1097.

she had summoned for that purpose. She then withdrew to a convent near the Vatican. Her tomb was formerly shown in the ancient chapel of S. Petronilla.

Pope URBAN II, having been driven from the Lateran in the sad year of 1093, possessed no other refuge in Rome than the Frangipani tower, (the ancient Coliseum). He was there accosted one day by a pilgrim, a countryman of his own, who prostrated himself before him. He had just arrived from Jerusalem, bearing with him sad tidings from that "widow of nations", now more than ever in servitude to the infidels. SYLVESTER II and GREGORY VII had already heard her lamentations, and had re-echoed them through Western Europe. Urban received Peter the Hermit most kindly and sent him to preach a holy war among the Princes and knights, who were wasting their strength in mutual slaughter. He himself convoked Councils to meet at Piacenza and Clermont-Ferrand, and soon the whole of Europe resounded with the cry of the French:— "Dieu le veut! Dieu le veut!"

A troop of crusaders, commanded by Robert, Duke of Normandy, and Stephen, Count of Blois, passed through Rome, in 1096, on their way to take ship on the Adriatic coast. These crusaders found the partisans of the antipope in possession of the interior of S. Peter's, while one of the towers was held by Romans who were faithful to Urban II. The schismatics seized upon offerings made at the shrine, and aimed stones from the scaffolding at the pilgrims at prayer, if they did not belong to Guibert's party.

These details will give an idea of the disorder and confusion into which Rome was plunged. In 1084 the chapels in S. Peter's had been seized upon by laymen, who, shaving off their beards and assuming mitres, personified Cardinals to foreigners whose confessions they heard, and whose gifts they received. At night they would rob, murder, and give way to abominable orgies in the neighbouring streets. It had required all Gregory VII vigour to put a stop to such abominations.

Urban II died on the 22ⁿᵈ July 1099, fourteen days after the taking of Jerusalem; but without having had the consolation of hearing the great news which had been the desire of his life. This illustrious Pontiff died in a tower of the city belonging to his friend Peter of Leon (Pier-Leoni), and not in the Lateran Palace: this fact alone suffices to show into what a state of ruin the old papal residences had fallen during the schism. Paschal II, on succeeding to the throne, devoted his first cares to removing the ruins. He rebuilt the church of the Quattro-Santi, which had been destroyed by the Normans, annexing to it a palace, in which he resided during the restoration of the Lateran Palace. His most important foundation was S. Maria-del-Popolo, near to the Flaminian Gate, close to where Nero's tomb had stood. Nero had committed suicide in the house of his freedman Phaon, not far from the Via Nomentana; but, according to Suetonius, his body had been brought to the Hill of Gardens, "Collis hortulorum", where the Domitian family were buried. The populace became superstitious, and thought that phantoms haunted the hill, so Paschal determined to sanctify the accursed spot by erecting a church. (1)

S. Maria-del-Popolo rises at the foot of the hill; it has been reconstructed by Sixtus IV and beautified by Julius II. Paintings by Pinturicchio and Annibale Caracci, sculptures by Contucci and Paolo Posi, have made it one of the most interesting monuments of modern Rome.

Perhaps it is the only church which takes its origin from the eleventh century; for those days of wretchedness only produced ruins for the ancient city. Nevertheless from this time art began to revive in Italy, and the architect Buschetto came from Dulichium (now Neochori or Cacaba) to Tuscany, (2) where he built the magnificent Cathedral of Pisa with treasures captured from the Saracens by the Pisans in the harbour of Palermo. At the same

---

(1) M. de Chateaubriand relates on this subject, in a note to his "Martyrs", a popular tradition current in Rome. "There was formerly, so it is said, at the Porta del Popolo, a great tree upon which a crow used to perch. A hole was dug at the foot of the tree, and an urn was found bearing an inscription to the effect that it contained Nero's ashes. The ashes were scattered to the winds, and, on the spot where the urn was found, a church was built, now known as S. Maria-del-Popolo." Montfaucon cites an inscription on the high altar of this church referring to this very tradition.

(2) So great were the mechanical talents of Buschetto that by aid of his inventions ten young girls could raise a weight which one thousand yoked oxen could not move, and no ship could take to sea. These marvels attested by his epitaph prove how much the Italians valued his talents.

time Desiderius, Abbot of Monte-Cassino, rebuilt the church attached to his monastery with fabulous splendour. He obtained marbles, columns, and capitals from Rome; workmen in mosaic, stone-masons, and painters from Constantinople; and he even had the servants belonging to the monastery instructed in these various arts.

This awakening movement was general; S. Edward built Westminster Abbey; S. Odilon brought marble columns for the new cloister at Cluny by way of the Durance and the Rhone. "I have found an Abbey of wood," he said, "and I leave one of marble." His successor, S. Hugo, built the splendid church attached to the monastery; it had five naves, sixty-eight pillars flanked with small columns, four belfries, and twenty-six bells.

In the seclusion of another monastery, at Pomposa, in the Duchy of Ferrara, a Benedictine monk, called Guido of Arezzo, was simplifying the art of music by the invention of the gamut. Guido was called to Rome by Pope JOHN XIX, who, as the learned monk himself tells us, considered his "antiphonary a prodigy, and did not leave his seat until he had learnt a strophe which he had never heard sung before; thus proving to himself what he had scarcely believed of others." Guido's health prevented his remaining in Rome in spite of the Pope's entreaties; he tells us that he could not endure "sea-side and marshy countries," so he returned to his monastery. He was a sincerely pious man, and, though his wonderful discovery was a boon to man, he required no reward beyond asking for a few prayers for his soul from those who profited by his discovery.

A general work of renovation went forward throughout society during the eleventh century. Ancient idioms were dying out, while new languages took their place; energy and activity prevailed, and only wanted proper control in order to work wonders. If crimes were greater than usual, so also were virtues. S. Romuald founded the Camaldoli; John Gualbert, Vallombrosa; S. Bruno revived the ancient "laures" of Palestine (1) for his order. Few centuries could boast of so many holy Kings: S. Henry reformed German administration, adding fresh lustre to a crown which had already been worn by S. Adelaide and S. Matilda; S. Edward drew up a code of laws which for long was the "palladium" of England; S. Olaf governed Norway; S. Canute Denmark; S. Charles the Good Flanders, S. Stephen was legislator and apostle of Hungary; and S. Margaret appeared as the Guardian Angel of Scotland.

It was about the end of the tenth or the beginning of the eleventh century that a special day was set apart for prayers for the dead, the day following the Feast of All Saints. This touching institution recalled to forgetful hearts the memory of those whom the year had snatched away; with one

---

(1) The "laures" of the East were villages of isolated huts which were inhabited by one or two monks at most. (Note by translator.)

hand it pointed to the tomb, with the other to the final meeting place in Heaven; while it called on suffering mankind to raise unanimous supplication for mercy to the throne of God. (1)

(1) The first idea of this institution belongs to S. Odilon, Abbot of Cluny. It was made general throughout Christendom by Sylvester II.

CHAPTER XII.

> Que dirai-je du peuple? C'est le peuple romain ! . . . Qu'y a-t-il de plus connu, dans les siècles passés, que l'insolence et le faste des Romains? C'est une nation qui ne sait ce que c'est que la paix, et qui est accoutumée à la sédition; une nation farouche et peu traitable jusqu'à présent, qui n'a jamais su se soumettre que lorsq'elle n'a pu résister. — *S. Bernard.*

TWELFTH CENTURY.

THE quarrel about investitures was long maintained: we have already indicated its origin; but it is necessary to give some account of its nature and results. Kings granted the investitures of bishoprics and abbeys inasmuch as they were fiefs depending upon the crown; but, instead of employing for this ceremony the standard or sceptre, types of the temporal power used in the case of all other fiefs, they bestowed on ecclesiastical titulars the cross and ring, distinctive marks of spiritual authority.

At first the Popes submitted to this in silence; but when GREGORY VII wished to improve the morality of the clergy, and found in their ranks only an obstinate resistance to all reform, he authoritatively proclaimed the rights which belonged to him as head of the Church. Accustomed as the clergy were to receive everything from the temporal power, their pastoral staff and great estates, they had lost sight of the common centre of faith, and were deaf to the teachings of the Apostolic See; the bonds which united them to the Roman Pontiffs being thus insensibly loosened it was easy to foresee that the time would come when Christendom should be split up into a number of national Churches, immediately under the influences of princes and subject to their control. We might add that, under these conditions, simony would be freely indulged in without any check whatever. Indeed so evident were these results that the Popes determined not to renounce their just pretensions. Very heavy responsibilities, in truth, rested upon the Church in consequence of the high position of guide and keeper of society which S. Bernard attributes to her; a position, indeed, which the opinion of nations had already granted to her before S. Bernard's time. It is difficult to realise the full weight of these responsibilities in an age when brute force was all powerful, and when open warfare raged between mind and matter; mind being represented by the only class which then cultivated it, and matter by the unbridled passions of uneducated humanity.

The first weed to be uprooted was that tendency to usurpation which threatened to destroy the only liberty left in Europe, that of the children of God. This liberty was the only safeguard to the people then, their only hope for the future. So long as the Church remained powerful, by means of her unity of action, her possessions and her privileges, despotism felt the curb and could not advance. The Church, placed on a height so as to see all things, watched and guarded everything, says S. Bernard. She protected the goods of shipwrecked persons and sheltered merchants and travellers from those who wished to detain them until ransomed; she also proscribed those cruel games which made sport of men's lives; in short she shielded the child's cradle and the bridal couch; upholding social rights, offering an asylum to all in sorrow, and hurling anathemas at those who caused their unhappiness. The laws of the Church became in various ways models on which the secular laws were based. Alone, among all laws, the rules of the Church allowed no torture, knew no distinction of persons, showed in fact in those early days the realisation of the most important improvements which have been subsequently introduced into later codes. (1)

---

(1) Unfortunately ecclesiastical laws applied only to clerics, the temporal authority refusing to subject the laity to clerical jurisdiction. What Europe gained thereby was the retention of torture, and the survival of a system of justice which had two weights and measures according to the condition of the individual. The superiority of ecclesiastical over civil law may be studied in the "Génie du Christianisme", Book VI, Ch. X. The best maxims of our codes are taken from the canons, yet it was this very canonical law which Henry II of England wished to make subservient to the barbarity of secular law. In this attempt he was stoutly opposed by S. Thomas à Becket; and for this opposition Henry put à Becket to death. The one represents the old spirit of barbarism; the other, the civilisation of the Gospel.

The maintenance of the rights and privileges of the Church became then the most important social question of the age; the Roman Pontiffs, in taking up their defence, only answered to the demands and wants of humanity. Moreover, in pursuing their claim with regard to investitures, the Popes acted with that spirit of moderation which was to be so ably recommended at a later date by the great Abbot of Clairvaux. Thus, at the coronation of the Emperor Henry V, the only condition Pope Paschal II exacted was that the Emperor should cease giving the staff and ring, undertaking on his part not to interfere with the royal prerogatives. (1) This compact was approved and signed by Henry's ambassadors, on the 5th of February 1111, in the forecourt of S. Peter's Basilica, and the Emperor made a stately entry into Rome to receive his unction. But, at the very moment the Pope was about to place the crown on his head, Henry refused to ratify by oath the undertakings his ambassadors had signed on his behalf; he went further, for he ordered the Pope and the Cardinals to be seized and guarded by his troops.

When the news of this outrage upon the pontiff had spread throughout the town a fierce outbreak took place; the populace attacked the Germans from all sides, pursuing them into the Leonine city, and killing them even under the portico of S. Peter's. The Emperor was himself thrown down, and wounded

---

(1) "Droit de régale": royal patronage over ecclesiastical preferments whereby the monarch kept their revenues during vacancies, and appointed successors to them. (Note by translator.)

in the face; he would even have fallen into the hands of the Romans had it not been for the devotion of Otho, Count of Milan, who remounted him on his own horse, and remained fighting on the spot until he was hacked to pieces.

Paschal at first bore his captivity with courage; but, at the end of two months, fear of a schism, and the grief he felt for the sufferings of those who shared his prison, proved more powerful than had been the fear of death: he therefore yielded up his claim to the investitures, and bestowed the imperial crown on Henry. The Pope's return to Rome was welcomed with transports of joy, the crowd so pressing around him as to delay his entry into the Lateran palace until nightfall. But, when the conditions of his return became known, a dull murmur of disapproval succeeded to the expressions of universal joy. From France, England, Spain, and from many of the towns of Italy, complaints reached Rome against this surrender of the imprescriptible rights of the Church. Paschal therefore called a Council, before which he laid his explanations. He said:— "We have made the Bishops and Cardinals take an oath for us that we would not trouble King Henry any more about the investitures, and that we would not excommunicate him. Now, though King Henry has ill kept his oath, we shall never excommunicate him . . . we leave him and his to the judgment of God . . . . But as to the agreement which we were compelled to sign, without the advice and written consent of my brethren, we confess it was badly done, and desire that it should be set right, leaving its correction to this assembly, in order that neither the Church nor our own soul may suffer any injury thereby."

Thereupon this Council solemnly condemned the royal claims to ecclesiastical investitures; and a General Council, assembled in the Lateran Palace in 1116, confirmed anew by its decrees the rights and privileges of the spiritual power.

The Emperor then marched upon Rome, where the divisions which existed between the Pope and the people seemed to promise him a better reception than the one he had formerly received. For two centuries the papal power over the Romans had been greatly counterbalanced by the lawless influence of a few families who, from the theatres, baths, and tombs of ancient Rome, which they had turned into fortresses, constantly threatened the maintenance of law and order. We have seen the Castle of S. Angelo successively held by Crescentius and Cencius; this latter had even erected a tower on S. Peter's bridge whence he levied toll on all passers by. The tomb of Cæcilia Metella, on the Appian Way, and that of the Plautia family near Tibur were casemated; the Coliseum became the head quarters of the Frangipani; the theatre of Marcellus, of the Pierleoni; and the Mausoleum of Augustus, of the Colonna. It may well be understood that the existence of these persons, independent of all authority by their position, was a constant source of trouble.

The administration of Rome was in the hands of a prefect, whose power, though often treated with contempt, was nevertheless the object aimed at by every ambitious man. In 1116 a vacancy occurring, some individuals elected the son of the last holder of the office, although he was but a youth; conducted him to the Pope's Mass on Holy Thursday, and suddenly, after the first prayer, requested him to confirm the election. The Pope thereupon excused himself from attending to civil affairs during the holy solemnity; but the tumult increased, continuing even on Good Friday while the populace were visiting barefoot the churches and the tombs of the martyrs; and on Easter Sunday Paschal was twice assaulted, near the Bridge of S. Angelo, by some armed insurgents who clamorously demanded him to confirm the people's election. The Pope endeavoured to calm the sedition by promising to give an answer within a few days; but the rioters would brook no delay, and fell to attacking houses belonging to the Pope's adherents, especially those of the Pierleoni which they dismantled. To restore order it would have been necessary to shed blood; this the Pope refused to do, withdrawing to Albano, and sedition remained rampant within the city.

This state of affairs offered the Emperor too favourable an opportunity to let slip. He was then in Italy occupied in preventing the fulfilment of Countess Matilda's will. She had died in 1115 leaving all her dominions to the Apostolic See. To possess Rome was the object of Henry's wishes; to attain it he sent presents to the rebels, and soon afterwards entered the city himself, and gave his daughter in marriage to the former commander of the Roman troops, a man who had proved false to Pope Paschal. He then demanded the imperial crown from the

Roman clergy; but they refusing to comply with his request it fell to the lot of Maurice Burdin, Archbishop of Braga, in Portugal, to perform this ceremony in S. Peter's Basilica. It is not hard to perceive, in the Emperor's anxiety for another consecration, an involuntary homage to public opinion, which held that the Church alone was the true depository of all power.

PASCHAL II was then in Campania; he died there in 1118 just as the force of the rebellion was spent, and as he was about to return to Rome.

It has already been stated that Countess Matilda died during this pontificate. This woman was possessed of an energetic spirit, and endowed with a courage that was almost superhuman. Always devoted to the Apostolic See, no matter who might be the reigning pontiff, she never gave way under reverses of fortune, not even when her lands were subjected to invasion: she hastened to every place, in the absence of the Emperor, retook her towns, drove out the imperial troops; and her people, astonished by the brilliant qualities she displayed, only knew her by the title of the great Countess. Having had no children by either of her husbands, Godfrey the Hunchback, Duke of Lorraine, and Guelph of Bavaria, she devised all her States to the Church, a last and magnificent token of a devotion which had ended only with her life. (1)

---

(1) This donation, renewed in 1102, had first been made under the pontificate of GREGORY VII. Matilda had then appeared at the Lateran in the chapel of S. Croce, which was situated in front of Constantine's baptistery, and there, in the presence

Matilda was buried in the church of S. Benedict, near Mantua; but, in the sixteenth century, URBAN VIII caused her remains to be brought to Rome, and commissioned Bernini to raise a monument to their memory in S. Peter's. The sarcophagus is surmounted by a shield wreathed in laurels; the famous scene between the Pope and Emperor at Canossa is sculptured upon it in bas-relief; armorial bearings are upheld by children, angels are represented in prayer, and above all stands a statue of the Countess, holding the sceptre in one hand, and with the other supporting the tiara and keys which she had defended so well.

Paschal's successor was Cardinal John of Gaeta, deacon of S. Maria-in-Cosmedin, who took the name of GELASIUS II. His election was followed by frightful violence: Cencio Frangipani, leader of the imperial faction, broke open the doors within which the Conclave was sitting, and, having seized the new Pope by the throat, flung him down, mangled him with his spurs, and dragged him to his own house, in which he imprisoned him. The Cardinals were similarly ill-used and imprisoned: but soon the prefect of the city and the Pierleoni sounded the alarm; the people rose up in arms, and the Frangipani taking fright fled, leaving their victim behind. This triumph of law and order was but brief; at the tidings of the election of Gelasius, the Emperor Henry

---

of several Roman nobles, she bestowed on S. Peter's church all her present goods and all she should acquire in the future, both on this side and beyond the mountains. "Propria clavigero sua subdidit omnia Petro." (Donnizone.)

set out himself for Italy, and managed to get into the Leonine city by night. He demanded that the Pontiff should admit his full and entire right to confer investitures; threatening, in case of refusal, to bring about the election of another Pope. Gelasius, awakened by the noise of the Emperor's arrival, escaped under cover of the darkness and a great storm; he reached the Tiber and managed to drop down it, safe and sound, in spite of darts hurled at him by the Germans who were guarding the banks; then, borne on the shoulders of Cardinal Alatri, on account of his great age, he took refuge in the Castle of Ardea. Later on he retired to Terracina and Gaeta.

The Emperor, enraged both at the escape and unshaken constancy of the Pontiff, set up Maurice Burdin in opposition to him. This man insolently assumed the insignia of papacy under the title of GREGORY VIII, and the Emperor insisted on his crowning him once more, for, at each new excess, he felt the necessity of securing the tottering diadem on his brow.

Gelasius only waited for Henry's departure to return to Rome; and, on the 21st of July 1118, he officiated solemnly in the church of S. Praxedes. But his courage had not sufficiently measured the danger: the Frangipani attacked him during the sacred office, and, after a fierce fight which lasted half the day, Gelasius managed with great difficulty to escape on horseback into the country, still wearing his pontifical vestments, and accompanied only by his cross-bearer. Gelasius now determined to retire to France, leaving

Burdin master of the tombs of the Apostles. But Burdin's authority did not extend far beyond the limits of the city; for, though he was supported by the imperial faction, he found steady and determined opposition from the people. The Bishop of Porto remained in Rome as Vicar of the lawful Pope; and so powerful was his influence that, on the death of Gelasius at Cluny in 1119, and the election in France of CALIXTUS II to succeed him, the Bishop of Porto had the courage to ascend the Capitol and request the people to ratify this election in the usual manner. The acclamations of the people were unanimous, their echoes resounding as far as the Basilica of S. Peter where Burdin sat in state.

Next year Calixtus set out for Rome, receiving on his way the homage of all the people of Provence, Lombardy, and Tuscany, who flocked round him to receive his blessing. When news of this was brought to Rome, Burdin felt no longer safe, so he withdrew to the shelter of the fortress of Sutri. Meanwhile the Roman militia marched forth a three days' journey to meet the Pope; every street was carpeted; children carried branches of trees as the people had done once before at Jerusalem; even Greeks and Jews joined in the general enthusiasm; and thus, amid the liveliest marks of rejoicing, amid hymns and prayers, the Pope was received into the city of Pontiffs.

Burdin was delivered by the inhabitants of Sutri into the hands of the pontifical troops, who, in cruel derision, conducted him to Rome seated backwards on a camel, whose tail he was made to hold, and covered with a bloody sheepskin, intended to be a hideous counterfeit of the red cope he had usurped. The excitement was so intense on his entry into the town that he would undoubtedly have been killed had not Calixtus interfered on his behalf. The Pope sent him to do penance in the monastery of Cava, near Salerno.

Rome now recovered, under the severe but just administration of Calixtus, that appearance of order and peace to which she had long been a stranger. The fortresses of the Frangipani were occupied or demolished, and brigandage ceased to reign supreme on the highways and in the churches. The churches had, in fact, continued to be the scene of such unbridled pillage that the General Lateran Council, in 1123, considered a special anathema necessary:—"We forbid laymen", runs one of its decrees, "under pain of excommunication, to remove offerings from the altars of S. Peter, the Saviour, S. Maria-della-Rotonda, or from any other altars or crosses; we also prohibit turning churches into fortresses, as thereby they are reduced to servitude. Should any one dare to stop, rob, take toll from or aggrieve any pilgrim going to Rome or other places of devotion, he shall be excommunicated until he makes restitution". (1)

Three hundred Bishops and more than six hundred Abbots were present at this the ninth Ecumenical Council, and the first of those that were to be held at the Lateran.

(1) Canons 14 and 16.

Meanwhile Calixtus was restoring aqueducts and public monuments; but the most remarkable event of his pontificate was the agreement which put an end to the long continued quarrel about investitures. It was in a vast plain near Worms, on the banks of the Rhine, the 23rd of September 1122, that the deed was proclaimed which marked the reconciliation of the Holy See and the Empire. This act defined, with strictest impartiality, the several rights of the two powers; to the temporal power, it granted the investiture, with the sceptre, of the prerogatives depending from the crown'; to the spiritual power, the investiture, with the staff and ring, of the churches and goods which particularly belonged to them. (1)

Very shortly these two principles were accepted throughout Europe. Calixtus had for successor Lambert, Bishop of Ostia, who took the name of Honorius II. This election was, to some extent, carried by force by the Frangipani faction; but Honorius refused to profit from a right acquired by violence, so he declined to ascend S. Peter's Chair until he had been proclaimed by a fresh assembly. But schism was only deferred for a short time. Yet, in order to prevent any competition, the Cardinals, seeing the life of Honorius in danger, agreed to place the choice of his successor in the hands of eight of their body. Four of these, immediately on the death of Honorius,

---

(1) In fact these were royalties, or rather rights and fiefs, belonging to the Church, which had not been bestowed by the crown. Now, according to feudal law, fiefs were only held from those who had conferred them.

elected Gregory, deacon of S. Angelo, who was himself one of the appointed eight electors, and proclaimed him Pope, against his wish, under the name of INNOCENT II. The other three electors, separating from their colleagues, met a few hours later in the church of S. Marco, and there, with the assistance of a small number of the clergy, acclaimed Peter of Leon, (Pier-Leoni,) one of their number under the title of ANACLETUS. This Pier-Leoni descended from a rich Jew who became a convert under Leo IX, and who introduced into his own name that of this illustrious Pontiff: his wealth and his alliances soon made him one of the most important men in Rome, and the Pier-Leoni became the most powerful rivals of the Frangipani in the struggle between the papacy and the empire. But, after nobly and courageously upholding the cause of the Popes, the Pier-Leoni had the misfortune to obtain the tiara. After the pretended election of Anacletus they even fell to plundering churches, among others S. Peter's, the richest of all, SS. John Lateran and Maria Maggiore, and by money obtained from melting down sacred vessels they bribed and won the leaders of the people over to their side. Innocent II, feeling that he was no longer safe in Rome, retired to France.

Thus Rome became again a prey to civil discord. In 1133 the Emperor Lothair III advanced to the city accompanied by Innocent; he encamped on Mt. Aventine, and vainly endeavoured to enter into negotiations with the antipope, who occupied the greater part of the city, and notably S. Peter's Basilica. The Castle of S. Angelo and other fortresses of the Pier-Leoni were then attacked; but they vigorously resisted, and, after seven weeks of fruitless efforts, the besiegers were compelled to return to Germany. It was during Lothair's stay in the capital of Christendom that Innocent crowned him and his wife, Richenza, in the Lateran Basilica, and presented him with the yearly revenues from Countess Matilda's domains.

S. Norbert, Archbishop of Magdeburg, accompanied Lothair as Chancellor. It is to be regretted that he has left no trace of his stay in Rome, whither he had come once before, during the pontificate of Honorius II, to petition for the confirmation of a religious Order which he had founded at Prémontré, in the diocese of Laon. It is therefore on Mt. Aventine, where the imperial army lay encamped, that one likes to think of this man, powerful in deeds and words, "potens in opere et sermone," whose voice the pillaging nobles and immoral clerics of Magdeburg sought to stifle in his blood. The sacred churches on the Aventine, SS. Maria, Alessio, and Sabina, often witnessed his fervent prayers.

Meanwhile Pier-Leoni succeeded in maintaining his authority in Rome, hateful though it was to the people. His reign continued for five years; but, when he died in 1138, it became necessary to bury him secretly in order to avoid an outbreak. The Cardinals of his party made haste to give him a successor; however this new intrusion proved but ephemeral. Everyone was weary of the schism; the Pier-Leoni submitted to the Pope, and the powerful voice of S. Bernard persuaded the intruder to sue for mercy and pardon.

At this time S. Bernard towered before Europe

in all the grandeur of his genius and virtues. During his youth he had been vainly tempted by the most violent passions; and, in the solitude of Clairvaux, honours and dignities had also in vain assailed him. He was one of those zealous men to whom God gives a fore-knowledge of heavenly things here below which apparently influences their words supernaturally. Simple monk as he was, for nearly fifty years he had been the counsellor of Christendom; his eloquence swayed nations, directed and governed Popes and Kings; no such power had been seen on earth since the days of S. Ambrose and S. Jerome; all the world bowed before him as to a Father of the Church.

In the Church of SS. Vincenzo-ed-Anastasio Rome preserves a precious memory of S. Bernard. The monastery of SS. Vincenzo-ed-Anastasio, situated ad aquas Salvias, was granted by Innocent II to a colony sent by the saint from Clairvaux under the charge of his disciple, Bernard of Pisa. Whenever S. Bernard came to Rome he stayed in this monastery. One day, when saying Mass for the souls in purgatory in a neighbouring chapel, he suddenly beheld a mysterious ladder like that of Jacob; it reached to heaven, and ransomed souls appeared to be ascending it in crowds. This chapel has ever since been an object of great veneration. Cardinals Farnese and Aldobrandini had it restored by Vignoli, and it bears the name of Heaven's Ladder (Scala Cœli).

S. Bernard returned to Clairvaux a few days after the suppression of the schism; he went alone, taking nothing except a few relics with him; but the whole population of Rome, clergy, people, and nobility, followed him with respect and thanksgiving as far as the Milvian Bridge.

Rome seemed henceforth to revive with new life; the churches, which had fallen into ruins during the usurpation of Anacletus, were restored; the divine office was again celebrated with pomp and fervour; exiles were recalled, and the abandoned towns of ancient Latium repeopled. At the same time the peace of the Church was consolidated by the second General Lateran Council in 1139. Roger, King of Sicily, alone refused to submit to papal authority. Innocent excommunicated him, and marched against him as far as San-Germano, at the foot of Monte-Cassino; but there he was suddenly surprised and taken prisoner by some troops belonging to the enemy. Roger only consented to acknowledge and release him after obtaining the investiture of the kingdom of Sicily, which had already been granted to him by the antipope Anacletus.

This captivity of a few days was like the prelude to fresh disasters. There was among the Romans an incessant restlessness which could not be satisfied either by peace or war; war decimated and ruined them; but peace gave a free vent to their unquiet passions, and allowed old memories of the Roman Republic to live again in their feeble intellects. Ever in conflict with Tusculum and Tibur, they desired to crush these intractable towns as their ancestors had crushed Veii and Fidenæ, so as to dominate Italy by the ascendency of their power. Innocent II would not lend himself to these dreams of foolish ambition; in 1143 he even granted an honourable peace to the Tiburtines, who had gloriously maintained a long siege. This forbearance on the Pope's part led to a sedition in Rome. Those who had been unable to conquer Tibur assembled tumultuously at the Capitol, tore up the treaty signed in S. Peter's name, and re-established the Senate, as though this ancient name contained in itself the whole secret of Roman greatness. This revolution dealt a fatal blow to Innocent; he suddenly fell ill, and all remedies failed to restore his exhausted strength. He was buried in S. Maria-trans-Tiberim, a church he had restored, and within which a vast mosaic commemorates him. He is represented near Jesus Christ and the Virgin, in company with SS. Peter, Calixtus, Julius and several other saints of the old and new law. Bethlehem and Jerusalem appear, as usual, in the background of the picture, with angels issuing from their gates.

S. Malachy, the illustrious Archbishop of Armagh, came as a pilgrim to the tomb of the Apostles towards the end of the reign of Innocent II. This holy prelate, to whom has been attributed a series of prophecies concerning the Popes who were to occupy the Apostolic Chair, spent a full month in Rome visiting the holy places, and seeking to obtain permission to lay aside the episcopal mitre in order to don the rough habit of the monks of Clairvaux.

Meanwhile the Romans boldly pursued their efforts to obtain the form of government they desired; they elected a patrician to replace the prefect to whom the Popes were in the habit of delegating their temporal authority; then they appropriated all the fiefs of the Church, leaving only for the support of the clergy offertories and tithes. Powerful families, like the Frangipani and Pierleoni, seeing in this new organisation only a lessening of their influence, stood outside the movement, and fortified their strongholds; but the greater part of the nobles, to whom the establishment of a senate appeared to give some sort of superiority, and the people, always eager for change, declared so vigorously against papal authority that Celestine II thought it wise to retire to Viterbo a few days after his election.

Arnold of Brescia now came to Rome to stimulate the spirit of sedition. He was a disciple of Abelard, and had assumed the monastic cowl in order to give greater weight to his words. For a long time he had overrun France, Italy, and Germany, accusing the clergy of crime on account of their wealth, and exciting the secular power against ecclesiastics. Arnold assumed the airs of a pious reformer, though his heart beat only with the fierce passions of a tribune; his discourses were consequently less addressed to those whom they most concerned than to the mob and wealthy persons to whom the riches of the Church were an object of eternal envy. Having been condemned and excommunicated by the General Lateran Council in 1139, it was a triumph for him, after Celestine's departure, to be able to enter the city of the Popes in spite of them, and to witness his doctrines put into practice by a people who proudly called themselves the Senate and People of Rome, "Senatus populusque Romanus".

Arnold now resumed his character of tribune with greater boldness than ever: in his orations one might have imagined that the Republic of Cato and Gracchus lived again, that the Capitol would once more rise from its ruins, and the dead legions again recover their eagles. But all his eloquence only produced anarchy and plunder. At his bidding the houses of ecclesiastics were sacked and demolished; S. Peter's was converted into a fortress, and every pilgrim robbed. Worn out with these labours the Romans found no strength to resist the attacks of the Tiburtines and the Pope.

CELESTINE II and LUCIUS II reigned only a few months. The latter died in Rome from the effects of an injury caused by a stone having been hurled at him by the partisans of Arnold of Brescia; but his successor, EUGENIUS III, succeeded, with the help of the Tiburtines, in lowering the pride of the Romans. He exacted from them suppression of the patriciate, and the re-establishment of the prefect in his dignity and office; he consented to the continuance of the senate only on condition that it submitted its jurisdiction to pontifical authority. The entry of Eugenius into Rome resembled a triumph; the populace held branches in their hands, even Jews accompanied the faithful, bearing on their shoulders the books of the law. People were in fact weary of anarchy and sighed for peace: nevertheless the desire for domination was not quite dead in some hearts; the senate in particular was much chagrined to witness the curtailment of their power as a political body, so they set to work to excite the passions of the populace against Tibur, whose arms had been more powerful than those of Rome. Eugenius owed too much to the Tiburtines to lend himself to the scheme of vengeance prepared by their enemies; but, fearing the results of popular excitement, he withdrew to the Vatican, which, with the Leonine city, formed a fortified place quite distinct from the rest of the town, having the Castle of S. Angelo as its main defence. Eugenius had been a disciple of S. Bernard. He was indeed that very Bernard of Pisa whom the great Abbot of Clairvaux had placed at the head of the monastery of SS. Vincenzo-ed-Anastasio: "a gentle and scrupulous soul, full of modesty and reserve, a mind more given to silence and contemplation than to the management of business." (1)

While Eugenius was at work at Clairvaux his chief occupation, according to the annals of that Abbey, had been "to look after the heating apparatus, and to keep fires for the monks who were overcome with cold after matins and only lightly clad." (2) Having become Prior of the monastery of SS. Vincenzo-ed-Anastasio, this humble monk still yearned for Clairvaux and S. Bernard: "O my father," he writes to him, "since I am far away from you my life is consumed with affliction, my days are passed in tears. Unhappy man that I am! I no longer hear your gentle voice, nor see your beloved face . . . . Grant, O my father, that I may leave this place to seek

---

(1) S. Bernard, ep. 237.
(2) For full details see the excellent "Histoire de S. Bernard," by the Abbé Ratisbonne.

some repose." Yet it was this man, who felt himself misplaced as superior of a monastery, whom the Cardinals singled out to place at the head of the world! "Is it not perfectly ridiculous," writes S. Bernard, "to take a poor little man, covered with rags, 'pannosum homuncionem' and make him lord over Princes, Bishops, kingdoms and empires! Do I say ridiculous! No, by no means, for it is an admirable thing to do!"

Admirable it doubtless was, for this poor monk, who had only possessed holiness, became from that moment endowed with both talents and strength. A few days after his election S. Bernard wrote to him, "The tidings of your elevation have spread through this country . . . and I have expected some messenger would come to assuage my sorrow, by saying: 'Joseph, your son, is well, and reigns over all Egypt' . . . So my son Bernard has become my father Eugenius; I trust that the Church may now also change for the better. How happy should I be could I see her, before I die, as she was in the first age, when the Apostles spread their nets, not to catch gold and silver, but to capture souls! This is what the Church expects of you."

S. Bernard maintained towards the Pope the same freedom of speech he had used to the disciple, and the Pontiff encouraged him therein by his respectful deference.

When Eugenius came to France, in 1147, he wished to revisit the monastery which recalled the sweetest memories of his life; and the monks were struck with admiration on discovering in the supreme pontiff the humble simplicity of a monk. Beneath his papal robes he always wore a woollen habit, and the rich coverings of his bed concealed the straw pallet of the Clairvaux dormitory. Eugenius III and S. Bernard died the same year, 1153. At his death Eugenius resided at Tibur, but his body was solemnly brought to Rome and buried at S. Peter's.

The spirit of independence continued to reign among the different classes of the Roman population; papal authority was not disputed, but it was constantly hampered in its action by jealous ambitions, so that the Popes continued to reside at the Vatican in order to be safe from violence.

Arnold of Brescia profited by this mutual distrust to re-enter Rome and again preach sedition. The senate received him eagerly, and the people broke into rioting.

There are always two classes of men in every town: one consists of loud talkers who try to domineer; while the party of quiet persons are often the stronger. One day, Arnold's followers attacked and wounded, in the Via Sacra, Gerard, the Cardinal priest of S. Pudentiana. The Pope, who was ADRIAN IV, thereupon placed Rome under an interdict, so that sacred services ceased in all the churches. This worked as the signal of reaction against Arnold and the senate: Arnold was driven away, and the senators found themselves compelled to go in person and ask forgiveness from the Pontiff. The following day, which was Holy Thursday of the year 1155, an immense crowd went to the Basilica of S. Peter to receive solemn absolution; and, after the ceremony,

Adrian, surrounded by Cardinals and Bishops, left the Leonine City, amidst hearty acclamations, in order to take possession of the Lateran palace.

Arnold of Brescia was arrested a few days later, brought back to Rome, and burnt. His ashes were flung into the Tiber.

The throne of Germany was at this time occupied by Frederick Barbarossa, the first Emperor of the House of Swabia. This Prince "sighed for the crown of the city, and of the world", as Otho of Freisingen tells us, and it was only in Rome that he hoped to obtain it. He therefore set out for Italy with his troops, thereby awakening many fears and many hopes. The Pope advanced to meet him beyond Viterbo; the Roman nobles sent ambassadors to offer him the imperial crown on behalf of their leader, on condition that he would free them from the yoke of the clergy, restore to Rome the empire of the world and her ancient splendour by re-establishing the senate and the order of knighthood, sanction ancient customs, present the city on entering the Capitol with five thousand pounds weight of silver, and that he would defend her against all insults, even to shedding blood. The ambassadors were to obtain the Emperor's oath to all these conditions. But Frederick roughly interrupted their oration by crying out:— "Rome is no longer what she once was", and, after curtly upbraiding them with their abasement and impudence, he dismissed them. The following night, by the advice of Adrian, the imperial troops occupied the Leonine City; and on the 18th of June 1155, at the hour of tierce, the

Pope bestowed upon Frederick, in the Basilica of
S. Peter, the sword, sceptre, and crown, amid German
shouts, which, say the chroniclers, "resounded like
thunder".

The Romans roused themselves at this clamour,
feeling indignant that the Emperor should have received from the Pope's hands what he had refused
from theirs. Accordingly they sallied forth from the
Castle of S. Angelo, and fell upon some Germans
who were still in the Basilica, killing them without
mercy. Frederick, who had already left Rome,
hurriedly returned, and a desperate fight ensued until
night-fall, when a thousand Romans were left dead
upon the field. Then the Pope and Emperor departed, and from this date Adrian IV seldom dwelt
in Rome. He died at Anagni on the 1$\underline{st}$ of September 1159.

ADRIAN IV is the only Englishman who ever
occupied S. Peter's Chair. His name was Nicholas
Breakspeare, and his youth had been spent in the
greatest poverty. Later on, he became Abbot of
Saint-Ruf, near Avignon, and then Cardinal-Bishop
of Albano. The dignities with which he was invested,
even the sovereign pontificate itself, changed in no
way the spirit of disinterestedness he had acquired
from his early struggles in life. As a child he had
begged for alms at the gate of S. Alban's Abbey,
in Hertfordshire; as supreme Pontiff, instead of
raising his family to worldly honours, he left them
poor like Jesus Christ. England greatly felt the
honour of one of her sons being enthroned on the
Apostolic Chair. Henry Plantagenet thus wrote to

Adrian:— "Your recent elevation has, like a radiant morn, dissipated the gloomy mourning of the Roman Church . . . But, above all, our West rejoices at having been worthy to give this new light to the universe, this sun of Christendom." As for Adrian himself, he once told John of Salisbury that he would rather have never left the quiet cloister of Saint-Ruf than be involved in all the difficulties of the papacy. "The Lord," he added, "has always made us grow up between the hammer and the anvil; and now, if it be His desire, He will lay His hand upon the burden with which He has laden us, for in truth it is beyond our strength."

John of Salisbury, who afterwards was Bishop of Chartres, came twice to Rome under the pontificate of Eugenius III and Adrian IV. The latter Pope was then at Benevento, whither John went to visit him, receiving a most affectionate welcome. Adrian admired alike his many attainments and frank speech. He admitted him to his own table, even insisting that they should use one plate and glass between them. The good understanding which had at first existed between Adrian and Frederick Barbarossa was soon disturbed, and the split between the empire and the priesthood became deeper and more intense. Adrian when writing to Frederick had spoken of the benefits (beneficia) of the papacy, the Emperor chose to take the word as signifying benefice, as though the empire were a fief of Rome; but, not stopping at this vain quibble, which the Pope repudiated, he claimed for himself regal prerogatives over the whole of Italy, thus reducing that country to the position of a mere dependency on his dominions. (1) "As, by God's will, I am Roman Emperor," he said, "I only bear an empty title, unless Rome be in my power."

These claims aroused national feeling in most Italian hearts, and it was then that the two great parties of the Guelphs and Ghibelines began to appear. The rallying cry of the Guelphs, who looked to the Pope for support, was the independence of Italy; the Ghibelines strove for German domination and relied upon the Emperor. These two parties were even represented in the Conclaves. Thus, on the death of Adrian IV, the votes of the Cardinals were divided between Roland Bandinelli, chancellor of the Roman Church, who had carried to Frederick Adrian's severe remonstrances, and Octavian, priest of S. Cæcilia, who was devoted to the Imperial cause. Roland received twenty-two votes, Octavian only three; consequently Roland was elected, and took the name of ALEXANDER; but, as he was being invested with the insignia of his office, Octavian violently snatched away his scarlet cope and placed it on his own shoulders. At the same time armed men broke into S. Peter's; Alexander and the Cardinals who had nominated him took refuge in one of the towers of the Basilica, where they were closely blockaded by Octavian's partisans, and only at length permitted to come out

(1) These royal prerogatives included the duchies, marquisates, counties or earldoms, consulships, rights of coinage, forage for the troops (fodium), market-tolls, high-way-tolls, mills, fisheries, all revenue arising from river dues, quit-rents, and poll-tax.

in order to be thrown into prison. But, after a week, the populace rose against the imperialists and the senate who were in league with them, and led by Hector Frangipani they released the Pope. Alexander III then made a progress through the city amid the heartiest acclamations and bell ringing. Nevertheless the outbreak of ill-feeling was too great to permit of Alexander remaining peacefully in Rome. He therefore withdrew to the neighbouring towns, and at Anagni, Segni, Ferentino, small towns on the road to Monte-Cassino, spent several tempestuous years of his pontificate. The papacy was always certain to find a last refuge among the children of S. Benedict.

The legitimate right of Alexander was undoubted, and incontestable; it would have received the universal acknowledgement of Europe, had not ambition had greater weight with Frederick than his devotion to the cause of Christendom. But Frederick had no intention of yielding the least of his claims on Italy, more particularly on the dominions of Countess Matilda, although Lothair had most deliberately acknowledged them to be the property of the Holy See. He therefore gave in his adhesion to Octavian, and for twenty years rent asunder the Church by a schism.

This is one of the most glorious epochs in the history of the papacy. Throughout it two men stood face to face: one governed all Germany, and claimed, in his quality of successor to the Cæsars, to be master of the world: he was young, ambitious, and full of pride. The other was a priest; humble and meek, driven a wanderer from town to town, for a rebel faction reigned in his capital, and an intruder sat upon his throne. But, feeble as he was, outraged and oppressed persons applied to him for justice. It was under the spell of his name that the Lombard towns united in a holy league to drive back foreign invasion; and, when at length Milan had fallen, when her churches had been overthrown, her walls destroyed, and the Emperor had uttered that ancient pagan sentence against the vanquished — "confiscation and slavery" — (1) Alexander's voice was raised in favour of the oppressed; at its sound Milan, in spite of the Emperor, sprang up again from her ruins, and the now enthusiastic populace built another capital close by, which they called Alessandria after the Pope, as though to proclaim their identity with his cause throughout the world. This bitter strife lasted fifteen years; it drained the resources of the empire, and witnessed the fall of two antipopes.

Rome remained under the power of Octavian during his life; but after his death, which happened in 1164, the Romans sent ambassadors to Alexander, who was then in France, beseeching him to return. At first he hesitated, but finally set out, and after a dangerous voyage, during which he had to put into Messina, Salerno, and Gaeta, landed at Ostia on the 20th of November 1165. Next day all the corporations and an immense crowd came out to meet him, bearing olive branches in their hands, and he was again solemnly put into possession of S. Peter's and the patriarchal palace.

(1) Voltaire speaking of Frederick's conduct in this matter says:— "This decree more resembles an order from Attila than an edict from a Christian Emperor."

This defection of the ancient capital from his cause greatly distressed the Emperor; he immediately left Lombardy, and marched with his forces towards the Marches and the Sabine country; but Ancona held out for a long time, so that he did not reach Rome until the 16th of July 1167. His first exploit was taking S. Peter's church, the portico of which he endeavoured to burn in order to force the garrison to capitulate; but the Castle of S. Angelo and the strongholds of the Frangipani withstood all his efforts. The imperialists, despairing of success, were compelled to bribe the people, who were moreover terrified by the prospect of war within their walls. Then Alexander and his Cardinals, disguised as pilgrims, secretly quitted the city and took refuge at Benevento. But the Frangipani still held out; Lombardy rose up in arms from one end to the other; a dreadful epidemic decimated the imperial troops, and Frederick, after being again crowned at S. Peter's, hurriedly left Italy.

He re-appeared, however; indeed he returned five times to the charge against the Lombards; but the defeat he suffered on the 4th of June 1176 so completely ruined his power that he was forced to send ambassadors to Anagni to sue for peace from Alexander III, from that very Pontiff whom he had contemptuously styled on the previous day "the Chancellor Roland". Alexander refused to treat with him without the concurrence of his faithful allies, the Lombard cities; but, in order to hasten negotiations, he set out in the direction of Venice and Ferrara. On Ash Wednesday 1177 the Pontiff, after celebrating Mass, embarked on the Adriatic Sea. At Zara, in Dalmatia, he was received with the greatest demonstrations of joy, which found vent in singing hymns of praise to God; at Venice, the Doge, Sebastiano Ziani, the senators, and clergy conveyed him in one of the Republican gondolas from S. Niccolò-del-Lido to the Lion of S. Marco, where the people kneeling awaited his fatherly blessing; at Ferrara, the Bishops, Rectors, Marquises, and Counts, with representatives from all the Lombard cities, assembled to hear him preach in the church of S. Giorgio.

"Dear children", said Alexander, "it is by a miracle of the divine power that an old and infirm priest has been enabled to resist the fury of the Germans, and to conquer a powerful Emperor without war; but this has been permitted in order that the world might see that it is impossible to fight against God. Now, though the Emperor has requested us on behalf of the Church and of the King of Sicily, and without your consent, to grant him peace, we have not yet agreed thereto, being mindful of the devotion and courage with which you have fought for the Church, and for the liberty of Italy. But, regardless of our dignity and great age, we have braved the dangers of the sea in order to come among you to deliberate whether or no we shall accept the peace that has been offered us."

At these words cheers resounded without the church, and one of the Lombard Chiefs thus spoke;— "All Italy throws itself at your feet to thank you, and testify to the joy it feels, for the honour you have conferred on your children by coming among them, in order to find and bring home the wandering sheep. We were among the first to oppose ourselves to the fury of the persecution which the Emperor raised against the Church and yourself. We went to the front to prevent him from oppressing Italy and the liberty of the Church, and, in so good a cause, we have been reckless of money, labour, losses, and dangers. Therefore, holy Father, it is meet that you should not accept the peace he offers you without our consent; for we have often refused it unless it included peace also with the Church. Moreover, we are quite willing to come to terms with the Emperor, and to concede to him all his ancient rights in Italy; but as to the liberty we have received from our fathers we shall part with it only with life."

This was a remarkable scene of simplicity and noble sentiment. The papal diplomacy, and that of its allies, is revealed in all its artlessness. The church of S. Giorgio has long ceased to be the Cathedral of Ferrara. Situated outside the town, stripped of those beautiful decorations which attract the curiosity of strangers, its name is but just mentioned in travellers's guides; yet Christians none the less go there to kneel within its walls, and the memory of Alexander and the Lombard League are well worth a few paintings by Scarsellino and Bonone.

One must ask forgiveness for laying so much stress upon details which do not essentially bear upon the subject of this book; but the life of Alexander III is so intimately bound up with Christian Rome, and is in itself so complete, that it is impossible to pass over in silence some of its most brilliant episodes.

From Ferrara the Pope returned to Venice, being followed thither by Frederick, after he had been absolved from excommunication. At Venice he received all the honours due to imperial dignity, and was led by the Doge to the vestibule of S. Marco where the Pope, accompanied by the Patriarch of Aquileia, the Archbishops and Bishops, who were seated and arrayed in their vestments, awaited him. Frederick threw himself at Alexander's feet, the Pontiff immediately raised him up, and gave him the kiss of peace; the Te Deum was then sung by an immense multitude, while the Pope and Emperor advanced to the altar holding each other by the hand.

Next day, the 25th of July, a pontifical mass was celebrated in S. Marco, at Frederick's request, who walked in front of the Pope to clear a way for him as he entered the church, holding his bridle and stirrup according to custom. (1) The 1st of August following, peace was solemnly sworn to in the great hall of the ducal palace. Frederick returned to the Church the possessions of which he had deprived her, and again forswore the schism. A truce of fifteen years was at the same time concluded with the King of Sicily, and one of six years with the Lombards. (2)

(1) This custom had prevailed since the time of the Emperor Lothair II.
(2) The Venetians have been proud to commemorate these glorious events. In the hall of the Great Council there are as many as ten pictures illustrating Alexander III; several of

Alexander III did not return to Rome till the following year; for the Romans, taking advantage of the troubles which distracted the Church, had formed a Republic under the direction of the Senate and refused to acknowledge the temporal authority either of the Pope at Anagni or of the antipope at Viterbo. But, when peace was concluded with the Emperor, the Romans understood that their revolution was at an end, and actually invited Alexander to return. The Pope made his entry conditional upon the senators taking an oath of fidelity and homage to him on their election; that the Basilica of S. Peter and the Prerogatives belonging to the Patrimony of the Church should be restored; that his safety, as also that of the Cardinals, and of all travellers coming to Rome either for devotion or business, should be absolutely guaranteed. These terms were accepted and sworn to by the senators, who then proceeded to Tusculum where the Pope was residing; on the 12th of March, 1178, the festival of S. Gregory, the Pope made his solemn entry into Rome, surrounded by crosses and banners which, contrary to custom, were carried a great distance out of the town to meet him. Shortly afterwards the antipope, who was John of Sturm, and had assumed the title of CALIXTUS III, threw himself at the feet of the Pontiff, was received with kindness and graciously pardoned.

these pictures are by Leandro Bassano, Tintoretto, and Paolo Fiammingo; the Emperor kissing the Pope's feet is by Federigo Zucchero. Several slabs of red marble in the vestibule of S. Marco mark the spot where the interview between Frederick and Alexander took place.

CHAPTER XII.—TWELFTH CENTURY.

This state of peace and concord lasted during the remainder of Alexander III life; he died on the 30th of August 1181, after a pontificate of twenty-two years, blessed by the affection of his subjects and the veneration of all Europe. Even Voltaire has praised his noble conduct; saying that he was the conqueror of the Emperor by his policy and the benefactor of the human race. (1)

Under his successor, LUCIUS III, the turbulent passions of the Romans once more broke loose. Lucius was obliged to flee from his capital in 1183; then, having re-entered by means of money contributed by Christian Princes, he once more found himself an object of hatred to the principal inhabitants. One day they gouged out the eyes of several clerics attached to his person, sparing only one in order that he might bring his unhappy brethren into the presence of the Pope. Lucius again left the city, withdrawing to Verona. URBAN III and GREGORY VIII passed the few years of their pontificate sometimes at Verona, sometimes at Ferrara or Pisa. (2) CLEMENT III entered into negotiations with the Romans at the beginning of 1188. They demanded that the town of Tusculum, which had always been faithful to the Popes, and had often successfully upheld their cause, should be made over to them; that its fortifications should be destroyed, and that the Apostolic See should give a pledge never to rebuild them. Clement III

---

(1) Essai sur l'Hist. gén., C. XLIV.
(2) Urban III died at Ferrara from the grief he experienced on receiving tidings of the reverses in the Holy Land.

was weak enough to consent to this agreement; and, when the Romans found themselves masters of Tusculum, the memory of their former defeats urged them on to ignoble vengeance. Tusculum was utterly destroyed, the houses being razed to the ground, so that the unhappy inhabitants, who were scattered over the slope of the hill, found no shelter except in huts made of leaves. These huts in the lapse of time grew into another town, which, in memory of its origin, retained the name of foliage—Frascati.

Since then, the site of Tusculum has remained bare and deserted. A few scattered stones, some mutilated inscriptions from which science can scarce extract a memory or an idea, are all the remains of Cato's fatherland, of the most renowned free city, "clarissimum municipium," (1) where Cicero, Lucullus, Gabinius, and Crassus had their luxurious country seats. The one thing that is recognised, and will always be so, is the high hill which commands a view over Rome, Tibur, Lake Regillus, and Mt. Albano, and on which once rose the white houses of Tusculum: "Superni villa candens Tusculi."

The final years of the twelfth century were terribly sad for Christendom. In the East the Crusaders lost the battle of Tiberias; Jerusalem herself fell before Saladin, while all the efforts of the third crusade only resulted in the capture of a few places on the sea coast. In the West a new heresy appeared, which attacked every basis of the moral law, and comprised the errors of every clime and age. Besides the two

---

(1) Cicero, "pro Fontino".

principles of the Manichees, it taught the negation of providential justice, contempt for the sacraments, and the substitution of chance for the almighty wisdom of God in the government of the world. This doctrine, contradictory in its principles and antisocial in its results, infected all the south of France and particularly the Albigeois. Germany and Italy were not more fortunate. Frederick Barbarossa died in Syria in 1190 from the effects of bathing, and the empire passed to his son, Henry VI, who for twenty years had borne the title of King of the Romans. This high sounding and fanciful title had been adopted by the Emperors of the Holy Roman Empire as the designation of their eldest son, as that of Cæsar had of old been selected by the Roman Emperors. It was a method of glorifying their lineage, and by degrees to render hereditary a crown which was constitutionally only elective. It was moreover a constant protest against the independence of Italy, and at the same time a support to that claim of universal dominion to which the monarchs of Germany aspired, a dominion of which Rome must be the centre. Henry received the imperial crown from the hands of Pope CELESTINE III, on the 15th of April 1191; and he at once set out for the conquest of the Two Sicilies. This war was marked by some most unworthy deeds. Part of the money with which it was waged had been extorted as the ransom of the gallant Richard I of England, who had been treacherously taken prisoner by Leopold of Austria as he was returning from the Holy Land, and sold to Henry VI. Little good could be expected from Princes capable of such felony. Tancred, whom the inhabitants of Palermo had elected as their King, being dead, Henry VI had his corpse dug up and beheaded; he also put out the eyes of Tancred's young son; but he himself soon afterwards died suddenly on the 28th of September 1197, being poisoned, it is said, by the hand of his wife Constance.

Let us take notice of the action of the papacy amid these calamities and crimes. Leopold of Austria and Henry VI were excommunicated for their perfidious conduct towards the English King; and, when they died, their bodies were left unburied, as the law ordained in the cases of criminals, until the ransom paid for Richard had been returned to England.

The pontifical anathema was also hurled at Philip Augustus to revenge the outraged chastity of a young girl who had been snatched from her father's house, for one day honoured as a wife, and then banished with contempt to a convent.

At the same time Cardinals, Bishops, and monks worked among the Albigeois, amid the burning ruins of churches and dwellings which had been devastated by the heretics, preaching and seeking to evangelise these undisciplined hordes. It was only in the next century that the struggle became both cruel and bloody.

Finally the voice of the Popes was heard, from North to South, summoning the Christian Princes, whose fierce rivalries with one another were deluging Europe with blood, to the holy war, and seeking to instill into them that noble spirit which begets great deeds. Thus Rome still remained the centre of that progressive movement with which Christianity sought to leaven society.

During the pontificate of Alexander III Rome witnessed the meeting of a General Council, the third held at the Lateran, but the eleventh of the Church. It was attended by Bishops from the most distant lands; one of them came on foot from the heart of Scotland; another was an Irish Bishop, whose only revenue was the milk of three cows. At the head of the Irish bishops was S. Lawrence O'Toole, Archbishop of Dublin. Among the decrees of this Council was one condemning the Albigensian heresy, that socialism of the twelfth century; another gave protection to lepers, those pariahs of the human race, to whom laws and custom allowed neither hearth nor home: this decree granted them houses, priests, and burying places, and exempted them from all taxation. Soon afterwards, in 1187, during the pontificate of GREGORY VIII, a poor French leper built a hospital and a church, under the invocation of S. Lazarus near the Vatican, for his fellows in misfortune; it is known as S. Lazaro-fuori-di-Porta-Angelica. The feast in memory of the brother of Martha and Mary was celebrated there on the day of Our Lord's Passion.

The Council of 1197 again renewed the prohibition of tournaments, and anathematized all those hordes of mercenary Brabançons, (1) Aragonese and Cotereaux, (2),

(1) Brabançons was a name given to adventurers who fought on whatever side they were paid best; they were so called because they chiefly came from Brabant. See "Le Grand Vocabulaire Français." Paris, 1768, etc. (Note by translator.)
(2) Cotereaux: ruffians who appeared in Gascony and Languedoc in the twelfth century. (Note by translator.)

who, having warred in every land, existed in times of peace only by murder and plunder. These wandering and lawless men were ever at the disposal of the nobles in their local quarrels. Offspring of the anarchy produced by the feudal system, they had become one of its most powerful weapons; and the Councils in excommunicating them, their adherents, and all who treated with them, only responded to the sad complaints of the miserable country folk.

Such were the forces upon which Christianity had to work in the Middle Ages; and doubtless it experienced quite as great a resistance, on the part of the bold and independent spirit which the Barbarians had introduced into Europe, as it had formerly encountered in the polished but corrupt manners of the Romans. It is true that in the Middle Ages nations were young, and they embraced the faith with holy ardour; long pilgrimages did not wither up their zeal; their devotion was enthusiastic; yet, in spite of every effort the Church had made, education was but little diffused, and such a spirit of independence and insubordination reigned, on account of the lawless state of government, that the faith was often debased, distorted, or adulterated with false beliefs and superstitious practices. Therefore the Church was frequently driven to employ force against men who only respected force, and this accounts for those numerous cases of excommunication which left the culprit isolated in the world, as though he were in the depths of a dungeon. But these extreme measures, those interdicts, above all, which laid whole kingdoms under the ban, and forced the pride of the guilty to bend beneath the weight of public sorrow, were of exceptional occurrence, which the peaceful development of Christian institutions tended each year to render less necessary. Universities sprang up under the influence of religion at Paris, Cambridge, Bologna, and Salamanca; on all sides monasteries increased in number and with them cities, for it is a remarkable fact that nearly every town of modern foundation derived its origin from a monastery; towns were thus sheltered from feudal oppression, and received the fostering care of the monks who looked after every want of mankind.

It was in the twelfth century that the Grand Order of the Trinity for the redemption of captives was founded by S. John of Matha and S. Felix of Valois. One day as John of Matha was saying Mass, his soul burning with that love which, according to the Apostle, is God Himself, "Deus charitas est", (1) a handsome figure, on whose breast shone a blue and red cross, appeared in a vision to him. He communicated his holy revelation to a recluse, and they fasted and prayed together for guidance and strength, after which they went to Rome where their institution was sanctioned and many disciples joined them. Before long these new warriors of Christendom were seen, clad in white, with a blue and red cross upon their breast, hastening through Europe, Asia, and Africa, collecting alms from the rich wherewith to ransom slaves.

(1) I Epis. Joan. IV, 8.

But Christianity did not stop at this; it adapted itself to all that was energetic and vital in the feudal system, in order to employ it for the welfare of mankind. The foundation of a hospital at Jerusalem, by some merchants of Amalfi and a Roman lady named Agnes, became the origin of the Knights Hospitallers of S. John, whose noble courage, purified by religion, never drew sword but in defence of Christendom. The temple of Jerusalem had need of servants and protectors, so the Templars devoted themselves to its defence. The German Crusaders found neither help nor shelter in Palestine, for no one understood their tongue; whereupon the Teutonic Knights of S. Mary sprang into existence to minister to the wants of their countrymen. Religious and military orders quickly increased; the twelfth century alone produced five, and before long they numbered thirty.

These religious troopers, uniting as they did the noble qualities of knighthood with the practice of Christian virtues, rendered very great services to society, as much by the resistance they offered to the enemies of the faith as by the influence they exerted on feudal customs. Feudal chivalry naturally looked for its models among these accomplished types of courtesy and valour. It imitated them by having its own watching over weapons through a night of prayer; it adopted their oaths to fight only in the cause of justice; and it realized better, in presence of these devoted lives, that a Christian knight must never turn recreant.

There had indeed never been a time when modifications were more necessary in the customs of the feudal system. The times had advanced; beneath the surface desire for emancipation was stirring among the people; the communes were in course of formation, constituting themselves into almost independent administrations, and thus becoming centres of free action outside the close system of feudal oligarchy. But it was not only the enfranchisement of the communes which threatened the power of feudalism; the creation of Universities, by spreading knowledge; the building of vast cathedrals, by developing and diffusing the love of art; the invention of the mariner's *compass and bills of* exchange, by giving a fresh *impetus to commerce;* the discovery of the Pandects of Justinian, which indicated what were the advantages of a settled and complete legal system; these were all so many blows struck at monopoly and absolutism. Feudalism could therefore no longer seek its strength in the number of its vassals or the loftiness of its towers, but in the idea that aristocracy is an association for promoting general welfare.

From whatever point of view this great social movement may be studied, Catholicism will be found at its head. Here the clergy established great markets, where commerce might be free from the exactions of the lords of the manor; there the canons of Councils created a legislation for the future, stamped with all the forethought and gentleness of the Gospel; it was in short the Church which multiplied schools and called forth art once more from the tomb. So early as the eleventh century, while still dull barbarism enslaved Europe, we behold the monks of Cava, of Subiaco, of Monte-Cassino, sending for sculptors and painters to decorate their churches: in the twelfth century the monk Azon built the Cathedral of Séez; but a few years before, Humbert, Archbishop of Lyons, ordered a bridge to be constructed across the Saône; in 1163 Pope Alexander laid the foundation of Notre Dâme at Paris; at the same time the druidical oaks of La Puisaye were cut down to form the timber work of S. Denis. The Cathedrals of Chartres, Modena, and Ferrara were rising; ten thousand workmen were building that of Strassburg; Diotisalvi raised the baptistery at Pisa; the great door of the Duomo of that city was cast in bronze by Buonanno; the leaning tower, "il campanile torto," this artist's masterpiece, claims admiration for its graceful and delicate architecture; and numerous master-workers in mosaic were brought from Constantinople by the Republic of Venice to enrich the church of S. Marco by their genius.

Rome alone, which ought to monopolize our attention, remained stationary amid the general activity. Only a few churches, SS. Tomaso-in-Parione, Salvatore-delle-Cupelle, and S. Matteo-in-Merulana, were either built or restored. The impetus had come from her; yet she herself scarcely felt it. (1) Behold how her energy,

---

(1) Those noble Pontiffs, who, by the insubordination of the Romans were driven to reside in the small towns of the patrimony of S. Peter, nevertheless did not forget Rome. Eugenius III, in 1145, constructed the portico of S. Maria-

which under the faithful inspiration of Catholicism could produce such masterpieces, sinks to petty strife, and mere childish efforts at securing independence. Still, even at Rome, an effort was made to promote organisation; made, it is true, entirely within the bosom of the Church: ecclesiastical law was also codified and arranged; the right of canonization, which had until then been exercised sometimes by the public voice, sometimes by the Bishops, was made a special pontifical function, and was reduced to a settled and uniform procedure. The proceedings of Conclaves were arranged in a more complete manner. Since the time of NICHOLAS II the Cardinals alone had been charged with the election of the Pope; by a decree of ALEXANDER III two thirds of their votes were now

Maggiore, which was supported by eight columns; ALEXANDER III placed in the same church two amboes for reading the epistle and Gospel; CLEMENT III added a palace to the Liberian Basilica: CALIXTUS II and INNOCENT II had also enlarged the Lateran. The Oratory of S. Nicolò dated also from CALIXTUS II, as did also the frescoes which ornamented the apse. Near this Oratory he had also constructed two chambers for the use of the Pontiffs. The schisms which had rent the Church asunder and the peace which he had concluded with the Emperor Henry V were recorded by his orders on their walls. Even the clauses of the treaty are reproduced. INNOCENT also added two chambers to those of Calixtus, wherein the crowning of Lothair was represented. In this picture particularly the King was depicted standing at the door of the Basilica, swearing, before being admitted, to respect the rights and honours of the city, with an inscription which, under Frederick Barbarossa, became the subject of bitter strife:—

"Rex stetit ante fores jurans prius urbis honores,
Post homo fit papæ sumit quo dante coronam."

required to make an election valid; then, when the name of S. Peter's successor was announced, majestic and symbolic ceremonies gave the highest tone of Christian dignity to his enthronement. (1) The Pope clad in a cope or red chlamys and wearing the tiara, or papal crown, mounted a white horse, and approached the Basilica of the Saviour amid the acclamations of the people. The noble simplicity of this triumphal procession recalled the entry of the Son of Man into Jerusalem, when He came full of meekness like a victim chosen for the sacrifice. The multitude cried out, as they had done at Jerusalem, "Hosanna, blessed is he that cometh in the name of the Lord, the King of Israel." (2)

It was in the apse of the Lateran church, that Mother church of the world, placed under the invocation of the Saviour and of those two prophets, SS. John the Baptist and John the Evangelist, upon whom divine knowledge had been so plentifully bestowed, that the throne of the Vicar of God was raised. There the nobility, magistrates, and people, came to kneel at his feet as though he were God Himself; then, lest the man should take to himself homage which was only paid to the Person he represented, he was led into the vestibule of the church, and, like a beggar, was placed on a seat level with the

(1) Most of these ceremonies were observed at the enthronement of Paschal II in 1099; but they were only first fully described in the Roman Ceremonial published in the twelfth century by the Chamberlain Cencio Savelli, who became Pope under the title of Honorius III.

(2) S. John XII, 13.

ground, while a voice proclaimed:— "Raising up the needy from the earth, and lifting up the poor out of the dunghill: That he may place him with Princes, with the Princes of his people." (1) The Pope then threw money three times among the people saying:— "Silver and gold are not for our pleasures; what I have, I give." (2)

He was then presented with a rod and keys, as being at once the great Justiciary of the world and the keeper of the gate of Heaven; he was girded with a red scarf, as a symbol of chastity, and to remind him of the poor he was presented with a purple purse, within which were twelve finely engraved stones intended to represent the seals of the twelve Apostles, and a piece of amber to recall the sweet odour of Christ, which, says S. Paul, should be found in us. When a Pope had not previously attained to episcopal dignity, his consecration took place in the Basilica of S. Peter by the Bishop of Ostia, assisted by the Bishops of Porto and Albano. The Archdeacon placed the pallium on his shoulders, fastening it at the breast and sides by three gold pins with hyacinth heads, and the Pope then ascended to the altar to offer the sacrifice of the Mass. After that he pronounced his profession of faith, took the oath, and

---

(1) "Suscitans a terra inopem, et de stercore erigens pauperem; ut collocet eum cum principibus, cum principibus populi sui." (Psalm CXII, 7 and 8.) It was from the recital of this antiphon that the seat in question was called "sedes stercoraria."

(2) "Argentum et aurum non est mihi ad delectationem; quod autem habeo, hoc tibi do."

announced his accession to all Christian people by a solemn declaration. The watchfulness he was now to observe over the nations was represented, in the ceremony, by peacock's feathers, which signified that the Pope was to have as many eyes as there were on the plumage of this bird.

Lastly no common terms were employed to express the magnificence and symbolic splendour of this majestic enthronisation. It was not said that the Pope was raised to the seat of the Apostle: the expression used was, "in apostolica sede sublimatus". Then also the new pastor of the great flock received at one and the same time the titles of Pope and of Pontiff: Pope, because he became the father of all; Pontiff, because henceforth he represented a mystical arch, thrown between God and man, between time and eternity.

CHAPTER XIII.

"Laboravi clamans, raucæ factæ sunt fauces meæ".
Ps. LXVIII, 4.

THIRTEENTH CENTURY.

O whatever high antiquity the origin of the distinguished families of modern aristocracy may be traced, it is only from the twelfth and thirteenth centuries, owing to the then general adoption of hereditary names, that their descent becomes unquestioned. These names made members of the same family joint partakers of their honour as well as of their shame; and fixed their traditions of glory and of power in the same line. Influence attaches itself to all that is great; in the eyes of men, people are great as much perhaps from past traditions, which surround them with glamour from their cradles, as by the magic of their own genius.

Previous to the twelfth century the Marquises and Counts, who lorded it over the small towns of Italy, were often merely adventurers; and we have seen the Pierleoni, the son and grandson of a Jew, rivalling in importance the ancient family of

Frangipani, whose very name recalled their good deeds to the populace of Rome; for it was by the generosity with which they had relieved the hungry in days of famine that they acquired their name of "bread-breakers", Frangipani, which henceforth became their patronymic. (1) This handing down of the family name and arms soon made the nobility a homogeneous and continuous body, jealous alike of their rights and privileges. Hitherto the nobility had in particular been attached to their fiefs; henceforth they prided themselves on their name; it became, in consequence, more difficult rapidly to attain to fortune, and the clearly defined grades established a permanent order in the hierarchy of the social state. It is therefore towards this period that first appear the great names of the Roman aristocracy.

The Cenci (Crescentii) tyrannized for long over Rome, during the tenth and eleventh centuries, from the summit of Hadrian's Mole, defying in turn both Popes and Emperors. But henceforth their star paled; and the name of that mighty race, which seemed to have sworn to destroy the power of the keys, "apostolicæ sedis destructor", scarcely ever is mentioned in history again.

About the same period the Frangipani had appeared, having made the Coliseum their stronghold. After a long domination they were driven out of it by the Annibaldi, whose own stronghold rose close by amid the very outbuildings of the Lateran; and

---

(1) The Frangipani claimed their descent from the "Anicia gens".

finally the Frangipani left Rome for their marquisate of Astura, in the kingdom of Naples.

So early as the twelfth century the Colonna had possessed, and sustained several sieges in, the mausoleum of Augustus. This family, which traced back to the ancient Counts of Tusculum, bore the name of a fief in the neighbourhood of Palestrina, supposed to have been the ancient Labicum. In Rome they inhabited the Palace of the Holy Apostles together with the surrounding quarter as far as the Square of S. Marcello. Outside Rome they owned a great number of places, including Palestrina, Zagarolo, Paliano, and Capranica. In a short time they were audacious enough to threaten the papacy itself, and from the rocky heights of Palestrina treated as equals with the Popes.

The Orsini, who were for long the rivals of the Colonna, take their glorious place in history with NICHOLAS III. Their Roman palace covered the Monte-Giordano, a hill composed of ruins near the bridge of S. Angelo, and stretched away to Pompey's theatre and the Campo di Fiore. They had, however, a Palace near S. Peter's, and were for long masters of the castle of S. Angelo.

The Savelli furnished two Popes during the thirteenth century, HONORIUS III and HONORIUS IV. At that time they dwelt on the Aventine and in the Vico de' Savelli near the chancellor's office; but in the fourteenth century they became masters of the theatre of Marcellus, which the Pierleoni had formerly possessed, and thence their rule extended to the banks of the Tiber.

The Cajetani, whose power was established under the pontificate of BONIFACE VIII, were originally from Catalonia, whence they had migrated and settled at Anagni. The tomb of Cæcilia Metella became their fortress, and BONIFACE VIII raised the battlements which still crown the edifice.

The Conti had for long been Counts of Segni in the Roman States. During the civil wars they, like other great families, possessed several strongholds in Rome. The ruined Torre dei Conti, on the site of Cæsar's Forum, is a most picturesque object. According to Petrarch, who probably referred to its height, the Torre was unrivaled in the whole world. This tower was the work of the architect Marchione d'Arezzo, who was instructed to build it by INNOCENT III and his brother, Ricardo Conti. But the greatest glory of the Conti family is that it produced several of the most illustrious Pontiffs of the Middle Ages; three Conti ascended the Apostolic Chair in the thirteenth century; INNOCENT III, GREGORY IX, and ALEXANDER IV; and during their reigns the authority of the Head of the Church was never more powerful and respected throughout the world. (1)

INNOCENT III was born at Anagni in 1161, and pursued his studies in the University of Paris, which

(1) The Conti family trace their origin from Trasimondo, Duke of Spoleto and Count of Capua in the seventh century. It has given four Popes to the Church. The last, INNOCENT XII, died in 1725. "This Pope", says M. Hürter, "had nine uncles, eight brothers, four nephews, seven great-nephews; what a promise for power and futurity! ... Alas, a century had not elapsed ere the last of the Conti was laid in his tomb." (Histoire d'Innocent III.)

was then esteemed as the source of all wisdom, the tree of life in the terrestrial paradise, the lamp destined to illumine the house of the Lord. The chroniclers of the time are never tired with praising it, and Innocent, who was then known by the name of Lotario Conti, gratefully remembered throughout his life the royal city of the Franks. He was raised to the Cardinalate by Clement III, who named him deacon of the church of SS. Sergius and Bacchus of which he had been Rector. Henceforth his virtues, knowledge, love of study, and retiring manner gave him a special place in public esteem and regard. Therefore, after several years had passed, on the death of Celestine III, a number of Cardinals, who had met in the Septizonium during the obsequies of the Pope, determined to confer the papal tiara on Lotario Conti. Lotario was not at the time present, being employed in rendering the last honours to the late Pope; but when the clergy had assembled for the election he heard with surprise his own name proclaimed, for he was one of the youngest dignitaries of the Church, being then only thirty-seven years of age. At first he refused, begging and entreating with tears that he might be left in his retirement; but the voice of the Conclave was like the voice of God, and finally he was compelled to yield. It is a strange fact that certain Popes, to whom historians have imputed pride and ambition, as for instance Gregory VII and Innocent III, have only ascended the throne upon moral compulsion.

Lotario was ordained priest on the 21st of February 1198; next day he received episcopal consecration in the Vatican Basilica, and took possession of S. Peter's Chair under the name of Innocent III.

Well was he named Innocent, say the historians of his time, for he was the friend of virtue and equity, the enemy of wickedness and vice. People spoke of wonders which had attended his election, which was even attributed to a divine revelation. "Innocent appeared so great to his contemporaries," says M. Hürter, "his influence over politics was so powerful and energetic, that they thought the invisible Head of the Church shed over him a special providence, which through him enveloped also the Church itself."

On the day of his enthronement the new Pope preached publicly at Rome, on the duties which were imposed upon him by the glorious title of "servant of the servants of God". "Oh, what anguish, what pain!" he cried, "let one day tell another what we endure; let one night relate our sorrows to the next; we have not the hardness of stone; our flesh is not made of brass. Nevertheless, in spite of all our weakness, God gives us strength."

The administration of Innocent III has remained justly celebrated. The Courts of Justice at Rome had for long been venal; advocates and lawyers purposely prolonged lawsuits in order to enrich themselves by despoiling their clients; but these abuses ceased on the accession of Innocent, for he himself sat and administered justice. — "Every morning, immediately after Innocent had said Mass, he proceeded to the consistory; around him the Cardinals were seated, while other distinguished ecclesiastics stood in front. It was there he received petitions from all who claimed his support, from whatever nation they came. Each request was received with kindly consideration; every endeavour to obtain redress of grievances, or some favour for churches, or some reform for religious orders, might count upon a friendly reception from him. Three times a week the consistory was public, and devoted to the solution of the most important legal questions, a custom re-established by this Pope after long disuse. During the debates, he paid the most careful attention to all arguments, critically examining every point, insisting on the production of detailed reports, proofs, witnesses and documents, whenever these became necessary. The prosecution and the defence were each allowed free play for throwing light upon the affair, without having any fear lest they might weary the Pontiff." (1) In the course of these cases, no matter how subtly or eloquently difficulties were raised, his judicial mind unravelled the true point of law with remarkable sagacity.

Soon from every quarter of Europe people came to Rome to submit their disputes to his judgment. He not only decided matters of litigation but, above all, endeavoured to restore peace between the contending parties. The most distinguished legal luminaries quitted their schools to come and hear him. When Innocent was forced by the Roman climate to seek one more suitable to his weak health, he was followed by an immense crowd, so that, like a general

---

(1) Hürter, Histoire d'Innocent III.

camping his army, he was forced to select places where there was abundance of food. At Viterbo forty thousand strangers referred their cases to Innocent, and it almost seemed that justice could only be obtained from him.

This great influence affected even Princes, no matter how great their defiance of pontifical authority might otherwise be. The Empress Constance confided the guardianship of her son Frederick II, King of Sicily, and the regency of that kingdom to Innocent III. John, leader of the Bulgarians, and Primaslaus, Duke of Bohemia, applied to him for the title of King; and Peter II of Aragon travelled to Rome to be crowned by him.

Peter set out from Provence with five galleys, disembarking on the $6^{\underline{th}}$ of November 1204 on an island formed by the two mouths of the Tiber. The Roman magistrates, the nobility, and several Cardinals, accompanied by two hundred horse, went to meet him and conduct him to the Vatican, where the Pope had ordered apartments to be prepared for his reception. The ceremony of coronation took place a few days later in the church of S. Pancrazio. The Bishop of Oporto anointed the King of Aragon, and Innocent invested him with the insignia of the royal dignity, the mantle, the tunic, the sceptre, the globe, crown, and mitre. Peter also wished to be knighted in the Vatican Basilica; he placed his crown and sceptre upon the altar, while the Pontiff buckled on the King's sword, symbol of strength and courage, which, by this ceremony, became specially dedicated to the cause of right and justice.

Five years later, in 1209, Otho of Bavaria came, in his turn, to ask the Pope to grant him the imperial crown. This ceremony took place in the Vatican Basilica, and when it was over both Pope and King went in procession through Rome accompanied by bell-ringing and the hymns of the clergy. Otho's chamberlains scattered money among the crowd, and the new Emperor gave a grand banquet to all the inhabitants of the city. The streets resounded with cries of joy; but, after a few days, the outrages committed by the Germans became unbearable; the Romans broke out into insurrection, and a dreadful conflict ensued. Otho lost eleven hundred horses and a great number of his followers. He demanded an indemnity, which the Pope refused; thereupon Otho quitted Rome.

Justice, universal and impartial, was the ruling passion of Innocent III. Insulted wives, abandoned wards, Ingeburg of Denmark, Mary of Aragon, Adelaide of Bohemia, Ladislaus of Hungary, all found in him an energetic and incorruptible defender. Old Raymond of Toulouse came as a suppliant to Rome: he was condemned by a Council and deprived of his possessions as being an abettor of heresy; but, before leaving the city, he sent his son to the Pope, remembering that Innocent had already taken his part against Simon de Montford. Innocent graciously received the young man, and said to him:— "Dear child, if you follow our advice you will never be deceived. Love God above all things, and serve him faithfully; stretch not forth your hands to grasp the goods of others, but defend your own against those who would despoil you of them; thus you will not be deprived of your heritage: in order that from this day you may be provided with one, we present you with the county of Venaissin, with Beaucaire and Provence. You will thus be enabled to live according to your rank. When the Church meets in another Council you will be able to bring forward your complaints against the Count of Montford." "Holy Father", said the youth, "do not be angered if I succeed in taking back from the Count of Montford the estates of which he has deprived me." "In whatever you undertake," replied the Pontiff, "may God grant that you both begin and end it well." (1)

This description of the pontificate of Innocent III especially belongs to the general history of the Church; but, in many ways, it also bears upon the history of Rome, on which city Innocent lavished his gifts, and where, in return for his benevolence, he only met with turbulence and ingratitude. The spirit of lawlessness had become engrained in this people; they could no longer submit to any rule however beneficial it might be. Innocent was obliged to withdraw from his capital in 1203; and like most of his predecessors, during the last two centuries, he resided at Anagni, Ferentino, and Viterbo, everywhere finding that respect

---

(1) Hürter, "Histoire d'Innocent III". — It was at the Lateran Council in 1215 that the Counts of Toulouse, Foix, and Comminges were deprived of their States. They had appeared before the Council, where they found in Innocent a judge who used every endeavour to prevent passion from obscuring truth. In carrying out the sentence of the Council, Innocent also gave evidence of his gentle disposition.

and obedience which the Romans refused him. But more fortunate than his predecessors, because he possessed more energy and determination, he succeeded in suppressing the rebels, the senate submitted to him, and even the prefect of Rome was compelled to beg for the investiture of his authority from the Pope.

During the pontificate of Innocent III all the offerings placed on S. Peter's tomb were entirely devoted to the relief of the poor. During a famine, the Pope himself supported eight thousand sufferers daily; besides this, he sent help and clothing to their homes; all grandeur and luxury were banished from the patriarchal palace, except the masterpieces and works of art which could not be indifferent to a Pontiff so gifted and refined as Innocent III. (1)

Immediately after he had ascended the throne he banished money changers and goldsmiths from the courts of the Lateran Palace. His table was of such frugal simplicity as to disgust the sensual appetites of certain prelates. After his meal he allowed himself a few minutes' rest; his doors were then thrown open for the reception of pilgrims, clergy, laymen, of any one in fact who desired to speak to him about the welfare of Christendom. "When the Pope had slept exactly an hour," says an eye witness, "I was introduced alone into his presence, and knelt down;

---

(1) Innocent III is the author of "Veni, Sancte Spiritus", falsely attributed to King Robert of France, and of "Ave, mundi spes". It is not quite so certain that he composed the "Stabat Mater", which is claimed by the Franciscans for a brother of their Order, who lived at the end of the thirteenth century, Fra Jacopone de Todi.

but he at once called me to him to receive the kiss of peace, which gave me good courage; after this he bade me sit at his feet and speak about my business." (1)

One day the Pope was told that some fishermen had brought up the bodies of some children in their nets, on drawing them in from the Tiber. The intense grief he experienced inspired him with a holy, noble, thought. He determined to devote his patrimony to building and endowing a house of refuge for foundlings. This house was erected on the site which had been occupied, as late as the eleventh century, by the hospice founded by King Ina for pilgrims from Britain. Some Brothers-hospitallers of the Order of S. Spirito, instituted by Count Guy of Montpellier for the relief of all human sufferings, were summoned to Rome to undertake the management of this new establishment. The church was dedicated to the Holy Spirit; a painting represented the children who were drowned in the Tiber; and the foundlings, redeemed by the Pope's charity, were clad in light blue to remind them that, being saved from death, they were henceforth the children and wards of heaven. The Hospital of S. Spirito was for long, and is perhaps still, the largest, finest, and best appointed establishment of its kind in Europe. Enlarged by Sixtus IV, enriched with the gifts of Roman Pontiffs and many wealthy noblemen, it contained separate wards for every form of disease and for invalids of every class. The wards for the clergy and for noble-

(1) Hürter, "Histoire d'Innocent III".

men were side by side with those for the foundlings and the poor. The boys were taught a trade, and were only left to their own resources when they were able to gain a livelihood. Very frequently the girls only left the hospital to marry, on which occasions they received fifty Roman scudi (about £ 10. 18. 0) for their dowry. Forty nurses were constantly employed to look after the foundlings. (1) This asylum contained a convent for nuns who undertook the girls' education, a monastery for the clergy who conducted the Church services, and competent masters to teach mechanical arts. It was a marvellous creation, so far in advance of the age which saw its birth and development that it needed centuries to elapse ere it was imitated by the other countries of Europe.

The keen sensibility of Innocent III was equally touched by every misfortune which afflicted Christendom: the desolation of the Holy Places, the sufferings of Spain, and the restless tyranny of several Princes, greatly disturbed him. His letters and his legates were ceaselessly traversing Europe, repressing injustice, preaching concord, and endeavouring to awaken in Christian minds some spark of that ardour felt in the days of the Council of Clermont and of S. Bernard. At his bidding, seventy thousand pilgrim warriors crossed the Pyrenees, hastening to the help of Alphonso IX, King of Castile; while at Rome a solemn procession was organised to entreat God to

---

(1) In addition, the Hospital of S. Spirito maintained more than two hundred nurses either in Rome or the neighbouring country.

grant victory to the Christian arms. This procession took place on the 17th May, in 1212. From early dawn the clergy assembled in the church of the Apostle; the men at S. Augustine's, the women at S. Maria Maggiore; thence they set out barefoot towards the Lateran Square, where the Pope, bearing the true Cross, and surrounded by Cardinals and Bishops, preached a sermon from the upper steps of the peristyle. Afterwards Mass was celebrated for men in S. John Lateran, for women in S. Croce-in-Gerusalemme; all the people fasting on bread and water as for a public calamity. Ten months later the Castilians gained that magnificent victory of las Navas de Tolosa which proved to be the beginning of Spain's freedom.

Soon afterwards another grand idea occupied the mind of Innocent III. He resolved to complete the disciplinary legislation of the Church, and oppose the authority of a Council to the new heresies. With this intention he summoned all the prelates of Christendom to the Lateran Palace. Seventy-one primates and metropolitans, four hundred and twelve Bishops, nine hundred Abbots and Priors of every order, responded to the Pontiff's appeal. Ambassadors from the Kings of France, Aragon, Sicily, England, Hungary, Jerusalem, Cyprus, from the Emperor of Constantinople, and from many Princes and towns, came also as representatives of the secular power to this Congress of Christendom. In short there were two thousand two hundred and eighty-three persons assisting in various capacities at this assembly. "Catholic Rome shone forth at that time with greater splendour than she had ever done before", says Hürter, "greater even than in antiquity in those days of her power. The presence of so many Princes of the Church gave a solemnity to the consecration of S. Maria-trans-Tiberim which had never been surpassed as an imposing display." (1)

The Council opened in the Lateran Basilica on S. Martin's day of the year 1215, and so great was the crowd which gathered for this ceremony that the Archbishop of Amalfi was suffocated under the portico. The Bishop of Liége appeared in a scarlet mantle and hat in his quality of Count; next day his costume was green as being a Duke; and it was not until the third sitting that he presented himself arrayed in episcopal vestments.

The first sessions of the Council were devoted to drawing up, clearly and precisely, articles of belief upon every question controverted by heretics. Heresy had, in fact, daily become more menacing. From Bulgaria to Spain wandered Catharists, Patarenes, and Boni-homines, strange names, which concealed a fierce hatred of all subordination and government, especially that of the Catholic Faith, which was the most energetic upholder of all rights.

In Italy, Lombardy was almost completely perverted; and error, spreading like leprosy, had even succeeded in tainting some towns in the pontifical domains. At Viterbo it gained over the municipal authorities; at Orvieto it obtained freer scope by the

---

(1) S. Maria had been completely restored throughout. Hürter, "Histoire d'Innocent III", tom. III, p. 250.

murder of the governor S. Pietro Parenzio. Society itself was in danger; for these sectarians boldly assaulted every one of those civilizing doctrines Christianity had preached to the world. They attacked marriage, and brought women down to the level of a plaything for man's caprices; they denied the existence of justice, holding that the spirit, tossed about as it was between two antagonistic divinities, became the mere slave of destiny; they recognised neither law nor duty, for they denied the existence of a future state; this lax morality was accompanied by austere practices and mystic rites, which, by over exciting the imagination of the initiated, enslaved them to the will-power of the Believers. It was in fact a kind of Freemasonry, for they formed the secret societies of the Middle-Ages; and, though oaths taken on daggers were not yet in vogue, haranguing and insult were not the only weapons employed in securing a triumph for the work of destruction. It can, therefore, surprise no one that the civilized world rose up as one man to repel this new inroad of Barbarians, that the Roman Pontiffs summoned the nations to arms, and blessed victories obtained in the name of law and order. Rebellion was no less a crime in the thirteenth century than at the present time. The least uprising against constituted authority, the propagation of doctrines subversive of public tranquillity, the formation of secret societies for effecting reforms by the commission of crimes, are now punished by society with the severest penalties, with infamy, perpetual imprisonment, and even death. In exactly the same manner society then defended itself against the

CHAPTER XIII.—THIRTEENTH CENTURY.

Catharists and Albigenses, on the universally accepted principle that self-preservation is the first law of nature. (1)

The disciplinary canons of the fourth Lateran Council are famous in the history of civil and ecclesiastical legislation. It was this Council which abolished judicial ordeal, ordered the publication of marriage banns, in order to prevent clandestine alliances, established free schools, and drew up those admirable rules of procedure of which modern laws are but a reproduction. (2)

S. Dominic assisted at the Lateran Council; he had come to Rome with Fulk, Bishop of Toulouse, in order to obtain the Pope's advice on certain plans he had formed for the conversion of heretics. Domingo de Guzman was one of those simple-minded steadfast men who are born for action, because they feel deeply, and are endowed with energy and constancy. His Christian love of simplicity had been long offended by the luxury indulged in by the dignitaries of the Church. Their cavalcades, their bands of servants, the effeminacy of manners displayed by these disciples of the Crucified, appeared to him to be the true cause of the downfall of the faith and the propagation of schism. At the same time he was horrified by the

---

(1) The cruelties committed during the war were the acts of only a small number of men; and no argument can be based on them against the right society possesses to reduce to order rebels against its laws. Moreover, INNOCENT III never ceased from recommending both justice and mercy to the crusaders.

(2) See Canons 11, 35, 36, 37, 38, 42, 48, and 51.

cruelties committed in the course of the war; he did not believe in the hardness of heart of misguided sectaries, and loudly denounced those outbursts of passion which culminated in burning towns, and slaughtering whole populations. Therefore, to some he constantly preached the spirit of poverty and humanity; to others, obedience and faith. Indefatigable in this pious mission he gathered around him a number of associates as poor as himself, and strict observers of all Christian virtues, who were known by no other name than that of Friars-preachers.

Innocent III and the Lateran Council feared the increase of religious orders; the Pope therefore advised Dominic to select a rule already approved by the Church for his institution. Dominic remained some time in Rome, praying that God would enlighten him as to the execution of his plan. One night, during his sleep, he dreamt that Jesus Christ was preparing to destroy the proud, the voluptuous, and the avaricious, when, suddenly, the Virgin appeased His anger by presenting two men to Him, one of whom Dominic recognised as himself, but the other he had never seen. On entering the Lateran next morning, the first person his eye fell upon was the unknown of his dream. This man was clothed in rags, and was praying with great devotion. Dominic threw himself into his arms, embracing him tenderly, saying :— "You are my companion; we are both following the same end; let us dwell together, and no enemy shall prevail against us." The legend informs us that henceforth they possessed but one heart and one soul in the Lord. This poor beggar was S. Francis of Assisi.

Francesco Bernadone, a few years younger than S. Dominic, was in fact "that other champion of the faith, whose deeds and words were once more to rally the scattered nations; that other spouse of poverty which, since Christ's death, had languished in obscurity and contempt unsought for by any one." (1) Dante represents them in the fourth heaven, surrounded by the glories of the sun, in company with SS. Augustine, Thomas Aquinas, and Bonaventure: "S. Francis burns with the infinite love of the seraphim, and the marvels of his life may only worthily be sung by the elect in the centre of glory; Dominic shines with the wisdom of the cherubim; he is indeed the chosen labourer in the vineyard of Jesus Christ; he is a torrent which rushes through the thickest undergrowth, and then flows on in streams of living water to fertilize the earth." It would be impossible to describe more nobly the different characters of these two great intellects. The burning mysticism of S. Francis made him, as it were, the poet of love. His hymns, his ecstasies, his simple yet sublime deeds, were all so many overflowings of love. Therefore he drew around him sensitive persons, whose imaginations were quickly influenced by mystic aspirations; they flocked to him in eagerness to exchange their passions and wealth for one spark of that immense charity with which he was consumed. Ten years later, withdrawing from the world, S. Francis had already five thousand disciples.

---

(1) Dante, "Paradiso", c. XI and XII.

In like manner the Friars-preachers increased throughout Europe. This infectious ardour to submit to austere rules, to be weaned from all enjoyment and be devoted to the welfare of mankind, was certainly a strange, even divine, ordinance. Monks were the forerunners of civilisation; they daily instructed the peasantry and townsfolk, opened schools, and taught in high places that poverty should be respected.

At the monastery of the Fratelli Minore di S. Francesco a Ripa, on the site of Cæsar's Gardens, is S. Francis's cell; in it may still be seen the crucifix before which he prayed, and the stone which served him for a pillow. At Assisi three fanes have been erected, one above the other, over his grave: the room which witnessed his birth and the prison in which his father confined him still remain; while the cottage in which he died has been preserved as a precious relic in the magnificent church of La Madonna degli Angeli.

S. Dominic only obtained the confirmation of the Order of Friars-preachers in 1216, under the pontificate of Honorius III. Honorius then presented him with the monastery of S. Sixtus for the accomodation of himself and his monks. There, however, they only remained a short time, taking permanent possession of S. Sabina, which was granted to them by the same Pontiff, as also a part of his family's palace on the Aventine. (1)

At S. Sabina the visitor is shown an orange tree planted by S. Dominic, his cell, the chapel in which

---

(1) Honorius belonged to the Savelli Family.

he prayed, and the one in which he and S. Francis spent several nights in heavenly conversation. It was at S. Sabina that the Friars-preachers first adopted the habit of their Order, and that S. Dominic, shocked by the idleness of the servants attached to the pontifical court, instituted for their benefit classes for religious instruction which classes have been continued throughout the following centuries.

But the monastery of S. Sixtus has preserved still nobler memories: first occupied by the saint, it afterwards came into the possession of nuns who were placed under his direction, and S. Dominic's memory remains living there through his miracles. One day, as he was preaching at S. Marco, a poor woman who had come to hear him lost her son. Returning home to find him dead she carried the body to the monastery of S. Sixtus, and implored the prayers of the preacher whose saintly eloquence had made her forget her maternal duties. Dominic prayed, and the child was restored alive to his mother. On another occasion at S. Sixtus he obtained the restoration to life of young Napoleon, Cardinal Stephen's nephew, who had fractured his skull by a fall from his horse. (1) It was also at S. Sixtus that the pious devotion of the rosary was for the first time put in practice at Rome.

The nuns who replaced the Friars-preachers at S. Sixtus's monastery were gathered from different

---

(1) Romae autem duo instituit monasteria, alterum virorum, mulierum alterum. Tres etiam mortuos ad vitam revocavit, multaque alia edidit miracula quibus ordo Praedicatorum mirificè propagari coepit. "Brev. Rom.", 4th August.

convents where they had lived without rule or discipline, and their first superior general was the Blessed Cæcilia, a Roman lady of the Cesarini family. Some of these nuns had dwelt, before removing to S. Sixtus, in a house close to S. Maria-trans-Tiberim and only consented to leave their retreat on condition that they were allowed to carry away a picture of the virgin attributed by tradition to S. Luke. But the people objected to the removal of this venerated relic, and it became necessary for S. Dominic to come by night and carry it away on his shoulders to its new home.

S. Dominic died at Florence in 1221; S. Francis at Portiuncula in 1226.

A few years before, in 1213, S. John of Matha, founder of the Order of the Trinity, had also ended his holy life at the monastery of S. Tomaso-in-formis, near the Claudian aqueduct on the Cælian Hill. This convent had been given to the Trinitarians by Innocent III. (1)

Thus Innocent III had the happiness of seeing three of the most illustrious men in the history of Catholicism. He also had the joy of receiving a Christian orator at the Lateran whom all Rome, including S. Dominic and S. Francis, flocked to hear; this was a poor Carmelite brother who is known as S. Angelo. But the consolation this revival of Christian life brought to Innocent III did not suffice to obliterate the sorrows which were exhausting his

(1) The convent of S. Tomaso-in-formis was abandoned by the Trinitarians during the residence of the Popes at Avignon, and the relics of S. John of Matha were taken to France.

life. Ceaselessly struggling with selfish interests, now in Germany, where elections to the throne led to endless conflicts, then in France where Philip Augustus reigned, or in England, then governed by John Lackland, he sought to quell ambitions and hatreds, in order to unite the powers of Europe once more in a new crusade. This great idea had induced him to leave Rome more hurriedly to put his plans into execution. But soon all the hopes he had entertained were shattered; he was overwhelmed with disappointment, and died at Perugia, on the 16th of July 1216, when scarcely fifty-five years of age.

"The reign of Innocent III was the most brilliant epoch of papal power", has said Daunou, a revolutionary writer. It is therefore not surprising to find an illustrious Catholic author, Montalembert, saying that Innocent probably was "the most thorough model for a sovereign Pontiff, the pre-eminent type of God's Vicar". If we seek traces of him at Rome we shall specially find them at the hospital of S. Spirito, that establishment which Laporte du Theil describes as "the largest, finest, and possibly the best appointed hospital existing at the present moment, not alone in the town which is the queen of cities, but in any civilised society in Europe". Again we shall find traces of him in the Lateran Basilica, the mosaics of which he restored, and we should have found them in S. Peter's, did the old Basilica still exist, for he enriched it with mosaics, crosses, chalices, and books of the Gospel bound in gold with chasings, pearls, and precious stones. He distributed ornaments and gifts of all kinds among twenty other churches; a gold cross is especially mentioned, as having been given by him to S. Maria-in-Sassia, on which Jesus Christ was represented dragging victory out of hell. Two sapphires shone at the extremities of its arms, and two garnets at the head. Moreover Innocent found out which churches were without silver chalices, and distributed among them one hundred and thirty three, each weighing one hundred marks. To these gifts may be added one which the inhabitants of Viterbo were compelled to make to the Vatican Basilica. Ever since the ruin of Tusculum, Viterbo had become Rome's most obstinate rival. The Romans carried it by assault in 1201, and, as a trophy of their victory, they brought a chain from one of its gates to Rome, and also the parish bell which they hung up at the Capitol. The inhabitants of Viterbo were furthermore obliged to pay an indemnity to replace the bronze doors of S. Peter's, and the Atlantes that had supported the holy water stoop, and which they were accused of having destroyed at the time of Frederick's invasion.

Innocent III was succeeded by Cencio Savelli, Cardinal-priest of SS. John and Paul, who was one of the most learned prelates of the Roman Church. Cencio took the name of HONORIUS III. (1)

He was, as already stated, the Pope who confirmed the Dominican Order. He also approved of

(1) Honorius III, before his election, was "Cameriere" of the Roman Church; he had published a book on the census of the Church. A ceremonial, which has been printed, is also due to him.

the rule of those hermits who now for ten years
had dwelt in the cave of Elias on Mount Carmel.
Soon after his accession to the pontifical chair Pierre
de Courtenay, Count of Auxerre, who had been
elected Emperor of Constantinople, came to Rome
with his wife Yolande in order to receive the imperial crown. The ceremony took place in the church
of S. Lorenzo-fuori-le-mura, on the Sunday of the
Good Shepherd in the year 1217. Honorius would
not allow the function to be performed in S. Peter's,
lest the Emperor might from that fact think himself
entitled to claim sovereign rights over Rome as the
successor of the Emperors of the East. A thirteenth
century fresco over the portico of S. Lorenzo represents the coronation of Pierre de Courtenay. Both
the portico and decorations date from the pontificate
of Honorius III.

Meanwhile, long wars had been devastating the
western Empire: three competitors for the crown,
Philip of Swabia, Otho of Bavaria, and, later on,
Frederick II of Sicily, had set Europe in flames by
their pretensions. The deaths of the first two clai-
mants left the field free to Frederick, who then
requested pontifical consecration, so that he might
add the title of Emperor to that of King of the Romans. But the Roman Court had decided objections
to the union of the Two Sicilies with the crown of
Germany, for thereby the patrimony of S. Peter
would be surrounded by imperial possessions. Nevertheless, there appeared to be such good-will in
Frederick's Government, he instituted such reforms,
was so deferential in his manner, and was apparently

so determined to further the conquest of the Holy Land, that Honorius felt obliged to sacrifice the temporal interests of the Roman States to the more important interests of Christendom. Therefore, on the 22nd of November 1220, Frederick and his wife Constance were solemnly consecrated in the Vatican Basilica. He then publicly renewed his vow to set out for Palestine within a year, and both he and Honorius proclaimed laws of great severity against the heretics.

Frederick had thus attained to the height of his wishes, he was both Emperor and King; his dominions extended from Aachen to Crotona and Agrigentum; but from that moment all his pledges and promises were also forgotten. What did the Holy Land matter to him, now that he was all powerful in Europe? One thing, however, would still flatter his ambition; the crown of Jerusalem. Without leaving Italy he sought to obtain it by means of that cunning and plausible hypocrisy which had already proved of good service to him. His wife, the Empress Constance, being dead, he solicited in marriage the hand of the daughter of Jean de Brienne, who had succeeded to the glorious kingdom of the Baldwins and of Godefroy de Bouillon. Brienne yielded to the combined entreaties of the Emperor and Pope; but, as soon as Frederick had become his son-in-law, the Emperor deprived him of his sceptre, the one and only consolation that had remained to the old crusader.

This contempt for his vows, and this insatiable passion for seizing and encroaching upon the rights of other powers, soon caused a serious breach between the Emperor and the pontifical see, the sad effects of which disturbed Europe during twenty-three years. Honorius III only saw the beginning of this misunderstanding; it is to the great honour of his memory that he nobly stood by Jean de Brienne, who had been despoiled and forsaken by the ungrateful man who had married his daughter. Honorius gave him the government of the lands of the Church from Montefiascone to Viterbo.

The restlessness of the Romans continued throughout the pontificate of Honorius to perpetuate a state of lawlessness and disorder within the city. The Pope was even compelled to quit Rome and withdraw to Tibur in 1225. Roman restlessness resembled an intermittent fever, attacks of which were yet to return for many years.

Gregory IX who, in 1227, ascended S. Peter's throne, was named Ugolino Conti; the remarkable energy of this old man of ninety, his learning, virtues, natural talents, and personal grace, worthily recalled his kinship to Innocent III. Gregory IX excommunicated Frederick II. Frederick's reply was to bribe a number of the Romans, among them the Frangipani, to acknowledge him as sovereign of Rome. These men suborned a portion of the populace to rebel and insult the Pope while celebrating Mass at S. Peter's, on Easter Monday of 1228. In consequence of this Gregory IX left Rome, retiring successively to Rieti, Spoleto, Perugia, and Assisi.

"Frederick II would have been without a rival on earth had he loved his own soul", says an old chronicler. (1) But Frederick only loved pride and sensual pleasure. For him there existed neither truth nor right: he valued only skill and power, both of which he thought he possessed. He even employed Saracen troops against the Pope; their outrages and wickedness actually disgracing warfare. Gregory IX retorted by commanding the strictest moderation on the part of the pontifical troops. "Nothing is more unworthy the soldiers of Jesus Christ", he wrote to his general, "than to slay those whose lives might be spared, or to mutilate and disfigure the image of the Creator ... Wherefore we order you to watch carefully over those who may fall into the hands of our troops so that no harm may befall them, and that they may be able to congratulate themselves on their captivity". These sublime precepts, thus taught in the thirteenth century, laid the foundation of a new law for Christian nations.

Peace was concluded between Gregory and Frederick on the 28th of August, 1230; Gregory even taking the part of his new ally against the opposition he encountered from his own family, and against the ever bitter enmity of the Lombard cities. Frederick paid no regard to his promises, his double-dealing being his real genius. But the aged Gregory would not let either the Church or the cause of righteousness become his victims. Therefore he again excommunicated Frederick on the 24th of March, 1239, and the struggle continued with greater fierceness than before. What most envenomed the strife was

(1) Quoted by M. de Montalembert in his introduction to "Histoire de S. Élizabeth".

Frederick's dissolute conduct; the King of Jerusalem had a seraglio of young Eastern beauties; and public rumour ascribed a horrible blasphemy to him, Frederick being supposed to have said that the "world had allowed itself to be deceived by three impostors, by Moses, by Jesus Christ, and by Mahomet".

The Romans had recalled Gregory IX after an inundation which had thrown the town into great distress, and they received him with expressions of great joy; but the underhand practices of Frederick always made the Pope's position difficult and uncertain in the Christian capital. He was in fact again driven to leave the city in 1232, and only returned after a victory gained in the very heart of the city by a party of the inhabitants over the prefect and hirelings of the Emperor.

The people, led by Giacomo Capocci, stormed the Capitol, and then went forth themselves to fetch back the Pope. But the internal quarrels fomented by his gold gave Frederick plenty of confidence. He therefore marched on Rome, and took possession of all the northern provinces of the domains of S. Peter. Even towns in the Roman Campagna capitulated, and, acting as a traitor to the Church, Cardinal Colonna waged war on behalf of the Germans in the neighbourhood of Palestrina.

"Now it is that we behold Gregory IX, this old man who was almost a centenarian," said M. de Montalembert, "plunging boldly into a hopeless struggle. Defeated and abandoned by all, besieged in Rome by Frederick, who was in league with the Romans themselves, he found in that supreme moment, despite his human weakness, that strength which belongs only to things divine. He withdrew from their sanctuary the relics of the Holy Apostles, had them carried in procession through the city, asking the Romans if they wished to see that sacred trust perish, for he could no longer defend it without their aid. This appeal touched them and they swore to die for him; the Emperor was repulsed and the Church was saved."

But these last efforts exhausted the small remaining strength of this noble Pontiff; he quietly expired a few days afterwards in the midst of his glory.

Frederick was then at Grotta-Ferrata, for he had no intention to go away from Rome; so the war continued under the pontificates of CELESTINE IV and of INNOCENT IV, with no further advantage to the Emperor than was to be gained by raiding the Roman Campagna. For a brief moment he was reconciled with Innocent IV, but soon deceived him as he had Gregory IX. Trusting in his good faith, Innocent set out from Rome to meet the Emperor. On reaching Sutri he learnt that every effort was useless, and that three hundred knights were advancing to capture him. Without losing a moment Innocent laid aside the insignia of his dignity, and, in the early hours of night, escaped on a fleet horse to Civita-Vecchia, where several Genoese galleys lay at anchor expecting him. Innocent was by birth a Genoese, of the illustrious family of Fieschi; his arrival at his native city, on the 5th of July 1244, was therefore welcomed with enthusiastic rejoicings. However, Innocent was only able to stay a few days at Genoa, for Frederick succeeded in cutting off his communications with the other countries of Christendom; and, as no Prince would risk the Emperor's anger by receiving him in his dominions, he betook himself to Lyons, a free city subject only to its Archbishop. There he summoned a Council to meet on the Feast of S. Peter 1245. This assembly opened in the presence of the Emperor of Constantinople and ambassadors from other Christian monarchs. Frederick was cited to appear: more than once he had demanded the convocation of a Council which should judge between him and the Pope; but, when the Council had assembled, he declined to appear before it. His bad faith and his usurpations were easily proved; and, on the 17th of July, 1245, this Prince, so proud and powerful, who, in the words of S. Louis, warred against God for his gifts, was solemnly deposed as being a perjurer, sacrilegious, a heretic, and a felon towards his subjects. When the Pope pronounced sentence each of the prelates held a lighted taper; and, when the fatal words were uttered, all these lights were suddenly extinguished. Those who assisted at this ceremony, say historians, were seized with dread, as though a thunder-clap had burst upon them accompanied by lightning; the Emperor's ambassadors groaned and struck their breasts, crying out, "dies iræ, dies illa, dies tribulationis et angustiæ, dies calamitatis et miseriæ." (1)

From that day Frederick's authority was set at nought by a great part of his dominions, and Henry, the Landgrave of Thuringia, was elected to fill his place. Meanwhile Frederick was marching on Lyons

---

(1) Sophonias, I, 15.

at the head of a powerful army; but had only reached Turin when he learnt that Parma was in insurrection in his rear. Returning immediately to Parma he surrounded and besieged it, giving orders to his army to build another city at its gates which he called Vittoria. But the inhabitants of Parma devoutly consecrated their city to the Virgin, and, displaying on their banners the picture of Mary, they resisted with marvellous resolution all the imperial efforts made against them. Already, during this war, Viterbo had set an example of similar heroism. The women of that town, even its young girls, had bravely gone down into the trenches to set fire to the enemies' war-engines; and Frederick had been compelled to retire from before that weak town. Parma was now to do what Viterbo had already done. In vain did Frederick order two or three of his Parmesan prisoners to be beheaded each morning in sight of the whole town; this sorrow only added to the hatred of the besieged. At length they sallied forth from the town, men armed with pikes, women with shards, and fell to killing and burning. In the evening, when Frederick returned from hunting, he found only a heap of ashes where the city of Vittoria had stood in the morning. This happened on the 18th of February 1246. The treasure and all the baggage had fallen into the hands of the conquerors; even the crown itself was taken and carried into Parma amid joyful cries and cheers from the populace. Frederick then gave way to boundless anger; he ordered that the Bishop of Arezzo, who had refused to curse the Pope, should be dragged by his hair to a gibbet and hanged; but a few years later, on the 12th of December 1250, Frederick also died, recommending his son to restore to the Roman Church all the rights which he had unjustly usurped, so that, on her part, she might protect him like a good mother.

Since the departure of Innocent IV for Lyons, Rome had remained without a master amid the general lawlessness. Powerless to conquer the opposition of the Pontiff, Frederick made no effort to establish himself securely in the ancient metropolis of the empire, allowing the senate to remain in possession of the Capitol. But, when Frederick had carried his claims and hatreds to the tomb, Innocent returned to Italy, passing through Genoa and Milan, where the Lombards, constant enemies of the imperial power, received him with transports of joy; he then went to Perugia, where he fixed his residence for several years.

Towards this period S. Clare, a spiritual daughter of S. Francis, died at Assisi. For forty-two years she had directed the Convent of S. Damiano, carrying to an heroic height the austerities of her life. The Pope and Cardinals assisted at her funeral, which was celebrated with trumpets and solemnities in which the people of Assisi heartily joined. S. Clare was buried in the church of S. Giorgio, near the tomb of S. Francis. (1)

Innocent only re-entered Rome in 1254, and his

---

(1) The Order of which S. Clare was the first superior bore in France the name of Clarisses, and in Italy that of poor women (delle povere donne). It has produced many branches

stay there was of short duration. The desire he felt to have the authority of the Apostolic See acknowledged, in the south of the Peninsula, made him set out for Campania, where death overtook him in December of the same year, and his body was laid to rest in the Cathedral of Naples. The pontificate of Innocent IV had lasted eleven years and a half; it was a very sad period, for, in addition to all the sorrows which afflicted Christendom, it witnessed the defeat of Mansourah and the captivity of S. Louis.

ALEXANDER IV, his successor, had, on one side, to struggle against Manfred, an illegitimate son of Frederick II, who had seized upon the Two-Sicilies, and, on the other, against the turbulent passions which kept alive ceaseless strife among the Roman families. To the domination of the Frangipani had succeeded that of the Annibali; to that of the Annibali the influence of a former governor of Rome, named Brancaleone. Powerless to repress the excesses which accompanied these contentions, Alexander left Rome, and retired to Viterbo, so long the enemy of the Popes, but now their devoted and faithful ally. Viterbo was the birthplace of S. Rose who had preached and converted, and whose pious life had just ended, at the age of twelve, in the perfume of sanctity which still lingers in her name. Alexander IV ordered that her body should be exhumed, when it was found to be in

---

under the names of Capucinesses, Annunciades, Cordeliers or Grey Sisters, Recollects, nuns of the Ave Maria, and Conceptionists. Not a century ago they possessed no fewer than four thousand houses.

a perfect state of preservation, in which condition it remains to our day at Viterbo.

Meanwhile wars, violence, and aggression went on from one end of Italy to the other: in the south there was Manfred; in the north Ezzelino di Romano, the faithful ally of Frederick II, who appeared by his cruelties to have undertaken the task of disgracing humanity. Excommunicated by the Popes, he boldly resisted them, even gaining over to his side his brother Alberic; but all the Lombard cities united against him, and by reprisals, which raise a shudder, succeeded in stamping out the entire race of tyrants.

It can easily be understood that amid such hopeless disorder, in the midst of crimes, wars, and wholesale destruction, despair should seize upon society, and that people should imagine there was no other way of appeasing the anger of heaven but by the practice of the most severe penance. At Perugia a band of Flagellants was formed who roamed through the streets, almost naked, flogging one another with leather thongs, imploring the mercy of God with groans and tears. Soon the nobility and the wealthy followed the people's example; their practises spreading like contagion even among women; but these last instead of wandering about, shut themselves up in their rooms and indulged in the most painful austerities. At Rome, throughout Italy, Germany, and Poland, long processions of Flagellants were met with; they went about in hundreds, nay even thousands; by night they carried tapers, while their doleful groans resounded throughout the cities and the country. Union, forgiveness of injuries, but, above all, the necessity for doing penance, was everywhere preached. Prisons were thrown open; exiles were recalled; one might have thought the world was coming to an end, and that fire from heaven was about to destroy the earth. Alexander IV held aloof from these strange proceedings, the dangers of which were not long in being developed. These crowds degenerated into licentious vagabonds, and the Flagellants, condemned on all sides,. were dispersed.

But, side by side with these outbursts of frenzied zeal, great virtues, noble talents, and holy lives were pleading for divine mercy. Brother John of Vicenza, a Dominican friar, strong in his love, went from town to town preaching peace and goodwill. At his voice nations forgot their mutual prejudices and jealousies; four hundred thousand men assembled to hear him on the plain of Paquera, three miles from Verona; and, amid pious enthusiasm, peace was sworn to throughout Lombardy.

A son of S. Francis, the great S. Anthony of Padua, strong in charity, whose eloquence was so captivating, and theological knowledge so profound, that Gregory IX called him "the ark of the covenant", "the holy depository of the sacred books", preached peace and concord. S. Anthony came to Rome in 1217, and obtained many conversions.

We must not forget S. Bonaventure, the seraphic doctor; S. Thomas Aquinas, the angel of the schools; and that Albert the Great (1) whom the admiration of his

---

(1) Albert the Great was born at Lowingen, in Swabia, towards the end of the twelfth century, and taught for a long

contemporaries has surrounded with a kind of superstitious halo.

Giovanni Fidanza, whose happy recovery from an illness while yet a child obtained for him the surname of Buonaventura, was born in Tuscany in 1221. He joined the Friars Minor at the age of eighteen, and soon the extent of his learning and the touching influence of his words raised him to the highest scholastic degrees in the University of Paris. S. Thomas having one day asked him whence he drew all his knowledge, Bonaventure pointed to the crucifix.

The Order of Friars Minor was at that time greatly divided; one section of it wished to relax the rule, the other to render it more severe. Finally both parties agreed to elect Bonaventure as General of the order; this accordingly took place, in 1256, in the Convent of Aracœli. (1) Bonaventure at once fully revived the ancient spirit of S. Francis;

---

time at Köln, where he acquired that immense reputation which induced Alexander IV to summon him to Rome and make him comptroller of the sacred palace. He was at Anagni, in 1256, with S. Bonaventure and S. Thomas, who had followed his classes at Köln. A lively dispute was then raging between the Mendicant Orders and the University of Paris. Doctor Guillaume de Saint-Amour had just published his book "Périls des derniers temps", in which it was stated that the apparition of these new monks was only one of the first calamities which announced the end of the world. SS. Bonaventure, Thomas, and Albert the Great, went to the Pope at Anagni to defend their Orders, and obtained the condemnation of the work.

(1) The Convent of Aracœli, first occupied by the Benedictines, was given, by INNOCENT IV, to the Franciscans in 1252.

and, during the remainder of his life, took an active part in directing the great affairs of Christendom.

Thomas Aquinas belonged to one of the most powerful families in the Kingdom of Naples. Brought up at Monte-Cassino, he felt at an early age that love for retirement and study which, at a later period, led him to flee from his family and country in order to submit himself to the law of S. Dominic. Thomas started for Rome, followed by his mother; she knocked at the gate of the convent of S. Sabina, in which he had sought shelter, and demanded to see him, uniting threats and entreaties to her request. All her efforts were vain; Thomas listened to the voice of God, and remained deaf to his mother's pleadings. His superiors then sent him to France in company with four monks of his order. But, one evening when resting by one of those clear springs which water the district of Aquapendente, Thomas's brothers surprised them, and, taking him prisoner, they tore his monk's habit to pieces, and shut him up in the castle of Rocca-Secca, which belonged to their father. There the youth had to submit to a lingering and painful persecution. Solitude was not distasteful to him, for prayer and reading transported his soul to a world where suffering is unknown; still all his affections and desires were wounded; even his chastity was attacked by the introduction of a young woman to his chamber, but Thomas drove her from his presence with a blazing torch, with which he stamped a cross upon the wall, and there and then consecrated his virginity to God by a solemn vow. His family grew weary at last of this useless strife, and allowed him to escape. One night he let himself down from his window and returned to S. Sabina, whence he proceeded to Köln and Paris, where his genius first began to shine forth in all its greatness. Later on. S. Thomas opened a public school of theology at Rome, where he taught for ten years. When the Popes withdrew from Rome to Anagni, Viterbo, and Perugia, he followed them, and continued his lectures in each of these towns. "He was the most learned man of his age", said Erasmus, "and no modern theologian can compare with him for exactitude, talent, and erudition." (1)

The Protestant Brücker goes even further:— "If he had lived in a more favourable time, and had been able to make use of the literature we enjoy, there is no doubt that he would have been considered one of the very greatest geniuses who have ever existed." (2)

It is to S. Thomas that the Church is indebted for the Office of the Blessed Sacrament, a work admirable for its depth of devotion, for the sublimity of its thoughts, and the fervour of its prayers.

The institution of the Feast of the Blessed Sacrament is one of the most sacred memories of the thirteenth century. A poor girl, named Julienne, prioress of the convent of Mont-Cornillon, near Liége, was favoured with several visions which appeared to point to the absence of a pious solemnity in the ceremonies of the Church. This humble woman at

---

(1) Comment. in epist. ad Rom.
(2) Hist. crit. et philos., tom III, p. 803.

once consulted her Bishop, reporting the words spoken to her by an interior voice, and, at her request, the Bishop ordained a special festival to be kept annually in honour of the dogma of the Eucharist. This Feast was celebrated, for the first time, at Liége in 1253, and at Rome in 1264, during the pontificate of URBAN IV, who, by a Bull, dated in the month of September that same year, prescribed its observance in all the churches of Christendom. The miracle which occurred about the same time in the town of Bolsena, when the Host, during the celebration of Mass by an unbelieving priest, suddenly became tinged with blood, added greatly to the homage and faith of the people towards the Blessed Sacrament of the Altar. Meanwhile, however, the pious idea of the nun of Liége met with many detractors and opponents. The Blessed Julienne died an exile from her native land for having endeavoured to honour the memory of the Last Supper in a special manner, and, on the death of Urban IV, the festival he had instituted fell into oblivion for more than forty years.

Urban IV (1) had been elected at Viterbo, in 1261, as the successor of Alexander IV. Before ascending the Chair of S. Peter he had been Patriarch of Jerusalem; and, in the various posts he had filled, had always distinguished himself by the moderation and sweetness of his character. Urban had no intention of entering into a struggle with the Roman populace. His predecessor had withdrawn to Viterbo

---

(1) The name of Urban IV was Jacques Pantaleon: he was a native of Troyes in Champagne.

to escape from the seditious spirit reigning within the capital; Urban, for a similar reason, selected Orvieto as his residence. But even there he did not escape the storm; the Orvietans rebelled against pontifical authority, seizing upon a fortress which belonged to the Church; Urban, who was ill, was compelled to escape in a litter to Perugia, where he shortly afterwards expired.

In his stead the Cardinals chose Guido Fulcodi, Cardinal-Bishop of Sabina, who was then on a mission in England. (1) On hearing of his nomination, Guido set out in haste for Italy, disguised as a mendicant friar, in order to escape the followers of Manfred who was in constant warfare with the Church. When he reached Perugia, where the Cardinals had assembled, he besought them to elect some person more worthy of the dignity; but they refused to do so. Guido was enthroned under the title of CLEMENT IV, and subsequently notified his accession to the Princes and Bishops of Christendom in a letter of noble simplicity. But it is in a letter he addressed to one of his nephews that the noble character of this holy Pontiff is most admirably revealed. To the honour of the Holy See, whose history is the only one which offers such numerous instances of humility and self-sacrifice, we here reproduce it.

"Many rejoice over our promotion; but we find

---

(1) Guido Fulcodi, or Foulques, was born at Saint-Gilles in Languedoc. He was successively a soldier, lawyer, and secretary to S. Louis; having become a widower he took orders, and was made archbishop of Narbonne and Cardinal.

therein cause rather for fear and tears. We alone feel the immense weight of our charge. In order therefore that you may know how to bear yourself on this occasion, learn that it should be with even greater modesty than before. We do not wish that you or your brother, or any one of our relatives, should approach us unless by our own command, for they would go away abashed and frustrated in their hopes. Do not on our account seek to marry your sister more advantageously; we would not approve of it, nor should we aid you therein. Nevertheless, if you marry her to some simple knight, we propose to give you three hundred pounds Tours currency. (1) If you aim higher, expect not one penny from us; even what we propose doing we desire shall be kept secret, and that only you and your mother shall know of it. We do not wish any of our relatives to be puffed up because of our elevation; but that Mabille and Cécile shall accept husbands as if we were a simple priest. See Gélie and tell her not to leave home but to remain at Susa; let her keep to due simplicity and modesty in dress, and on no account permit herself to present petitions for anyone, for they will turn out useless for the person on whose behalf they are made, and hurtful to herself. Bid her refuse any present offered if she wishes for our goodwill. Salute your mother and your brothers. We do not write to you nor to members of our family with the bull (the leaden seal), but with the seal of the fisherman which the Popes use in their private

---

(1) About three hundred pounds.

affairs. Given at Perugia, the day of SS. Perpetua and Felicitas, in the year of Jesus Christ 1265."

Shortly after the election of Clement IV, Charles of Anjou, the brother of S. Louis, hastened to Italy to take possession of the kingdom of the Two Sicilies, which the Popes had granted him as a fief of the Church. He made his entry into Rome on the eve of Pentecost, and, without paying any regard to Clement who dwelt at Perugia, he quartered a portion of his suite in the patriarchal palace of the Lateran. The Romans received Charles with noisy acclamations. This Prince's character, his military habits, and his relationship to the most powerful Kings of Europe were so many inducements to make him their ruler; and the Romans fancied they could use his protection as a powerful weapon against the bold forays of Manfred, and perhaps even against the domination of the pontifical See. Therefore they elected him senator for life, and, under this title, abandoned to him the whole administration of the city. Thus was the papal authority completely annihilated: Clement realising this reasserted his claim as legitimate lord of Rome, and Charles's senatorial functions were limited to three years. Clement subsequently sent four Cardinals to the Count of Anjou with the deed of investiture to the kingdom of the Two Sicilies; while, on the 29th of May, the standard thereof was solemnly presented to him before the altar of S. John Lateran. On the 6th of January of the following year Charles and Beatrice of Provence received the Royal crown in S. Peter's from the hands of the Cardinal Albano, the Pope himself not being present at the ceremony. The Popes had for long feared to enter Rome, which had ceased to be under obedience to them.

The destruction of Manfred's power and his own death quickly followed the opening of the campaign by Charles of Anjou; but a new claimant thereupon appeared from Germany in the person of young Conradin, the grandson of Frederick II. Neither the threats of the Pope, nor the fulminations of the Church, could arrest his advance. His ambassadors actually dared to enter Rome with banners unfurled, where they were received by the Romans with pomp, and the magistrates of the city gave them a solemn audience in the Capitol. The chief of these magistrates was a son of King S. Ferdinand, named Henry of Castile; he had succeeded Charles of Anjou in the title and duties of Senator of Rome. This Prince, whose long sojourn in Barbary had only left him the merest pretence of religion, now boldly betrayed the friendship which united him to Charles of Anjou, and the fidelity he owed to the Pope. He unfurled Conradin's banner, and, being in right of his office master of Rome, he forcibly seized all the treasures of the churches, the sacred ornaments and trusts which the faithful were in the habit of placing under the safeguard of respect due to the holy places. In particular the Lateran and the Basilicas of SS. Paul, Sabbas, Basil, and Sabina were disgracefully pillaged. Some time afterwards Conradin passed through Rome, where Henry of Castile received him with the honours reserved for royalty: but a catastrophe was at hand. Defeated at Tagliacozzo and betrayed, Conradin was imprisoned by Charles of Anjou; two months later the head of this young and last scion of the House of Swabia lay bleeding in the market place of Naples.

Some writers have sought to accuse Clement of complicity in this tragic execution; but these suspicions are disproved by history. Clement even severely reproved Charles of Anjou for his cruelty. Clement IV died at Viterbo in the same year as Conradin. His habits were extremely austere, his prudence perfect, while his talents as lawyer and orator made him one of the most eminent men of his age.

It was during his pontificate that the confraternity of the Gonfalone, the most ancient Roman brotherhood, was instituted. It was formed, under the direction of S. Bonaventure, by a certain number of young men who sought in this holy union strength to resist the temptations of the world, by devoting their time to deeds of piety and charity. Clement IV granted them several indulgences, and henceforth the brothers of the Gonfalone marched in processions beneath the shadow of Mary's standard. One day, during an insurrection, they seized upon the Capitol, and waving the banner of the town they defended order and papal authority against the ambition of nobles and the unbridled fury of the mob. It was on this occasion they took the name of the Gonfalone or Standard, in order to mark, says Hélyot, that beneath the standard of their city, of country, and of justice, they had restored liberty to the city of Rome.

The costume of this confraternity was a white linen sack bearing at the height of the shoulder a shield charged with a parti-coloured cross, white and red; from the belt hung a rosary and a scourge. Their meetings were at first held in S. Maria Maggiore; but the number of the brethren increased so rapidly that the Popes assigned them hospitals and churches in various quarters of the city, while S. Lucia-della-Chiavica became the headquarters of the association. (1)

Nevertheless Rome was ceasing more and more to be the centre of action in Christian affairs. Given over at this time to the quarrels of the Orsini and Annibaldi, a prey to hopeless anarchy, Rome still proudly refused to accept the sovereignty of the Pope, who would have made her the capital of the Universe. Thus the Pontiffs, after receiving the tiara at S. Peter's tomb, always returned at once to the neighbouring towns. Several elections took place at Viterbo during the second half of the thirteenth century; it was there indeed, but not without strenuous opposition, that the constitution of GREGORY X, which ordained absolute seclusion for the Cardinals during a Conclave, began to be put into practice. It is no longer in that ancient and venerable sanctuary of Councils, at

---

(1) Scarcely had the confraternity of the Gonfalone been started ere four others arose under the invocation of the Nativity of our Lord, the Nativity of our Lady, of the Innocents, and of S. Helena. The headquarters of these four confraternities were at the church of Aracœli. They acknowledged the Confraternity of the Gonfalone as their mother, and joined themselves to her, whereupon she assumed the title of Archconfraternity. The chief duties of the members of this pious association were to visit the sick, give dowries to poor girls, and collect alms for the redemption of Christian slaves.

the Lateran, that the great assemblies of Christendom were held, but in a far distant town, away beyond the mountains. Twice during the thirteenth century Lyons witnessed the gatherings of the prelates of the world within its primatial palace. The Council which assembled there in 1274 was presided over by S. Gregory X, the peacemaker of Italy; and among the Fathers present were SS. Bonaventure, Filippo Benizzi, and Pietro Celestino; Thomas Aquinas was expected, but God called him away while on his journey thither.

At Rome what little authority the magistrates were able to exert was as a rule centred in the hands of the Senator, who was elected by the people; even a Pope, MARTIN IV, became a candidate for that dignity, in order that he might secure some influence in the city. (1) The decree by which he was elected affords a curious evidence of the jealous pretentions of the Roman people:—

"In the year 1281, on Monday 10th March, the Romans having assembled, according to custom, at

(1) The election of Martin IV took place six months after the death of Nicholas III, not thirty three months as recorded by M. Valéry in his "Itinéraire". The Conclave was then divided into the Orsini party and that of Charles of Anjou. The Orsini had placed one of their side at the head of the government of Viterbo, where the Cardinals were assembled; but Charles of Anjou succeeded in stirring up the people who rushed to the episcopal palace, dragged the Cardinals of the Orsini faction out of it, and locked them up in a room the doors and windows of which they walled up; then they took off the roof of the Conclave Hall, in order to oblige the Cardinals to proceed at once to the election of a Pontiff.

the summons of the town-crier, before the palace of the Capitol, the noble Lords Pietro dei Conti and Gentile degli Orsini, senators and electors nominated by the people, taking into consideration the virtues of our Holy Father, Pope Martin IV, and his love for the city, have committed to the said Lord Pope, not on account of his pontifical dignity, but because of his noble descent, the government of the Roman Senate and its territory, during his lifetime. They have given him full power to rule either alone or by proxy, and to institute one or more senators for as long as he pleases and at such salary as he may appoint. He may also dispose of the revenues belonging to the city of the Romans, bestowing what he thinks proper on the senators and other officials of the city. He may suppress rebels and disobedient persons by such punishments or other methods as may commend themselves to him as just; provided that all the above shall in no way diminish or increase the people's rights or those of the Roman Church in electing a senator after the life of Pope Martin; but that each shall preserve their entire rights."

Conti and Orsini read out this deed to the people who accepted and confirmed it.

During all the time this pretended independence of the city of Rome lasted, arts, letters, in fact everything that constitutes the intellectual life of a nation, remained as though paralyzed. If occasionally monuments were still raised within its walls this was done by order of the Popes, who, whether near or far away, never neglected the city sanctified by the martyrdom of the Apostles. We have already mentioned the works of Innocent III. Nicholas III rebuilt part of the Basilica of S. Peter, enlarged the Vatican, and laid out a large garden enclosed by walls and towers. During the pontificate of Innocent IV the church of S. Maria-in-Via was erected; this church became renowned for its miraculous Madonna; it also gave a title at a later period to the devout Cardinal Bellarmine, who ornamented it with stucco-work.

Honorius IV constructed a palace near S. Sabina, and dwelt there for a considerable time. It was in this palace the Conclave assembled on the death of Honorius; but the air proved so unwholesome during the summer months that many Cardinals died, and the rest dispersed without having appointed a successor to the throne. Girolamo Ascoli alone remained at his post; he succeeded in keeping off the pestilential vapours by kindling great fires daily in spite of its being the dog days. The other Cardinals only rejoined him in the winter, when Girolamo Ascoli was unanimously elected. He took the name of NICHOLAS IV. This Pontiff rebuilt the apses of SS. Maria Maggiore and Giovanni Laterano, ornamenting them with mosaics. The mosaic in S. Maria represents the coronation of the Virgin; that of the Lateran discloses, in three compartments, a symbolic image of the truths of the faith. At the foot are nine Apostles, divided from one another by palms and cypress trees, two monks are kneeling; these monks are of much smaller dimensions than the Apostles; one holds a square, the other a hammer; they are in fact the two masters of the work:

Giacomo Toriti, the painter, and Giacomo Camerino, his associate. The second design is separated from the first by the Jordan, an emblem of baptism, the river serving as the base of the upper composition. The baptism of Our Lord is moreover represented at the point where the arms of the cross intersect in the centre of the picture. Above the instrument of our redemption hovers a dove, from whose beak flows a small streamlet of water which bedews the cross, and forms a pool at its foot from whence issue the four great rivers mentioned in Genesis, symbols of the four Gospels. Two deer approaching to slake their thirst at the pool prefigure future conversions of the Gentiles. Betwixt the several branches of these streams rises a city, above which tower SS. Peter and Paul, signifying the Church. An angel, holding a drawn sword, is stationed before the gate. Finally, standing by the cross are Mary blessing Nicholas IV, SS. Peter, Paul, the two SS. John, Francis of Assisi, Anthony of Padua, etc. The figure of Mary is the largest, those of the Apostles, of other saints and of the Pope, are notably smaller. The third plan fills up the concavity of the tribune and entirely consists of a miraculous picture of the Constantine Basilica. This picture, remarkably majestic in character, was removed by Nicholas IV from the old to the new wall, and stands out from a light blue background, surrounded by a golden aureole.

At the end of the Lateran stands the cloister of the ancient monastery, which probably dates from the thirteenth century. The portico is supported by little columns of marvellous variety and grace.

These columns are either twisted or fluted, single or in groups; garlands of mosaic twine around them; their capitals representing, without any fixed design, animals, flowers, fruit, and small figures. They possess all the richness and freshness of the middle ages. The following inscription formerly was to be seen on the walls: —

> "Et stabiliantur animo qui canonicantur
> Ut conjungantur lapidesque sic policentur."

CELESTINE V, Nicholas IV successor, was eminently holy. Pietro di Morone was born of humble parents about the beginning of the thirteenth century. He preferred a life of solitude from his earliest years, living in dark caverns on the wildest mountains. One of these caves near Sulmone on Monte Morone was his retreat during five years and from it proceeded his appellation. He left this refuge when the land was being cultivated and sought another. Zealous disciples soon submitted to his rule, and raising an Oratory under the invocation of the Holy Spirit these new hermits took the name of Celestines. After the death of Nicholas IV political passions prevented the Cardinals from coming to any agreement as to his successor for two years, when they suddenly remembered the solitary of Sulmone and meditated his election as head of the Church. The deed of election was unanimously signed, and five deputies were sent from the conclave to convey it to him. On reaching Monte Morone he was discovered in an almost inaccessible grated cell, attenuated by age and mortification. He wept and prayed on being informed of his election, but finally resigned himself to God's will. Meanwhile, Cardinals, religious, laymen, the two Kings of Sicily and Hungary, the nobility and people hastened to Sulmone to do homage to the new pontiff. Peter mounted an ass, the two kings holding the bridle, and thus they reached the little town of Aquila where the ceremony of his consecration was held.

The reign of Celestine V (the name he assumed) was not a happy one. In his ignorance of mankind he easily became a victim of intrigue. The King of Sicily induced him to reside in Naples, to the great vexation of the Cardinals who saw him thus at the mercy of this Prince; for, while the Pope practised the severities of a monastic life in a wooden cell contrived in the palace, the government of Christendom was left in the hands of subordinates who abused the Pontiff's holy trust. Celestine felt his own incapacity of bearing the burden imposed upon him, and wanted to abdicate; but this the Neapolitans would not hear of, and, after a solemn procession ordered by the Pope for the purpose of obtaining light from God, the people loudly implored him not to resign. Celestine pretended to acquiesce, and a Te Deum was enthusiastically sung. Nevertheless scruples of conscience continued to assail the Pope, and when he compared court life with one of solitude he was seized with bitter regret. Not only did he find himself powerless to save the souls of others, he doubted whether he should save his own. Having therefore summoned the Cardinals on the 13th of December 1294, he resigned his power, and took off the insignia of papacy in order to re-assume the lowly habit of a monk.

His successor was Benedetto dei Cajetani, Cardinal-priest of SS. Martino-e-Silvestro, who took the name of BONIFACE VIII. The reign of this Pontiff was a period of great trouble, the violent passions of which have left deep marks in history. Dante Alighieri, the Ghibelline poet, called Boniface the Prince of the new Pharisees, a man of blood and crimes, the bold usurper of Celestine's throne. (1) Since then a great number of historians, following the poet's lead, have described Boniface either as a knave, ready to promise, slow to perform, or as a trickster who made the humble Celestine imagine he heard mysterious voices which advised his abdication; in short, the accounts given by several contemporaries have been rejected with contempt or boldly falsified, in order to make way for absurd fables.

The first thought of Boniface VIII was to restore the Apostolic See to S. Peter's tomb; he therefore left Naples early in January 1295. The inhabitants of Anagni, his fellow townsmen, received him with dancing, and every possible expression of joy. A body of Roman nobles came to meet him, and offered him the position of Senator; Boniface accepted this dignity, and entered Rome surrounded by a large cavalcade. The clergy burnt incense, and sang hymns of thanksgiving; the Kings of Sicily and Hungary held the bridle of the Pope's horse as they had done for Celestine when he entered Aquila. Boniface pro-

---

(1) See the "Inferno", c. XXVIII; and the "Paradiso", c. XXVII.

ceeded first to S. John Lateran, and then to S. Peter's, where he was crowned and took an oath to preserve intact the faith and discipline of the Church.

But many persons held that the abdication of Celestine V was null, and that the Pope had no right to lay aside his high functions. The Papacy, they said, came from God alone; He alone had the right to grant it, and He alone could take it away. It was feared that the malcontents might influence Celestine, or that, at least, they might make use of his name to create trouble in the Church. Boniface therefore resolved to place his predecessor beyond the reach of hostile suggestions. He caused the late Pope to be arrested when about to embark for Greece, and brought to Rome, where Boniface received him with great courtesy, gave him much praise, and sent him to Anagni, finally permitting him to dwell in the castle of Fumone in Campania. (1) There Celestine lived in a small cell, though, as Stefaneschi asserts, he might, had he chosen to do so, have occupied a larger apartment, "nolens laxioribus uti"; being kept under supervision until his death, which happened a year and a half after his abdication. He was canonized by Clement V, and bears the name of S. Peter Celestine in the Church.

Boniface VIII had an unbending nature and at times was even harsh; never yielding except for the public good. "However strong and energetic his convictions might be," says Cardinal Wiseman, "how-

---

(1) These are the very words of Fleury, who is undoubtedly beyond suspicion, l. XXXIX.

CHAPTER XIII.—THIRTEENTH CENTURY.

ever severe he was in his manner of procedure, he continually endeavoured to make sovereigns sheathe their swords, and respect the rights of neighbours weaker than themselves, and unite all their energies to compass the great object of the Church at that period, that is to say, the destruction of the Saracen's ever increasing power." In short if war did come to trouble him at the gates of Rome, it may be possible to attribute it to some other reason than his mere selfish ambition.

The Colonna family, one of the most noble in Rome, had acquired great power in the city by their wealth and generosity. It was Cardinal Giovanni Colonna who, in 1216, founded the magnificent hospital of S. John Lateran, and who, on his return from Palestine, whither he had gone as legate of the Apostolic See, brought to Rome, and placed in the church of S. Praxedes, the column at which Jesus Christ had been scourged. (1) Two other Cardinals of the same family, Giacomo and Pietro Colonna, adorned the façade of the Liberian Basilica with the vast mosaic which is now at the back of the loggia of Benediction. Giacomo Colonna also made the Basilica his residuary legatee. Another Colonna presented Aracœli with a mosaic which long adorned the forecourt of the monastery. Generous and powerful they were often holy. The nuns of Palestrina, who had been called to Rome by Honorius IV, had solemnly conveyed the body of their foundress, the

---

(1) This column of black and white marble, about a metre in height, is still one of the principal treasures of S. Praxedes.

B. Margarita Colonna, and buried it with every mark of veneration in the church of S. Silvestro-in-capite.

But, on the other hand, since the defection of Cardinal Giovanni, who had warred against the Church on behalf of Frederick II, the Colonna had led the Ghibelline party. In spite of this, however, that powerful family had given their votes to Boniface in the Conclave which had elected him, and at first it was one of his firmest supports in Rome. But, suddenly, a fierce division arose among the members of that family. Cardinal Giacomo Colonna was violently attacked by three of his nephews, Matteo, Odone, and Landolfo, who accused him of keeping possession of their patrimony. Boniface supported their claims and furthermore demanded that a pontifical garrison should be admitted to the fortress of Palestrina, which was a fief of the Church; for he feared the alliance which existed between the Cardinal and the House of Aragon, which at that time was at war with the Holy See. (1)

Giacomo Colonna and his nephew, Cardinal Pietro, at once unfurled the standard of revolt. They even went further, and disputed the legality of Boniface's title, although they had themselves sanctioned it by their votes in the conclave; and they actually affixed their protest to S. Peter's altar. So bold an act might not go unpunished. Boniface cited the Colonna to appear before his tribunal, and, on their refusal, he stripped them of their dignities. A war then

---

(1) M. Leo, professor at the Protestant University of Halle, says, "The Colonna were the allies of the Kings of Aragon and Sicily; therefore the Pope considered they were traitors to the States of the Church."

broke out, which was contested with bitterness on both sides. The Colonna no longer gave the Pope any other name than Benedetto Cajetani, and called the people to arms against him whom they accused of usurping the Chair of S. Peter. On his side Boniface preached a crusade against these new schismatics, and he caused their palaces at Rome to be demolished. The pontifical army easily took possession of Nepi and Zagarolo, and proceeded to besiege Palestrina, which ended by falling into their power. S. Peter's standard already waved from the city walls when the Colonna issued forth, presenting themselves before Boniface arrayed in black with ropes around their necks. (1) They threw themselves down before him, and besought his pardon. One cried out:— "I have sinned, my Father, against heaven and before thee, and am no more worthy to be called thy son." The other added:— "Thou hast afflicted us because of our sins." Boniface raised them up, forgave and absolved them from all the censures they had incurred. But he firmly determined not to leave the strong position of Palestrina any longer in the possession of this family; so he demolished the town, deprived it of its Bishopric and Cardinal's title, removing all its rights and privileges to another city which he ordered should be built at a short distance from Palestrina. However,

---

(1) Memoirs taken from the Secret Archives of the Vatican and published in 1795 by Petrini. Palestrina, having been captured before any interview had taken place between the Colonna and the Pope, disproves that there was any arrangement between them, as Dante asserts in Canto XXVII of the Inferno.

the Pope's wishes were not entirely carried out; and, later on, he restored their lands to the inhabitants of Palestrina, on condition that they were held in fief to him, and no longer to the Colonna.

Let us now turn away from these sad scenes and observe the virtues Rome witnessed in the closing years of the thirteenth century. As we have already stated the illustrious Colonna family did not merely produce bold warlike chieftains; it is even remarkable that, at this very time, side by side with the proud governors of Zagarolo and Palestrina, history tells of a humble monk, Egidio Colonna, who, after studying under S. Thomas Aquinas, taught at Paris and became tutor to the young Prince who was one day to be Philippe le Bel. The hermits of S. Augustine elected him as their General in a chapter held at Rome in 1292, and soon afterwards the Archbishopric of Bourges was bestowed upon him as a striking token of esteem for his merits.

S. Raymond Nonnatus came twice to Rome during the thirteenth century in his capacity of Procurator-General of the Order of the Brothers of Mercy, founded by S. Peter Nolasco. He was sent to obtain the approval of the rule of the new institute. During the last days of his life, he was named Cardinal of the title of S. Eustachio.

The monastery of S. Sabina, now belonging to the monks of S. Dominic, received during the thirteenth century SS. Hyacinth and Ceslas, two Polish brothers, and an illustrious Spaniard, S. Raymond of Penafort.

Rome also beheld Raymond Lullus, the knight-errant of the faith, and William Durandus the Speculator, one of the most illustrious professors of the university of Bologna. In 1295 Lullus deposited his "Arbor Scientiarum" and his "Ars Generalis" for the discovery of truth on S. Peter's altar. Durandus died at Rome in 1296 after performing the functions of Governor of S. Peter's patrimony, and General of the pontifical troops. His tomb may be seen in S. **Maria-super-Minervam**, a church built on the ruins of a temple of Minerva, which had been erected by Pompey on the field of Mars in thanksgiving for his triumphs.

S. Louis did not come to Rome; but the great and holy King, who had been canonized by Boniface VIII at Orvieto, on the 11th of August 1297, was represented, in the Christian capital, by another S. Louis, his great-nephew, son of Charles the Lame, King of Naples. This young Prince came to Rome to embrace the rule of S. Francis. He pronounced his vows, on Christmas Eve, in the monastery of Aracœli, renouncing, in favour of his brother Robert, all his rights as heir-presumptive to the throne of the Two Sicilies. The Pope appointed him Bishop of Toulouse, permitting him to retain, under an ecclesiastical mantle, his habit of Friar Minor. But this zealous religious could not long submit to any relaxation of discipline, so, on the 5th of February, S. Agatha's day, clothed only in a friar's rough habit and girdle, he went barefoot to the Vatican from the Franciscan monastery on the Capitol. He was followed by respectful crowds which completely filled S. Peter's where he preached to them. Next year S. Louis of Toulouse died at Brignolles in Provence at the early age of twenty-three. (1)

As the fourteenth century drew near, an extraordinary movement took place at Rome and throughout Europe. Aged men had said that, by an ancient custom of the Church, every hundredth year was marked by singular graces to all who visited the tomb of the Apostles at that time. According to some a plenary indulgence was obtained; others affirmed that it was an indulgence of one hundred years for every day of the year. Boniface vainly examined the archives of the Church for some clear evidence of this privilege; but, none the less, people persisted in their own opinion; centenarians were consulted, and all agreed as to the antiquity of this belief. Accordingly, on the evening of the first of January 1300, the Romans hurried with extraordinary eagerness to the Vatican Basilica. The crowd continued to increase for two months. Boniface, from the summit of the Lateran palace, perceived men and women thronging the approaches to S. Peter's tomb, their serried ranks also covering the Ostian Way, on which stood the Basilica of S. Paul. The Pontiff did not wish to oppose this devotion, and, by a Bull of the 22nd of February, he granted a plenary indulgence, applicable every hundred years to all who, being truly penitent and having confessed their sins, should daily

---

(1) The Versailles Museum possesses a fine portrait of S. Louis of Toulouse. The ornaments of this picture are in relief and enriched with gold. By some persons it is attributed to Giotto.

visit the churches of the Apostles for thirty days. Foreigners might obtain the same indulgence by visiting the stations for only fifteen days. (1) Immediately vast multitudes flowed in from Italy, Germany, France, England, in fact from every country into which Christian civilisation had penetrated. Old men arrived supported by their children; the sick were borne in litters. During the remainder of that year, two hundred thousand pilgrims were at Rome, if we believe Giovanni Villani who was present. Dante was also there, and, in his "Inferno", compares the rolling waves of souls to the tumultuous agitation of pilgrims crossing the Bridge of S. Angelo in opposite directions. (2) Elsewhere Dante describes their astonishment and admiration on beholding S. John Lateran. (3) It must indeed have been a grand sight, this assemblage of all tongues and all

---

(1) The indulgence granted by this Bull did not bear the name of Jubilee; but the populace immediately gave it this name, as may be seen from Dante's verses written about this period: "l' anno del Giubbileo, sù per lo ponte" . . . (Inferno, c. XVIII.) Later on, the Pontiffs recognised this title in their Bulls. The first was in one given at Avignon by CLEMENT IV, on the 27th of January 1848, which fixes the indulgence granted by Boniface VIII at every fifty years; recalling therein the Jubilee of the Mosaic Law. ("Extrav. com. de pœn." C. II.) The Jubilee was later on attributed to every thirty-third year by URBAN VI, in memory of the years of Jesus Christ's life, and, finally, PAUL II ordered that it should be celebrated every twenty-five years. See following chapters XIV and XVI.

(2) "Come i Roman per l'esercito molto", etc. Inferno, c. XVIII, st. 16 and 11.

(8) "Paradiso", c. XXXI.

nations, forgetful alike of birth, prejudices, rivalry, ambition, and hatred, meeting thus in brotherly love to mingle their thoughts and hopes in **adoration** and **prayer.**

CHAPTER XIV.

> Rien n'est égal à toi, ô Rome, bien que
> tu ne sois presque plus qu'une ruine.
> *Hildebert, Archbishop of Tours.*

FOURTEENTH CENTURY.

AS years rolled by, Christian civilisation developed, while its sphere of action grew larger. Christianity's first self-imposed duty, after the iron age of barbarism was over, was to settle the civil government of nations as well as possible, and fit man once more for the practices of social life which he had lost. The grand work of the Church was to make laws, repress tyranny, and instruct nations on religion and morality. This was not all; it soon encouraged all intellectual impulses, the fine arts and letters as well as legislation and scientific discoveries. Religion consecrated magnificent monuments in monasteries and towns; Greek mosaics with hard lines, and backgrounds relieved by gold, no longer sufficed; these gave place to brilliant paintings remarkable for their colouring and perspective, to large frescoes which covered bare walls and recalled heavenly subjects in God's house. Cimabue,

Giotto, Orcagna, Fra Angelico da Fiesole belong to this century, and their works manifest the highest stage in devotional art.

Architecture had already during two centuries produced some fine masterpieces; but its development had been chiefly in the North. Italy was as yet unable to present buildings which could compare with the conceptions of Robert of Luzarches and Erwin of Steinbach. But the time was at hand when the genius of Greece and Rome would revive on this privileged Christian soil.

Arabian art was also to become magnificent with Catholicism. Its slim columns were grouped together into clusters, or transformed into bold pillars; its want of proportion and many varied ornaments were combined, producing constant contrasts between the small and the gigantic. In short, from the empty whims of fancy, Catholicism developed that style which is both mysterious and solemn, and which perhaps corresponds best with the severity of her dogmas.

The choice of a style of architecture for Christian monuments was not the same throughout Christendom; it varied and was influenced by the traditions and character of nations.

Until the fourteenth century, Italian art remained undecided between Northern and Southern influences and traditions; but finally it adopted the Greek style. This period was indeed marked not only by a revival of the arts, but most of all by that of literature.

Dante was a Catholic, a serious reflecting poet; a theologian, mystic as a monk, yet terrible as a prophet of evil; scornful and malevolent as a politician. Petrarch was more like a minor Grecian poet, although the modesty of his passion was utterly unknown to antiquity. Boccaccio alone belongs wholly to pagan traditions; he imports the character of Lucian, the licentiousness of Petronius, to the banks of the Arno, where they unfortunately met with a too fertile soil.

If we enquire into what influence this great intellectual movement had on Rome, we must admit that it had none whatever at this period. Since the Popes had lost their power over Rome, the city of the Cæsars had lost all its influence over the world. Its separation from the papacy had never been greater than in the fourteenth century, for it was then that the emigration to Avignon took place, when the history of Rome, for seventy one years, became almost foreign to that of the Church.

But, before these days of isolation and solitude began, the Church experienced times of bitter strife. A new revolt of the Colonna, and the quarrels which arose on the often disputed question of ecclesiastical immunities between Philippe le Bel, King of France, and Boniface VIII, brought about a deplorable condition between the powers. Boniface assembled a Council at Rome in 1302, and published the famous Bull "Unam Sanctam", in which the rights and functions of the spiritual and the temporal power were clearly laid down; the "two swords" as the Pontiff called them. The true meaning of this Bull was that Kings like nations were subject to the unchangeable laws of justice; when they did not fulfil the duties imposed upon them they fell beneath the spiritual sword appointed by God to cut down and uproot all moral evil from Christian society. (1)

This exposition of doctrine was received in France with violent opposition, and Philippe le Bel sent William de Nogaret secretly into Italy to carry off the Pope. Boniface was at Anagni, employed in drawing up a new Bull against Philippe le Bel, when on the 7th of September, 1203, William de Nogaret entered the city, accompanied by Sciarra-Colonna at the head of three or four hundred men. They cried:—"Death to Pope Boniface! Long live the King of France!" The Governor and citizens yielded, some to the influence of money, others to fear; the pontifical palace was taken after a slight resistance, its treasury sacked, while cardinals and attendants fled and dispersed.

On hearing the attack Boniface put on the ornaments of his dignity; assuming S. Peter's mantle, and the tiara, that ancient crown which report traced to the time of Constantine, and holding the keys and cross he knelt before the altar. (2) "Since,

---

(1) The following are a few passages from the Bull:— "Uterque ergò est in potestate ecclesiæ, spiritalis scilicet gladius et materialis; sed is quidem pro ecclesiâ, ille verò ab ecclesiâ exercendus; ille sacerdotis, is manu regum et militum, sed ad nutum et sapientiam sacerdotis. Oportet autem gladium esse sub gladio, et temporalem auctoritatem spirituali subjici potestati ... Veritate testante, spiritalis potestas terrenam potestatem instituere habet et judicare si bona non fuerit..., ergò si deviat terrena potestas, judicabitur a potestate spiritali."

(2) According to some authorities he seated himself on the papal throne.

like Jesus Christ, we are betrayed, we will at least die as a Pope should die," he said. When Nogaret and Sciarra entered his presence, they threatened to carry him off to Lyons to be deposed by a General Council, which they bade him convoke. Sciarra went so far as to add outrage to threats; though the report is doubtful that he actually laid hands on the successor of the Apostles. (1) To all these insults the Pontiff boldly replied:— "Here is our head, here is our neck; we are ready to suffer all things for the liberty of the Catholic Church. Pope and legitimate Vicar of Jesus Christ, we will patiently bear being condemned and deposed by heretics; we desire to die for the faith of Christ and for His Church." (2)

The conspirators then placed guards around the palace, and Boniface remained a prisoner within it for three days. But a reaction promptly took place without. The inhabitants of Anagni, ashamed of their weakness, took up arms to the cry of "Long live the Pope; death to the traitors!" Then fiercely attacking Colonna's partisans they drove them both from palace and city. Boniface, freed from his enemies, set out for Rome, with the intention of summoning a Council; but the violent emotion he had experienced had exhausted his strength already much impaired by

---

(1) It is not surprising that Sciarra was accused of violence; this was not his first attack on either the Pope or the treasury of the pontifical court; Villani has the following:— "In questo avenne che Sciarra-Colonna veggendo, al mutare della corte di Alagni, le some delle arnesi e'l tesoro della chiesa, le rubò e prese e menolle in sua terra." Giov. Villani, VIII, 21.

(2) Rom., ap. Rub., p. 213.

eighty-six years. On feeling the approach of death he made his profession of faith in the presence of the Cardinals, according to the custom of the sovereign pontiffs, and expired.

The character of Boniface VIII is one of the most difficult to treat impartially, for, like all strong willed men, he had many enemies; this much, however, is certain, if he aroused bitter hatred in some, he was also surrounded by many devoted sympathisers. The Romans, notoriously impatient of the papal yoke, remained firmly attached to him; they placed their confidence in him because he was strong. The republic of Pisa, by a spontaneous act, placed itself under his direction; Velletri selected him as its governor; Florence, Bologna, Orvieto raised marble statues to him, and, when he was at war, sent troops to his aid; it is even related that women, not being able to fight themselves, recruited soldiers for his service. (1)

Boniface, although he would not brook any contradiction to his wishes, was never revengeful nor tyrannical. At the very time he was delivered out of the hands of Nogaret, during that very crisis in which Sismondi represents him as being mad with rage, Rinaldo of Anagni, his chief betrayer, was brought a prisoner before him. The Pope, however, pardoned him. (2) It is difficult to express how great was popular indignation on learning that the Pope had been made prisoner. We may believe Dante

---

(1) Petrini's "Mémoires".
(2) This fact is related by Cardinal Stefanesius.

on this subject, when, in the twentieth canto of his "Purgatorio", he puts the following words in the mouth of Hugh Capet:— (1)

> "I see the flower-de-luce Alagna enter,
> And Christ in His own Vicar captive made;
> I see him yet another time derided;
> I see renewed the vinegar and the gall.
> And between living thieves I see him slain.
> I see the modern Pilate so relentless", etc. (2)

Yet Dante was a Ghibelline, and had been driven out of Florence by the partisans of Boniface, whom he did not spare in his writings.

Moreover, no Pope has ever been more abused than was Boniface, particularly by the Colonna, who scattered pamphlets against him all over Europe; but the iniquities they laid to his charge "were not believed", says a historian, "because, with great evidence of piety and humility and much devotion to the Blessed Virgin, he never failed to visit the Lateran Church and that of the Crucifix, where daily he remained for two long hours in prayer." We possess two prayers by Boniface; one to Jesus crucified, the other to Our-Lady-of-Sorrows, and they bear witness to the grace within his soul. The same feeling of ardent piety induced Boniface to give greater solemnity to the feast of the Apostles, Evangelists, and to the four great doctors, Ambrose, Jerome, Gregory, and Augustine. We must also not forget that he decreed the canonization of S. Louis in 1297. On this occasion Boniface preached two remarkable ser-

---

(1) "Veggio in Alagna entrar lo fiordaliso . . . ."
(2) Longfellow's translation of Dante.

mons, taking for his text Our Lord's words which are so often quoted by kings:— "Reddite quæ sunt Cæsaris Cæsari et quæ sunt Dei Deo."

In spite of his stormy pontificate he nevertheless left monumental evidence of his passage at Rome. We must specially mention the Gothic baldacchino which overhung the altar of S. Boniface in the ancient Vatican Basilica, and the graceful balcony of Blessings, at the Lateran. This balcony, built on the occasion of the Jubilee, was at the end of the Council Hall, on the left of the spot where the obelisk now stands. It projected over the square, and was adorned with Corinthian columns. Many coloured marbles covered the outer walls, while, within, large frescoes represented the baptism of Constantine, the building of the Lateran, and the proclamation of the holy year. These paintings were executed by Giotto.

BENEDICT IX, who succeeded Boniface VIII, reigned but eight months; it was on the death of this holy Pontiff that the election of Bertrand de Goth, Archbishop of Bordeaux, took place at Perugia, the new Pope assuming the name of CLEMENT V. Instead of coming up to the tomb of the Apostle to receive the pontifical crown, Clement insisted on being consecrated at Lyons and fixed his residence in France. From this period, namely 1305, Rome has her separate history, sad and disturbed, which nevertheless we must follow without considering that of the Popes who succeeded one another in Provence.

The unhappy Italian cities were then rent asunder by the conflicting passions of Guelphs and Ghibellines, the whites and the blacks. Cardinal Napoleon Orsini related that "Rome fell into ruins, S. Peter's patrimony being pillaged by men who were more robbers than governors."

In addition to these misfortunes came the terrible conflagration, on the evening of the 23rd of June 1308, which reduced to ashes the ancient and venerable Basilica of S. John Lateran. It destroyed the choir, the principal nave, the canons' residences, and the greater part of the palace, melted the silver tabernacle of the high altar, and the faithful were beginning to deplore the irreparable loss of the table on which S. Peter had offered up mass, when they heard that some brave men had rescued it from the flames and placed it in a chapel. This conflagration plunged Rome into a melancholy stupor. It was looked upon as a divine punishment; the streets and churches were filled with lamentations, while numerous processions traversed the city imploring the mercy of heaven.

At the same time efforts were made to restore the Mother church of the world from its ruins. Men, women, children, nobles, rich and poor, everyone indeed, lent a hand to this work; CLEMENT V energetically encouraged this generous action by sending large sums of money and by granting indulgences. The restoration of the Basilica was not, however, completed, and, although in 1334 BENEDICT XII sent further sums for its reparation, Petrarch a few years later lamented the neglected state in which this mother of all churches was left. — "The Lateran is falling to pieces", he exclaimed, "its roof has gone, it lies open to the winds and storms." The poet adds, personifying Rome, "I have as many wounds as I have churches and palaces." (1)

"The Church is the Sun, the Empire the Moon of Rome", cries Dante, "but now she is deprived of both luminaries, and is thus doubly an orphan."

It would be thought that Rome, thus degraded and ruined, must have lost all her former prestige. Of all her past greatness there remained only a few crumbling Basilicas and her name which still held the world in awe. One of the Popes at Avignon once remarked, "Whether one likes or dislikes it, Rome must ever be the capital of the world." Thus it was not in Provence that Emperors desired to be crowned, but in the city of the Cæsars, at the tomb of S. Peter. Clement V promised Henry of Luxembourg that he would go to Rome and consecrate him on the Purification A.D. 1312; but, being detained by several matters of importance in Provence, he appointed a commission of five Cardinals to represent him at the ceremony. Before leaving Germany, Henry took an oath to the Archbishop of Trier to defend the Catholic faith, exterminate heretics, protect the Pope, make no alliance with his enemies, and maintain the rights of the Apostolic See. But serious difficulties awaited him at Rome. The King of Naples was, in fact, master of part of the city, and was strongly supported by the Orsini. On Henry's side were the

---

(1) The destruction of S John Lateran affected the whole of Christendom. Dante, recalling the ancient glory of the Lateran, amid the splendours of his "Paradiso", writes:—

      ". . . . . "Quando Laterano
      Alle cose mortali audo di sopra."

Colonna; he seized the Cælian Hill and the Lateran palace, within which he took up his quarters; but, when he sought to reach S. Peter's, the troops of the King of Naples attacked his own, and succeeded in driving them back after a bloody conflict. Henry felt he was not strong enough to renew the struggle, so gave up his intention of being consecrated in the Vatican Basilica, and received the imperial crown, on the 29th of June 1312, in the Lateran sanctuary.

These internal dissensions, which existed among the principal families in almost every town of Italy, became a constant source of agitation, until it appeared that there no longer existed either law or tradition. What was instituted in the month of October ceased to exist ere the middle of November, unbridled licence reigned supreme. Robbery and assassination were rife; the streets were battle-fields, the houses fortresses. At Recanati, a furious mob indulged in wholesale slaughter; the dead were buried in public squares, houses were razed to the ground, while the populace indulged in every excess. This state of lawlessness ended by producing a host of petty tyrannies. Those families who mostly triumphed in these struggles established and consolidated their power over their fellow citizens. The Visconti became masters of Milan, the Scaligeri of Verona; Mantua, Ravenna, Rimini, each had its lord, or leader of the people, until, in the absence of any strong authority either at Rome or in Germany, Italy became split up into small principalities, jealous and independent of one another.

Louis of Bavaria wished to profit by this disorganisation of the Italian powers in order to extend his dominion over the peninsula. He had been elected Emperor on the death of Henry of Luxembourg; but as he had intermeddled in imperial affairs before the Pope had confirmed his election, and upheld the Visconti who were at war with the Church, JOHN XXII refused to acknowledge him. None the less, Louis continued to pursue his ambitious plans. In the month of February 1327, he assembled troops at Trent, held a Council with the Ghibelline leaders, then crossed the Alps and entered Milan.

It was then that Petrarch wrote his appeal to the Italian nobles beginning "Italia mia," etc. (1)

On hearing of the German prince's advance Rome was greatly disturbed. The people feared that the nobles wished to surrender their city to the King of Naples who, being its Senator, had appointed Count Anguillara and Annibale di Annibaldi to be his lieutenants. They accordingly mutinied. Sciarra-Colonna was named leader, and they gave him a council of fifty-two citizens to aid him in the government. The Romans next sent ambassadors to Avignon, requesting the presence of the Pope, and threatening to yield up the city to Louis of Bavaria should the Pope continue to reside in France.

John XXII expressed his willingness to yield to the wishes of the Roman people; but an accumulation of business still retained him. Further overtures were made by the Romans on several occasions; but, as these also proved fruitless, they gave way to bitter lamentations, writing, "On our knees we implore your

---

(1) Canzone IV, Petrarca.

Holiness to come at once, without further delay, and personally visit your first See, which you have apparently forgotten. Otherwise we declare that henceforth we shall hold ourselves blameless before God and all the heavenly host, before the Church itself, and before the whole of Christendom, should any misfortune occur, or if the children, deprived of their father's presence and leadership, should go astray."

The Pope's reply contains the following words, which were only too true, "As far as the state of Rome is concerned you know whether peace and safety reign there."

Meanwhile Louis of Bavaria had taken Pisa after a stout resistance. On the 2$^{\underline{nd}}$ of January 1328 he reached Viterbo, and on the 7$^{\underline{th}}$ of the same month entered Rome. At first he lodged in the Vatican, but after four days he crossed the Tiber and made his head-quarters at S. Maria-Maggiore, from whence he could command a view of the whole city. Louis was accompanied by a great number of mendicant friars, who were then in rebellion against the Pope on the much discussed question as to the poverty of Jesus Christ. This invasion of schismatics was a cause of great sorrow to the faithful at Rome; several ecclesiastics fled; the city lay under an interdict; bells were no longer rung; divine service was suspended, except in a few churches which had been invaded by monks of the imperial suite. Louis wished to employ force in order to overcome this opposition from the Catholics, and Sciarra-Colonna willingly made himself the agent of his will. But all their efforts and threats were in vain, and one of the Vatican Canons hid the holy winding sheet thereby causing great consternation among the townsfolk.

It was under these sad circumstances that Louis' coronation took place. We have heard Dante call the Empire "the Moon of Rome". He also calls Rome the spouse of the Empire. "Come," he says to Albert of Germany in his immortal poem, "come and see thy weeping Rome, a forsaken widow, who appeals to thee day and night, crying — 'Come Cæsar, why art thou not with me?'" Dante held that as a divine right from God the empire of the world belonged to Rome, and that the Emperors drew their rights from the Romans. Petrarch shared these views, as also did Rienzi at a later date; indeed more than once they had been openly expressed in assemblies at the Capitol. It was doubtless to show them respect that Louis of Bavaria summoned the people and promised to protect and raise them up once more. Cries of "Long live our lord, the King of the Romans!" answered these promises; his anointing was then fixed for the following Sunday, 17$\underline{\text{th}}$ of January. It took place at S. Peter's; the King and Queen being crowned by Giacomo Albertino, Bishop of Castello, who had been deposed by the Pope. After the ceremony Louis ordered three decrees to be read, in which he bound himself to maintain Catholic faith, to honour the clergy, and to protect orphans and widows; afterwards he attended a stately banquet which lasted till night-fall.

From this moment Louis of Bavaria exercised all the rights of sovereignty at Rome. Several times he was seen presiding at meetings of the people in S. Peter's Square, seated on the upper steps of the peristyle, arrayed in purple, crowned and holding the sceptre and globe. Around him thronged prelates, nobles, advocates, and judges. On these occasions Louis decreed laws; at one assembly he actually pronounced a solemn sentence of deposition against John XXII, whom he styled Jacques de Cahors, loading him at the same time with epithets of heretic, simoniac, mystic antichrist, and precursor of antichrist.

One man could not endure the insult offered to the Vicar of Jesus Christ: this was Giacomo Colonna. He went to the Piazza S. Marcello, and there in the presence of more than a thousand persons read aloud a papal Bull against Louis of Bavaria, which no one had yet dared to publish. Afterwards he exclaimed, "I protest against what Louis of Bavaria has done, and I maintain that Pope John is a Catholic, and the legitimate Pope. He who styles himself Emperor is not one; but is excommunicated with all his adherents . . ." Giacomo Colonna offered to prove his words by argument, or, if need be, by the sword on neutral ground. He then affixed the Bull to the doors of S. Marcello, mounted his horse and leaving Rome withdrew to Palestrina. Louis of Bavaria sent armed men in pursuit, but they failed to come up with him. (1)

---

(1) Giacomo Colonna was appointed Bishop of Carpentras by John XXII; he was much attached to Petrarch who dedicated the poem to him beginning "O aspettata in ciel, beata e bella anima . . . . ." Canzone I.

The Emperor now determined to give John XXII a successor, and, in order to secure the assent of the Romans, he first of all drew up a constitution which made it obligatory for a Pope to reside constantly at Rome, and forbade him to go further away from the city than a two days' journey without obtaining the consent of both clergy and people. In case of unauthorized absence, and after three warnings, the Pope was to be deprived of all right to his dignity. This constitution was promulgated on the 23rd of April 1328. On the following 12th of May, Feast of the Ascension, Louis of Bavaria placed Pietro Rainalucci, a friar Minor, born at Corbario, beneath a canopy outside S. Peter's, as his candidate for the papacy. In order to preserve some appearance of an election, Giacomo Albertino thrice asked the people if they would accept Brother Pietro di Corbario as Pope. Some persons who had desired a Roman pontiff hesitated, but fear carried the day, and they answered:— "So be it." Albertino then read the decree of election, the Emperor rose, named the new Pope NICHOLAS, giving him the ring and cope, after which they proceeded to the Basilica with great pomp. Finally on May 22nd the ceremony of enthronement took place. Louis of Bavaria had spent the night at S. Lorenzo-fuori-le-mura; the antipope with his Cardinals met him at S. John Lateran, whence they proceeded to S. Peter's. The King presented the red cap to Pietro di Corbario, and finally insisted on being crowned a second time, in order that he might say that his election had been confirmed by a Pope.

This intrusion and violence were fortunately of

short duration. Louis was driven back from Campania, and the Romans, weary of schism and of the interdict laid upon them, raised cries of death against both Germans and antipope. Prudence compelled the Emperor to retreat towards the North, and Pietro di Corbario followed him. On his departure he was hooted by the populace who flung stones and killed some of his people. Then the whole population went forth to meet the Cardinal-Legate who was welcomed with shouts of "Long live Pope John; long live the Holy Church!" All the acts and decrees of Louis of Bavaria were burnt on the square before the Capitol; and some young people, with that deplorable levity which turns the most sacred things into ridicule, went to the cemeteries, digging up the bodies of Germans, dragging their disfigured remains through the streets and flinging them into the Tiber.

The Catholic clergy, who had withdrawn from the city in consequence of the interdict, now hastened to re-enter Rome on the departure of the antipope; the holy winding sheet, which had been secreted by a few Romans in the church of S. Maria-della-Rotonda, was brought back with great pomp to S. Peter's, and, at the same time, ambassadors set out for Avignon, bearing declarations of fidelity from the city to the Apostolic See. Indeed several times the Romans renewed these declarations; acknowledging that to the Pope alone, so long as he lived, belonged the lordship of the city of Rome; that they had grievously offended, in receiving Louis of Bavaria and his troops, and by allowing Louis to be crowned Emperor, and Pietro di Corbario elected antipope.

This state of submission was maintained for several years, which were years of quietude and peace. But the Queen-City never ceased reminding the Popes that the sanctuaries of the Apostles were deserted and forsaken since they had resided at Avignon. BENEDICT XII sent fifty thousand florins for the restoration of palaces and churches, among others, of S. Peter's and S. John Lateran; but this proved merely a fleeting help, which only slightly delayed the ruin that was threatening every monument in the city; so Rome continued to lament and entreat.

On the election of CLEMENT VI Rome sent eighteen of her citizens, selected from various ranks of the people, as deputies to the new Pope. The envoys made three requests to the Pontiff:— first, that he would accept the dignities of Senator, Captain, and other magistracies of the city; but they added this offer was not made to him as Pope, but as Lord Roger de Maumont; secondly, that he should come to Rome, to the chief Basilica S. John Lateran, his own proper seat; and, thirdly, that he should reduce the period of the Jubilee to fifty years, seeing that but few men lived one hundred years.

Clement accepted the positions offered to him, with, however, a reservation as to his sovereign rights, which it appeared were not acknowledged by the envoys. He excused himself from going forthwith to Rome; and, finally, he issued a Bull in which, after comparing the indulgence of the hundredth year with the Jubilee of the Mosaic Law which occurred every fiftieth year, a period of grace and mercy, he fixed the indulgence in like manner. By this Bull visiting the church of S. John Lateran was required in addition to visiting the churches of SS. Peter and Paul, which alone had been exacted by the Bull of Boniface VIII.

Among the Roman ambassadors who went to Avignon was a tavern-keeper's son who had acquired great influence at Rome by his learning and profound knowledge of national antiquities: he was intriguing and ambitious, gifted with a shrewd mind, able to profit by opportunity, and endowed with that burning eloquence calculated to excite the masses. He was known as Nicholas Laurentii (Nicholas the son of Laurence), according to the prevailing custom of joining the son's name to that of the father; his full name had been commonly abbreviated into Colà di Rienzi. (1) Rienzi was a notary; and, while carrying out duties which brought him into constant contact with the people, he constituted himself, according to his own statement, the advocate of orphans, widows, and of the poor. He went beyond this. One of Rienzi's brothers had been murdered, and, being unable to bring the assassin to justice, he resolved on changing the Roman constitution, and on freeing the city from aristocratic tyranny. With this object in view, he mingled more than ever with the populace, became the mouthpiece of their complaints, and was soon reputed to be the most eloquent man among

---

(1) Rienzi was born in 1313 in the Regola Quarter, on the banks of the Tiber, near the church of S. Tommaso and the Quattro capi bridge. His father kept an inn; his mother washed linen and was a water-carrier.

the Romans. He had been attached to the embassy at Avignon on account of his eloquence, even Clement VI was charmed by it, so that when Rienzi returned to Rome his influence became paramount. He gave orders that a ship disabled by tempests bearing a woman in tattered garments, with dishevelled hair, clasping her hands and gazing upwards, should be painted on the outer wall of the Capitol which overlooked the Forum. The word ROME was written above the picture. Not far from it were represented four other wrecked vessels, each bearing a female corpse, over each of these were the words:— BABYLON, TROY, CARTHAGE, JERUSALEM. The waves were upheaved by four rows of winged animals which blew trumpets. In front were lions, wolves, and bears, with the inscription:— "Behold the powerful Barons!"; dogs, swine and goats followed, labelled "Evil Counsellors"; after which came sheep, dragons, and foxes, bearing the legend, "Weak Judges"; and finally appeared cats, hares, she-goats, and monkeys, with the words, "These are the Brigands, Murderers, Adulterers, and Robbers among the people." (1)

The populace was moved by this allegorical picture, which made them look upon Rienzi as a saviour who would once more revive the glories of ancient Rome. At first Rienzi contented himself with the title of Provost, being careful to associate the Bishop of Ostia with his government as the Pope's Vicar;

---

(1) A detailed description of this painting is to be found in "Rienzi et Rome à son époque" by Félix Papencordt.

he soon, however, aspired to the title of Tribune, and was duly proclaimed from the Capitol: "Tribune of liberty, peace, and justice, illustrious liberator of the Roman Republic."

Rienzi had appealed to religion to take some share in the revolution he contemplated. Thus he chose the Feast of Pentecost to overthrow senatorial power, and, before ascending the Capitol, he began the day by having thirty masses of the Holy Ghost celebrated in the church of S. Angelo-in-Pescaria, which was near his dwelling. In his code of government he curiously mixed up religious with civil ordinances. Side by side with the severe penalties incurred by murder, robbery, and adultery, were the *obligations for* annual confession and communion enforced by confiscation of one third of the worldly goods of those who neglected these duties.

Rienzi gave out that he was the elect of the Holy Ghost, and, as such, on solemn occasions he wore a white chlamys (candidatus Spiritus Sancti); he promulgated laws, levied troops, sent ambassadors to all the powers, endeavouring to persuade them to join what he called the league of the good state; he created new tribunals, and organized a vigilant police throughout the extent of his administration.

The great Roman families, whose undisciplined pride kept up a state of perpetual lawlessness within the city, were the first to feel the weight of his attacks. He took away their privileges, and was merciless towards all disturbers of good order, so that Rome was very shortly freed from those malefactors who had infested her. — "Forests no longer conceal robbers," says a contemporary writer, "oxen may again plough the soil, pilgrims again visit the holy places, and merchants, travelling in security, may at night leave their goods by the way side, and be sure to find them untouched on the following morning; tyrants tremble with fear, while honest folk rejoice at being freed from bondage." But, with success, the pride of the Tribune increased. He gave splendid banquets during which his praises were sung; he flung money to the people as though he were a King, and, on one occassion, when going to S. Peter's, shops were actually pulled down in order to widen the streets for him. Rienzi, at length, forgetful of his origin and popular name, resolved on being dubbed knight by the chief magistrate. The church of S. John Lateran was selected for this ceremony, and, as watching arms was usually preceded by a bath, in order to render the knight as clean and spotless as honour, Rienzi bathed in the marble basin which had been used, according to tradition, at the baptism of Constantine, and in which he had been cured of leprosy. The Tribune then slept in that consecrated space surrounded by the ancient porphyry columns which had been brought to the Lateran by Sixtus III. In the morning, Mass was celebrated in the Balcony of Blessings, and Rienzi, after his spurs and sword had been buckled on, turned towards the people, and the following proclamation was read out:—

"To the glory of God, of the Apostles SS. Peter and Paul and John the Baptist, to the honour of the Holy Roman Church, our mother, for the prosperity of the Pope, our lord, for the prosperity of the holy city of Rome, of sacred Italy, and of the whole Christian faith, We, Nicholas, knight, candidate of the Holy Spirit, austere and clement deliverer of Rome, lover of Italy, friend of the universe, and august Tribune, wishing to imitate the liberty of ancient Roman princes, make known to all that the Roman people has recognized from the advice of wise men that it still possesses the same authority, power, and jurisdiction over the universe which it had from the beginning, and that it has revoked all privileges granted to the prejudice of that authority. We, therefore, in order not to appear ungrateful and miserly of the gift of the Holy Spirit, and so as no longer to allow the rights of the Roman people and of Italy to perish, do declare and pronounce that the holy city of Rome is the capital of the world, and foundation of the Christian religion; and that all the cities and all peoples of Italy are free, and Roman citizens." (1)

Rienzi furthermore declared that the Empire and the Emperor's election belonged to Rome and all Italy; and he cited the various pretenders to the imperial crown to appear before him "and other officers of the Pope and Romans," adding, "all without prejudice to the authority of the Church, of the sovereign Pontiff, or of the sacred College."

The apartments of the Lateran were then turned into banqueting-halls, and red wine poured in streams from the nostrils of the horse of Marcus Aurelius in the Piazza. (2)

(1) See Villani, XI, 89; Rinaldi, 1347, nos. 16 and 17; and Fleury, Book XCV.
(2) This statue now stands on the Capitol Square.

All this took place on the 1st of August 1347. On the 15th of that month Rienzi was solemnly crowned during Mass. The Prior of the Lateran offered him an oak crown; the Prior of S. Peter's, ivy; the Dean of S. Paul's, myrtle; the Prior of S. Laurence's, laurel; the Prior of S. Maria-Maggiore, olive; the Prior of the Hospital of S. Spirito a crown of silver and a sceptre; and the Syndic of the people one of silver surmounted by a cross. These seven crowns represented, so it was said, the seven gifts of the Holy Ghost.

Some persons, overwrought by the remembrances of ancient days, received the Tribune's ostentatious proclamation with enthusiasm. Petrarch was of their number; he had long been attached to Rienzi by the similarity of their studies, so it appeared to him that virtue had no home on earth except in Rienzi's heart. (1)

Rienzi had not in principle attacked the sovereignty of the Apostolic See; but several of the rights he

---

(1) Io parlo a te peró ch' altrove un raggio
    Non veggio di virtù ch' al mondo è spenta.

  Byron has also paid his tribute of homage to Rienzi:—

    "Then turn we to her latest tribune's name,
    From her ten thousand tyrants turn to thee,
    Redeemer of dark centuries of shame —
    The friend of Petrarch — hope of Italy —
    Rienzi! last of Romans! While the tree
    Of freedom's withered trunk puts forth a leaf,
    Even for thy tomb a garland let it be —
    The forum's champion, and the people's chief —
    Her new-born Numa thou — with reign, alas! too brief."
            Childe Harold, canto IV, stanza CXIV.

had arrogated to himself were incompatible with that sovereignty. Clement VI complained bitterly on this point, and summoned the Romans to withdraw their obedience from the Tribune, and to remain faithful to their oaths and duty. Meanwhile Rienzi triumphed in a bloody battle against the Colonna, four powerful barons of that family losing their lives in the fight: on this occasion the Tribune proudly said to his sword:— "To-day thou hast struck off an ear from that head which neither Pope nor Emperor has dared to touch."

But, at the same time, a conspiracy was being plotted against him by the nobles; the people also abandoned him, and on the 15th of December 1347, after only a seven months' dictatorship, Rienzi fled in disguise to Naples. Three years later he returned to Rome; but it was then the time of the Jubilee, and the Romans were much too happy, at the concourse of foreign pilgrims, to wish to fall out with the Pope. Rienzi was thus forced to leave his native land a second time. He went to Bohemia, where he was arrested and handed over to Clement VI who kept him prisoner at Avignon.

The Jubilee of 1350 produced a general commotion throughout Europe, more marked than even in 1300. Neither the extreme cold, nor the rains which followed it, nor the difficulties of travelling, sufficed to damp the fervour of the pilgrims. What was most remarkable among them was the order maintained, which was entirely due to the religious object of the journey. Neither pillage nor quarrelling was permitted; everything was paid for in good faith; while the hostelries were given up to Southerners, who could ill withstand the severe weather, Germans and Hungarians slept in the fields around large fires. During the year 1350 there were often more than a million strangers in Rome, and never less than two hundred thousand. At each religious solemnity, and particularly when the holy winding sheet was exposed to the veneration of the faithful, several unfortunate persons were suffocated in the crowds.

The greed of the Romans was disgracefully exhibited during this period. Not content with the enormous profits resulting from this pilgrimage, they determined to augment them by claiming the monopoly of food, which they always sold at high prices. They even went further; they rose in rebellion against the Cardinal-legate, who, in order to assist the pilgrims, had reduced from two weeks to one, and finally to one day, the period necessary for obtaining the indulgences. They assaulted the Legate's palace, slew several of his servants, and, during a procession, his hat was pierced by an arrow.

S. Peter's patrimony then fell a prey to frightful anarchy, and the populace, enriched by the Jubilee, gave way to excesses and disorder. INNOCENT VI, who succeeded Clement VI in 1352, wrote saying, "To remedy these evils, we shall shortly send back to Rome our dear son Nicolaum Laurentii, a Roman knight, hoping that his misfortunes will have taught him wisdom, and that, giving up his early dreams, he will, with his great energy, oppose the designs of the wicked, and favour the goodwill of those who desire peace and the public welfare." (1)

Cardinal Gilles d'Albornoz, the Legate, accompanied Rienzi: at first only two places, Montefiascone and Montefalco, were willing to receive him; but he soon gained possession of Toscanella, and was then able to keep the field. At Rome leaders and laws had alike disappeared; "there were but robbers within and without", says Mattei Villani, "pilgrims and other strangers were like sheep among wolves". Rienzi was received at Rome with shouts of joy; but he was no longer the young tribune of 1347. Age and a prison had dulled him; his very appearance had grown heavy and vulgar; and, in order to govern, Rienzi found it necessary to employ all the resources of that masterful spirit which had survived the memory of his power.

The Romans *still* gave him the title of Tribune; but the Pope only styled him knight and Roman Senator. Now Rienzi restored order and peace in the administration of the city; but he also burdened it with new taxes; he put to death several leading men on the grounds that they were sedition-mongers and agitators, so that his yoke became equally unbearable both to the people and nobles. Public ill-will suddenly showed itself in a violent outbreak. On the 8th of October 1354, the Capitol was assailed by a furious crowd shouting, "Kill! kill! death to the traitor Colà di Rienzi! death to the author of the salt-tax!" Rienzi replied by cries of "Long live the people!" and from a lofty window he

(1) Rinaldi, 1353, No 5.

waved Rome's standard, but was only answered by a volley of arrows. Then disguised as a groom he mingled with the furious crowd who had poured into the Capitol, exciting them to pillage by his own example. He was in the act of escaping, bearing a mattress on his shoulders, when he was recognised, flung to the ground, pierced by a sword and his hands cut off, after which he was disembowelled, and dragged to the Colonna palace, where his mutilated remains were suspended from a forked gibbet.

There is no evidence to show that the Romans desired to throw off pontifical authority during the years following Rienzi's death. Cardinal Albornoz succeeded in bringing back the townsmen of S. Peter's territory to obedience, and the peace which reigned there during his administration bears witness to the greatness of his genius. He it was, according to Papencordt, who laid the foundation of the modern pontifical States. (1)

Charles of Luxembourg came to Rome with his wife, the Princess Anne, in 1355, and received the imperial crown in the Basilica of S. Peter, from the hands of Cardinal Bertrandi, who had been given full powers for that purpose from Innocent VI. After

---

(1) The legation of Albornoz did more towards consolidating the temporal power of the Popes than could have been done by the most successful wars. It is related that Urban V one day asking him to render an account of the funds sent to him, Albornoz called up a cart filled with keys and locks: "It is in that your money has been spent", said Albornoz to the Pope, "I have made you master of all the towns, the bolts of which are before you."

the ceremony, the Emperor mounted his horse and rode across the city to the Lateran Palace, where a great banquet had been prepared for him; afterwards, under pretence of going to the chase, he went to S. Lorenzo-fuori-le-mura to sleep, in order to fulfil the promise he had made to the Pope to quit Rome the very day of his consecration.

Thus the Popes attached great value to their title of Lords of the Eternal city; yet that city languished in degradation and neglect. For more than fifty years, during which the Apostolic See had been transferred to Avignon, not a single Pope had visited the tombs of the Apostles. URBAN V felt deeply how much this abandonment had afflicted Christendom; therefore immediately after his election, in 1362, he announced his intention of returning to Rome, and gave orders to restore the pontifical palaces at Rome and Viterbo. On the 19th of May, 1367, he embarked at Marseilles on board a Venetian galley, which was escorted by numerous ships magnificently equipped by Queen Joanna of Naples and the Republics of Pisa and Genoa. Urban was received at Genoa, Porto-Venere, the port of Pisa, Piombino, Corneto, Viterbo, everywhere in fact, with the greatest honour and the liveliest expressions of joy. When he disembarked from his galley he found the shore covered with silk tents hung with foliage, and in their midst an altar erected at which was celebrated a Mass of thanksgiving. The Roman deputies came to meet him as far as Corneto bringing the keys of the Castle of S. Angelo, and offering him full lordship over the town. Urban received them kindly; but, before entering Rome, he decided to dwell some time at Viterbo, perhaps with a view of studying the disposition and character of the people among whom he now found himself. This disposition soon showed itself with all the ardour characteristic of southern races. The people of Viterbo, joyful that the Pope had returned, spent several days in holiday-making; after which they fell out with the servants of the Cardinals, and cries of "Long live the people! down with the Church!" resounded in every street and square. The populace rushed to arms; several Cardinals were ill-treated, and for three days such disorder reigned in the city that alarm was felt for the life of the sovereign Pontiff. Fortunately this sudden outburst soon died away. The townspeople, ashamed at having allowed themselves to be led away without reason, brought their weapons and the chains used for barricades as a mark of repentance; after which they hung the most guilty among themselves at the doors of the insulted Cardinals.

A month after these scenes of riot, Urban V entered Rome accompanied by two thousand men-at-arms. The clergy and people went forth to meet him, singing praises to God, after which they brought him to the Vatican, where he was installed, after having prayed at S. Peter's. Henceforth all Pontiffs resided at the Vatican. Only two or three Popes during the twelfth century, notably Adrian IV and Eugenius III, had sought shelter therein from the evil passions which surged in the town, the Lateran having always been the patriarchal palace. Since the conflagration of 1308, followed by that of 1360, the

Lateran was no longer habitable: so the successors of the Apostle betook themselves to the spot hallowed by his martyrdom, as though to become guardians of his tomb.

When the papacy returned, and again took up its residence at Rome, there existed 414 churches of which 252 were parish churches; but of these last forty-four were without priests, and eleven were completely destroyed. Each of the others had only one or two priests to perform divine service. As to the monuments, we have heard Petrarch's lamentations. "They shake! they fall!" cried he, "ruitura tremunt." Doubtless the population had also decreased; but in this respect we are in want of accurate statistics. According to Cancellieri it was reduced to 17,000 souls in 1377; but if we follow the computation of Papencordt it was still 60,000 in 1362. Petrarch appears to support the latter opinion:— "We wandered", said he, "through that city, which, on account of its size, appeared to be abandoned, and which nevertheless contains an immense population." (1)

The rage for antiquarian research at this time was seen in tournaments and wrestling matches in the Coliseum, thus imitating ancient shows in the amphitheatre. Notably, on the 3rd of September, knights from all parts of Italy were seen to enter the lists against bulls; eleven of these animals were slain, and eighteen warriors were left dead in the arena. Urban V spent three years either at Rome or in the neighbouring towns, whither he generally

---

(1) Rer. fam., Epist. VI.

retired during the summer heats. In the month of March 1368 he had the heads of SS. Peter and Paul taken out from beneath the altar of the Holy of Holies at the Lateran, and exposed for veneration from the top of the outer tribune. For their reception he subsequently ordered two new reliquaries, which were not completed until the following year; they were reputed to be worth thirty thousand gold florins. These reliquaries were silver busts with gilt heads, representing the two Apostles. S. Peter was clad in pontifical vestments, wearing the tiara in the shape of a cone bearing three crowns, blessing with one hand and holding the keys in the other. On their breasts a gold fleur-de-lis was displayed studded with precious stones, a splendid present from King Charles V of France.

Furthermore Urban repaired the Lateran Basilica, and constructed the rich Gothic baldacchino over the high altar. It is upheld by four columns, and surrounded by gilt railings.

Pierre de Lusignan, King of Cyprus, and Queen Joanna of Naples profited by Urban's sojourn at Rome to pay him a visit. They were in Rome on the fourth Sunday of Lent, a day on which the Pope blessed a golden rose which he afterwards presented to some eminent personage. On this occasion Urban favoured the Queen of Naples with the rose; thereupon Joanna, holding the rose, rode on horseback through the streets of the city, surrounded by a gallant company of Cardinals and gentlemen.

The blessing of the golden rose dates from the eleventh century. On the day of the ceremony the

Pope and the Cardinals, arrayed in scarlet, went in procession to the Basilica of S. Croce-in-Gerusalemme, where Mass was said and the rose blessed.

The Emperor Charles IV came to Rome a second time during the residence of Urban V, and the Empress, who had not yet been crowned, then received royal unction. Historians relate that, during the Mass which was celebrated at this function, the Emperor, as a deacon, handed the book and corporal to the Pope; "but", adds Fleury, "he only read the Gospel on Christmas Day". After her coronation the Empress mounted her horse and rode across Rome to the Lateran Basilica.

Scarcely had the German Emperor departed ere another came to perform homage to the Vicar of Christ, and, strange to relate, this was an Eastern Emperor, heir to that throne of Constantinople which had always looked with jealousy upon the spiritual primacy of S. Peter's! No Emperor from the East had come to Rome since Constans II, who had pillaged it after putting its Pontiff to death. Since that period, the growing hatred and separation between the two cities had been completed by schism, when suddenly a Prince, called John Palaiologos, appeared from the Levant, craving for help and protection from the Mussulmans, who, not content with the conquest of Palestine, were already thundering at the gates of Constantinople. Urban V commissioned four Cardinals to receive the Emperor John's profession of faith. The Emperor repaired to the church of S. Spirito where he pronounced his profession of faith, according to the Catholic rite, signed it with his own hand in vermillion affixing to it a gold seal. The following Sunday, being the 21st of October, 1369, the Pope on leaving the Vatican seated himself on a throne placed above the steps leading to S. Peter's. He was arrayed in pontifical ornaments and surrounded by Cardinals and Bishops. Then John Palaiologos approached, prostrating himself three times; and on reaching the Pope he kissed his feet, hands, and mouth. The Pope raised him up, and led him into the Basilica, while the people sang the Te Deum.

This reconciliation with the East raised false hopes. The Greek Empire continued to exist only by permission of the Sultans, and the last off-shoots of this race of the Lower-Empire were so debased by contact with Moslem morals that nothing could be expected from them. John Palaiologos left Rome at the beginning of 1370; it does not, however, fall within the scope of this work to relate the excesses and vices which stained the last days of his life. The year 1370 also witnessed the departure of Urban V for Avignon; he felt that his presence was necessary in order to put an end to the endless quarrels which existed between the Kings of France and England. Vainly did the Italians endeavour to withhold him; in vain did S. Brigit of Sweden threaten him with divine wrath if he crossed the Alps; thoughts of charity and of peace had inspired the resolution he had formed, and nothing could turn him from it. He embarked on the 5th of September, but had scarcely reached Avignon when he was seized with a serious illness from which he died.

S. Brigit belonged to the royal family of Sweden. At thirteen she married a young nobleman named Wolf-Gudmarson, on whom some hagiographers have bestowed the title of Duke of Nericia (Orebro). Eight children were born of this marriage. Afterwards Wolf and Brigit lived in a state of continence; they made a pilgrimage to S. James of Compostella together, having agreed that they would both enter religious life, when Wolf was overtaken by death. Brigit's fervent piety greatly increased by meditation and penitence. The most severe mortifications became habitual to her; she was one of those souls whose complete detachment from all worldly objects leads them to entire absorption in all that appertains to heaven. At first this holy widow lived in the convent of Wadstena, which she had founded in the diocese of Linköping, but soon left it for Rome where she long resided. In the sixteenth century a church was built on the Piazza Farnese on the very spot where her house had stood. Among the relics of this church were a crucifix, a prayer-book, and a black cloak which had belonged to S. Brigit.

Meanwhile, Catherine, the youngest of Brigit's daughters, left her husband Edgar, in 1350, in order to visit her mother at Rome and gain the indulgence of the holy year. Catherine was remarkable for her beauty, and gifted with all the charms of youth in addition to those of a pure heart and soul. Edgar and she had respected virginity in marriage, as many a wedded pair had done in the early ages of Christianity. When Catherine arrived in Rome that unfortunate city was a prey to utter lawlessness. Terrible licentiousness prevailed, and Brigit was compelled to conceal her daughter in order to save her from the dangers which became more threatening when by Edgar's death his wife was left a widow at the early age of eighteen. Then the concealment in which they lived failed to screen her from annoying pursuit. Their visits to hospitals and churches were watched; and one day when they were making a pilgrimage to the Catacombs of S. Sebastian they were assailed by some men in the pay of a young Count who aspired to Catherine's hand. Fortunately the street was so blocked by drivers that, with their aid, Catherine succeeded in gaining the shelter of a neighbouring house. Similar attempts were repeated on several occasions; and when Brigit and Catherine undertook some pious journey to Umbria, Tuscany, or Sicily, desperate efforts were made by some of the Roman nobility to separate them. God, however, watched over Catherine; every plot was defeated, and His blessings were poured forth upon her in her enforced retirement; this holy young woman no longer left her room except to visit the nearest churches; but, in order to have the poor near her, so as to help and comfort them, she and her mother established a hospital close to her house destined more particularly for northern pilgrims.

Thus passed Catherine's saintly life until S. Brigit resolved to sail for Palestine and offer up prayers on Calvary. Catherine accompanied her, and visited Jerusalem, Nazareth, and Bethlehem. But this long, trying ourney exhausted Brigit's strength, and, feeling that her end was approaching, she hastened back to Rome where she wished to die. This time the two saints went to reside with the nuns of S. Clare, at the convent of S. Lorenzo-in-Panisperna, on the Viminal. In this place, sanctified by the martyrdom of S. Laurence, Brigit breathed her last. Her mortal remains were at first laid in the convent church, but were subsequently removed by her daughter, in accordance with her last wishes, to the convent of Wadstena in Sweden.

The memory of S. Brigit still lives in the convent of S. Lorenzo-in-Panisperna where she had dwelt, in the Catacombs of S. Sebastian whither she had often repaired in pilgrimage, and in the Basilica of S. Paul where she had several of her revelations. The crucifix which addressed her is religiously preserved in this Basilica; it is exposed to view on the first day of each month and on Good Friday. This crucifix is larger than life size, the head of Christ is turned very much to the right side, His expression being life-like with a look of intense pain.

S. Catherine of Sweden had placed herself under the protection of S. Sebastian, and spent long hours almost daily in his Catacomb. She returned once more to Rome in 1375 in order to accelerate S. Brigit's canonization, after which she returned to Wadstena to die near her mother's tomb.

In contrast to S. Catherine of Sweden there appeared another saint, also a S. Catherine, who lived and was in Rome at the same time; a saint whose great virtues equalized the positions of the poor dyer's daughter and the daughter of a King. Catherine of Siena from her earliest years felt that attraction to heaven which is a characteristic mark of predestined souls. She made a vow of virginity at eight years of age; when only ten she endeavoured to conquer sleep for the purposes of meditation and prayer, and her days were spent in nursing the sick, particularly those whose contagious diseases cooled the zeal and the charity of many. Such an existence as Catherine's, secluded and devoid of worldly knowledge and education, might be expected to pass away unnoticed in solitude. But, during the Middle Ages, people believed in virtue, and it often happened that a poor nun proved herself to be as powerful by her good deeds as a King might be by his victories. Thus the Florentines, in 1375, turned to Catherine, the daughter of Benincasa the dyer, to negotiate their reconciliation with Gregory XI, whose authority they had set at nought. Catherine set off for Avignon, clad in the habit of the Third Order of S. Dominic; she succeeded in allaying the Pope's anger, obtaining his pardon for those who had sent her; then, going beyond the scope of her mission, she strongly urged on Gregory the necessity of his no longer abandoning the sanctuaries of the Apostles and the cities of Italy, leaving them without either protector or guide. From this time until her death Catherine of Siena took part in all the great events of Christendom. From her father's workshop she passed to princely courts; and from peaceful solitude to the strife of faction; yet everywhere she appeared to be at home, because in her solitude she had imbibed the spirit of peace and charity which placed her above all the tumults of the world. Her great characteristic was an unlimited confidence in divine protection. Urban VI desiring to confide some negotiations with the Neapolitan Court to her and to S. Catherine of Sweden, the latter was terrified at the thought of two young girls braving the dangers of the inns and roads alone, but Catherine of Siena was not alarmed. She is reported to have said, "Had SS. Agnes and Margaret been thus cautious they would never have gained the crown of martyrdom."

S. Catherine of Siena died in 1380 at Rome, whither she had been summoned by Urban VI that he might utilize her influence in suppressing the Western Schism. She was buried in the Dominican Church of S. Maria-della-Minerva. (1) Several sanctuaries were afterwards raised under her invocation. The most ancient was near the Minerva; but, in the sixteenth century, this was forsaken in favour of the church and convent of S. Catherine on Mount Magnanapoli, near the Piazza Trajano. (2) It was also in the sixteenth century that certain Sienese, who had formed themselves into a confraternity, dedicated the ancient church of S. Nicholas, which stood in the Strada Giulia, to their holy patroness. This confraternity granted dowries to poor Sienese girls.

(1) Cardinal Antonio Barberini caused the little room she had occupied to be transported to his church, and turned it into a private chapel. The church and convent of the Minerva, originally occupied by the Greek monks of S. Basil, were, during the pontificate of Gregory XI, granted to the Order of S. Dominic, to which Order S. Catherine of Siena belonged.

(2) The name of Mount Magnanapoli (Balnea Pauli Emilii) was given to that part of the Esquiline which is nearest the Piazza Trajano.

On the death of Urban V at Avignon, GREGORY XI had ascended the Apostolic throne. The Romans feared that the new Pope, being also a Frenchman, would not come to reside among them. Nevertheless they despatched a solemn embassy to express their wishes to him, and, as Gregory XI did not at once comply, they entrusted Lucca Savelli with a fresh mission in 1376. "The Romans wish to have their Pope at Rome," said Savelli, "for he is the Roman Pontiff, so called by all Christians, ... otherwise be assured we shall provide a Pope who will henceforth reside at Rome." Whatever may have been the effect of this threat it is a fact that Gregory had intended, after his election, to re-establish the Apostolic Chair at S. Peter's tomb. Froissart says, "Also, from his childhood, he had promised God that if, during his lifetime, he was ever promoted to the high and most worthy dignity of the papacy, he would, so far as in him lay, only keep his Apostolic seat where S. Peter had kept it." (1) The reproofs of S. Catherine of Siena had strengthened his resolve, and he persevered therein in spite of great difficulties, and, above all, of the opposition of the King of France. "Holy Father," said the Duke of Anjou, "you are going to a country and among people who do not love you overmuch, and are quitting the fountain of faith and the kingdom in which the Church has more influence and worth than elsewhere in the world; and, by your act, the Church may fall into much tribulation; for if you die there, as is probable from what your doctors say of your health, it will

(1) Chronicles 11, ch. XX.

happen that the Romans, who are a strange and treacherous people, will become masters and lords of the Cardinals, and will compel them to elect a Pope of their own choosing." (1)

Gregory did not allow himself to be shaken by these words. He set out in the month of September 1376, and three months later reached Ostia. The Cardinals who were in Rome had signed an agreement with the Romans by which the latter undertook to acknowledge the free and complete lordship of the Pope over the city, as they had done before with Urban V, and to hand over all bridges, gates, and towers to his keeping. On his side the Pope promised to preserve the rights and privileges of tribunals intact, on the sole condition that all magistrates should swear fealty to him.

Gregory XI left Ostia on the 16$\underline{\text{th}}$ of January 1377, after celebrating Mass, and sailed for Rome on board a galley. The banks of the Tiber were covered with crowds of people eager to see and welcome him. The Pope landed not far from S. Paul's where he wished to hear Mass, then, mounting his horse, with his Cardinals around him, he crossed the city to S. Peter's, the Piazza of which was illuminated, while the church was resplendent with light from eight thousand silver and gold lamps. On the following days Gregory went to S. John Lateran and S. Maria-Maggiore, as though to retake possession of those holy, ancient, Basilicas.

These first rejoicings on his return were soon disturbed by the secret ambition of the principal-

---

(1) Froissart, II, ch. XX.

functionaries of the quarter (Caporioni), who, having grown accustomed to absolute independence, impatiently endured the sovereignty of the Pope. Exhausted by their opposition Gregory XI withdrew for some time to Anagni. Towards the close of 1377 he returned to Rome where he was attacked by the sickness which was to prove fatal. At this critical time Gregory XI was horrified by thinking of the schism which might follow on his death; so he drew up a decree authorizing the Cardinals to meet where they pleased, and to elect a Pope by a simple majority of votes without waiting for any Cardinals who might be absent. Gregory even sanctioned an election which might take place before the Conclave assembled.

This Bull only preceded the Pope's death by a few days; he breathed his last on the 27th of March 1378, and was buried in the church of S. Maria-Novella, of which he had formerly been rector. The belfry of S. Maria-Maggiore which is the highest in Rome dates from his pontificate. Gregory also built the lateral doorway of the Lateran Basilica which, during the sixteenth century, was replaced by a double portico raised by Sixtus V. The doorway built by Gregory XI was of Gothic architecture and Parian marble; it was surmounted by a kind of baldacchino upheld by two columns resting on the backs of lions. Panvinius described it as being wondrously beautiful.

Scarcely were the obsequies of Gregory XI concluded before officers from the town presented themselves to the Cardinals demanding an Italian Pope, who would restore the long abandoned palaces and

Basilicas, and who would bring back to obedience those towns within the papal territory which, since the Popes had resided out of Italy, had declared their independence. At the same time discontent had arisen at Rome. The peaceably inclined withdrew from the city, and great numbers of mountaineers, placing their services at the disposal of the popular passions, seized upon the gates and bridges. The Cardinals, terrified at the threatening storm, quickly agreed upon the choice of a Pontiff, and, on the day following their assembling in Conclave, they elected Bartolomeo Prignano, Archbishop of Bari, by two successive ballots, resulting in a majority of more than two-thirds of the votes.

Before the election was proclaimed, the populace had assembled in the Vatican Square, and thence fierce shouts of:— "We want a Roman Pope!" resounded throughout the Conclave. Froissart relates that bloody threats mingled with the cries and tumult:— "Have a care, have a care, my lords the Cardinals, that you give us a Roman Pope who will dwell among us; otherwise we shall make your heads redder than your hats." (1)

The Archbishop of Bari was not a Roman; that was in truth the reason why the Cardinals had elected him, for they did not wish to appear to yield to violence; but he was an Italian, and they had hoped this would quiet all those who objected to a French Pope. Nevertheless there was such indignant shouting that terror reigned in the Con-

---

(1) Book II, chap. XXI.

clave, the Cardinals fearing to proclaim their choice. On the other hand the populace, indignant at being kept waiting, broke into the palace, and scattered the members of the sacred college. Some sought refuge outside Rome, others in the Castle of S. Angelo. Cardinal Tebaldeschi, a Roman, remained alone in the Vatican; a rumour had been circulated that he had been elected, so the crowd threw themselves at his feet to offer their homage. But Tebaldeschi refused these honours, saying:— "The Archbishop of Bari has been elected; he is more worthy than I." This news calmed the sedition; the choice of the Archbishop was approved by both magistrates and people, and, during the following days, he took possession of S. Peter's Chair surrounded by all the dignitaries of the Church, who had returned to assist at this ceremony. The sixteen Cardinals who had assisted at the Conclave afterwards wrote to the other six who, since Gregory XI departure, had remained at Avignon to apprise them of URBAN VI accession and acquaint them with the circumstances attending his election. The Cardinals at Avignon approved and acknowledged the new Pontiff; they even sent orders to the governor of the Castle of S. Angelo, who was a Frenchman, and had applied to them for orders, to hand over the Castle to Urban.

This peaceful state of things lasted from the month of April 1378 till the month of July of the same year. But the severity of the Pope, who had no indulgence for ambition or immorality, together with his abrupt manners, alienated people from him by degrees. Learned lawyer as he was, enemy to simony and luxury, and hard upon himself, Urban VI would have been a great Pontiff had he, to his other qualities, united evangelical mildness, which, far from denoting weakness, would have strengthened his influence. The indiscretion of his zeal too frequently compromised its effect; and, in the end, thirteen Cardinals withdrew from him. They retired to Anagni on pretence of spending the summer away from Rome; but, once there, they no longer concealed their intention of proceeding to the election of another Pope. So long as they had been in Rome, they said, they were under the dominion of violence, and consequently any acts in which they had taken part must henceforth be considered of no effect.

Urban went first to Tivoli to watch his opponents, and then sent troops to prevent them from receiving assistance of any kind; but these troops were defeated by Bernard de la Salle, a Gascon captain in the pay of the Cardinals at Anagni. The fugitives filled the streets of Rome with clamour and disturbance, and, in their rage, fell upon the French, pillaging their houses, and imprisoning a great number. From that moment terror seemed to be ceaselessly threatening the lives of those foreigners who had not quitted the city.

Meanwhile the Cardinals at Anagni retired to Fondi, in order to be under the more immediate protection of the Count of that town, he being in open revolt against Urban VI. Three of the Cardinals who had remained in Rome now joined them, and, on the 20th of September 1378, having assembled in conclave, they elected Robert of Geneva, Cardinal priest of SS. Apostoli, who took the name of CLEMENT VII.

Urban's position became difficult, for all the members of the sacred college, with the exception of Tebaldeschi, had forsaken him; and it is probable that even Tebaldeschi was only kept back by the illness which carried him off a very few days after the departure of his brethren. On the other hand, the governor of the Castle of S. Angelo declared for Clement VII; and the King of France, the Queen of Naples, and the King of Castile similarly gave up Urban for Clement.

Thus Europe found itself divided between two Popes; consciences were uneasy, and a fierce war broke out through the whole peninsula. It was under these circumstances that Urban VI summoned Catherine of Siena to Rome, hoping to receive help and strength from her in the midst of the dangers which surrounded him. Catherine urged submission and fidelity upon the clergy; she wrote to the Cardinals upbraiding them for their treason, to the King of France urging him to withdraw from the schism, and with pious fervour she occupied herself with endeavouring to restore unity. Unhappily all her efforts proved fruitless; hatred and animosity reigned, and for nearly forty years Christendom was torn asunder by internal dissensions. "Doubtless", says Froissart, "future ages will wonder at these things, and how it came about that the Church could fall into such troubles, and remain in them so long. But it was a wound sent by God to warn and make the clergy reflect on their want of dignity and luxurious habits; nevertheless, the greater part took no heed . . . therefore things went very ill; and if our faith had not been held in the hand and grace of the Holy Spirit, who enlightens hearts that have missed their way, and keeps them in unity, it would have sunk or fallen."

We have already mentioned the outrages committed on foreigners in Rome; but, on the other hand, the partisans of the antipope showed no greater mercy to the Romans. "They kept", says Froissart, "a great number of hirelings in the fields and villages, these made war on Rome and S. Peter's borough, harrying them day and night by assaults and skirmishes." The Castle of S. Angelo was moreover in the hands of the French, and those who were within it caused great trouble to the Romans, "ceux qui éstoient dedans faisoient moult de déstourbiers aus Romains". The Romans thereupon called German mercenaries to their help, and then attacked the Vatican Quarter; they even dared to lay siege to the Castle of S. Angelo, the garrison of which at last surrendered, their lives being spared ("sauves les vies"). Overjoyed at this victory, the people demolished the fortifications of the Castle, and burned all the borough of S. Peter.

However, the French, or rather the Bretons, as Froissart calls them, were not long in re-appearing. One evening they entered by the Neapolitan Gate, and advanced towards the Capitol where the council had assembled; then, "lowering their swords and spurring their horses", they charged the multitude upon the square. The crowd consisted of "all the most notable people in the town", says Froissart, "and among the dead were seven bannerets, quite 200 seigneurs, and a great number of the lowest ranks of the people". The terror into which this sudden attack threw Rome was so great that the Bretons were enabled to withdraw unscathed, leaving the Romans "in great agony of heart". (1)

Pope Urban now took into his pay the celebrated English captain, John Hawkwood, and "made him master and governor of all the war". (2) Hawkwood had a stout heart that knew no fear; his battle cry was: "Crux Christi, protege nos!" He marched at the head of the Romans against the Bretons, cut them to pieces and took their leader, Messire Sevestre Budes, prisoner.

It may well be believed that such a war must have exhausted the Roman resources, (3) and on Urban VI return he was received with neither rejoicings nor marks of honour. The Pope, being near his end, turned his thoughts towards religion. The institution of the Feast of the Visitation of the Virgin is due to Urban VI, also the second reduction in the period of the Jubilee to thirty-three years in commemoration of the years of the life of Jesus Christ. He

---

(1) II, ch. XLIX and L.
(2) The name of this illustrious warrior has been mangled by the chroniclers. Froissart calls him Haccoude; elsewhere he is styled Agúto, Agu, or even Falcone in bosco, an Italian rendering of the English Hawkwood. M. Valéry, in his "Itinéraire", gave him the name of Jean Aucud. His tomb is in the church of S. Maria-dei-Fiore at Florence.
(3) It is said that the population of Rome had then fallen to 13,000 souls.

also decreed that the festival of the Holy Sacrament should always be celebrated, even during times of Interdict. Until then only the Feasts of Christmas, Easter, Pentecost, and the Assumption enjoyed this privilege. (1)

On the death of Urban VI the Cardinals elected Pietro Tomacelli, who took the name of BONIFACE IX, to replace him. Tomacelli was a man of no experience in affairs of state, but was gifted with that easy eloquence and graceful carriage which sometimes supply the place of real talent.

In 1393 Boniface concluded a treaty with the Romans which shows clearly enough what was then the condition of the town. Under this agreement the Pope selected the senator, who received his pay from the town; and this magistrate in the discharge of his duties was to be recognised by all other officials in the city. The Romans were to be responsible for the safety of the roads to Rieti and Narni and the way to the mouth of the Tiber. Clerics and officers belonging to the pontifical court had their own jurisdiction and distinctive tribunals. Officers of the republic were charged with the assessment of taxation, from which those in the employ of the pontifical court were exempt, as well as hospitals, and churches. By another article the Senator and magistrates could not deprive of their arms either clerics or laymen, who were attached to the person of the Pope, or

---

(1) A last decree of Urban VI granted one hundred days' indulgence to those who accompanied the Blessed Sacrament to the sick.

Roman clerics in general. Doubtless a spirit of mutual distrust may be observed in this arrangement; but, none the less, the pontifical power went on openly consolidating itself. It had succeeded in securing some form of independence, and, by nominating the Senator, it directly influenced public administration. About one hundred years later, Cardinal Egidio of Viterbo wrote:— "Through the great power of virtue alone, the Pope succeeded in governing all things at Rome according to his will."

But, if on the one hand the Senator depended upon the Pope, he was also dependent upon the magistrates, who were to act with him as advisers, and upon the bannerets, or "Caporioni", who exercised great influence in their respective quarters. These bannerets ill brooked a superior authority, and, by means of their daily intercourse with the inhabitants, they constantly impeded its action. In 1394 they even incited the populace to rebel both against the Senator and the Pope, and there is no knowing to what excesses they might have gone had not Ladislas, who happened to be in Rome, strenuously opposed them. Boniface profited by these disorders to repair the Castle of S. Angelo which he surrounded with new fortifications.

The popular disturbances were followed by some daring efforts on the part of the nobility. Nicolò and Giovanni Colonna determined to take away the lordship of Rome from the people. Assembling a certain number of their friends one night in January 1400 they entered the town by the Porta del Popolo, with a vast parade of arms and horses, and went straight to the Capitol; but no one declaring in their favour they were obliged to disperse before daybreak. Thirty-one of their accomplices were taken and hanged.

The miseries of these days of trial gave rise to another devotional imposture resembling that of the Flagellants. Some men appeared dressed in white sackcloth, branded with red crosses on their breasts, which crosses were carefully kept moistened with oil, in order that they might always appear to be bleeding. They passed themselves off as prophets; one said he was Elias descended from heaven; they threatened the world with confusion and calamities, as punishment for the schism and disorders to which it was abandoned. Their strange dress, their terrible threats, and the deep feeling of unrest which attacks people in troublous times, powerfully affected the populace. Men and women arrayed themselves in white sackcloth, forsook their homes, and, during thirteen days, wandered about in processions, singing doleful hymns, especially the "Stabat Mater". These penitents had no other refuge by night than churches and monasteries in which they lay promiscuously, no other food by day than the produce of the fields which they plundered. Complaints were raised against them; one of these impostors was convicted at Acquapendente of a very atrocious crime punishable by law with the stake; he was at once burned to death, and this severe act of repression led to the dispersal of the initiated. (1)

---

(1) For fuller information on the White Penitents, see S. Antoninus and Platina, "in Vita Bonifacii IX".

Side by side with this licentious hypocrisy, which, under a myth of piety, imposed on some really fervent souls, it is comforting to notice that the spirit of religion perpetuated itself, in spite of the depravity of the age, and even found new outlets in touching devotions. It was the fourteenth century that gave birth to that holy custom of reciting the Angelus, as the church bell announces the approach of night. This custom was first observed in France in the diocese of Saintes. John XXII solemnly approved of it, and extended it to Rome with a grant of indulgences in a Bull of 7th of May 1327. (1)

Among the foundations belonging to the period under description is one which is little known, yet greatly deserving of notice, for it bears witness to a desire among the Romans to sanctify, by the purest symbols, those spots which had been tainted by the vices of old days. (2) We refer to S. Maria-di-Grotta-Pinta in the Campo di Fiori. The name of Flora and the Floral games recall all the worst and most

---

(1) It was only in the next century under Calixtus III, and in France under Louis XI, that the Angelus began to be rung at mid-day.

(2) As it is impossible to mention all the foundations laid at Rome during these devout and generous ages, reference can only be made to those distinguished by some special mark; for this very reason there is one which may not be passed over in silence, namely, S. Bernard at the column of Trajan, a monument of piety raised by a holy priest, who, after building it, made it the headquarters of a confraternity placed under the invocation of the holy name of Mary, whose members distributed every Sunday bread and clothing to poor families.

shameful passions of paganism, the most hideous vices bedecking themselves in poetic garb in order to veil their loathsomeness. Now the Christians thought there was no better way of blotting out these foul memories than by placing, on the spot where they believed Flora's circus had stood, a statue of the Virgin, that "Chaste Mother of God", that "Gate of Heaven" as the Church calls her. This statue was placed deep within a grotto, where it received veneration. Later on it was removed to S. Lorenzo-in-Damaso; but the Orsini family erected a church dedicated to the Conception of Mary near the spot on which it had stood. This church was opened on the 8th of December 1343, and took the name of Grotta-Pinta in memory of la Madonna di Campo di Fiore.

The Savelli also consecrated to God the small ancient temple which now ornaments the Piazza di S. Maria-in-Cosmedin. This temple, circular in shape, is surrounded by graceful Corinthian columns. Its entablature and roofing were gone, and part of the wall of the nave was destroyed; but none the less the genius of Greece was still living amid its ruins, giving them wonderful beauty. It is not known to what divinity this building was dedicated. Its small dimensions, the authority of some medals, and its proximity to the Tiber, on the banks of which it would appear Horace places the temple of Vesta, have led to its receiving the name of that goddess. Other opinions assign it to Hercules, some have even recognised it as the temple consecrated to Pleasure. This ruin then lay unknown, the forgotten fragment of a dead religion, when the Savelli raised it up again, and devoted it to the worship of the true God, under the name of S. Stephen. It is now dedicated to the Virgin, and it may perhaps be some remembrance of Vesta, the goddess of fire, which has obtained for it the popular name of La Madonna-del-Sole.

In 1370 Gregory XI granted the church of S. Marcello-al-Corso to the Servites, or Servants of Mary, an Order specially devoted to the veneration of the Virgin, and which, a century earlier, had been founded by some Florentine merchants. This Order already counted a saint among its members, S. Filippo Benizzi.

The religious Order of Mt. Olivet had also, from its origin in 1319, placed itself under the protection of the Virgin. Thus more man became corrupt the more fervent were the prayers poured forth by Christian hearts to the pure and spotless Queen. (1) The first establishment of the Olivetans at Rome was at the church of S. Maria-Novella, in the Via Sacra; that of the Jesuats, a monastic institution also dating from the fourteenth century, who owed their origin to B. Giovanni Colombrini, at the church of SS. John and Paul, and at the church of S. John of Malva beyond the Tiber. (2) While the genius of Christianity thus multiplied charitable and pious works in Europe, the Friars Minor and the preaching Friars

---

(1) Dante's homage to Mary must not be forgotten:
"Vergine madre, figlia del tuo figlio,
Umile ed alta più che creatura,
Termine fisso d'Eterno consiglio, etc."
                Paradiso, Canto XXXIII.

(2) The Order of the Jesuats was suppressed in 1668.

were spreading throughout Hungary, Walachia, Syria, and all Asia, bearing the Gospel as far as India, and even to the mysterious kingdom of Cathay. Blessed Oderic of Friuli evangelised the shores of Malabar, Java, Ceylon, and Thibet. Raymond Lullus was martyred on the African shore, while in Europe itself some noble hearts, Gerson among the number, worthily upheld the cause of religion and virtue.

Then arose, under the auspices of Boniface VIII, that great Roman university known as La Sapienza, because she taught that the fear of God was the beginning of all science and wisdom, "initium sapientiæ timor Domini". (1) Then, by order of different Councils, Chairs were established for teaching the Hebrew, Arab, and Chaldean tongues at Rome, Paris, Oxford, Bologna, and Salamanca. (2) The desire for study became so general that the literati, philosophers, and poets received as much flattery as princes. People bowed before them, gave them the best places, and literary enthusiasm attained to such a pitch that ancient triumphs were revived in their honour. The triumph of Petrarch at the Capitol is well known. The University of Paris had offered him these honours, but Petrarch desired to be crowned on the very spot where, according to tradition, Horace and Virgil had received their crowns. One may easily imagine how great a charm this memory must have had for a poet

---

(1) These words of the Psalmist were adopted as the motto of "La Sapienza". The Professors and students of La Sapienza were exempted from all taxation by Boniface VIII.

(2) Council of Vienne in 1311.

and student like Petrarch, and for the Roman masses who were now beginning to be smitten with a passion for antiquity.

The ceremony took place on Easter Day, the 8th of April, 1341. Petrarch wore the robe King Robert had taken from his own shoulders and placed upon those of the poet when he quitted Naples. Around him thronged the most distinguished citizens clad in green. Twelve youths belonging to the first families of Rome preceded him, arrayed in scarlet; behind him came the Senator, Count Orso d'Anguillara, the members of the Council, and a great crowd eager to see and applaud him. When they reached the Capitol, Count Anguillara placed the crown upon the poet's brow, and, after long speeches, letters patent as laureate were presented to him in the name of the Senate and the people.

This triumph was complete; yet, like all human vanities, it left but emptiness and bitterness in the heart of him who received it. In his old age he wrote, "This crown has made me neither wiser nor more eloquent; it has only served to let envy loose against me, and to take away the calm I formerly enjoyed. Since that day, I have ever had to be on my guard; every pen, every tongue has been sharpened against me; my friends have become enemies; I have carried about with me the punishment of my boldness and presumption." (1) Petrarch also said, "It is a sad thing to have contemporaries!"

(1) "Senil.", Book XV, ep. I.

CHAPTER XIV.—FOURTEENTH CENTURY.

Side by side with letters, science and art had also taken an unexpected development. A monk, Berthold Schwartz, discovered the explosive properties of nitre; another, Roger Bacon, or perhaps a cleric named Alessandro Spina, invented the telescope. An immense revolution took place in music, through the various modifications in the duration of sounds introduced by Jean des Murs; so, in every sphere of art, painters, sculptors, and architects, encouraged by Bishops and monks, created masterpieces.

We must go back to the thirteenth century for the origin of those rich miniatures which illuminated missals and antiphonaries, generally produced by the genius and patience of monks whose names are often unknown. A few of them are, however, mentioned by the chroniclers; for instance, Franco Bolognese and Oderigi d'Agobbio, who were summoned to Rome in the early years of the fourteenth century in order to illustrate the palace books. Dante has immortalised their memory in the eleventh canto of his Purgatorio:

> "Oh dissi lui, non se' tu Oderisi,
> L'onor d'Agobbio, e l'onor di quell' arte,
> Ch' alluminare e chiamata in Parisi?
> Frate, diss' egli, piu ridon le carte,
> Che pennelleggia Franco Bolognese:
> L'onore e tutto or suo, e mio in parte."

Mosaic withstood the general decadence better than any other art, and its productions were very numerous at Rome. But the great workers in mosaic came from Byzantium, and it was not until the thirteenth century that the Byzantine school began to give way to the Italian. Giacomo di Turiti, Giacomo di Camerino, Gaddo-Gaddi founded the Italian school; then it suddenly soared upward with the flight taken by painting in the fourteenth century, acquiring unlooked for perfection at the hands of Giotto.

Giotto had devoted himself to the study of nature; he profited by the impulse Cimabue had given to art in developing an expression and truthfulness unknown to the painters of the Byzantine school; but the greatness of his genius carried him far beyond the teachings of his master. Boniface VIII called him to Rome, and rewarded him with six hundred gold ducats for the first works with which he decorated the tribune and sacristy of S. Peter's. (1) Giotto now attached himself to the Pontiff; he multiplied his works in the sanctuary of the Prince of the Apostles, presented a Christ on the Cross to the Church of La Minerva and produced that remarkable mosaic of S. Peter's bark which still decorates the porch of the Vatican Basilica. Vasari describes it as a wonderful work, "cosa miracolosa"; the countenances of the Apostles, the movement of the sea, the gradation of shades were all rendered by means of small fragments of glass as perfectly

---

(1) Only some vestiges of these works of Giotto remain in the sacristy of S. Peter's; they represent Jesus Christ, the Apostles, the Virgin, the beheading of S. Paul, and are all treated with remarkable grandeur of style. See the interesting pages M. Rio has devoted to the first Italian masters in his work "l'Art Chrétien." At S. John Lateran may be seen a portrait of Boniface VIII by Giotto.

as though they had been painted by the most skilful brush. (1)

Giotto was assisted in this work by Simone Memmi and Pietro Cavallini, a Roman. Cavallini decorated a great number of Roman churches with his works, either in painting or mosaic. They were to be seen at S. Maria-trans-Tiberim, and at the churches of SS. Chrysogonus, Cæcilia, Francis, and Peter. The mosaic on S. Paul's façade was by Cavallini; it represented Jesus Christ, surrounded by a brilliant circle, upheld by four angels. The Saviour is in the act of blessing. To his right, between the windows, were the Virgin and S. Paul; to the left, SS. John the Baptist and Peter. But Cavallini's masterpiece was the vision of Augustus at Aracœli. The Tiburtine Sibyl was represented showing the Virgin and Infant Jesus surrounded by a brilliant glory to the Roman emperor.

To his talents as a worker in mosaic, Cavallini united those of a distinguished sculptor; but what is more remarkable in his works is the fervent piety they reveal. The most celebrated of all his works was the crucifix which addressed S. Brigit.

Amid this advance of the arts, we again notice no architectural structure worthy of mention. The only important monuments which may possibly date from this period are a portion of the main building of the Capitol, erected by order of Boniface IX, and the fortifications of the Castle of S. Angelo carried out

---

(1) Giotto received 220 florins for this mosaic from Cardinal Stefanesius, the nephew of Boniface VIII.

by Nicolò d'Arezzo during the reign of the same Pontiff. Thus architecture remained dead in the capital, at the very time she was filling other cities in Italy with her masterpieces. Then, in truth, the cathedrals of Florence, Milan, Siena, and Orvieto, the Campo-Santo of Pisa, the belfry of S. Maria-dei-Fiori, the Chartreuse of Pavia, S. Petronio at Bologna, and the Abbey of Montreale were either already in existence or rising amid the applause of all Europe. But at Rome internal divisions, and the absence of the Popes, checked the genius for great undertakings, which require peace and comfort for their development; public spirit had lost that energy which it still preserved in other parts of Italy; while the duty of building churches was left to confraternities, who proportioned the importance of their works to the narrowness of their means.

But it happened that distant people desired to have their national Church at Rome, accompanied by a hospital for their pilgrims. This desire arose more especially after the institution of the Jubilee, when, from all parts of the world, Christians flocked to the tombs of the Apostles to find themselves with neither protection nor shelter; it was then that the need of a common rallying place for each country was recognised. So it came about that the Germans founded, towards the end of the fourteenth century, a church and hospital destined for the reception of pilgrims from Germany and Flanders. On laying the foundations of this church an ancient statue of the Virgin was discovered seated between two kneeling figures, which were supposed to represent the faithful, whence originated the name of S. Maria-dell'-Anima. Before long arose the churches of SS. Louis of France, Nicholas of Lorraine, Catherine of Siena, S. Julian of Belgium, S. Anthony of Portugal, S. James of Spain, S. Andrew of Scotland, S. Yves of Britanny, S. Ambrose of Lombardy, S. Athanasius of Greece, S. Jerome of Slavonia. Rome was not only the centre of Christianity, but the great assembly of Christianity itself, represented at once by her misfortunes and glories, and by what she had of poorest and most illustrious.

END OF VOLUME I.

INDEX.

Abachum, S., 83.
Abbundantius, S., 315.
Abbundius, S., 315.
Abelard, 397.
Abondanza, S., 134.
Abraham, 161.
Achilleus, S., 34, 44.
Adalbéron of Rheims, 313.
Adalbert of Friuli, 301.
— of Prague, S., 307, 315.
— of Tuscany, 297.
Adalgise, 281.
Adam, 67, 162.
Adelaide, S., 306, 377.
— of Bohemia, 435.
Adrian I, 8, 164, 196, 210, 234, 248—253; 257, 259, 289.
— II, 9, 280—282; 287.
— III, 9, 283—284; 290.
— IV, 13, 401—405; 518.
— V, 15.
— VI, 18.
Æneas Sylvius, see Pius II.
Æsculapius, S., 315.
Æthelnoth of Canterbury, 371-372.
Aetius, 154.
Afferrano, 35.

Agapetus I, S., 6.
— II, 10, 298, 300.
—, S. and M., 52.
Agatha, S., 163, 165, 267, 317.
Agatho, S., 8, 219.
Agiltrude, 282.
Agilulphus, 184.
Aglais, 91, 92.
Agnes, S., 63, 67, 92—94; 117, 165, 527.
—, Empress, 353—354; 372.
—, foundress of hospital in Jerusalem, 420.
Agrippa, 206—207.
Alaric, 144—148; 150, 170.
Alatri, Card., 388.
Alberic of Camerino, 295-296.
— the Patrician, 296-298; 301.
— di Romano, 461.
Albert the Great, 462—463.
— I of Germany, 502.
Albertino, Giacomo, 502, 504.
Albina, 126, 143.
Albornoz, Card. Gilles, 515-516.
Alcuin, 241.
Aldobrandini, Card., 394.
Alexander I, 2, 52, 82.
— II, 12, 337, 345, 350—353.

INDEX.

Alexander III, 14, 405—413, 417, 422—423.
— IV, 14, 430, 460, 462—463; 466.
— V, 17.
— VI, 18.
— VII, 19.
— VIII, 20.
—, S. and M., 51.
— of Lyons, S. and M., 52.
— Severus, 72—73; 79, 81, 89, 114.
Alexis, S., 92, 157.
Alfano of Salerno, S., 372.
Alfred K. of Northumbria, 213, 214.
— the Great, 290.
Algardi, 93.
Almachius, 75—76.
Almachus, *see* Telemachus, S.
Alphonso IX of Castile, 439.
Alypius, S., 144.
Amalasontha, 175.
Amandus of Maestricht, S., 214.
Ambrose, S., 35, 85, 122—123; 134, 256, 394, 495.
Ammianus Marcellinus, 133.
Ampère, 209, 282.
Anacletus I, S., 2, 36—38; 71, 104, 107, 109.
— II, *see* Pietro di Leone.
Ananias, 340.
Anastasia, S., 35, 39.
Anastasius I, S., 5, 116, 130, 156.
— II, S., 6.
— III, 10, 294.
— IV, 13.

Anastasius, the antipope, 9, 275.
— II, Emperor, 227.
—, the Librarian, 35, 98, 116—118; 135—136; 195—196; 198, 221, 238—239; 245, 251, 262, 276, 281, 287.
Ancharius, S., 290.
Ancillon, 328.
Ancus Martius, 32.
Andronicus, 26.
Angelico da Fiesole, Fra, 490.
Anguillara, Count Orso, 500, 544.
Anicetus, S., 2, 66.
Anne, Empress of Charles IV, 516.
Annibaldi, the, 428, 460, 472.
Annibale di Annibaldi, 500.
Anselm, S., 258.
Anselm of Lucca, *see* Alexander II.
Anselm of Canterbury, S., 371—372.
Anthasia, S., 258.
Anthemius, Emp., 155.
Antherus, S., 3, 71.
Anthony, S., 51, 121.
— of Padua, S., 462, 476.
Antonina, 187.
Antonines, The, 51.
Antoninus Pius, 2, 47, 50, 88.
Antoninus, *see* Marcus Aurelius.
Antoninus, S., 539.
Apollinaris of Hierapolis, the Apologist, S., 55.
Apollonius, the Senator, S. and M., 54.

Apronian, 143.
Aquila, 37, 77.
Aratore, 189, 223.
Arcadius, Emp., 109.
Archimedes, 171.
Arialde, S., 355.
Aristarchus, 29.
Aristides, the Apologist, S., 55.
— of Smyrna, 89.
Aristotle, 171, 173, 185.
Arius, 118, 133, 150, 173.
Arnobius, 30.
Arnold of Brescia, 397—398; 401—402.
Arnulf, Emp., 282, 325.
Arsaces, the proconsul, 92.
Arsenius of Engubbio, 275.
Artemius, *see* Anastasius II.
Ascoli, Girolamo, *see* Nicholas IV.
Asella, S., 126, 127.
Astolf, K. of the Lombards, 228, 242—243; 246, 248, 258.
Athalaric, 189.
Athanasius, S., 120—122; 132, 134, 212.
— of Naples, S., 290.
Athelm, 306.
Athenagoras, the Apologist, 55.
Attalus, Emp., 145.
Atticus, 315.
Attila, 153, 170, 236, 407.
Audifax, S., 83.
Augustine, S., 29—30; 35, 123—125; 130, 134, 143— 144; 147—148; 153, 176, 234, 445, 495.
— of Canterbury, S., 194.

Augustus Cæsar, 40, 102, 121, 192, 206, 207, 320, 547.
Aurelian, 146, 182, 216.
Ausonius, 129.
Azon, 422.

Bacon, Roger, 545.
Bæda, 213, 247.
Balbina, S., 119.
Balbinus, 4.
Barberini, Card. Antonio, 527.
Baronius, Card., 29, 35, 121, 190, 275, 285, 287, 289, 292— 294; 300, 303, 336, 348.
Bartholomew, S., 315.
Basil, S., 134, 212, 318.
—, an assassin, 232.
— II, Emperor, 334.
Basilissa, S., 35, 38.
Bassano, Leandro, 412.
Batrachos, architect, 113.
Beatrice of Provence, 469.
Belisarius, 155, 176, 181—182; 187—188; 284.
Bellarmine, Card., 475.
Bellay, Card. J. du, 157.
Benedict, S., 134, 176—181; 197, 223, 284, 406.
— Biscop, S., 214.
— of Aniane, S., 290.
— I, 7, 192.
— II, S., 8, 219.
— III, 9, 274—277.
— IV, 10, 292.
— V, 10, 304.
— VI, 10, 305.
— VII, 11, 305.
— VIII, 11, 330, 333—335; 369.

Benedict IX, 11, 335—336; 338, 358, 496.
— X, 12, 16, 346—347.
— XI, 16.
— XII, 16, 497, 506.
— XIII, 20, 110.
— XIV, 20, 114, 263.
—, *see* Pierre de Lune.
Benincasa, 526.
Benizzi, S. Filippo, 473, 542.
Benoist de Matougues, 128.
Berengar I, 281, 295.
— II, 301—303.
Bérenger of Tours, 349, 370.
Bernadone, Francesco, *see* S. Francis d'Assisi.
Bernard, S., 379, 380—381; 393—394; 399—401; 439.
— de la Salle, 533.
— of Pisa, *see* Eugenius III.
Bernini, 134, 165, 387.
Bernwald of Hildesheim, 314.
Bertaire, Abbot, 284.
Bertrand de Goth, *see* Clement V.
Bertrandi, Card., 516.
Bessarion, Card., 318.
Bibiana, S., 165—166.
Biondo, 35.
Birinus, S., 213.
Blesilla, 126.
Blondel, David, 275.
Boccaccio, 491.
Boethius, 170—175; 223.
Bollandists, The, 60.
Bonaventure, S., 445, 462—463; 471, 473.
Boniface, S. and M., 91—92.

Boniface, S. (Winfrith) 231, 240—241; 326.
— I, S., 5, 150, 168.
— II, 6, 257—258.
— III, 7, 214.
— IV, S., 7, 208, 214, 222, 266.
— V, 7, 215.
— VI, 9.
— VII, (Franco), 10, 15, 305—306.
— VIII, 15, 430, 479—480; 482—483; 485—487; 491—496; 507, 543, 546—547.
— IX, 17, 537—539; 547.
— III, of Tuscany, 362.
Bonnetty, 320.
Bonone, 410.
Borromeo, *see* St. Charles.
Borromini, 102.
Bosio, 65.
Boso of Burgundy, 277.
Bossuet, 133.
Bouquet, Dom., 255.
Brancaleone, 460.
Brennus, 146.
Brigit of Sweden, S., 522—525; 547.
Brücker, 465.
Bruno, S., 369—370; 377.
—, *see* Gregory V.
— of Segni, S., 372.
— of Toul, *see* Leo IX.
Brutus, 24.
Budes, Sevestre, 536.
Buonanno, 422.
Burchard, Bishop of Wurzburg, 240.

Burdin, Maurice, 13, 386, 388—389.
Buschetto, 375.
Bussières, Baron de, 102.
Byron, Lord, 512.

Cadalous, 12, 351.
Cæcilia, S., 63, 75—76; 265—268.
Cæcilia Cesarini, Blessed, 448.
Cæcilius, 69.
Cæcilius Metellus, 73.
Cædwalla, 213.
Cæsar, Julius, 24, 81, 144—145; 159.
Cæsarius, the deacon, S., 44, 83, 116.
Cæsarius, S., brother of S. Gregory, 134.
Cæsarius of Arles, S., 205.
Caius, S., 4, 63, 71, 78.
Caius, the writer, 108.
Cajetani, The, 430.
—, Benedetto dei, see Boniface VIII.
Calepodius, S., 3, 4, 63, 77.
Calixtus I, S., 3, 4, 63, 71—73; 76, 82, 119, 265, 396.
— II, 13, 389—391; 423.
— II, (antipope), 13.
— III, 17, 540.
— III, see John of Sturm.
Callinicus, 226.
Calliopas, 217.
Camden, 25.
Camerino, Giacomo, 476.
Camillus, 158.
Campulus, 253, 255.

Cancellieri, 519.
Candida, S., 85.
Canute, 371—372; 377.
Capellari, see Gregory XVI.
Capocci, Giacomo, 455.
Caracalla, 79, 199.
Caracci, Annibale, 194, 318, 375.
Carloman, 180, 258.
—, see Pepin.
— of Bavaria, 282.
Carpophorus, S., 166.
Cassiodorus, 170, 172, 189.
Castorius, S., 166.
Castulus, S., 84, 90.
Cataline, 22.
Catherine of Siena, S., 168, 525—528; 534.
— of Sweden, S., 523—525; 527.
Cato, 398, 414.
Cavallini, Pietro, 547.
Cécile, a relative of Clement IV, 468.
Celestine I, S., 5, 150, 152.
— II, 13, 397—398.
— III, 14, 415, 431.
— IV, 14, 456.
— V, S., 15, 473, 477—480.
Celestius, the heretic, 151.
Celsus, 70.
Cenci, The, 428.
Cencius, 351, 357, 384.
Ceolfrid, S., 241.
Ceolwulf, S., 258.
Cesarini, The, 448.
Ceslas, S., 484.
Charitana, S., 56.

Charito, S., 56.
Charlemagne, 107, 225, 249—252; 254—259; 261—264; 292, 302, 325, 331.
Charles Martel, 180, 237.
—, the Fat, 282.
— the Simple, 282.
— the Good, of Flanders, 377.
— of Anjou, 469—471; 473.
— II, the Lame, of Sicily, 485.
— Borromeo, S., 138, 222.
— IV, of Luxembourg, 516, 521.
— V, of France, 520.
Chateaubriand, 23, 197, 214, 281, 375.
Childeric III, 240.
Christopherus, 10, 293.
Chromatius, S., 84, 186.
Chrysanthus, S., 63, 84, 285.
Chrysostom, *see* S. John.
Ciampini, 163.
Cicero, 22, 189, 261, 276, 283, 317—318; 364, 414.
Cimabue, 489, 546.
Clare, S., 459.
Claudia, wife of Pudens, 25.
—, mother of S. Eugenia, 85.
Claudian, 53.
Claudius, 84.
—, S., 166.
Clement I, S., 2, 37—38; 198.
— II, 12, 337—338; 369—370.
— III, 14, 413, 423, 431.
— IV, 15, 467, 469, 471, 487.
— V, 16, 496—498.
— VI, 16, 506, 508, 513—514.
—, VII, 18.

Clement VIII, 19.
— IX, 19.
— X, 19, 210.
— XI, 20.
— XII, 20.
— XIII, 20.
— XIV, 20.
— III, *see* Guibert.
— VII, *see* Robert of Geneva.
— VIII, antipope, 17.
— of Alexandria, S., 55, 69.
Cletus, S., 2.
Clotilda, S., 168.
Clovis, 168.
Colombrini, Blessed Giovanni, 542.
Colonna, The, 384, 429, 481—484; 491, 495, 499, 513.
—, Egidio, 484.
—, Card. Giacomo, 481—482.
—, Card. Giovanni, 455, 481—482.
—, Giovanni, 538.
—, Landolfo, 482.
—, Blessed Margaret, 482.
—, Matteo, 482.
—, Nicolo, 538.
—, Odone, 482.
—, Card. Pietro, 481—482.
—, Sciarra, 492—493.
Comestore, 35.
Commodus, 54.
Conon, 8, 219.
Conrad, 371.
Conradin, 470—471.
Constance, Emp. of Henry VI, 416, 434.
—, Emp. of Frederick II, 452.

Constans II, 216—218; 235.
Constantia, d. of Constantine I, 117.
Constantine, antipope, 8, 247.
— the Great, 22, 63, 96—99; 103—104; 109, 111, 113, 115—121; 131, 134, 152, 162, 167, 187, 195—196; 210, 228, 253, 257, 496.
— IV, 219.
— V, 236, 242, 258.
Constantinus, 8.
Constantius Chlorus, 114.
— II, 121, 131—133.
Conti, The, 430.
—, Lotario dei, see Innocent III.
—, Pietro dei, 474.
—, Ricardo dei, 430.
—, Ugolino dei, see Gregory IX.
Contucci, 39, 375.
Coppi, 298.
Coquerel, 356.
Cornelius, S., 3, 4, 71, 79.
—, Lentulus, 159.
Crassus, 414.
Crescentia, S., 222—223.
Crescentius, S., 51.
— of Rome, 305.
—, the Younger, 308—311; 316, 384.
Cunegund, S., 330, 333.
Curtius, 200.
Cyprian, S., 70, 71, 79.
Cyriaca, S., 63, 88, 111, 201.
Cyriacus, S., 83.
Cyril of Alexandria, S., 168, 212.

Dafrosa, S., 165.
Damasus I, S., 5, 126, 131, 133, 135—137; 369.
— II, 12, 338.
Daniel, 66, 223.
Dante, 196, 445, 479, 483, 487, 490, 494—495; 498, 502, 542, 545.
Daria, S., 63, 84, 285.
Daunau, 244, 449.
David, 129, 311—312.
Decius, 80, 90, 159.
Demas, 29.
Demetria, S., 165.
Demetriades, 143.
Deodatus I, S., 7, 214.
— II, 7, 218.
Desiderius, 248—249.
—, see Victor III.
Diderot, 192.
Diocletian, 71, 78—84; 90, 93, 166, 186, 223.
Dion Cassius, 72.
Dionysius, S., 4, 123, 234.
—, the Areopagite, 28, 245.
—, of Alexandria, S., 70.
Dioscorus, 68.
Diotisalvi, 422.
Docibilis of Gaeta, 284.
Dolabella, 135.
Domenichino, 72, 126, 164, 194, 318.
Domitian, 43—44.
Dominic, S., 158, 288, 443—448; 464.
— Loricatus, S., 338.
Domitian, 43—44; 319.
Donatus, 276.

Donnizone, 387.
Donus I, 8, 105, 218.
— II, 10, 305.
Duncan, 371.
Dunstan, S., 306.
Durandus, William, 484—485.

Eberhard, Count, 352.
Edgar, husband of S. Catherine of Sweden 523—524.
Edward the Confessor, S., 376—377.
Egidio of Viterbo, Card., 538.
Eginhart, 256.
Eichhorn, Prof., 365,
Eleutherius, S., 3.
Elfege of Canterbury, S., 371.
Elias, 451, 539.
Elijah, 68.
Elizabeth of Hungary, S., 454.
Elpis, 173.
Emerentiana, S., 94.
Emiliana, S., 191.
Emmelia, S., 134.
Ennodius of Pavia, 131.
Epaphras, 28.
Epaphroditus, 28.
Epictetus, 70.
Epiphanus of Salamis, S., 126.
Epipodius of Lyons, S., 52.
Equitius, a priest, 118.
—, Senator, 177.
Erasmus, 465.
Erwin of Steinbach, 490.
Ethelwulf, 276.
Eubulus, 25.
Euclid, 171.
Eudocia (Athenaïs), 164.

Eudoxia, 36, 154, 163.
—, the Younger, 155.
Eugenia, S., 85, 86.
Eugenius I, S., 7, 218.
— II. 9. 270, 302, 333.
— III, Blessed, 13, 394, 398, 399, 400—401, 404, 422, 518.
— IV, 17.
—, S., 51.
Eulalius, an antipope, 5, 167.
Euphemius, 157.
Eusebius, S., 4, 131.
—, the historian, 25, 72, 134.
Eustachius, S., 52, 54.
Eustochia, S., 126, 128, 149.
Eutropia, 121.
Eutyches, 150, 173.
Eutychian, S., 4, 78.
Evaristus, S., 2, 37.
Eve, 67.
Evellius, S., 81.
Evelpistus, S., 56.
Exhilarat of Naples, 233.
Ezechiel, 64, 148, 160, 184.
Ezzelino di Romano, 461.

Fabian, S., 3, 71.
Fabiola, S., 126, 128, 141.
Fabricius, 189.
Farnese, Card., 394.
Fausta, 98.
Faustina, 88.
Favorinus, 70.
Felicianus, S., 84.
Felicitas, S., 51, 52.
Felix I, S., 4, 71, 73.
— II, S., 5, 6, 132, 133.
— III, S., 6, 196.

Felix IV, S., 6, 191.
— V, (antipope), 17.
—, S., 51.
— of Valois, S., 419.
Ferdinand of Castile, S., 470.
Fiammingo, Paolo, 412.
Fidanza, Giovanni, see St. Bonaventure.
Fieschi, The, 456.
Fisher, S. John, 157.
Flavia Domitilla, 44, 81.
Flavius Clemens, 43, 81.
Fleury, 304, 310, 354, 480, 511, 521.
Flodoard, 294—295.
Florentius, 180.
Formosus, 9, 282, 286.
Fortunatus of Fano, 230.
Frances, S., (Francesca Romana), 73.
Francis d'Assisi, S., 158, 445—448; 459, 462-463; 476, 485.
Franco, see Boniface VII.
Franco Bolognese, 545.
Frangipani, The, 384, 387—388; 390—392; 397, 408, 428—429; 453, 460.
—, Cencio, 387.
—, Hector, 406.
Frederick of Lorraine, see Stephen IX.
— Barbarossa, 402—408; 411—412; 415, 423, 450.
— II, 434, 451—461; 470, 482.
Froissart, 528—529; 531, 534—536.
Fulgentius, S., 169, 173.

Fulk of Toulouse, 443.
Fulrad, 107, 240, 244.

Gabinius, 414.
Gaddo-Gaddi, 546.
Galilei, Alessandro, 102.
Galla, 173, 175.
Gaume, 265.
Gebhard, see Victor II.
Gelasius I, S., 6, 152, 202.
— II, 13, 315, 387—389.
Gélie, relative of Clement IV, 468.
Genseric, 153—155; 170, 218.
Geoffrey, Card., 368.
George of Præneste, 247.
Gérard of Burgundy, see Nicholas II.
— of Rheims, 312.
—, Card., 401.
Gerbert, see Sylvester II.
Gerbet, Mgr., 119, 161, 224, 236, 340.
Germanus of Auxerre, S., 205.
Gerson, (Charlier), John, 543.
Gervasius, S., 156.
Getulius, S., 50.
Ghibellines, The, 405, 496, 500.
Giacomo di Turiti, 546.
— di Camerino, 546.
Gibbon, 193, 245, 319, 364.
Giotto, 490, 496, 546—547.
Giovanni Patrizio, 137.
Giswulf of Benevento, 230.
Giulio Romano, 23.
Glaber, 331, 335, 353.
Glycerius, 156.
Godfrey the Bearded, 346—347

Godfrey the Hunchback, 362, 386.
— de Bouillon, 542.
Gorgonia, S., 134.
Gracchus, 398.
Gratian, John, *see* Gregory VI.
Gregory Thaumaturgus, S., 70, 80.
— Nazianzen, S., 134.
— —, S., the Younger, 134.
— of Nissa, S., 134.
— of Tours, S., 35, 63, 107, 190, 205.
—, the Arian, 121.
— I, S., 7, 105, 158, 163, 175, 177—178; 183—184; 189, 190—196; 198—199; 201—205; 216, 222—223; 228, 251, 289, 321, 495.
— II, S., 8, 231—234; 237.
— III, S., 8, 201, 235—238.
— IV, 7, 9, 270—271; 287.
— V, 11, 307—309; 312.
— VI, 11, 335—336.
— VII, S., 12, 108, 344—347; 349—350; 352—358; 360, 362—367; 369, 373—374; 379, 386, 431.
— VIII, 14, 413, 417.
— IX, 14, 430, 453—456; 462.
— X, Blessed, 15, 472—473.
— XI, 16, 526—530; 532, 542.
— XII, 17.
— XIII, 19, 364.
— XIV, 19.
— XV, 19.
— XVI, 20, 194.
— VIII, *see* Burdin.

Gruter, J.-P., 82.
Gualbert, John, 377.
Guelph of Bavaria, 306.
Guelphs, The, 405, 496.
Guéranger, Dom., 76.
Guercino, 164.
Guibert, 12, 362—363; 367—368; 373.
Guido d'Arezzo, 376.
— di Crema, 14.
—, the artist, 194.
— of Spoleto, 281—282.
— of Tuscany, 295—296.
— Fulcodi, *or* Foulques, *see* Clement IV.
Gundobald, 172.
Gunther of Köln, 278—279.
Guy of Montpellier, 438.
Guzman, Domingo de, *see* St. Dominic.

Hadrian, 50—52; 54—55; 110, 114, 159.
Halinard of Dijon, 370.
Hawkwood, Sir John, 536.
Hegesippus, S., 61.
Helena, S., 114—116; 274.
Heliogabalus, 114, 210.
Helmold, 368.
Hélgot, 471.
Hénault, 274.
Henry the Fowler, 301, 307.
— II, S., 330, 333—334; 343, 377.
— III, the Black, 336, 338, 344.
— IV, 351—355; 358—363; 366—368; 372.

Henry V, 382—383; 385, 387—388, 423.
— VI, 415—416.
— VII, 498—500.
— of Thuringia, 457.
— II of England, 381, 403.
— of Castile, Senator of Rome, 470.
Heraclius, 210, 225.
—, son of Constantine IV, 219.
Hermas, 29.
Hermes, S., 54, 186.
Herod, 164, 368.
Herondina, S., 198.
Hierax, S., 56.
—, the heresiarch, 79.
Hilary, S., 6, 163.
— of Poitiers, S., 134.
— of Arles, S., 168, 205.
Hildebert of Tours, 489.
Hildebrand, see Gregory VII.
Hilduin, 279.
Hippolytus, S., 70, 86, 89.
—, S. and M., 88, 197.
—, a priest, 89.
Homer, 185, 269.
Honesta, 231.
Honorius I, 7, 105, 215, 222, 288.
— II, 13, 391, 393.
— III, 14, 112, 158, 424, 429, 446, 450—453.
— IV, 15, 429, 475, 481.
— II, see Cadalous.
—, Emperor, 140, 145, 182, 206, 215.
Horace, 51, 164, 541, 543.
Hormisdas, 6, 196.

Hosius, 134.
Hugh of Provence, 296—297.
— the Great, 300.
— Capet, 405.
Hugo, S., 369, 376.
Humbert of Marolles, S., 214.
—, Card., 346, 349, 370, 371.
—, Archb. of Lyons, 422.
Humphrey de Hauteville, 343.
Hürter, 430, 432, 433, 436, 438, 441.
Hyacinth, S., 484.
Hyginus, S., 2.

Ignatius of Antioch, S., 47, 49, 198.
— of Constantinople, S., 290.
— Loyola, S., 156.
Ina, 241, 438.
Ingeburg of Denmark, 433.
Innocent I, S., 5, 145, 150—151; 156—157.
— II, 13, 392—396; 423.
— III, 14, 241, 360, 430—437; 439—441; 443—444; 448—450; 453, 475.
— IV, 14, 456, 459—460; 463, 475.
— V, 15.
— VI, 16, 514, 516.
— VII, 17.
— VIII, 18.
— IX, 19.
— X, 19.
— XI, 19.
— XII, 20, 430.
— XIII, 20.
Irenæus, S., 55, 61, 89.

Irene, wife of S. Castulus, 90.
—, sister of S. Damasus, 137.
Isaac of Ravenna, 215.
Isaias, 21, 40, 144, 184, 291.
Ishmael, 211.

Jacob, 161, 394.
Jacopone de Todi, Fra, 437.
Jacques de Cahors, *see* John XXII.
Jager, Abbé, 365.
Januarius, S., 51.
Jean de Brienne, 452—453.
Jeremias, 276, 292, 339.
Jerome, S., 25, 64, 70, 125—129; 139, 141—143; 147—149; 153, 176, 276, 394, 495.
Joan, Pope, 274.
Joanna of Naples, 517, 520.
John the Baptist, S., 98—99; 118, 160, 215, 221, 369, 424, 476, 510, 547.
John the Evangelist, S., 44, 98—99; 107, 118, 180, 215, 301, 419, 424, 476.
—, S. and M., 135.
— Chrysostom, S., 81, 134, 186, 235, 269.
— I, S., 6, 174.
— II, 6.
— III, 7, 197.
— IV, 7, 215—216.
— V, 8, 219,
— VI, 8, 227, 230.
— VII, 8.
— VIII, 9, 275, 281—283.
— IX, 9, 286.
— X, 10, 295—296.

John XI, 10, 296—297.
— XII, 10, 301—304; 306, 312.
— XIII, 10, 304—305.
— XIV, 11, 305.
— XV, 11, 309.
— XVI, 11, 307, 309.
— XVII, 11, 330.
— XVIII, 11, 330, 372.
— XIX, 11, 15, 335, 376.
— XXI, 15.
— XXII, 16, 500, 503—505; 540.
— XXIII, 17.
— of Bulgaria, 434.
— Damascene, S., 200.
— Lackland, 449.
— of Matha, S., 419, 448.
— Philagathus, 11, 15, 309—310.
— Platys, 220.
— of Salisbury, 193, 404.
— of Sturm, 14, 412.
— of Velletri, *see* Benedict X.
— of Vicenza, Fra, 462.
Jonah, 67.
Jordanus, 232.
Josephus, 40.
Josue, 161.
Julian the Apostate, 135, 165.
—, S., 51.
Julienne, Blessed, 465—466.
Juliana, 143.
Julius I, S., 4, 72, 122, 131, 216, 396.
— II, 18, 164, 375.
— III, 18.

Justin Martyr, S., 55—56; 61, 69.
— I, 173.
Justinian, S., 51.
— I, 183, 187, 421.
— II, 219, 225—226.
Juvenal, 30, 34, 38, 61, 103, 158.

Kilian, S., 241.

Lactantius, 134, 186.
Ladislas of Naples, 538.
Ladislaus of Hungary, 435.
Lamartine, 322.
Lambert *or* Lamberti, 281—282.
Lando, 10, 295.
Laporte du Theil, 449.
Latinus Pacatus, 150.
Laurence, S., 39, 86—88; 111, 113, 197, 201, 525.
—, an antipope, 6, 168.
—, a Christian, 68.
— O'Toole, S., 417.
Lazarus, 68, 137, 417.
Lea, 126.
Leo I, S., 5, 152—155; 162, 164, 236.
— II, S., 8.
— III, S., 8, 253—256; 261—263; 287, 366.
— IV, S., 9, 105, 111, 272—276; 287, 290, 348.
— V, 10, 293.
— VI, 10, 296.
— VII, 10, 298, 300.
— VIII, 10, 12, 303—304.

Leo IX, 12, 338—341; 343, 345, 370, 392.
— X, 18, 350.
— XI, 19.
— XII, 20.
—, *or* Gregory, an antipope, 11.
—, father of John XVI, 309.
— III, the Isaurian, 227, 230, 232, 235—236.
— of Nonantula, S., 307.
— of Ostia, 295.
—, the historian, 361, 482.
Leontius, 225—226.
Leopold of Austria, 415—416.
Liberius, S., 5, 122, 131—133; 137, 159, 253.
—, S. and M., 56.
Licinius Crassus, 159.
—, the Emperor, 165.
Linus, S., 25, 37.
Liudprand, King of the Lombards, 228, 233, 236, 239, 259.
—, the historian, 294—296; 303.
Longfellow, 495.
Lothair I, 264, 270—271; 273, 302, 333.
— II, 277—280; 411.
— III, 392—393; 406, 423.
Louis I, le Débonnaire, 250, 264, 271, 302.
— II, 271—272; 278—279.
— IV, 499—505.
— IX, of France, S., 457, 460, 467, 469, 485, 495.
— XI, of France, 540.

INDEX.

Louis of Toulouse, S., 485—486.
Lucian, 491.
Lucina, S., 36, 38, 81, 91, 95, 109.
Lucius, I, S., 3, 71.
— II, 13, 398.
— III, 14, 413.
Lucretia, 130.
Lucullus, 139, 414.
Lucy, S., 165, 288.
Luden, 340, 355.
Luke, S., 29, 448.
Lullus, Raymond, 484—485; 543.
Lupus, an Abbot, 276.
Lurion, 232.
Lusignan, Pierre de, 520.

Mabille, a relative of Clement IV, 468.
Mabillon, 176, 179, 181, 257.
Macarius, 236.
Maccabees, The, 50.
Macbeth, 371.
Macrina, S., 134.
Mæcenas, 164.
Mahomet, 211, 455.
Maistre, Xavier, de, 208, 229.
Majorian, 155.
Malachy of Armagh, S., 396.
Mallio, 35.
Mammæa, 81.
Manes, 79.
Manfred, 460—461; 469—470.
Maphœus Veggius, 236.
Maratti, Carlo, 194.
Marcella, S., 121, 126, 128, 141, 146—148.

Marcellina, S., 122, 134.
Marcellinus, S., 4, 63, 83—84; 116.
Marcellus I, S., 4, 71, 95, 131.
— II, 18.
Marchione d'Arezzo, 430.
Marcion, 55.
Marcius, 56.
Marcus Aurelius, 37, 47, 52—55; 58—59; 511.
Margaret, S. and M., 527.
— of Scotland, S., 377.
Marinus, Duke of Rome, 232.
Marius, S., 83.
Mark, S., Pope, 4, 84, 119, 131.
Marozia, 294—298; 301.
Martha, S., 83.
— of Bethany, S., 417.
Martial, 25, 150.
—, S., 51, 103.
Martin I, S., 7, 216—217; 220, 235.
— II, or Marinus, 9, 283.
— III, or Marinus, 10, 298, 300.
— IV, 15, 473—474.
— V, 17.
— of Tours, S., 143, 180, 299.
— Polonus, 275.
Martina, S., 86.
Martinelli, 35.
Martinianus, 32.
Mary of Bethany, S., 417.
— of Egypt, S., 283.
— of Aragon, 435.
Marzia, 68.
Matilda of Germany, S., 308, 377.

Matilda of Tuscany, 362, 385—387; 393, 406.
Matthew, S., 46, 203.
Matthias, S., 201.
Maurice, S., 90.
—, the Emperor, 191.
—, an officer, 215.
Maurus, 177.
Maxentius, 22, 95—96; 131.
Maximian, 78.
Maximin, 79.
Maximus, S., 265—267.
—, the Patrician, 139, 154.
Mayeul, S., 306, 344.
Melania, the Elder, S., 141—144.
—, the Younger, S., 142—143.
Melchiades, S., 4, 131.
Melito of Sardis, 55.
Memmi, Simone, 547.
Methodius, S., 290.
Michael, S., 311.
— Angelo (Buonarroti), 164, 194.
— Cærularius, 341.
Miltiades, the Apologist, 55.
Minutius Felix, 69.
Modestus, S., 222—223.
Monica, S., 124, 184.
Montalembert, 449, 454—455.
Montanus, 55.
Montesquieu, 325.
Montfaucon, 118, 288—289; 375.
More, S. Thomas, 157.
Moses, 67, 161, 455.
Müller, Johann von, 365.
Muratori, 294, 296, 300.

Murray, John, 105,
Murs, Jean des, 545.

Napoleon, Cardinal Stephen's nephew, 447.
Naises, 183.
Nathan, 311.
Nemesian, S., 51.
Nepos, 156.
Nepotian, 121.
Nereus, S., 34, 44.
Nero, 1, 22, 28, 30—32; 34—35; 39, 43, 47, 52, 81, 103—104; 121, 146, 154, 166, 210, 236, 257, 274, 320, 368, 374—375.
Nerva, 146.
Nestorius, 150, 159, 173.
Newman, Card., 133.
Nibby, 289.
Nicholas I, S., 9, 277—278; 280, 290.
— II, 12, 347, 349—350; 423.
— III, 15, 429, 473, 475.
— IV, 15, 475—477.
— V, 17, 165.
—, S., 200.
— Breakspeare, *see* Adrian IV.
Nicolò d'Arezzo, 548.
Nicostratus, S., 166.
Nilus of Rossano, S., 307, 309—310; 316—318.
Noah, 67.
Nogaret, William de, 492—494.
Nonna, S., 184.
Norbert, S., 393.
Novalis, 324.
Novatian, 3.
Novatus, the heresiarch, 79.

Novatus, 56—57; 59—60.
Numerian, 63, 285.

Octavia, 175, 258.
Octavian, *see* Augustus.
—, *see* John XII.
—, 13, 14, 405—407.
Oderic of Friuli, Blessed, 543.
Oderigi d'Agobbio, 545.
Odilon of Cluny, S., 344, 369, 376—378.
Odo of Cluny, S., 298—299; 344.
Odo of Canterbury, S., 306.
Odoacer, 156, 169.
Offa, 241.
Olaf of Norway, S., 377.
Olympia, 165.
Olympius, Emperor, 156.
—, Exarch, 216—217.
Omar, 212.
Onesimus, 28, 52.
Onesiphorus, 28.
Orcagna, 490.
Origen, 46, 70, 72, 89.
Orosius, 72, 144.
Orsini, The, 429, 472—473; 498, 541.
—, Gentile degli, 474.
—, Card. Napoleon, 496.
Oswi, 213.
Otho I, 300—305; 307, 312.
— II, 306, 308, 312.
— III, 157, 307—311; 314—316; 318, 330.
— IV, 435, 451.
—, *see* Urban II.
— of Freisingen, 402.

Otho of Milan, 383.
Ovid, 141, 156, 258, 282.

Pagi, 353.
Palaiologos, John, 521—522.
Palladius, 150.
Pammachius, 141—142; 148.
Pancirole, 35.
Pancratius, S., 38, 73, 77, 92.
Pantaleon, Jacques, *see* Urban IV.
Pantaleone, the Consul, 345.
Panvinius, 35, 101, 530.
Papencordt, Felix, 508, 516, 519.
Paschal, antipope, 8, 219, 220.
— I, S., 9, 76, 264—270; 290.
— II, 13, 167, 369, 374—375; 382—383; 385—387; 424.
— III, *see* Guido di Crema.
—, 253, 255.
Pastor, a priest, 57, 60.
Paul, the Apostle, S., 21, 25—29; 32, 35—39; 48, 52, 64, 77, 81, 106, 108, 118, 197, 201, 215, 221, 266, 268, 304, 308, 359, 368, 476, 510, 519, 546—547.
— I, S., 8, 245—247; 265.
— II, 18, 487.
— III, 18.
— IV, 18.
— V, 19, 246.
—, S. and M., 135.
—, the Deacon, 221.
—, the Exarch, 232—233.
— of Samosata, 79.
Paula, S., 126—128; 141.

Paulina, S., 85.
Paulinus, S., 105—106; 125, 129—130; 134, 142—143.
Pelagius I, 7, 197.
— II, 7, 112, 189, 190—191; 197—198.
—, the heresiarch. 150—151.
Pepin, 170, 240, 242—244; 258, 264, 302, 326.
—, (Carloman), 250, 254, 256.
Perret, Louis, 67.
Peter the Apostle, S., 1, 11, 25, 27—28; 30—34; 36—39; 56, 60—61; 64, 70, 77—78; 103—104; 106—108; 111, 118—119; 131, 136, 147, 163—164; 189, 197, 215, 242, 244—247; 250, 252, 263—266; 268, 281, 290—291; 302—304; 308, 331, 359, 368, 387, 396, 476, 497, 510, 519, 528, 547.
—, the Exorcist, 83, 116.
—, an antipope, 8.
—, see John XIV.
—, Duke of Rome, 226.
—, brother of John X, 296.
—, prefect of Rome, 305.
— of Alexandria, S., 202.
— II, of Aragon, 434.
— Damian, S., 337—338; 346—348; 372.
— the Hermit, 373.
— Nolasco, S., 484.
— of Sebaste, S., 134.
Petrarch, 430, 491, 497, 500, 502—503; 511, 519, 543—544.

Petrini, 483, 494.
Petronax, 180.
Petronilla, S., 246.
Petronius, 491.
Phaon, 374.
Phidias, 23.
Philagathus, 11, 15, 309—310.
Philemon, 27—28.
Philip, S. and M., 51.
—, an antipope, 8.
— I, of France, 354.
— II, Augustus, 416, 449.
— IV, le Bel, 484, 491—492.
— of Swabia, 451.
Philippicus-Bardanes, 226-227.
Phocas, 208, 210.
Photius, 275, 277, 342.
Pier-Leoni, The, 374, 384—385; 387, 392—393; 397, 427, 429.
Pierre de Courtenay, 451.
— de Lune, 17.
Pietro Celestino, or di Morone, see S. Celestine V.
— di Corbario, (Rainalucci), 16, 504—505.
— di Leone, 13, 392—393; 395.
— Parenzio, S., 442.
Pilate, 368.
Pinian, 142.
Pinturricbio, 39, 375.
Pius I, S., 2, 57—61, 66.
— II, 17, 170.
— III, 18.
— IV, 18.
— V, S., 18, 158, 283.
— VI, 20.
— VII, 20.
— VIII, 20, 111.

Pius IX, 20, 113.
Placidia, 155.
—, Galla, 162.
Placidus, 177.
Platina, 539.
Plato, 171.
Plautilla, 35, 81.
Plautius Lateranus, 98.
Pliny, 108, 113, 159, 200, 207, 253.
Plotinus, 70.
Plutarch, 70.
Poggio Bracciolini, 189.
Polycarp, S., 52, 61.
Pomarancio, 135, 166.
Pompeianus, 145.
Pompey, 485.
Pontanus, S., 3, 71.
Porphyrius, 70.
Porzio, 35.
Posi, Paolo, 375.
Prætextatus, S., 3.
— the Senator, 133.
Praxedes, S., 38, 57—61; 63, 81, 186, 265, 267—269.
Praxiteles, 23.
Priam, 147.
Prignano, Bartolomeo, *see* Urban VI.
Primaslaus of Bohemia, 434.
Primitivus, S., 51.
Primus, S., 84.
Principia, S., 128, 141, 146.
Prisca, S., 73, 78.
Priscilla, 4, 5, 7, 26, 57, 59—60; 63, 77.
Proba, 143, 173.
Processus, 32.

Proculus, 81.
Propertius, 29, 158.
Prosper, S., 72, 168, 205.
Protasius, S., 156.
Prudentius, 89, 109, 136.
Ptolemy, S., 54.
Publicola, 142—143.
Pudens, 25—26; 56—58; 60, 267.
Pudentiana, S., 2, 25—26; 56—61; 63, 186, 265, 267—268.
Punicus, 57.
Pythagoras, 316.

Quadratus, the Apologist, S., 55.
Quintilian, 276.
Quintilius Varro, 51.
Quintus, 317.

Raphael, 23.
Ratchis, 180, 258.
Ratisbonne, Abbé, 399.
Raymond, C. of Toulouse, 435.
— Lullus, 484—485.
— Nonnatus, S., 484.
— of Penafort, S., 484.
Redempta, S., 198.
Remigius, S., 168.
Remus, 196.
Rhotaris, King of the Lombards, 259.
Richard of Cluny, 274.
— of Aversa, 350.
— I, of England, 415.
Richenza, the Empress, 393.
Richer, 313.
Ricimer, King of the Suevi, 155—156; 163.

Rienzi, Colà di, 502, 507—516.
Rinaldi, 511, 515.
Rinaldo of Anagni, 494.
Rio, M., 546.
Robert, father of John XV, 309.
— I, of France, 330, 369, 437.
— Wiscard, 350, 362—364.
— of Geneva, 16, 534.
— of Normandy, 373.
— of Sicily, 485.
— of Luzarches, 490.
— of Naples, 544.
Roger of Sicily, 395.
— de Maumont, *see* Clement VI.
Rohrbacher, 229, 333, 371—372.
Roland of Parma, 358.
Roland Bandinelli, *see* Alexander III.
Romanus, Pope, 9.
—, a monk, 179.
Romuald, S., 307, 311, 314, 377.
Romula, S., 198—199.
Romulus, 196.
— Augustulus, 156, 256.
Rose, S., 460.
Rossi, Comm. di, 62—63; 112.
Rousseau, J.-J., 24, 206.
Rudolph of Swabia, 361, 367.
Rufina, S., 85, 135.
Rusticiana, 173.
Rusticus, the prefect, 56.
—, nephew of Gregory VII, 363.

Sabellius, 79.
Sabina, S., 38, 54, 158.
Sabinella, 57.

Sabinian, 7, 214.
Saint-Amour, Guillaume de, 463.
Saladin, 414.
Sallust, 83, 146.
Salviati, Card., 156.
San Angelo, Fra, 448.
Savelli, The, 429, 446, 541.
—, Cencio, *see* Honorius III.
—, Lucca, 528.
Saul, 312.
Sauros, 113.
Scaligeri, The, 499.
Scarcellino, 410.
Schwartz, Berthold, 545.
Schmid, Dr., 365.
Scholastica, S., 134.
Scipio, 283.
Scopas, 207.
Sebastian, S., 39, 63—64; 85—86; 90—91; 163, 525.
Sebastiano Ziani, 409.
Secunda, S., 85.
Semiramis, 144.
Seneca, 61.
Septimus Severus, 81, 208.
Serapia, S., 54.
Serena Augusta, 81, 82.
—, Stilicho's wife, 144.
Sergius Paulus, 28.
— I, S., 8, 213, 220—221; 230.
— II, 9, 271—272.
— III, 10, 293—294; 296.
— IV, 11, 330.
—, an antipope, 9.
Sericius, S., 5, 131.
Servius Tullius, 282.
Servulus, S., 198.

Severani, 106.
Severianus, S., 166.
Severina, a Roman lady, 2.
Severinus, Pope, 7, 215.
Severus, a Christian, 68.
—, the Emperor, 155.
—, S., 166.
Sigonius, 368.
Simeon of Armenia, S., 372.
Simetrius, S., 59.
Simon Magus, 29—30; 247.
—, son of Gioras, 43.
— de Montford, the Elder, 435—436.
Simplicius, S., Pope, 6, 152, 164—165.
—, S. and M., 166.
Sisinnius, Pope, 8.
—, an antipope, 9.
Sismondi, 245, 495.
Sixtus I, S., 2, 52, 65.
— II, S., 3, 63, 71, 87.
— III, S., 5, 150, 153, 159—161; 510.
— IV, 18, 375, 438.
— V, 19, 37, 289, 530.
Smaragdus, 210.
Socrates, 133.
Solomon, 106.
Sophonias, 457.
Soter, S., Pope, 3.
Sotera, S., 85, 134.
Spina, Alessandro, 545.
Staël, M^{de.} de, 52.
Stateus, S., 51.
Stefanesius, or Stefaneschi, Card., 480, 494, 547.
Steffens, Henry, 365.

Stephen, S., protomartyr, 84, 113, 197.
— I, S., 3, 63, 71, 83, 346.
—, who died before consecration, 8, 240.
— II, 8, 240—245; 326.
— III, 8, 247—248.
— IV, 9.
— V, 9, 283—286.
— VI, 9, 286.
— VII, 9, 296.
— VIII, 10, 299—300.
— IX, 10, 346—347; 371.
— X, 12.
— of Blois, 373.
— of Hungary, S., 377.
Stilicho, 144.
Suetonius, 30, 374.
Suidger, *see* Clement II.
Sulpicius Severus, 143.
Suzanna, S., 78, 82.
Sylla, 319.
Sylvanus, S., 51.
Sylverius, S., Pope, 6, 187—188; 220.
Sylvester I, S., 98—100; 104, 107, 111, 118, 131, 195.
— II, 11, 119, 292, 312—314; 330, 358, 373, 378.
Sylvia, S., 191, 194, 289.
Symetrius, S., 274.
Symmachus, S., Pope, 6, 168, 195—197; 201, 205, 253.
—, the Patrician, 139.
—, father of Boethius, 173-175.
Symphorian, S., 52.
Symphorianus, S., 166.
Symphorosa, S., 50—51.

Tacitus, 31—32; 103, 328.
Tanaquil, Caia Cæcilia, 73, 129—130.
Tancred de Hauteville, 343.
— of Sicily, 416.
Tarcisius, S., 83.
Tarquinius Priscus, 73, 319.
— Superbus, 315, 319.
Tasso, 24.
Tebaldeschi, Card., 532, 534.
Telemachus, S., 140.
Telesphorus, S., Pope, 2, 52, 65.
Tempesta, 166.
Terence, 276.
Tertullian, 25, 29, 43, 46, 53, 69—70; 81, 95, 119, 153, 202.
Tertullus, 177.
Theodatus, 175—176.
Theodolinda, 184.
Theodora, 187—188.
— of Rome, 293—295; 301, 305.
— II of Rome, 294.
Theodoret, 115, 132.
Theodoric the Ostrogoth, 168—175; 189, 196, 223.
Theodorus, I, 7, 215—216.
— II, 9.
—, an antipope, 8, 219-220.
— of Amasia, S., 209.
Theodosius, 109, 120, 144, 150, 206.
— III, 227.
Theophylactus, 8.
—, an Exarch, 227.
—, see Benedict IX.
Theopista, S., 52.

Theopistus, S., 52.
Therasia, S., 129, 134.
Theutberga, 277—279.
Theutgaud of Trier, 278.
Thomas the Apostle, S., 304.
— Aquinas, S., 158, 445, 462—465; 473, 484.
— à Becket, S., 381.
Tiberius Cæsar, 145, 154, 320, 356.
— Apsimar, 226.
Tiburtius, S., 63, 75, 84, 265—267.
Timothy, 25, 28, 32—33; 37.
—, or Timotheus, son of Pudens, 56—57.
Tintoretto, 412.
Titus, 28.
—, the Emperor, 36, 40—41, 43.
Tomacelli, Pietro, see Boniface IX.
Toriti, Giacomo, 476.
Totila, 107, 173, 176, 180—183.
Toton, Duke, 247.
Trajan, 2, 37, 48, 52, 54, 97.
Tranquillinus, S., 84, 108.
Trasilla, S., 191.
Trasimondo of Spoleto, 430.
Tropez, S., 81.
Tullia, 164.
Tullus Hostilius, 32.

Udalric, S., 300, 306.
Urban, I, S., 3, 26, 71—76; 266.
— II, 12, 314, 367—370; 373—374.
— III, 14, 413.

Urban IV, 14, 466—467.
— V, 16, 102, 516—522; 528—529; 532—534; 536—537.
— VI, 16, 487, 527, 531.
— VII, 19.
— VIII, 19, 86, 196, 387.
Ursinus, 5, 133—134.

Valentine, S., 38, 216.
Valentinian III, 109, 115, 153-155; 162—163.
Valentinus, Pope, 9.
Valerian, 83.
Valerianus, S., 74—75; 265—266.
Valéry, M., 473, 536.
Varro, 282.
Vasari, 546.
Ventura, Padre, 86.
Vespasian, 40—41; 140, 146, 319.
Vestina, S., 156.
Victor I, S., 3, 52, 66.
— II, 12, 344—346; 371.
— III, Blessed, 12, 366—367; 376.
— IV, *see* Octavian.
Victorinus, S., 166.
Vigilius, 6, 188—189.
Villani, Giovanni, 487, 493, 511.
—, Mattei, 515.

Virgil, 64, 206, 320, 543.
Visconti, The, 499—500.
Vitalianus, S., 7, 218.
Vitalis, S., 51, 156.
Vitiges, 176, 181.
Vitruvius of Rouen, S., 205.
Vitus, S., 222—223.
Voigt, 365.
Voltaire, 24, 211, 225, 290, 358, 407, 413.

Waldrada, 277, 279—280.
Whiston, W., 40.
Wilfrid of York, S., 214.
William of Aquitaine, 298.
— Rufus, 372.
Winfrith, *see* S. Boniface.
Wiseman, Card., 365, 480.
Wulf-Gudmarson, 623.

Xystus *see* Sixtus.

Yolande, Empress, 451.

Zachary, S., Pope, 8, 180, 239—240; 259.
—, the Chamberlain, 220—221.
Zeno, S., 63.
Zephyrinus, S., Pope, 3.
Zoe, S., 85, 108.
Zozimus, S., Pope, 5, 150—152.
Zucchero, Federigo, 412.

ERRATA.

Page 20 line 29 read Capellari for Capellani.
" 35 " 8 " exaltari for exultari.
" 84 " 32 " Chromatius for Chromatis.
" 178 " 22 " ad fines terræ for ad finis terræ.
" 178 " 30 " Vicovaro for Vicovario.

www.ingramcontent.com/pod-product-compliance
Lightning Source LLC
Chambersburg PA
CBHW031932290426
44108CB00011B/532